26-45

Handbook of
Physical Distribution Management

Handbook of Physical Distribution Management

Third Edition

Edited by

John Gattorna

Gower

First published 1970
Second edition 1976
Reprinted 1978, 1980, 1981

Third edition published 1983 by
Gower Publishing Company Limited
Aldershot, Hants, England

British Library Cataloguing in Publication Data

Handbook of physical distribution management.
    —3rd ed.
    1. Physical distribution of goods—Management
    I. Gattorna, John
    658.7 882   HF5415.7

    ISBN 0-566-02219-2

Printed and bound in Great Britain by
Biddles Ltd, Guildford and King's Lynn

Contents

Foreword

by SIR ROBERT LAWRENCE, CBE, ERD

Chairman, The Institute of Physical Distribution Management

During the past decade, since the first edition of this handbook, the function of physical distribution has undergone dramatic changes. From being the Cinderella of business, the activities which comprise the total distribution cycle have received increasing management attention, and the role of the distribution manager today bears little resemblance to that of ten or so years ago. The future is likely to be even more dramatic in terms of change. We enter a phase of new technology, new transport techniques, high energy costs, and increasing pressures to preserve the environment. The successful distribution manager will be one who is thoroughly trained in these new techniques and who keeps himself abreast of developments.

The role of the distribution manager is predicted to develop even further into that of total logistics management, and the opportunity for enhancing the professional status of those who work in this area has never been better.

It is appropriate that *Handbook of Physical Distribution Management* should now be revised and updated. The Handbook has become a standard work of reference for students and managers alike, and Dr. Gattorna is to be congratulated on his painstaking editing of the new material.

I am sure that it will prove useful and valuable.

Preface to the Third Edition

For over two decades the distribution literature has promoted the potential benefits of an integrated approach to managing the distribution function. In some cases this potential has been realised, but generally distribution practitioners have found it exceedingly difficult to bridge the gap between their actual practices and procedures and the potential expounded in the literature.

Too much emphasis has hitherto been placed on 'what' might be achieved rather than the more pragmatic issue of 'how' such improvements could actually be achieved. Consequently, the third edition of the handbook has been revamped and redrafted in a bid to redress the previous imbalance. It represents a state-of-the-art review of proven practices, and attempts to explain 'how' improvements may be achieved in lieu of extending the theory.

Essentially it is a book written for distribution practitioners by distribution practitioners who are at the forefront of their respective specialties within the distribution field. This new edition contains virtually eighty-five per cent new material and is organised in such a way that each section is a useful free-standing reference in a logical sequence to provide the all-important sense of continuity throughout the length of the text. The topic coverage is wide and has been consciously stretched to include pre-production as well as the usual post-production activities; in this regard the full logistics spectrum is covered.

This work should provide an everyday reference facility to practising distribution managers and help them get closer to the greater efficiencies which general management is increasingly demanding of the function; hopefully it will go at least part of the way towards fulfilling this demanding purpose. My special thanks to all the contributing authors, many of them personal friends, who through their professionalism and co-operation have made my task that much easier, and finally, my thanks also go to the publisher who has shown confidence in the end result, from the early days when a third edition was first mooted, and waited patiently for it to materialise.

John Gattorna

Notes on contributors

George Brimstow (Delivering goods for export) originally joined Thomas Meadows & Co. Ltd. with the intention of gaining a few years' experience, and now thirty years later is still adding to that experience. He is currently Director in charge of Administration at Meadows after holding various management appointments and latterly specialising in European operations. Mr. Bristow maintains a strong interest in the Meadows training programmes and development of training material, including the now well accepted *Understanding the Freight Business.*

Chris Bushell (Rail freighting) is Assistant Editor of the monthly magazine *Railway Gazette International.* He joined the magazine in 1966 as an Editorial Assistant and was appointed Assistant Editor in 1975. He is the author of many articles in both British and overseas journals on transport matters, particularly railways.

David Farmer (In-coming materials management: a case of reverse distribution) is Professor of Management Studies at Henley, the Administrative Staff College. Prior to becoming a management teacher he had fifteen years industrial purchasing and marketing experience in four industries. He is the co-author of five texts, including the best selling European book *Purchasing Principles and Techniques,* Pitman, 3rd edn. He has lectured in every Western European country, Eastern Europe, Australasia and the United States, and was the first European to attain a doctorate in a topic associated with purchasing. He recently became the first European to have a Professorship conferred as a result of his work in the purchasing field.

Ken Firth (Materials handling system design and warehouse operation; Warehouse design and layout; Automated and mechanised warehouses), following war service in the Parachute Regiment, resumed an interrupted education by attending a full time Management Studies course at Leeds. After eight years in sales/production co-ordination with a switch-gear manufacturer, he joined Dexion Limited and served with that company for fifteen years in a variety of capacities, rising to Senior Project Manager. Since 1970 Mr. Firth has been a member of staff of the National Materials Handling Centre and is currently Assistant Director. At the NMHC he has prime responsibility for in-career educational courses, membership services, and information. Over the past twenty-five years he has travelled widely in relation to his work on the continent of Europe, North America and the Far East.

John Gattorna (General Editor and author of The total distribution concept; Distribution as a marketing variable; Auditing distribution performance) is a faculty member within the School of Marketing at the University of New South Wales, Australia. Before taking up his current position early in 1980 he was Senior Research Fellow in Marketing and Logistics Systems at Cranfield School of Management. During five years at Cranfield he became well known in Europe for his teaching, research and consultancy activities. Dr. Gattorna has also developed customised in-company logistics seminars for several major U.K. and European companies. He also takes a keen interest in retailing and has worked with major U.K. and Australian retail chains on a variety of matters. Dr. Gattorna has published (and is currently working on) a number of books and articles in his specialist interest areas, and is widely known for his expertise with the Delphi forecasting technique.

F. E. Harper (Vehicle maintenance) is General Manager of Cameron Commercial Vehicles Limited. Before joining his present organisation, Mr. Harper was employed as Group Technical Manager of Roadships Limited, Group Transport Manager of Tunnel Cement Limited, Chief Engineer of Hall and Ham River Limited, Transport Engineer for Schweppes Limited and Workshop Controller for Keith and Boyle Limited. He has been a council member of the Institute of Road Transport Engineers for many years.

John Kelly (Vehicle purchasing, replacement and costing), a Cambridge Economics graduate, worked in the metals and chemicals industries, before becoming Managing Director of Davies' and Robson (Southern) Ltd., in May 1975. This Company is one of the leading Management Consultancy organisations specialising wholly in transport and distribution. He is also a Director of Freight Software Systems Ltd.

Richard A. Lancioni (Energy: its impact on distribution) is Professor of Marketing and Logistics and Director of Logistics Program at Temple University. Professor Lancioni holds a BA in Government Administration from Lasalle College, an MBA in Marketing from Ohio State University and a Ph.D in Logistics from the Ohio State University. He has spent six years in industry with Standard Tank and Seat as Controller, and with Alcoa Aluminium as a Distribution and Marketing Analyst. Professor Lancioni taught marketing and economics at Ohio State University. He has published articles in all the major marketing and logistics journals.

Sir Daniel Pettit (Trends in distribution/delivery operations) has recently retired from executive duties after a long and distinguished career in distribution. Immediately prior to retirement Sir Daniel was Chairman of the National Freight Corporation, before which he was Chairman of SPD Limited, having joined Unilever in 1948. He was also Chairman of the NEDC Distributive Trades and served on the Waste Management Advisory Council. Among his many activities he is a Council Member (and Past President) of the Chartered Institute of Transport, Council Member of the Confederation of British Industry and British Road Federation, Member of the National Ports Council, Fellow of the British Institute of Management, and Member of the Institute of Grocery Distribution.

Alan Rawnsley (Containers, unitisation and packaging) is an independent business consultant specialising in the transport, electrical and mechanical engineering industries. He has worked as a ceramics engineer with Plessey and spent two years as an operations analyst with the European O.R. Group of N.C.R. in Holland, followed by a short term as financial analyst with Chrysler International. He was a market analyst and later, market research and planning manager with International Combustion Limited, before becoming marketing services manager with G.E.C. Diesels Limited where he was involved with transport systems.

David Ray (Inventory management; Profitable distribution cost analysis) is a former adviser to the various operating divisions of GKN Distributors Limited on all aspects of inventory control. He was previously Senior Research Fellow in Distribution Costing Systems at Cranfield School of Management and is now National Planning Manager with Johnson & Johnson Limited.

David Ross (Air freighting) began his career in freight forwarding in the North of England. Since joining British Airways he has specialised in marketing and is currently Head of the Distribution Advisory Service. This department specialises in evaluating distribution systems and recommending the optimum mix of surface and air transport for companies with worldwide distribution systems.

Philip B. Schary (The market place view of customer service) is Associate Professor of Business Administration at Oregon State University. He holds a bachelor's degree from St. Louis University, an MBA from University of California at Berkeley, and a Ph.D from UCLA. He is currently American Editor of the *International Journal of Physical Distribution and Materials* Management and is also on the Board of Reviewers for the *Journal of Business Logistics*. He has written papers and articles which have appeared in a variety of academic and trade journals in marketing, transportation and business logistics. He was also co-author of *Customer Service and Distribution Strategy* (London, Associated Business Press, 1979). Dr. Schary has served as a transportation officer in the U.S. Air Force, as a market analyst for Douglas Aircraft Company, Lockheed Electronics Corporation and the Flying Tiger Line, and as a business economist for the Atlantic Richfield Corporation.

Tage Skjøtt-Larsen (Distribution information systems) is Associate Professor of Transportation and Business Logistics at the Copenhagen School of Business Administration and was Visiting Research Fellow at Cranfield School of Management in 1976/77. He has written several articles in the distribution area and is a co-author of the recently published text, Customer Service and Distribution Strategy.

Alan Slater (Choice of the transport mode; Load planning) is currently National Distribution Manager for Sony (UK) Limited. Educated at Bradford and Liverpool Universities in economics and management, the majority of his experience has been in the field of distribution and logistics. Previous industrial experience includes employment at Plessey Telecommunications Ltd., Rank Radio International, and BOC Ltd. He also lectures on transport and distribution topics and has written a number of articles and papers.

Alan Waller (Use and location of depots; Computer techniques for siting depots), now Head of the Distribution Studies Unit at Cranfield Institute of Technology, spent five years in Production Management and Management Services with the British Steel Corporation after graduating in mathematics from Oxford University. Since studying for an MSc in Operational Research and Statistics at Cranfield School of Management, he has, in addition to a number of lecturing appointments, spent eight years in Management Consultancy and was Head of the Operational Research Group for Coopers and Lybrand International Management Consultants. He joined the National Materials Handling Centre in 1979 as Assistant Director, in order to develop a new MSc course in distribution technology and management. He has carried out numerous assignments in distribution, production and related areas over the UK and Europe. He has a particular interest in the application of computer systems in distribution planning, and has been heavily involved in the design, development and implementation of computer systems in this area. He has also published and lectured widely on this subject.

Felix Wentworth (Distribution management in the company organisation) was one of the pioneers of physical distribution management in Britain. In 1965 he was appointed Distribution Director of Schweppes, one of the first people in the country to hold this title. He also conducted the British Institute of Management's first series of seminars and forums on distribution. Since 1969 he has divided his time between consultancy and senior general management. He is a board member of the Centre for Physical Distribution Management, and Managing Director of Chubb Hennessy Ltd.

F. W. Wilson (Distribution budgeting and control systems) is currently Chief Executive Officer of Texport Terminals Ltd. Prior to this appointment he was involved in the development of terminals for the vacuum packaging of clothing, granular materials, and foams, etc., for the SPD Group. He has had previous experiences in hanging garment operations with Unilever associated companies in Europe, Canada, and South Africa.

John Wilson (Security in distribution) was formerly the Company Security Officer for Yorkshire Imperial Metals Limited. His role was primarily advisory to the Board and to the numerous factories in the group, on all matters of security policy and practice. A former Detective Chief Inspector in Leeds City Police, Mr. Wilson is a Fellow and Governor of the Institution of Industrial Security and National Chairman of the Industrial Police and Security Association. He is also co-author of two standard text books for Institution examinations, *Practical Security in Commerce and Industry* (Gower, 4th edition, 1983) and *Security Manual* (Gower, 4th edition, 1983).

F. H. Woodward (Road freighting; Delivery vehicle design), is Transport Services Executive with the Plessey Company Limited. He has been involved in industrial distribution management for the past twenty years. Before that he served in the Royal Air Force on a permanent commission. Mr. Woodward heads a division of the Plessey Company responsible for all transport services including the distribution of all its goods. He is the author of *Managing the Transport Services Function* (Gower, 2nd edition, 1977).

Illustrations

Figure

Figure

Figure

Figure

Figure

PART ONE

Distribution Management

Overview

The concept of managing the distribution function as an integral systems-oriented flow of materials and information has been around long enough for something practical to have emerged. And yet, we still find a profusion of differing interpretations over terminology and application issues.

In Chapter 1, Gattorna attempts to eliminate these semantic difficulties and offer a new clear logic for practitioners to use. The major focus is on the concept of 'trade-off' which he regards as central to the successful management of the distribution function. A four-tier hierarchy of trade-offs is proposed, and the implications of these in terms of information requirements and corresponding analysis are highlighted.

Gattorna continues in this illuminating vein in Chapter 2, where he makes the point that is too often overlooked by top management and operational distribution men alike, i.e. that distribution is a key element in the marketing effort of a company, charged with the task of fulfilling the demand created by activities in the areas of product, pricing, and promotions. This point is reinforced by the explanation of how the requirement for distribution varies along the life-cycle of a typical product. Chapter 2 also contains some very valuable insights into the managerial content of the distribution function within the firm's overall marketing plan, a subject all too often omitted, or treated superficially.

In Chapter 3, Schary continues with this market oriented approach to managing the distribution function with a very comprehensive coverage of customer service, which in effect is the output of all effort within the function.

Schary also adopts a systems-oriented view of this facet of distribution and makes the very valid point that customer service is a 'product' in its own right, a philosophy which is certainly not lost on service type companies, but not always recognised by product type companies.

Various methods of assessing the perceptions of customers to the service being offered are documented, all of which have been proven in field experimentation. Finally, in Chapter 4 Wentworth addresses the pragmatic and sometimes political question of how to organise the corporate distribution function in order to realise some of the aforementioned concepts in practice. In general terms, there is no single prescriptive answer to this issue – it largely depends on the existing norms and culture of the organisation and the type of industry involved. The reality is that organisations cannot be dismantled and put together again in a new ideal configuration. Instead, we must start from where we are and evolve gradually, preferably with some overall scheme in mind towards which we can work with phased changes. At all times, however, keep in mind the basic premise that however the distribution function is organised, or wherever it is located within the corporate management structure, it is still by its very nature a marketing variable. Correspondingly, for best results, it should be so organised and located as to allow it to function effectively in this mode.

1

The total distribution concept and its practical implications

John Gattorna

Definitions

The terminology which surrounds the topic variously known as 'product flow', 'physical distribution', 'logistics', 'materials management' or 'materials control' can be confusing because these terms tend to be used indiscriminately and sometimes interchangeably in the business literature.

The all-embracing word is 'logistics', which covers the movement of all materials, that is, the movement of raw materials from their sources to the processing point (materials management), and the movement of finished products from the plant through various channels of distribution to the ultimate customer (distribution), as depicted in Figure 1:1.

LOGISTICS = MATERIALS MANAGEMENT + DISTRIBUTION

Logistics is concerned with flows – flows of physical entities and flows of information related to those entities. In this handbook, however, the primary emphasis will be on the distribution of finished product (distribution) rather than the control of material flows into the production process (materials management). This whole subject area is becoming increasingly vital as industry begins to realise that management of the distribution resource is a key determinant of corporate performance.

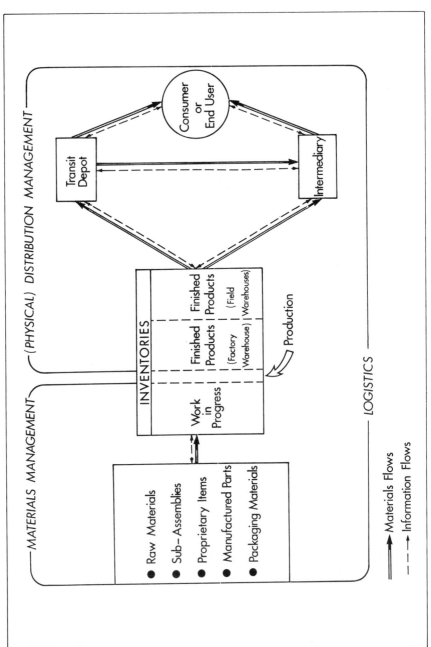

Figure 1:1   Logistics – the management of materials flows and information flows

Trade-offs

While the supply of materials to production facilities and the subsequent distribution of finished product to customers is an activity with a long history, the 'management' of this process as a unified entity (the total distribution concept or TDC) is a relatively recent phenomenon. Nevertheless, the movement towards TDC has come about through a realisation by industry that if the total cost and customer service implications of managing the distribution function as a complete entity are fully considered, then profit and competitive advantages are achievable.

In effect, the total distribution concept uses the 'systems' approach, the aim being to gain an optimum or best solution overall (in whatever terms have been decided), even at the expense of sub-optimum performance in one of the constituent elements of the distribution mix (Figure 1:2) – which is here defined as the combination of facilities, inventory, transportation, communications, and unitisation/materials handling.

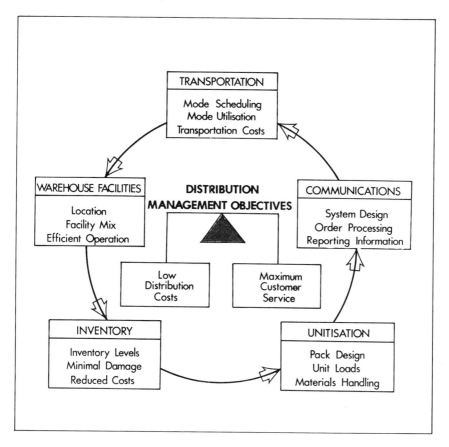

Figure 1:2   The distribution mix and some decision areas

Typically, management attempts to handle the complex problems posed by the increasing cost of distribution have been of a piecemeal nature, that is, individual activity centres have been examined for possible improvements, seemingly without regard for the effects that any change might have on other activity centres. For example, attempting to cut costs in transportation might well lead to disproportionately higher costs in inventory holding elsewhere in the system.

It is because of the dangers of such sub-optimisation that the integrated systems approach to managing distribution has begun to win favour, although diffusion of these ideas throughout industry has been slow the world over. The implication is that management is able to recognise, and is prepared to take advantage of, the 'trade-offs' which are found to be present in any given situation. (A 'trade-off' occurs when costs are consciously incurred in one activity centre in order to achieve increased benefits from another activity centre, or from the aggregated effect of other activity centres. In all cases the objective is to achieve a net gain.) In turn, appropriate information support systems must exist to enable correct judgements to be made – this is the task of the all-important communications element of the distribution mix.

The successful identification of cost trade-offs is the crux of logistics systems engineering, and is thus the key to enhanced corporate profitability (because it produces additional funds either through cost saving or revenue generation, or both). However, trade-off analyses can be complex and time-consuming because the process requires detailed consideration of all relevant activity centres within the logistics system, and the listing of all the alternative methods of performing their respective functions. Trade-offs appear at four different levels and each of these is reviewed below.

1   *Intra-element trade-offs:* trade-offs which occur within individual elements of the distribution mix, for example, the decision either to use one's own fleet, or hire a contract haulier. Similarly, in warehousing, the decision may lie between using and operating one's own facilities or leasing a public warehouse.

2   *Intra-functional trade-offs:* trade-offs which occur between elements of the distribution mix. The trade-off of this type which did much to establish the concept of physical distribution management (PDM) in the US during the 1960s is that relating to the use of premium transportation. For example, the use of air freight, although apparently more expensive than the alternative surface modes, is capable of reducing order cycle times, field inventories, and packaging requirements to such an extent that the overall effect is a net saving. Figure 1:3 depicts another example of intra-functional trade-off, i.e, by increasing the number of regional depots. The total cost of distribution may be reduced despite increased stockholding costs.

3   *Inter-functional trade-offs:* trade-offs which occur at the interface between distribution and other functional areas within the firm as depicted in Figure 1:4. Regardless of who has direct managerial responsibility for a particular activity, all functions affected by that activity should have some input to the decisions

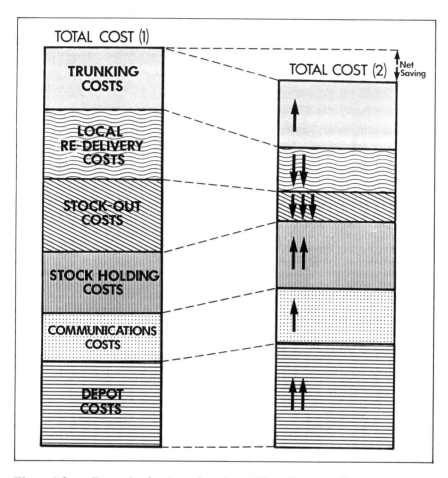

Figure 1:3   Example of an inter-functional (Type 2) trade-off

being made. The classic example is that of product packaging which has two
distinctly different tasks – promotion and protection. But the package which best
protects a product may well be unsuitable for promotional purposes. Another
example may be that of marketing people wanting to offer high levels of product
availability together with a wide product range – this obviously poses problems
for the distribution function which can usually only be resolved to best effect by
exploring the trade-off alternatives.

4   *Inter-organisational trade-offs:* trade-offs between the firm and other (external)
organisations as depicted in Figure 1:5. The manufacturer/processor should be
concerned about, and attempt to influence, the passage of his product as it moves
through the distribution channel; to achieve this, delicate inter-organisational
relationships may have to be developed. Often, however, there is a tendency for
a company to ignore the progress of its product down the channel once legal

ownership has passed to an intermediary. But what if that or another intermediary is inefficient in distribution resulting in poor customer service? The ultimate customer will probably attribute these inefficiencies to the manufacturer of the product rather than to the intermediary. Apart from channel intermediaries, the distribution function comes into regular contact with outside service organisations such as haulage and shipping contractors, public warehouses, shipping agents, etc., and in all cases proper working relationships have to be developed in order for the company to achieve its own objectives. At the same time due recognition must be given to the objectives of other channel parties.

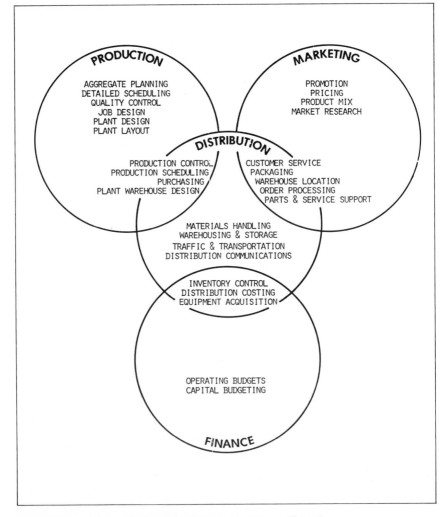

Figure 1:4   Interrelationships between corporate functions

A totally integrated distribution approach demands that the responsible distribution executive should closely examine each of the above types of inter-relationships and seek to capitalise on any trade-off opportunities which are present, the ultimate objective being either to:

(i)   provide the least total cost distribution system for a pre-determined level of customer service (note the emphasis on total cost, meaning all relevant costs

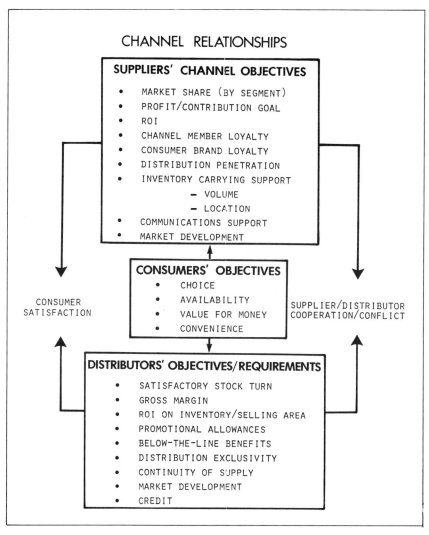

Figure 1:5   Channel relationships with inter-organisational trade-off potential

within or outside the distribution function).

or

(ii)   within given cost constraints, provide the highest possible level of customer service.

Either approach is acceptable, although the author prefers (i) because it implies cost-effectiveness. The one actually adopted will depend on the organisation concerned and its particular operating philosophy. However, it is not possible to provide 'maximum' customer service for 'minimum' cost – by definition the two cannot be achieved coincidentally.

Customer service – the other side of the coin

In many organisations attention has for too long been focused upon the potential for cost reduction within the distribution activity rather than upon the wider issue of devising integrated distribution policies which impact on both costs and revenues. (Perhaps this is understandable when the cost of distribution as a percentage of net sales can run as high as 35 per cent.) Indeed, there may be circumstances where higher total distribution costs can be justified, because of the incremental or geared effect produced on sales. Ultimately, the only thing which really matters is the output, that is, provision of a cost-effective level of customer service. But the cliche about providing 'the right product in the right place at the right time' implies a degree of integration within the firm that few companies can boast.

Implicit in the above, and central to any understanding of the possibilities that an integrated approach to distribution can provide, is the concept of the corporate system. Such a company-wide orientation may require a radical re-appraisal both in terms of policy determination and organisational structures. It also requires recognition at a high level within the company, that the provision of a distribution service, and the level at which it is sustained, is a strategic issue of the greatest importance.

Conclusion

The concept of total distribution, which is embodied in the ideal of an integrated systems approach to managing the distribution task, is essentially an attitude, a philosophy, a conviction. The total distribution concept is concerned with:

(i)   the relationships inside the distribution function and between the other functions and distribution;

(ii)   co-ordination within and between the functions in pursuit of the company's corporate objectives.

If the urgency and relevance of this concept are appreciated within the organisation as a whole, then realisation of the potential it offers will follow despite the technical and organisational challenges which will be encountered.

In summary, the total distribution concept (TDC) amounts to:

1   A continuing search for 'trade-offs' (all types).
2   The development of information systems sophisticated enough to support the demands of trade-off analyses.
3   Having the personnel capable of conducting the analyses and making appropriate decisions.
4   Winning top management support for the concept through demonstrated results, or even before any results are achieved.

2

Distribution as a marketing variable

John Gattorna

Irrespective of how the distribution function is organised and located within the firm (there are many variants in this regard), it remains a key variable in the Marketing Mix, which comprises four elements, i.e., Product, Price, Promotion and Distribution. Sadly, however, there is too little recognition of this fact.

The all-important interface between distribution and the other elements of the marketing mix can be explained quite simply as follows. Marketing activity in the areas of product, price and promotion has the primary task of creating demand for the company's product(s) in the market place. The distribution executive (which may be organisationally separate from or form part of the marketing executive) then has the task of ensuring that the demand so generated is actually serviced or fulfilled as depicted in Figure 2:1.

What is too often overlooked is that even when the product, its price and its promotion all come together to create a desire to purchase in the mind of the consumer, no sale can be achieved if the product does not actually arrive at a point where it is exposed to consumer attention. So, the distribution element of a product is a vital part of the value package represented by the product. Without it the value package is incomplete. Unfortunately, too many executives, in manufacturing/supplier companies particularly, have a bad case of marketing myopia – they tend to concentrate only on the tangible aspects of the product itself and lack awareness of the additional, albeit tangible, attribute which involves the timely positioning of the product.

Despite this, it is encouraging to find non-distribution executives becoming increasingly interested in the possibilities and potentials of a professional approach to distribution. Ten years ago this attitude was not at all evident – at that time the only people who seemed interested in distribution were those who actually worked at it

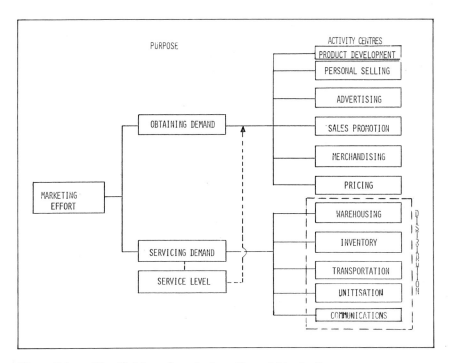

Figure 2:1   The division of marketing effort within the firm

professionally – the converted. Now, attitudes are changing, not through the pioneering efforts of distribution 'missionaries', but simply because of the economic realities which have become progressively harsher during the closing years of the 1970s and promise little respite in the 1980s.

The product life cycle concept and distribution

Following on the theme that distribution is a marketing variable it is pertinent to introduce another key marketing concept, the product life cycle (PLC). This seemingly simple notion suggests that products move through identifiable stages during their life which typically exhibit the patttern shown in Figure 2:2.

The principle generally thought to underlie the PLC concept is that of 'diffusion', i.e., knowledge about a new product diffuses through the population over time in a geometrical progression, thus creating the growth pattern in sales found for many new (and successful) products.

In lay terms the PLC model postulates that if the product is successful in its initial introduction into the market (and many new products fail at this stage), then as the product becomes established, repeat purchase grows, word of mouth spreads, the

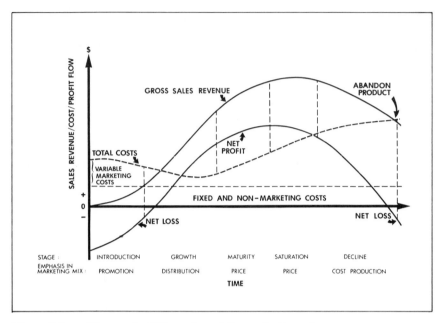

Figure 2:2   The product life cycle and the marketing mix

more cautious are persuaded to try the product, and the rate of sales growth increases.

Often, competitive organisations, seeing new sales potential, attempt to imitate the product and in so doing add their weight to the promotion expenditure which in turn tends to accelerate the increase in total sales. It is during this accelerated growth period of the life cycle that the distribution element has a vital role to play. If, through poor organisation and operation of distribution resources, the demand for the product is not met, sales and sometimes even customers are lost. The reader may even recall examples of such situations occurring in his/her own experience.

Later on in the cycle, sales of the product slow as it moves into the maturity and saturation stages of its cycle; hence the emphasis on trimming costs in the face of stiff price competition and consequent pressure on margins. Again, a cost-effective distribution system can play a major part in sustaining the sales pattern. Each of the stages in the PLC, and the corresponding dominant marketing variable at each stage, is depicted in Figure 2:2.

Distribution in a marketing planning context

The marketing planning process in many companies is substandard or superficial at best and non-existent at worst. Often, plans which are called marketing plans are no more than product plans, a fact which tends to reinforce the above claim that companies are too product oriented. The distribution component is either completely missing or at best covered very superficially.

This in turn makes life very difficult for the distribution executive in such companies which as a consequence is operating in a virtual planning vacuum and at best can only work on a day-to-day operational basis. Ideally, the marketing planning process (and distribution's part in that process) should follow the logic depicted in Figures 2:3a, b, c and d.

Together, these four diagrams trace the planning process from the corporate level, through the marketing (function) level, to the distribution (element) level. For perhaps the first time we have a logic diagram of how the distribution element fits into a marketing planning framework. In particular it is significant that distribution

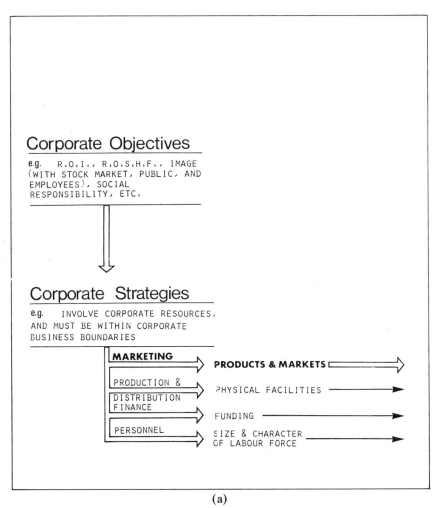

(a)

Figure 2:3   Distribution in a marketing planning context

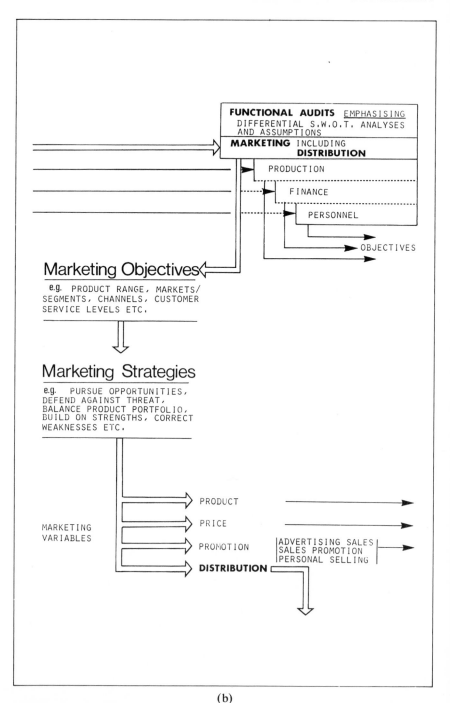

(b)

Figure 2:3   continued

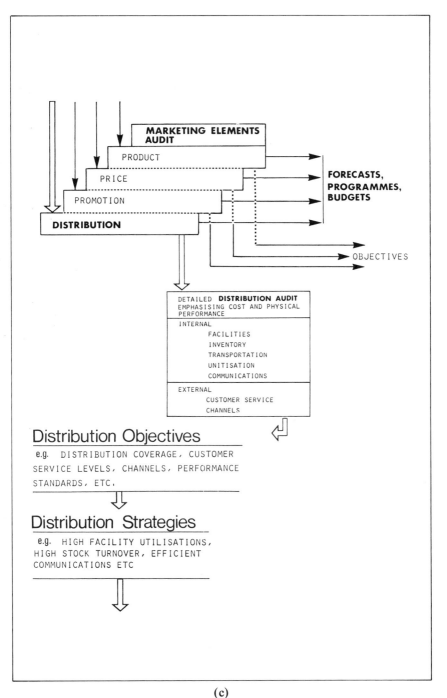

(c)

Figure 2:3 continued

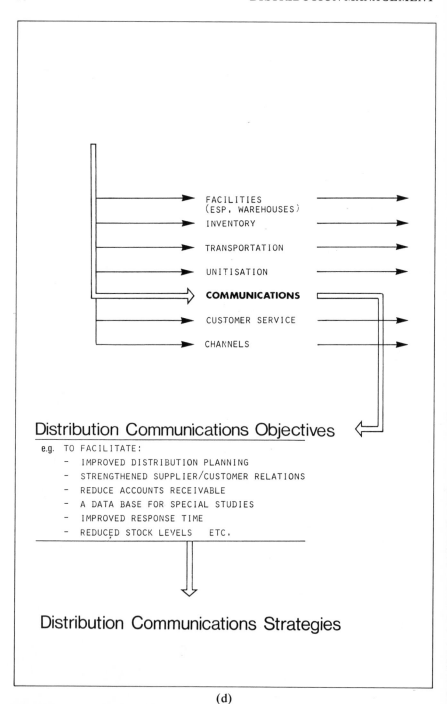

(d)

Figure 2:3   concluded

objectives (and their supporting strategies) can only be set *after* a full audit of the current system capability (the subject of the distribution audit is addressed in Chapter 22). Also significant is the fact that the issues of channel selection and customer service levels are very much a marketing executive responsibility and must therefore be included among the list of marketing objectives. At a later stage in the process the distribution executive sets its own internal customer service operating objectives and strategies which of course must be consistent with those already defined by marketing executive.

To assist the reader in following the important topic contained in Figures 2:3a, b, c and d, and to avoid difficulties with semantics, the relevant terms are defined in Figure 2:4.

OBJECTIVES: Define *what* is to be achieved and should generally be quantifiable and measurable.

STRATEGIES: Define *how* the set objectives are to be achieved.

POLICIES: *Guidelines* adopted in implementing the strategies selected. In essence, a policy is a summary statement of objectives and strategies.

OBJECTIVES, STRATEGIES AND POLICIES must be established for each level of the business.

PROGRAMMES: The aggregation of specific sub-objectives, supported by more detailed strategy and action statements. A programme includes individuals *budgets, forecasts* and a *consolidated budget*.

MARKETING AUDIT: A *situation review* of the company's current marketing capability.

DISTRIBUTION AUDIT: A review of the distributions system's *current capability*.

SWOT ANALYSIS: A *summary* of the audit which focuses on key factors only, e.g., a list of internal *differential* strengths and weaknesses vis a vis competitors and key external opportunities and threats.

ASSUMPTIONS: Lists the *major* assumptions upon which the plan is based.

MARKETING PLAN contains:
- Swot analysis
- Assumptions
- Marketing objectives
- Marketing strategies
- Programmes

Figure 2:4   Marketing and distribution planning terminology

It is impossible to develop and implement a successful distribution strategy within the firm until and unless the marketing objectives have been clearly defined and communicated to the distribution executive. Obviously, a disciplined approach to marketing planning will facilitate the achievement of this condition.

Once this is done, the distribution executive can be relied upon to mobilise its resources to achieve the desired result. Of course, it may well be that the task imposed by marketing is clearly beyond the resources currently available. This is why there has to be close liaison – so that such a situation does not arise in unforeseen fashion.

As mentioned already, the major policy inputs from marketing to distribution concern such vital matters as what market segments are to be serviced and at what differential levels of service. These latter decisions cannot and should not be left to the distribution manager; it is not his job to make assessments of this nature. And yet, this is often what happens. As customer complaints come in to the company as a result of such an approach, it is the distribution executive which is (often incorrectly) accused. In fact the responsibility must lie with the marketing and sales personnel who have effectively abdicated one of their primary responsibilities.

Areas of distribution and marketing interaction

There are nine main areas of interaction between distribution and marketing as follows:

1	Product design	this can have a major effect on warehouse and transportation utilisations (and therefore costs).
2	Pricing	obviously, distribution must provide the most cost-effective service possible in order to contribute to the company's competitive ability as manifested in its pricing policies.
3	Market and sales forecasting	the forecast made by marketing will largely dictate the level of distribution resources which will be taken on to perform the physical task involved in moving products to customers.
4	Customer service policies	if marketing opts to offer a very responsive level of service to customers, distribution resources in the form of facilities and inventory will need to be very considerable.
5	Number and location of warehouse	this is really a distribution decision area which in essence attempts to develop a distribution facilities network configuration which is appropriate to the task being required of the distribution system.
6	Inventory policies	such policies, whether set by the distribution or marketing executive or anyone else for that matter, will have a significant bearing on the costs of

operation and the extent to which desired levels of customer service are achieved. This is an emotional area within most organisations with several functions attempting to influence the level of inventories for their own particular purpose.

7   Order processing   this is the procedure followed upon receipt of a customer order and if carried out quickly and efficiently is a major factor in keeping unnecessary cost down on the physical side of distribution, as well as helping to ensure that promised delivery deadlines are met consistently.

8   Channels of distribution   the decisions taken as to through what channels (e.g., direct to customer or via various types of intermediary, etc.) will greatly influence the level of distribution resources required by the company. As channels change, so too will the resources requirement.

9   Trade practices   in this context, the procedures and practices commonly followed in the particular industry in which we operate. These too will dictate to some extent the type, quantity and configuration of our distribution system.

Obviously, the above examples describe just a few of the ways in which distribution and marketing interact along the nine dimensions listed; many others exist.

Conclusion

It is clearly vital to work towards a closer liaison between marketing and distribution people in the company, irrespective of the organisation structure as it currently exists. In the end, the output of all the various marketing-related activities which take place in a company is the provision of customer service, i.e., ensuring that customer demands (within reason) are met by way of desired products when and where required and in the requested quantities. The customer is not interested in how the supplying company is organised, the problems a supplier encounters in production or distribution, or even the in-company politicking which inevitably goes on between the various functions. Customers are only interested in results in the form of products delivered as per order instructions. For many supplying companies this will be the way forward during the 1980s. Getting organised to achieve the desired result, consistently, will become a major competitive factor in what for many industries is an increasingly hostile competitive environment. If marketing people can become more aware of the importance of the distribution variable and use it to their advantage, a whole new vista of commercial success is awaiting those who try and succeed.

3

The market place view of customer service

Philip B. Schary

Customer service is one of the most misunderstood areas of physical distribution management. Conventionally it is recognised as the quality of the performance of the physical distribution system. It has usually come to mean the dimensions of the order cycle and fulfilment which enhance the sales of an organisation. One writer has described it in various system-performance terms as follows:

1   The elapsed time between receipt of an order at the supplier's warehouse and the shipment of that order from warehouse.
2   The minimum order size or assortment limits which a supplier will accept from its customers.
3   The percentage of items in a supplier's warehouse which might be found to be out-of-stock at any given point in time.
4   The proportion of customer orders filled accurately.
5   The percentage of customers or the volume of customer orders which describe those who are served (orders delivered) within a certain time period from the receipt of the order at the supplier's warehouse.
6   The percentage of customer orders which can be filled immediately upon receipt at a supplier's warehouse.
7   The proportion of goods which arrive at a customer's place of business in saleable condition.
8   The elapsed time between the placement of an order by a customer and the delivery of goods ordered to the customer's place of business.
9   The ease and flexibility with which a customer can place his order.[1]

   Customer service is a balancing component that incurs costs in order to provide distribution system performance to meet customer needs. There is, however, a major difficulty. The descriptions above are laudable objectives but they do not necessarily take account of what the customer actually needs or wants as a member of the distribution pipeline.

While the conventional concept of customer service can be described in production-oriented terms, it ignores the relationship between buyer and seller, and the fact that the performance of distribution activities has as much impact on the buyer and his operating system as it does on the seller's. Failure to have a product in stock at the time that a customer asks for it creates a cost to the customer which may not be trivial. The variability of transit time with which an order is delivered can affect a customer's inventory more than it does the supplier's.

Customer service therefore describes an interface between systems as well as involving a system of its own. Elsewhere customer service has been described as 'a system organised to provide a continuing link between the time that an order is placed and the goods are received on a continuing long-term basis.'[2] Standards of inventory performance and delivery are only meaningful within the context of relationships between customer and supplier, for their influence on the operations of both parties, and ultimately for how they influence the customer's decisions about patronage with suppliers.

Three problem areas then emerge from this larger view of customer service:

1 The internal co-ordination problems for suppliers to combine differing functional areas into one co-ordinated effort.
2 The impact, and the ability of the customer to perceive this impact on the performance of his own organisation.
3 The development of systems which span both organisations such that decisions which have mutual impacts are made and managed jointly.

The conventional view concentrates on the first problem; this is the focus of most management discussion of the area, directed to topics such as how much safety stock to hold in inventory, or setting monitoring programs for delivery programs. To be sure, there is some acknowledgement of customer response in the design of combinations of service performance.[3] However, is this actually an extensive effort? The further recognition of systemic impacts which cross organisational boundaries 'are almost unrecognised with a few exceptions.'[4] In the discussion which follows, we will explore this broader perspective of customer service, examining it as an on-going system involving both supplier and customer. At the present time, this approach raises more questions than it answers. However, customer service can hardly avoid consideration of its impact on the customer.

Customer service as a product

When a firm sells and processes the order for a product, it is actually creating two products. The first is the one that the customer expects to buy; the second is the output of the seller's distribution system, the order-processing and delivery activities which place the product where the customer expects it to be, whether as an off-the-shelf item for immediate sale or as a planned production order. While the first product determines the initial order, the second determines the volume of repeat business because it affects the customer's cost of doing business with the supplier.

This second product can also be complex, because it involves the sustained output of an interactive system. The attributes that customers prefer in customer service generally reflect the long-term consistency of performance of the system – in particular, reliability of delivery within specified time constraints, and maintaining stock availability for a specific portion of times demanded. There may be requests to adapt the supplier's system to special demands of the customer, such as expedited orders, compatibility of materials handling systems, and requests for order status information. These attributes of the second product can be important to customers because the characteristics of a supplier's distribution can affect the buyer's own costs of processing orders and holding stock.

As a product, customer service should therefore contribute to corporate profits rather than be seen as merely incurring costs. The service should provide tangible benefits which the customer can recognise and use, and increase profit for the supplier. The relationship can be seen in Figure 3:1 which compares the level of service and hypothetical benefits with the costs involved. Line C describes how costs increase with the general level of service, slowly at first but accelerating as higher levels are established.

The benefits of low levels of service described by line R would also begin at low levels, but would soon create strong customer response in terms of revenue as service levels increase, leading to a position where revenues from service exceed the cost. There would presumably be some point, S*, where this difference (and therefore profit) is maximised. Conceptually the above description may be easy to recognise. However, it is much more difficult to achieve in practice.

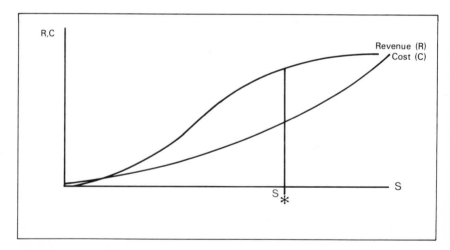

Figure 3:1   Market response to customer service

There are several reasons for this. First, customers in general may not be equipped either to recognise or to respond to different levels of service. If their supply acquisition system operates on a weekly monitoring cycle, changes of delivery time may not be observed. Second, customer service becomes a dominant variable in vendor selection only under certain conditions. Product marketing takes place generally within the context of the product life cycle. Sales of the tangible product of the firm undergo several transitional stages; sales are initiated as the product is introduced, increase rapidly through the growth stage, achieve a limit at maturity where growth occurs (if at all) only as fast as the market as a whole, and finally decline. These are shown in Figure 3:2. The value of the product life cycle concept is that it identifies characteristic strategies and decision imperatives for marketing strategy as each stage is reached. It also helps to define the specific tasks for distribution.

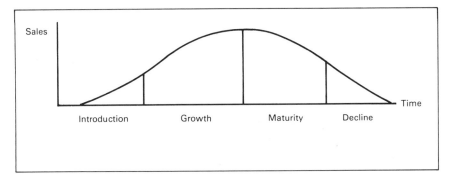

Figure 3:2   The product life cycle

New products are introduced with uncertainty about the level of demand. The requirement of customer service is to maintain the pace of supply to match that of demand. The functional emphasis is on forecasting sales in order to set production schedules and place stocks in readiness for anticipation of sales growth. This process continues through the growth cycle. At maturity however, service becomes more dominant in overall strategy. The emphasis is on achievement and maintenance of wide distribution. Service then becomes part of a bargaining relationship between suppliers and members of the channel of distribution. Service strategies are then useful in building and holding loyal relationships between customers and suppliers. The fact that most products are in the mature stage of the product life cycle makes the role of service crucial in holding sales at their peak level.

Elements of customer service strategy

Customer service is both decision and process. Decisions are concerned with the types of service attributes to provide, levels of service, and other commitments of resources both in the long and the short term. Processes are concerned with the sequence of activities necessary to fill orders. Process decisions are concerned with the design of the system and operating parameters.

Process elements

Some writers such as La Londe and Zinszer distinguish three groups of customer service elements:[5]

1   pre-transaction elements.
2   transaction elements.
3   post-transaction elements.

Pre-transaction elements are concerned with customer service policy as a basis for process decisions.

Transaction elements involve the activities in the actual processing of orders. The order process is generally described by a set of performance dimensions. Those quoted most commonly include:

1   product availability – usually described as a percent of items or orders filled from stock on hand.
2   order cycle time – described in terms of average time for delivery and the variation in the actual measured times experienced.
3   order status information – described in terms of whether it is provided or whether the customer can interrogate the system.
4   order preparation – described in terms of the ease with which orders can be entered into the system. It also includes common coding systems and freedom from error.
5   order size and frequency – these are the result of policy decisions.

Post-transaction elements are the aftermath of the order process and include customer complaints, product recall and replacement. Customer service activities embrace the entire physical distribution system since they are the output of that system. Normally the activities of the service product has direct impact on industrial buyers and intermediate sellers who are the receivers in the logistics pipeline. However, the final consumer may also react to the effect of service failures through products which are out-of-stock or which take abnormally long to deliver. Customer service thus produces effects at two levels: the final market and at the intermediary stages of distribution, where the effects may be entirely different. If products are out of stock, consumers can react in a variety of ways: to ignore it, to substitute within the store, to look at other stores or just not to buy the product. In some cases the impact of the stock-out has led to temporary loss of market share[6] and changes in attitudes toward the store.[7] However, the permanent market impact of stock-outs on consumer patronage has been hard to measure.

At the retail store level, service failures have been more direct and abrupt. A study by Shycon and Sprague noted that retail chain store buyers tend to punish the seller for failures in service; a failure to maintain stock led to resistance to promotional efforts and new product introductions, going far beyond the immediate loss of sale. Ultimately service failures can lead to permanent loss of markets.[8]

Studies of industrial markets[9] have indicated that industrial buyers place a high priority on the quality of distribution service, ranking it first or second in importance, even surpassing price and product quality. These studies have dealt with standardised products in which several sources were available, in hypothetical markets. Other empirical studies, however, have supported these findings.[10]

Part of the difficulty in measuring market response is the difficulty of establishing service as a primary factor in determining revenue. Service is seldom employed alone; it is usually used in conjunction with other parts of the marketing mix, and thus becomes difficult to isolate for measurement purposes. Because it is most prominent at the time of product maturity, it is important at a time when competition is also at its most intense. It is a retention strategy, to hold sales volume and market share. The effects are thus asymmetric. Failures are noticed, but over-achievement goes unrecognised. Hutchinson and Stolle comment:

> [While] the *sales effects* of different levels of service can be determined with successful accuracy, their measurement does present more difficulty because they are less visible . . . As for the effects of providing really good service, these are more difficult to measure precisely because the results are often clouded by other marketing actions of the company and of competitors.[11]

Customer service as a strategic element is important, operates at several levels in the channel and produces effects which are hard to measure. It is the manifestation of the performance of a system which must be carefully co-ordinated and controlled in order to produce the specific attributes of service required by the market. Strategy, then, requires consideration of two aspects: determining what the market wants, and how to supply it. We will consider the supply side of the problem first because it is the most directly visible concern of distribution management.

The supply dimension of customer service

One writer[12] has divided customer service into two perspectives, identified as 'tactical' (short-term) and 'strategic' (long-term). Decisions relating to the operation of the order process are short-term; those relating to positioning of distribution centres would be long-term.

Short-term perspectives

In the short-term, most firms concentrate on two major service problems: management of order cycle time and stock availability. Other elements of customer service may be important but they are specific to individual customer requirements.

Order cycle time is generally divided into three components: order acquisition, internal processing, and delivery to the customer. Acquiring the order involves some form of communication from the customer to the order processing unit in the firm, whether by company salesman taking an order and mailing it or by a customer's computer placing an order with the supplier's computer. There are many short-term problems involved in scheduling the receipt of orders: common item coding, compatibility of different electronic data processing systems, the mode of order transmission and the ease with which the customer can place an order in the system. These are predominantly technical problems, although they may also involve inter-organisational adaptation.

Internal processing involves the flow of documentation and activities associated with the order, warehouse operations assembling the order, and finally preparing for shipment. In a study of six English companies, order processing was generally found to take some combination of either a sequential or a parallel path. [13] Typical systems are shown in Figure 3:3.

In sequential processing, each stage waits on the previous one, creating the potential for delay at each stage. However, the need for co-ordination is reduced because each stage is completed before the next one begins. In a parallel system, several activities are performed simultaneously, such as documentation, warehousing, and transportation planning, all on the assumption that there will be few irregularities. Under this system, elapsed time for internal processing can be substantially reduced, provided that there are no difficulties such as mismatching of inventory records with actual stock-on-hand, or uncertainties involving the release or scheduling of orders.

The final activity stage sometimes involves transportation by an independent contract carrier. This normally implies a potential loss of control, although in fact carrier service may operate on precise schedules so that the control issue is reduced in importance. A performance monitoring system may be incorporated here as a means of assuring this control.

In the short-term, the controllable elements in the system are somewhat constrained. Scheduling of customer orders, internal processing schedules and selection of carriers are all changeable to some degree, but many of the basic elements of the system are usually fixed, such as the mode by which orders are transmittted, or the mode of transportation used. Changes in these components are more difficult to implement without advance planning.

Stock availability is traditionally regarded as a problem in inventory investment. Inventories are customarily determined first by considering the service levels required and then by seeking to minimise costs within this service constraint. The service level can be varied for different classes of products, using techniques such as ABC analysis in which high demand, highly competitive or urgently needed items are given a high priority with high planned-for service levels, where low volume, non-urgent items are given lower service levels.

Recently, Herron proposed a different orientation. Instead of minimising cost for a given service level, profit should be maximised, by analysis of the profit consequences of stock-outs versus implementing an expediting procedure with premium transportation. [14] The essential characteristic is to recognise expediting as a

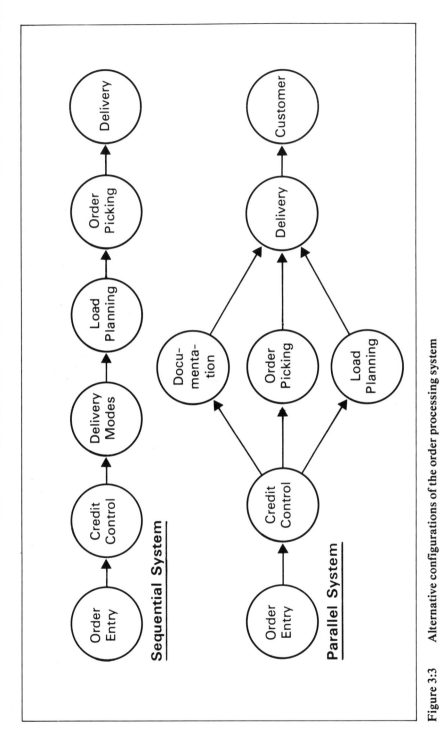

Sequential System

Order Entry → Credit Control → Delivery Modes → Load Planning → Order Picking → Delivery

Parallel System

Order Entry → Credit Control → Documentation / Order Picking / Load Planning → Delivery → Customer

Figure 3:3   Alternative configurations of the order processing system

necessary part of the service system, and to incorporate the incremental costs involved into an item-by-item profit analysis.

Longer-term perspectives

In the longer-term context of strategic decisions, there are many options available which are not possible alternatives in a short-term policy. Some possible strategic changes might include:

1   Development of improved computer-based order processing systems to reduce internal delays, transcription errors and to provide increased control information.
2   Changes in order profiles of customers through price or service incentives so that quantities, frequencies, and timing of their demands can be shifted to fit the requirements of the system.
3   Changes in location of fixed facilities such as warehouses and distribution centres in order to provide faster delivery from field stocks.
4   Replenishment of inventories through improved monitoring systems to match demand patterns among customers.
5   Development of specific transportation routing patterns from supply point to customer, to recognise costs, demands and product characteristics of particular markets.

Strategic decisions usually involve considerable outlay of funds and long-term commitment. These have both advantages and disadvantages associated with them. One advantage is that substantial cash outlays become barriers to immediate imitation by competitors. Placing a new distribution centre close to a strategically important market may provide immediate service advantages over competition and longer-term cost advantages for initiators, compared with competitors who may be forced to use public warehouses or initiate their own operations later at higher capital costs. The disadvantage is that in a period of rapid technological and market change it may be difficult to fully realise the advantages originally conceived for the investment, as materials handling and computer systems, for instance, become obsolete and have to be replaced by newer investments.

The marketplace and customer service

Marketing strategy generally involves monitoring the corporate environment to identify specific opportunities which match what the organisation is potentially able to offer. Customer service is a strategic marketing factor within physical distribution to match a need of a customer with a physical distribution service offering. The risks of failure are sufficiently high to make understanding the customer's service needs extremely important.

The assumption behind customer service is that it influences buyer selection in the market. Service must therefore reach those who are influential in the buying decisions and the attributes of service should match the needs of these decision makers. The first issue has been examined by investigation of service perceptions within a major food product market in the United Kingdom.[15] Five suppliers in the market were selling directly to major grocery store chains. The research involved interviews with buyers, store division managers, store managers and warehouse managers of several of these store chains. The objectives were to establish whether there were consistent perceptions of service between organisations and also whether perceptions of service differed within these organisations. If there were consistent differences, the market might be divisible into market segments with differing patterns of service which have been demonstrated elsewhere.[16] Those managers interviewed were asked to place the five suppliers in rank-order based on customer service, to list the criteria that they used, to rank these criteria, and then to rank-order each supplier against these criteria.

The results showed considerable diversity in the use of customer service criteria. Figure 3:4 is the aggregated rank-ordering or criteria of head-office buyers, calculated by combining rank orders and number of mentions into a common scale. The results showed product availability to be the dominant issue. However, the next two items on the list, promotion and representation, are not ordinarily considered as physical distribution variables. In fact the next PD variable does not emerge until rank No. 4, which indicates some confusion about what constitutes customer service in the minds of the particular buyers surveyed.

Variable	Rank
Product availability	1
Promotional activity	2
Representation	3
Order status	4
Distribution: direct or via depot	5
Delivery time	6
Pricing	7
Merchandising	8
Product positioning	9
Invoice accuracy	10
New product introductions	11
Advertising	12

Figure 3:4   Perception of customer service factors by head-office buyers

The role of the individual within the organisation is also important in determining which factors are most important. Buyers appeared to perceive service variables differently from other individuals. They stressed product availability more heavily. Other groups emphasised particular problem areas but without any consistent pattern.

These data therefore stress the importance of identifying the target of service if it is to be an influential factor in doing business.

A further dilemma was introduced when rank orders of suppliers were compared with their scores on specific attributes using the Spearman rank-order coefficient. The results of the analysis showed that only in about half of the individual cases were the overall ratings of suppliers highly correlated with any one of the attribute elements listed in the rank-ordering. The element that was most frequently mentioned was 'delivery time'. One of the most surprising results in several cases however was the complete irrelevance of some of the most commonly identified elements in the overall supplier rating.

Another study of appliance dealers in England asked dealers to evaluate their suppliers on several dimensions relating to the total constellation of influences which exist between supplier and buyer. The results were then combined by factor analysis, a statistical technique for determining the underlying structure of responses. Five factors emerged from the data:

1   Contact by suppliers with the dealer, such as frequency with which the representatives call, identifying delivery times, ease of general standing.
2   General standing in the trade such as complaints, and an image of general standing.
3   Pricing, reflecting profitability of the product item, discounts, perceived product value.
4   Delivery, including logistics factors such as order cycle time, availability from stock, willingness to deal with special requests, accuracy of performance on specified delivery dates.
5   Back-up services, such as promotion, product line, spares support, credit, knowledge by representatives.

The supplier involved in the study was generally most preferred by these dealers based on the full range of marketing variables: product, promotion, pricing, etc. However, it was the worst among all suppliers mentioned in general trade relationships and delivery. Among these small firms, delivery (i.e. customer service), emerges as a distinctly identifiable factor in supplier-dealer relations.

Given the importance of customer service which this research and that cited earlier has shown, how do we determine which factors are important? The most direct way is to start either by asking the customer to list the factors which are important or to begin with a pre-established list and ask him specifically to identify the degree of importance of each factor. Bender, for example, describes procedures for developing customer service surveys.[17] The danger is that there may be undetermined influences outside of the specific context of service which can distort the findings. In addition, without the context of a decision situation, the responses become answers without commitment and may, therefore, not be of any use in explaining actual behaviour. All surveys must therefore be related to a specific context of trade relationships to be meaningful.

An alternative is to present several hypothetical situations carefully arranged to test the levels of pre-identified customer service variables, and ask the respondent to determine which scenario he prefers. The technique, known as 'conjoint analysis' or 'trade-off analysis',[18] then translates these preferences, by means of computer algorithms, into utility values which demonstrate how much relative value a customer places on speed of delivery, for example, versus product availability or other aspects of service.

To demonstrate the use of this approach, data from the same set of appliance dealers is shown here. Four variables were identified as important to these dealers: elapsed order cycle time, the reliability of these delivery times, the degree to which dealers could expect products to be available from stock and information on orders. The technique is thus a verbalised experiment, using hypothetical situations.

Each of these variables was described alternately at specific levels of service in combination with other variables, and also at differing levels. Delivery time was indicated to be two weeks, four weeks or six weeks. Reliability of this time was either 'reliable' or 'unreliable'. Products were available from stock either 80 per cent or 50 per cent of the time and order status information was either 'regular' or 'irregular'. Each level of each service variable was then combined with levels of other variables to create distinct scenarios depicting hypothetical suppliers. The potential list of 24 combinations was reduced to nine through a process of elimination of implausible or obvious choices. The results are shown in Figure 3:5.

Variable and Level	*Units of Utility*
Order to delivery time:	
2 weeks	+12.64
4 weeks	+ 2.37
6 weeks	− 15.11
Reliability of delivery times:	
reliable	+15.39
unreliable	− 15.39
Products available from stock:	
80 per cent	+ 7.64
50 per cent	− 7.64
Information on orders:	
regular	+ 5.42
irregular	− 5.42

Figure 3:5   Service preferences of appliance dealers
From Christopher, Schary and Skjøtt-Larsen

These utilities can then be added together. For example, the ideal position in this case is two weeks' delivery, with reliability, with 80 per cent delivered from stock on hand and with regular order status information. The question then is which service variable would the customer be most willing to sacrifice. The answer in this case is order status information. Similarly a combination of four weeks' delivery, with reliability, with 80 per cent from stock and regular information (total utility of 30.82) can be compared with two weeks but irregular delivery, 80 per cent from stock and order status information (utility of 10.31). Obviously regularity of delivery over-shadows other elements in the combinations presented here.

The use of conjoint analysis has demonstrated that service attributes can be determined in a manner similar to that of identifying desirable product attributes in other aspects of marketing. Again the problem of the decision context becomes important. Another crucial problem is that of determining the point of decision and where these attributes will be the most influential variables in determining vendor selection. This aspect appears to be even more difficult to resolve.

Future directions

This discussion of customer service has been concerned primarily with short-term decisions. Strategy becomes important in the design and development of fixed facilities such as distribution centres, and also in the development of computer-based data processing systems. The use of customer service as a strategic element in itself however has been missing from management discussion.

In abstract form, customer service is a variety-absorbing mechanism. Customers, and the demands by customers, produce variety in the pattern of orders, in service standards required, and in the degree of co-ordination required. Customer service is a mechanism by which this variety can be absorbed without disrupting the operations of the supplying organisation. Service becomes a buffering system to match customer needs while simultaneously protecting the supplier against random disturbances. The ability to absorb variety is then the degree of competitive advantage over other firms in the marketplace which customer service provides for an organisation.

Absorbing variety can be accomplished through heavy investment in safety stocks or through co-ordination. Safety stocks and routinely fast response in effect protect supplying organisations from the buffering that the variety of demands imposes. However, this is also accomplished at a high price: investment in stocks and expenditure on premium transportation.

The alternative solution is, in effect, to create a system operating between customer and supplier which emphasises co-ordination so that complex demands and supply arrangements, such as production schedules and delivery requirements, can be specifically matched to the needs of the other party. This creates complex organisational requirements with dangers of overloading the internal communications network with signals from customers. The problems of dealing with customer service competition is becoming increasingly intense and can only intensify in the future. The organisational question confronting management is how to meet such competition a) without creating heavy investment requirements and b) without impairing the supplier's organisation.

References

1   James L. Heskett, 'Controlling Customer Logistics Service', *International Journal of Physical Distribution,* June 1971, pp. 141–5.

2   Martin Christopher, Philip Schary and Tage Skjøtt-Larsen, *Customer Service and Distribution Strategy,* London: Associated Business Press, 1979, p. 4.

3   William D. Perrault and Frederick A. Russ, 'Physical Distribution Service: A Neglected Aspect of Marketing Management', MSU *Business Topics,* Summer 1974, pp. 37–45.

4   Jay W. Forrester, 'Industrial Dynamics', *Harvard Business Review,* July–August 1958, Vol. 36, pp. 37–66.

5   Bernard J. La Londe and Paul H. Zinszer, *Customer Service: Meaning and Measurement,* Chicago: National Council of Physical Distribution Management, 1976, pp. 272-80.

6   Philip B. Schary and Boris Becker, 'The Impact of Stock-Out on Market Share: Temporal Affects', *Journal of Business Logistics,* Vol. 1, No. 1, 1978.

7   Philip B. Schary and Martin Christopher, 'The Anatomy of a Stock-Out', *Journal of Retailing,* July 1979.

8   Harvey N. Shycon and Christopher Sprague, 'Put a Price Tag on Your Customer Service Levels', *Harvard Business Review,* July–August 1975, pp. 71–8.

9   W. D. Perrault and F. A. Russ, 'Physical Distribution Service: Industrial Purchase Decisions', *Journal of Marketing,* April 1976; and Peter M. Banting, 'Customer Service in Industrial Marketing: A Comparative Study', *European Journal of Marketing,* 1976, Vol. 10, No. 3, p. 140.

10   Peter S. Banting, 'Customer Service in Industrial Marketing: A Comparative Study', op. cit.

11   William M. Hutchinson and John F. Stolle, 'How to Manage Customer Service', *Harvard Business Review,* November–December 1968.

12   David P. Herron, 'Managing PDM for Profit', *Harvard Business Review,* March–April 1977, pp. 121–32.

13   Martin Christopher, Philip Schary and Tage Skjøtt-Larsen, *Customer Service and Distribution Strategy,* London: Associated Business Press, 1979, Ch. 3.

14   Herron, op. cit.

15   Christopher, op. cit., Ch. 4.

16   Peter Gilmour, 'Customer Service: Differentiating by Marketing Segment', *International Journal of Physical Distribution,* 1977, Vol. 7, No. 3, pp. 141–9.

17 Paul S. Bender, *The Design and Operation of Customer Service Systems,* New York: AMACOM, 1976.
18 William D. Perrault and Frederick A. Russ, 'Improving Physical Distribution Service Decisions with Trade-off Analysis', *International Journal of Physical Distribution,* 1977, Vol. 17, No. 3, pp. 117–27.

4

Distribution management in the company organisation

Felix Wentworth

Physical distribution management is a relatively new concept, which has not yet won acceptance in every company and is still in the process of finding its right level within company hierarchies. What this level should be largely depends on the nature of the business, in each case, and on the importance of the physical distribution function to the company. The golden rule, as Bernard Shaw once said, is that there are no golden rules. Nevertheless, broad patterns and guidelines are beginning to emerge.

Reasons for management's interest in physical distribution

A good way to start approaching the problem is to determine how and why physical distribution (PD) comes to be an area of interest to top management in the first place. There are four main reasons; two negative and two positive:

1 The management conflicts which arise in the absence of physical distribution management (PDM).
2 The rapidly rising cost of physical distribution.
3 The opportunities for cost reduction in PD.
4 The opportunities for PD to assist the marketing effort.

Management conflicts

Traditionally, before the acceptance of the PD concept, companies have generally allocated its subfunctions among other departments (in something like the way shown in Figure 4:1). The objectives of each of the three are likely at times to diverge.

Production departments like to minimise production costs by having long runs at a steady rate; at the same time being aware of the lack of space at factory warehouses and so preferring to send as much of the stocks as possible out to depots, particularly when sales run low and stocks build up. Sales departments prefer to have high stocks at times of high demand and certainly not to run out of stock; they like to have many depots in order to give good customer service, with short production runs of every product to ensure full availability and frequent replenishment of depots. Traffic managers, wherever they may be placed in the hierarchy, like best to accumulate replenishments until they have full lorry-loads. Controllers or finance chiefs are anxious to reduce costs all round and to reduce the investment required in the form of stocks of all kinds.

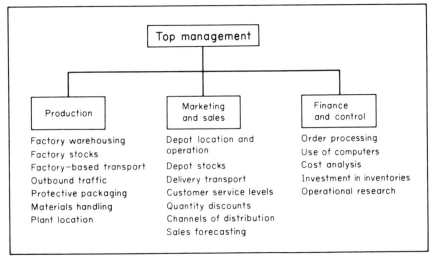

Figure 4:1   Traditional allocation of physical distribution subfunctions or areas of interest among other departments

Under such an organisation – which may be looked on as a first-generation situation – chief executives are likely to have to intervene from time to time in order to resolve the conflicts, and are probably only too well aware of the limited means at their disposal for making the best decisions when a cost or benefit trade-off situation arises. Physical distribution is a complex area and requires special skills for its successful management.

Fragmentation of responsibility for physical distribution also has the drawback that it makes it difficult and sometimes impossible for top management to hold any specific individual responsible for particular cost elements, such as transport, warehousing or inventory. Each of the functional heads can always find a legitimate excuse for 'passing the buck' to one of his colleagues, since these subheadings are so closely interdependent.

Rising costs

A number of factors are simultaneously helping to drive distribution costs up faster than costs in other sections of business activity. In the first place,the component costs of distribution have been going up relatively fast: distribution is labour-intensive, and the wage costs of transport and warehouse staffs have been rising rapidly in recent years. This is especially true of drivers: their high earnings in the past were generally gained by working long hours and they have begun to press for shorter hours without loss of earnings, as well as participating in the general pressure for higher wages. Warehouse costs, too, have risen disproportionately because of the shortage of suitable land and accommodation. At the same time, inventory-carrying costs have climbed in step with the rise in the general level of interest rates.

A second important cause of rising distribution costs is the greater intensity of competition. This has led to a great proliferation of product lines as a matter of marketing strategy, with an ever-quickening tempo of new products, wider ranges and new packaging. Old slow-moving lines have not been discarded at anything like the same rate. As the range widens, so the costs of distribution – and, no doubt, of production – have been driven upwards.

The increased competitiveness manifests itself also in customer attitudes that expect prompter, better and more frequent deliveries from suppliers, exhibit a diminishing readiness to hold stocks themselves, and a pressure on the part of marketing management to gain an advantage by out-performing competitors.

The third force tending to drive distribution costs up is the increasing internationalisation of trade, with goods moving over ever-greater distances and so incurring greater transport costs.

The result of these various trends is that distribution costs now occupy, particularly in the area of consumer products of all kinds, a position which is often second only to the cost of the raw materials. Depending on the type of product and its value, and on how they are defined, distribution costs can account for anywhere between 5 and 40 per cent of the total selling price.

Cost-reduction opportunities

Peter Drucker, that apostle of modern management techniques, pointed out in 1962 in an article in *Fortune*, 'The economy's dark continent', that almost 50 cents out of every dollar the consumer spends on goods go to activities that occur after the goods are made; he has described physical distribution as 'the last frontier of cost reduction'. Other areas of business activity have already had the spotlight of attention focused on them: production is ever more mechanised and even automated; the office has its computers; sales has broadened into marketing and become more scientific in the process. Now it is the turn of physical distribution.

Some of the opportunities for cost reduction lie in bringing a higher calibre of management and the benefits of modern technology to bear upon each of the component subfunctions of distribution: industrial engineering methods, the application of standards, the increased use of mechanisation for loading and unloading and improved packaging all fall into this category. But for the rest, there are opportunities that arise solely from the fact that the components are united under a single management. This expresses itself in two ways: optimising cost trade-offs and what may be called the synergetic effect.

Cost trade-offs.   One example is the speed of replenishment of stocks: the faster this can be done, the lower can be the safety stocks held at a depot. Somewhere the balance between the two has to be struck. Another example occurs when calculations arrive at an economic order (replenishment) quantity which is less than a full vehicle load yet the closer to full vehicle loads one can get, the lower are the unit costs.

The synergetic effect.   This term is used to describe the 'two plus two equals five' kind of situation, where the whole is greater than the sum of its parts. In the present context it refers to areas of cost-reduction opportunities which arise out of bringing transport and storage together. One example is the ability to relate their combined impact to customer service needs. A second example may be found in the strategic location of depots, which is partly also a multiple trade-off case.

PD as an aid to marketing

By taking the measurement and investigation of consumer service levels as its starting point, physical distribution management is in a unique position to adjust its service, in agreement with marketing management, in such a way as to increase customer satisfaction and so gain a competitive advantage. This may take the form of faster and more reliable delivery, greater stock availability, service in new geographical areas, or a special degree of collaboration with the receiving facilities of major customers. In addition, differential distribution cost analysis is able to help marketing management to evaluate alternative distribution channels and to construct rational quantity discount scales.

These are the kinds of reasons that are prompting the top managements of companies to take an interest in physical distribution and to give consideration to the consolidation of the various relevant subfunctions under a single physical distribution manager.

Should PDM be a staff or a line function?

Having decided to appoint a physical distribution manager, top management still has to decide on the form which his responsibility should take. Should it be 'staff' – that is, advisory – or 'line' – that is, in the line of control? There can be no general rule; the form of organisation must be that which is most appropriate to the particular operations and objectives of distribution in a particular firm in any particular time.

PDM as a staff function

Figure 4:2 shows a typical organisation of the physical distribution department in order to fulfil a staff function. This type of physical distribution department concentrates on planning and measuring activities. Setting it up does not require any substantial reassignments of people or reallocations of lines of authority. Consequently, it is relatively easy to implement and is frequently the initial form of organisation adopted by a company just moving into acceptance of the total distribution concept. It may involve the creation of a whole set of positions that had not previously existed in the company.

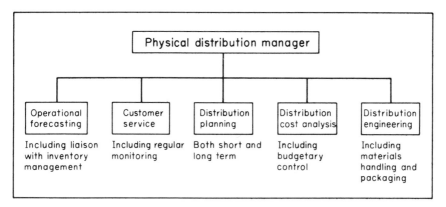

Figure 4:2   The physical distribution manager in a staff role

This arrangement is relatively simple, which does not mean it is ineffective. By the use of budgets, performance standards and various other guidelines, distribution managers can, as staff managers, go a long way towards effectively controlling the cost- and service-influencing efforts of personnel who are not directly answerable to them. In one company, an annual distribution expense of £8 million was effectively managed by one manager with a three-man headquarters department.

The main drawback of the staff role is that it is capable of running into entrenched opposition, or at least passive resistance on the part of line personnel who, in the last resort, can claim the right to follow their own judgement rather than that of the physical distribution manager.

The main advantage is that, relatively quickly and painlessly, a company can begin to apply and reap the economies of the new physical distribution skills, supported by operations research and advanced computer capability.

PDM as a line function

Figure 4:3 shows the organisation of a physical distribution department as it might appear in a line role. In this form of organisation, the physical distribution manager is directly supervising the efforts of personnel who are 'doing' rather than 'planning'. This puts him in an operational role. Because such an organisation probably requires the transfer of personnel who were previously reporting to other managers, it is more likely to encounter opposition from them, and is somewhat more difficult to implement. However, in a given situation it may be the only way to secure the necessary integration of essential functions.

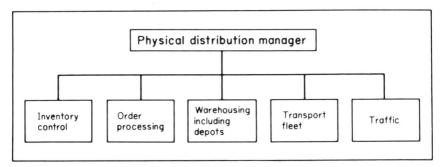

Figure 4:3   The physical distribution manager in a line role

The advantage of a line form of responsibility of this type is that it helps to create a strong unity of purpose among the staffs engaged in the various subfunctions concerned, with better co-operation with each other and probably better morale after feeling for years they were the 'Cinderellas' of the company. It may also lend weight to physical distribution managers' claims, if any, to be ranked equal to colleagues controlling production and marketing.

The main disadvantage of a line-only organisation is that, unless the physical distribution manager is a man of exceptional gifts and industry, he cannot by himself carry out the various analytical and planning functions described in the staff-type organisation. In that case his team may be eager to get on with their task, but without knowing in which direction to go.

PDM as a combined staff and line function

The answer to the dilemma posed by each of the other two forms of organisation may well be a combination of both, with the physical distribution department fulfilling both a staff and a line role. Figure 4:4 gives an example of a department organised along these lines. Such a solution to the problem may, however, be inappropriate in particular cases – for example, it may be top-heavy in a small company, or it may cut across an established form of regional organisation in a large one.

Probably the soundest approach for a company in which the solution is not self-evident is to call in expert assistance from outside to help determine the optimum distribution system and its needs from a planning and control point of view, and only then to develop the organisational framework best suited to operate it.

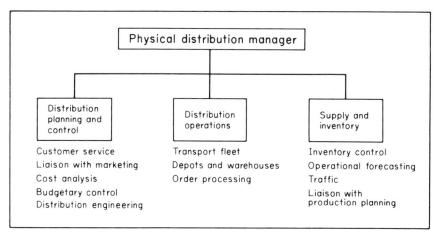

Figure 4:4   The physical distribution manager in combined line and staff roles

Position of PDM in the company hierarchy

The instinctive view of most physical distribution managers would probably be that they should occupy a place on a par with the other two functional departments (production and marketing) and with such other executive functions as purchasing, finance, R & D, etc. There is much to support this view: first is the fact that the essence of distribution's role is to act as the pipeline connecting production to marketing's customers. As a bridge between them, it ought to command equal status. As a cost (or profit) centre it can also often claim parity with the others. A third argument is that physical distribution fulfils a dual role which serves the interest both of production (assisting a smooth level of production by cushioning the ups and downs of sales) and of marketing (satisfying customer demand); if it is subordinated to either of the other two a certain bias is likely to enter into the approach to physical distribution's role, to the detriment of the other. Finally, it must be recognised that a fully fledged distribution function embodies a variety of special skills which is quite comparable in scope and complexity with those comprised in modern marketing, or in production; neither a production nor a marketing man is likely to be able to acquire a sufficient understanding of those in addition to his own to be able to supervise them effectively.

A growing number of companies have accepted the force of these considerations by appointing distribution managers or directors on equal terms with production and marketing managers, and responsible to the managing director. Before 1960, the title of physical distribution manager was practically unheard of. By 1974, according to a survey published by the Whitehead Consulting Group Ltd,[1] in no less than 22 of the respondent companies physical distribution was represented in its own right by a director on the board of the company with the title of distribution director. This trend has continued, albeit at a slow pace, over the succeeding six years.

Nevertheless, there may be good reasons in some instances for placing physical distribution under either the production director or the marketing director. One such reason may be to avoid increasing further the burden on the managing director; so many additional functions nowadays claim the need to report direct to him (for example, training, long-range planning, management services, and computer services, in addition to the more familiar production, marketing, purchasing, finance, personnel, R & D, secretary, exporting, etc.) that he must find some way to group them and reduce their number.

Another reason for not immediately appointing someone to a senior rank may be connected with the availability of suitable candidates. Physical distribution is such a young science that there are still only a few qualified men and most of them are relatively young. A more mature man with the right kind of background and enough interest can learn by doing but it may be wiser to leave him at middle-management level while he does it.

Likewise, a brilliant younger man may receive better acceptance from his marketing and production colleagues if for a time he is placed under the protective wing of one of them, who will thereby acquire a kind of proprietary interest in him and in physical distribution. Otherwise these senior men may react instinctively in a hostile manner to the sudden appearance of what appears to them to be a rival.

Yet another reason why top management may wish to proceed with caution is if it is only half convinced of the validity of the physical distribution concept. In such a case it is then up to physical distribution managers to seize the opportunities open to them, and to demonstrate in practice why physical distribution is of vital concern to their company. Lastly, the very nature of the business may dictate the solution. If marketing is by far the dominant management function of a particular company, this could make it essential that distribution objectives should be subordinated to those of marketing; and likewise with production.

One organisational solution, adopted by 18 per cent of respondents to the Whitehead Survey, is to group production and distribution management together under the title 'operations' – sometimes with the inclusion of purchasing.

In any case, functional relationships in any dynamic company are generally of a fluid nature, and no single solution should be regarded as final. In some degree, theoretical solutions may have to be modified according to the personalities, experience and special skills of the managers concerned. As people move, or are moved into, out of and within the firm, so the human structures called organisation must be manipulated and bent so as to make the best use of the available management material and make the greatest contribution to achieving the objectives of the company.

Collaboration with other departments

One of the most important functions of chief executives is to ensure a close collaboration between the various departments reporting to them. If each department operates as a separate entity and pursues its own objectives – however desirable – in isolation, conflicts of interest will inevitably arise at times between different departments which the chief executive will then, usually with inadequate information at his disposal, have to resolve.

A survey carried out by A. T. Kearney and Company in Britain, the USA and Germany revealed that in Britain there is a much stronger tendency than in the other countries for departments to be meticulous about not treading on each other's preserves. According to this doctrine, it is wrong for a member of one department to get together with his opposite number in another one: rather, he should pass a communication upwards to his departmental head who will then, in theory, communicate with the head of the other department and so down the line. While this may appear somewhat exaggerated, it contains a kernel of truth.

In its new and exciting role, physical distribution management must, above all, work together with the other departments, not only at the top level but all the way down the line. In co-operation with the marketing department, it must develop and monitor customer service standards; with brand management, action must be taken to support marketing strategies; with production planning, it must influence the length of production runs and manage inventories and traffic schedules to the best advantage; with the control or finance department, it must control the investment in inventories and assist in profit planning. It can advise production management on plant location, work with sales department and computer services on forecasting, and evaluate for the marketing department the alternative costs of using different channels of distribution. If the lines of communication between them all are not wide open, physical distribution management is likely to fail in its endeavours.

The dangers and shortcomings of suboptimisation of a total system through each department in a business pursuing its own optimum are beginning to be well understood. Indeed, the basic reason for breaking the total continuum or spectrum of business activity into separate manageable lumps, namely that it is too complex to manage as a whole, is being challenged by the development of computer applications. The computer is capable of handling great complexity, and the trend in the future will certainly be towards a greater degree of integration between functional departments, based on a mutual interdependence through the computer.

Some companies have, indeed, taken a step in this direction by setting up an overall computer-based logistics, or materials management department, whose function is to control and optimise the total flow of materials through the company system. Such a department need not be very large, and its function may be more akin to a total management information system than to a physical distribution management department as it is now understood. In any event, it seems clear that, whatever organisational structures are now in course of development for the management of physical distribution, there will be still more changes to come in the future.

Qualities required of physical distribution managers

Figures 4:5 and 4:6 are examples somewhat idealised, of a job description (Figure 4:5) and job requirements (Figure 4:6) for distribution management in a grocery products manufacturing company. How many distribution jobs at present embrace this scope, and how many men could fulfil the requirements, are matters of conjecture, but at least they may help to indicate what should be aimed at.

General. The distribution manager will report to the marketing director. He will be responsible for achieving the company's distribution objectives by the development of the lowest-cost distribution system consistent with marketing objectives, and for advising management on distribution planning, both short and long term.

Specific objectives
1 *Delivery service:* to provide a reliable delivery service to customers by the management of order-taking and processing, inventories, warehousing and transport.
2 *Marketing support:* to assist in establishing standards for customer service by geographical market, by customer class and by product groups, consistent with marketing policy, and to implement and monitor these.
3 *Inventory management:* to budget and control inventories of finished goods in the light of customer-service policies, sales forecasts, production constraints and investment policies.
4 *Cost control:* to prepare expense budgets for the total distribution process for approval by the marketing director and controller; to analyse variances; to take or recommend action to conform to the budgets.
5 *Warehousing and depots:* to determine warehousing needs, negotiate satisfactory rates for outside warehousing and organise warehousing procedures; to conduct short- and long-term studies of depot needs in co-operation with production department.
6 *Systems design:* to bring the distribution system as a whole continually up to date, based on regular analyses of the company's product mix, sales needs and costs.
7 *Organisation:* to staff his department and plan for the development and promotion of its personnel; to establish an effective organisation structure to plan, control and operate the distribution system.
8 *Protective packaging:* to suggest or approve containers so as to meet the materials-handling requirements of the customer and the company.
9 *Improvement:* to aim to achieve for the company a leading place in the field of transport and distribution within the food industry by continual improvement through innovation; constantly to seek ways of increasing efficiency and productivity and of reducing unit costs in all stages of distribution.

Figure 4:5   Job description for a distribution manager for a grocery products company

Relationships

1 *Director of marketing:* report to him and keep him informed on all transport and distribution matters; seek advice and direction from him.
2 *Sales manager:* co-ordinate with him in establishing customer-service standards; advise him on related costs.
3 *Brand managers:* co-ordinate with them to support marketing strategies and advise them on related costs.
4 *Production director:* co-ordinate with him the inventory needs with actual and planned production capacities.
5 *Controller:* assist him in profit planning by establishing transport and distribution budgets and analysing variances.
6 *Transport manager:* to obtain functional guidance and to direct and advise him on his operations.

Figure 4:5   continued

Education or advanced training. He should either have a bachelor's degree, preferably in economics, mathematics or a branch of science, or have qualified by examination for membership of a professional institute.

Experience and knowledge. He should have a minimum of five years' experience in transport and distribution, preferably in the food industry, with at least two years as departmental head, or as a deputy in a large concern.

He should have a reasonable understanding of the principles and practice of customer-service analysis, inventory management, sales forecasting, warehousing, depot location and planning, materials handling, order processing, and transport planning, costing and control. Finally he should at least be aware of the available computer packages, and familiar with those situations within the distribution area where computer technology could be usefully applied.

Personal. He should be a man of sound practical and technical judgement, with ambition and self-confidence. The ability to work without close supervision, to plan ahead, to delegate work through others, to show resourcefulness and creativity in solving complex problems, and to present written and verbal proposals effectively to top management, are all desirable characteristics.

He should preferably be a family man, active in community or association affairs and of above average intelligence. He will be 35 to 45 years old, in good health and neat in appearance.

Figure 4:6   Job requirements for the distribution manager described in Figure 4:5

Reference

1   Whitehead Consulting Group, *A National Survey of Physical Distribution Management*, 1974.

PART TWO

Storage Facilities

Overview

This section of five chapters is devoted to the topic of storage facilities and related matters. In Chapter 5, Waller explains the role of depots, their size, throughput and location. Warehousing cost relationships are explored, as also are the transport cost relationships involved in linking storage facilities to each other, and to the customer. Waller extends his treatment into Chapter 6 where the emphasis is on computer techniques for siting depots; single-depot and multiple-depot location cases are examined. An example is also given of a simple computer software package suitable for analysing the storage facility requirements of a particular system. Waller completes his comprehensive review of the subject with a discussion of custom designed systems models. Firth takes up the storage facility topic from a different angle in Chapter 7 where he focuses on the functions provided by such a facility, rather than on where it should be sited. He deals with the issues of cost, operational effectiveness, and design before going on to materials handling.

In Chapter 8, Firth covers a range of issues of practical importance to the distribution operations executive, i.e. alternative storage layout schemes, order-picking, goods receiving and despatch areas as well as the ancillary areas usually associated with a warehouse, i.e. offices, maintenance and battery charging facilities for fork lift trucks. Finally, in Chapter 9, Firth reviews automated and mechanised devices which are fast becoming commonplace within the modern warehouse. These include automated storage and retrieval systems, carousels, high speed carton packing systems, and wire in-floor guidance systems.

In all, this section provides an exhaustive and practical coverage of the storage element of the distribution mix.

5

Use and location of depots

Alan G. Waller

Distribution studies

A review of the role of depots in a company's distribution system, and of the most cost-effective number, size, and location of depots to fulfil this role, requires an understanding of the existing and likely future demands on the company; of the factors, internal and external to the company, that might provide opportunities or constraints relevant to distribution, and of the alternative distribution policies for satisfying demand under these conditions.

There are many reasons why companies undertake such distribution studies. These may be linked with changes in company structure, in the size and location of demand, in customer service expectations, in product characteristics, in costs, in legal requirements, or in technological advances in materials handling and storage, and in transport.

Figure 5:1 shows an analysis of the reasons behind sixteen distribution studies in which the author has been involved. The list of ten possible reasons is not intended to be exhaustive, but it serves to give some indication of the factors, or combination of factors, underlying such studies.

The role of depots

Distribution is often described as 'getting the goods from where they arise to where they are wanted, in the right form, at the right time, and at the right cost'. It can be seen from this that distribution is much more than transport alone, and that depot facilities are often justified and indeed essential. Production and supply cannot be

REASON FOR STUDY	1	2	3	4	5	6	7	8	9	10	11	12	13	14	15	16
Increasing sales volume	✓	✓	✓	✓	✓											
Customer service inadequate	✓	✓				✓	✓							✓		
Rationalisation following merger																
Increasing costs		✓				✓	✓	✓	✓	✓						
Inadequate storage facilities	✓		✓									✓				
New products	✓						✓					✓				
New sales areas	✓			✓		✓							✓			
Production rationalisation													✓	✓		
Change in legislation							✓								✓	
New technology															✓	✓

NOTE: The analysis was derived from reasons given for commissioning a distribution study

Figure 5:1   Reasons for distribution studies – an analysis of sixteen studies

instantaneous, but demand can be, and it can often be adequately met only by the storage of goods near the market place. Even given good demand forecasting, it is often not possible to match the rate of production with the forecast demand. The need for long production runs to reduce set-up times, or the incidence of seasonality in demand over the year, can often lead to intermediate storage requirements. Cost trade-offs in transport can also justify some intermediate transfer or storage facility. The economies of employing bulk transport from ports or factories, together with the use of smaller vehicles for final delivery, can lead to the use of depots. Savings in materials handling and movement resulting from unitisation, together with a need to deliver assembled orders of goods from various sources, can also justify the costs of specialised break-bulk and order-picking and assembly facilities. Thus intermediate warehouse or depot facilities may be necessary to provide working or safety stocks of goods, as a transfer point for transport operations, or as break-bulk and order-assembly operations.

Decisions in distribution

Decisions relating directly to the nature and size of specific depot locations must be based upon an understanding of how that depot would operate. These decisions therefore interact with the wider range of planning and operational decisions in distribution. These decisions can, for any particular company, be categorised according to the planning horizon involved in making the decision.

```
STRATEGIC: for example:
                  – Warehousing technology
                  – Number of depots
                  – Size of depots
                  – Location of depots
TACTICAL: for example:
                  – Transport methods
                  – Vehicle fleet mix
                  – Direct delivery policies
                  – Inventory levels
OPERATIONAL: for example:
                  – Vehicle routing
                  – Load planning
                  – Overtime levels
                  – Depot replenishment
```

Figure 5:2   Possible hierarchy of decisions in distribution

Figure 5:2 sets out a possible hierarchy for decision-making. Strategic decisions might be reviewed every three to five years, say, whereas tactical decisions might be reviewed every year or so. Operational decisions are those necessary to continue with the operations of the company, and are likely to be made many times each year. The detailed content and classification will vary from one company to another, but a hierarchy will always exist.

These decisions are practically all interrelated. For example, the best location for a particular depot will depend upon which factories are supplying it, which customers it is supplying (which in turn depends on the location of other depots), on the methods and costs of trunk and final delivery transport used, on the quantity and nature of the throughput, and so on. Furthermore, although the hierarchy of decisions in Figure 5:2 demonstrates that the shorter-term decisions such as vehicle routing are made within the constraints imposed by longer-term decisions such as depot location and customer zoning, it is also clear that these longer-term decisions have to be based upon assumptions about the resource, cost and service implications of these shorter-term decisions. Before looking at techniques that will help in handling these complexities, it is worth-while studying the nature of the costs in distribution.

Costs in distribution

Decisions regarding the use of depots involve a consideration of the complex trade-offs between various cost and customer service aspects. The costs to be considered will depend upon the nature of the distribution study and upon the particular company, but can include:

(a) warehousing – for example, the costs associated with:
  – receipt
  – storage
  – picking
  – assembly
  – packing
  – dispatch

(b) transport – for example, the costs associated with:
  – supply
  – trunking
  – final delivery

(c) lost sales – the cost of inadequate customer service

(d) inventory – the cost of capital tied up
  – the cost of obsolescence and spoilage

(e) communications and information handling – for example, the costs associated with:
  – order receipt and entry
  – order processing
  – inventory planning, control and replenishment
  – management information

(f)   packaging   – inner
                         – outer
(g)   production – for example, the costs associated with:
                                 – storing
                                 – handling
                                 – manufacturing

We shall discuss each of these cost elements briefly before studying in more detail the warehousing and transport costs.

Warehousing cost

Depot costs depend primarily upon the volume and nature of the throughput, together with the storage and handling methods employed. They may also depend upon a number of other factors, including the location of the depot. The total warehousing cost may vary significantly according to the number of depots utilised.

Transport cost

The cost of transport depends primarily upon the type and amount of goods carried from location to location, the method (or mode) of transport, and the distance between locations. Where more than one location is served on a single vehicle trip, the separation of cost becomes more difficult. Clearly, the positioning of the depots in the system will affect the source and destination locations served by the transport function, and transport costs may therefore vary significantly with the number and locations of depots.

Cost of lost sales

It is clear that this is a fundamental consideration in determining the right depot structure. In theory this could be represented by varying demand according to stock levels and stock proximity to the customer, and the speed of the order processing cycle. In practice, it is usually viewed as a constraint which is imposed on the distribution system, which might determine the overall stock levels, and which might lead to a minimum number of stock points at some maximum distance from the customer, and a minimum frequency for final deliveries.

Inventory costs

The formulation of inventory policies is fundamental to determining the stock hierarchy on which a warehousing structure might be based, and indeed the distribution study should ideally be carried out hand in hand with an inventory study. The costs clearly vary with the depot structure, and are often represented implicitly as part of the warehousing costs.

Communications costs

These may vary significantly for different depot configurations. The costs that vary may be included implicitly as part of the warehousing costs.

Packaging costs

It may be important to consider these costs if there is a significant trade-off between, for example, increased packaging and lower handling and transport costs. The transport and warehousing costs can be structured to represent particular standards of packaging and unitisation.

Production costs

These can in some cases vary under different distribution policies because of the different throughputs of different products required at each factory to supply the required demand most cost-effectively.

Selecting the right costs

What is needed in a strategic distribution study is an understanding of how the total of these cost elements varies with the number, location, functions and throughputs of the depots in any distribution system considered. This is best carried out by incorporating the likely operational cost implications into comparative analyses to find the best alternative distribution systems, and then comparing the advantages of these against the capital costs of making the required changes, treating capital and revenue implications as in a normal investment appraisal project.

The costs selected for a particular study must depend upon the particular requirements and characteristics of that study, but before discussing the problems of defining the distribution system, we will firstly look in more detail at the warehousing and transport costs.

Warehousing cost relationships

The planned and actual functions and throughputs of a depot will determine the depot facilities and the nature of the costs incurred. The costs include those associated with:

- land (for example rental costs)
- buildings (for example rent, rates)
- storage and handling equipment (for example maintenance)
- services (for example electricity)
- labour (for example pickers, packers)
- supervision (for example depot management)
- consumables (for example packing material)

Finding out the nature of warehousing costs

It is necessary to be able to reflect the likely cost implications of each of these cost elements, under various possible distribution structures. This means finding out how the costs vary, for example under different throughputs and locations, and requires a careful analysis based upon existing or planned warehousing operations. It may be necessary to use existing cost information that is not directly applicable, and therefore requires further manipulation before it is meaningful in this context. For example, in one study the author was involved in, some 40 per cent of one depot's costs were found to be shown as maintenance. Further examination revealed that this nearly all comprised an unusually large roof repair bill, and the true average annual cost of maintenance was some 10 per cent of the cost represented. Adjustment of this unrealistic figure reduced the depot costs for use in subsequent analysis by more than 30 per cent.

Regression analysis to study the pattern of depot costs is often useful, as shown in Figure 5:3. However, one danger here is to use information based upon a range of

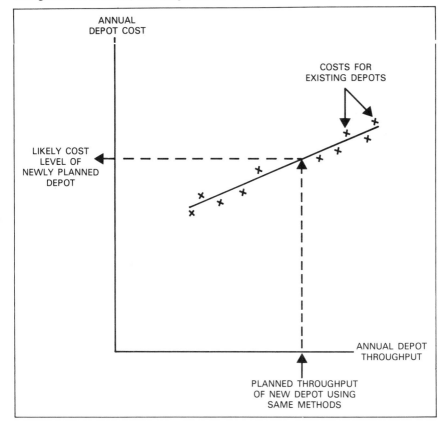

Figure 5:3   Use of regression analysis

current depot throughputs as a basis for estimating the costs of much higher throughputs. This can be quite misleading, as is seen from Figure 5:4 where further economies of scale are ignored in the analysis.

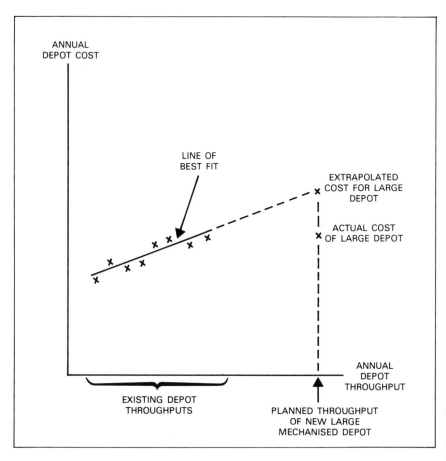

Figure 5:4   Misuse of regression analysis

The implications of depot cost relationships on total warehousing costs

At its simplest, the depot cost might turn out to be a constant amount per tonne of goods throughput. This implies that there are no fixed costs associated with operating the depot, and that the variable costs are the same, no matter what the level of throughput or the geographic depot location. This relationship is shown in Figure 5:5, and might hold under certain considerations where third party facilities are being used, with certain ranges of throughput.

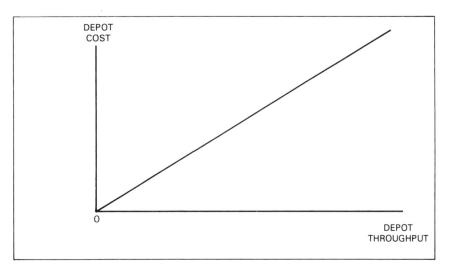

Figure 5:5   Simple variable depot cost relationship

If this cost relationship holds for all depot locations and depot sizes, then the total warehousing cost is the same for all distribution structures. This is shown in Figure 5:6.

Fixed depot costs

It is more usual for some costs of a depot to be incurred, irrespective of how much or how little throughput is experienced. Such costs would normally be termed the fixed costs of the depot, and might include factors such as rent and rates, and some aspects of administration. Clearly these so-called 'fixed costs' could be increased or reduced in the longer-term by contracting or expanding, or mechanising the depot, but for a specific type of depot operation they would be inevitable, and could change the relationship to that shown in Figure 5:7.

In the case where these fixed costs exist, the total warehousing cost will increase as the number of depots in the system increases. In particular, if this fixed cost, and the corresponding variable cost per tonne, are more or less the same over all possible depot locations, then the total warehousing cost for differing numbers of depots will be as shown in Figure 5:8.

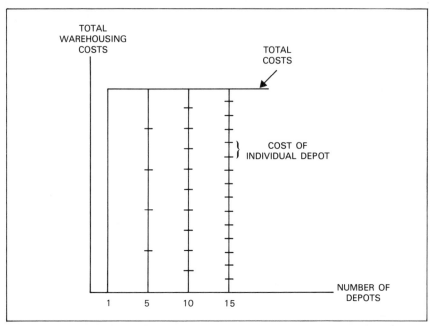

Figure 5:6   Total warehousing costs for simple variable depot cost
relationship

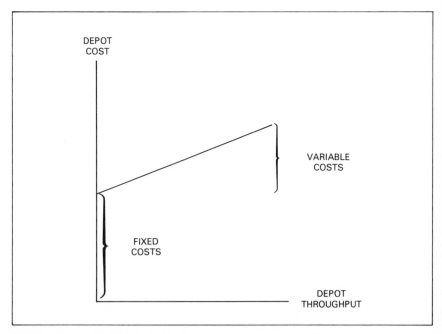

Figure 5:7   Depot costs with fixed and variable elements

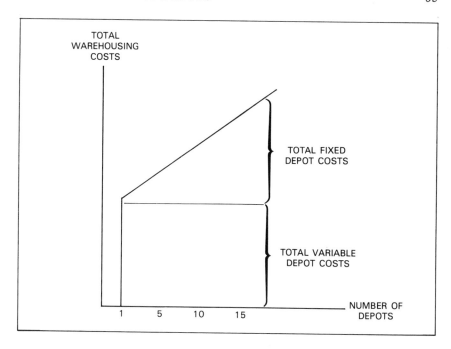

Figure 5:8   Total warehousing costs for depots with fixed and variable cost elements

Economies of scale

The 'fixed' costs discussed above can in the long run be reduced under low volume throughputs, and removed altogether by closing the depot down. Conversely, for high volume throughputs, the variable cost per ton can often be reduced by investment in handling equipment and automated systems. Furthermore, proportionally less stock is needed to support a high level of throughput than that required to support a low level of throughput. For these reasons there are often economies of scale in the warehousing operation that are reflected in Figure 5:9. This relationship might in practice be a number of jumps and bumps, but for purposes of analysis can often be represented by a smooth curve.

Diseconomies of scale

There is some evidence to suggest that at very high levels of throughput, economies of scale cease to apply, and problems of control are experienced. This could be reflected in increased marginal costs at very high throughputs, as shown in Figure 5:10.

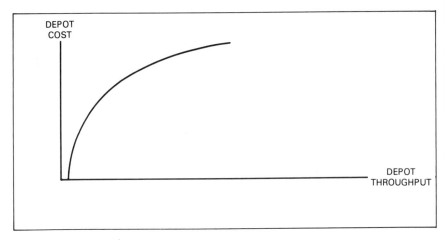

Figure 5:9   Depot cost relationship with economies of scale

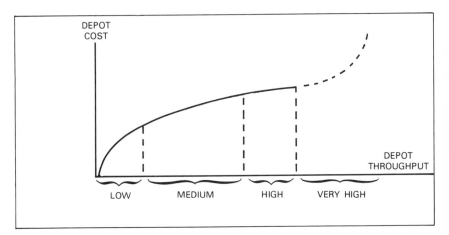

Figure 5:10   Depot cost relationship with diseconomies of scale

The effect of the type of cost relationships discussed above is that normally the total system warehousing cost increases with the number of depots in the system as shown in Figure 5:11.

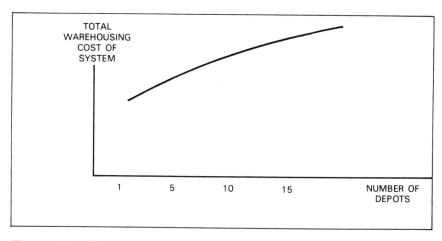

Figure 5:11   How total warehousing costs vary with the number of depots

Transport cost relationships

Transport costs are incurred because demand for goods is geographically removed from where the goods arise. The key variable affecting cost therefore is the distance over which the goods must be carried. The cost relationships are complicated in practice by the existence of intermediate storage and handling points. The nature and positioning of these, together with the product and demand characteristics, will directly influence the choice of transportation mode, and consequently the costs involved. Two distinct types of transport operation can occur, each requiring different costing approaches. These are single drop deliveries, where all goods are delivered to one destination, and multi drop deliveries, where goods are delivered to several destinations on the same trip.

For each of these types of operation, goods may be carried by a company's own fleet, or by third party carriers. In the latter case the costs may be more easily represented, as they are shown explicitly in the trade terms negotiated, however in the long-run such terms are likely to be continually adjusted to reflect the carrier's own actual costs, so for purposes of analysis, and as a basis for long-term decisions, it is often more meaningful to analyse distribution costs in a way that reflects the actual delivery operations.

Single drop loads

These include what are often termed 'trunking' operations, normally the transport of large shipments from factories to warehouses, and also customer deliveries, either direct from factories or from warehouses where a load is destined for one customer only. The costs of the method used may include a number of major elements:

(a)   costs to recover the capital outlay of vehicles, waggons or aeroplanes;

(b)   costs of maintaining the vehicles;

(c)   costs of setting up and maintaining the transport network. For road operations these are recovered by the excise licensing arrangements;

(d)   costs of running the vehicles, comprising mainly fuel and labour.

In practice the resulting costs tend to depend upon four basic factors, which in themselves influence the choice of transport mode:

(a)   the total annual volume of goods carried along a route;

(b)   the required frequency of movement;

(c)   the distance and geography involved;

(d)   the product characteristics (for example, density, value, fragility, perishability).

The costs can be further complicated by the likelihood on any particular route of obtaining a return load. (This explains why, for example, the tariffs for transporting goods from the North to the South in Italy are greater than for an identical return trip.)

For a particular choice of transport mode, the costs are likely to comprise a cost per tonne, varying with the distance travelled. At its simplest this will be a constant cost per tonne-kilometre, as shown at Figure 5:12.

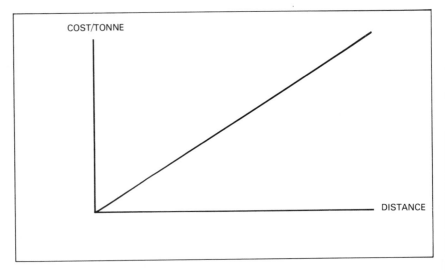

Figure 5:12   Simple transport cost relationship

With additional allowance for the cost of loading/unloading, a fixed cost is introduced into this relationship, as shown at Figure 5:13. This can be further complicated by, for example, the costs of overnight stops to conform with driver's hours regulations, as shown in Figure 5:14. When a choice of transport modes exists, for example in the choice of larger vehicles for longer distances, a composite cost relationship might exist, as shown in Figure 5:15. These relationships can be built up from information derived to show variable cost/kilometre and fixed daily costs for particular types of vehicle.

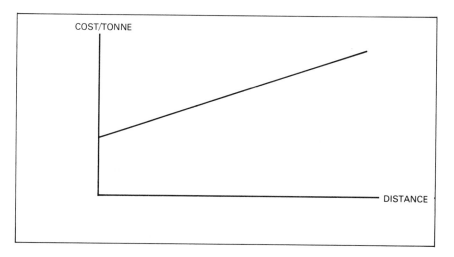

Figure 5:13   Transport cost relationship with fixed and variable cost/tonne elements

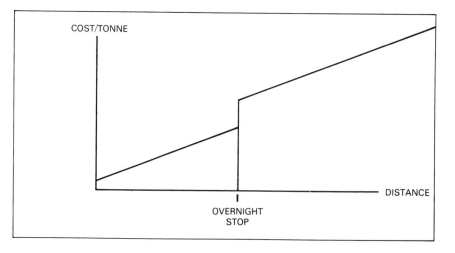

Figure 5:14   Effect on transport costs of overnight stops

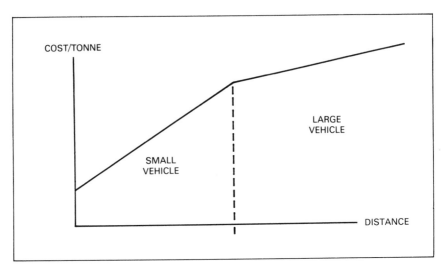

Figure 5:15   Composite transport cost relationship

Multi drop delivery

Occasionally the cost relationships may be similar to those incurred in single drop loads. However, in many cases an additional major influence on the costs of delivery to one outlet will be the ability to combine this with deliveries to other outlets in the vicinity, thus increasing the size and utilisation of the delivery vehicle, and so reducing the delivery costs. Where deliveries for any one trip are concentrated in a particular geographical area, it is useful to regard the distance travelled in two components – the 'stem' distance, being the distance to and from the zone, and the 'zone' distance, being the distance travelled within the zone. In cases where the zone distance is independent of the depot location, this may be regarded as fixed for different depot locations, the changes in the stem distance alone need to be considered when restructuring the distribution network.

When the zone distance needs to be considered, this can be approximated by devising a relationship between cost and a number of variables, for example:

(a)   size of zone;
(b)   number of customers in zone;
(c)   the volume of demand;
(d)   vehicle capacity;
(e)   average drop size;
(f)   customer service requirements, often measured by a minimum number of calls per week or month.

The use of such a relationship enables the expected number of vehicle trips to be calculated and costed out.

Where time constraints on delivery driver's hours are also important, additional variables are required:

(g)   unloading times, which may vary by the size of individual drops and according to the product mix;
(h)   driving times.

The derivation and use of such relationships is in many cases necessary in order to represent the cost implications of vehicle capacity and driver's hours constraints under varying stem distances resulting from alternative depot locations. It is generally not feasible, and indeed unnecessary, to attempt to schedule vehicle trips in order to obtain such information for use in depot location studies.

How transport costs vary with the number and locations of depots

Final delivery is often two to three times more expensive than a trunking operation, when measured in cost/tonne-kilometre. This is, as we have seen, one reason for locating depots near demand centres. The more depots in the system, the closer they may be on average to the demand centre, and so the greater the distance travelled at the more economic rate. This will be true up to the point when there are so many depots that their diminishing size makes the trunking operation uneconomic, and costs would tend to start to increase. This is shown at Figure 5:16.

Total distribution costs

One of the key aspects of distribution planning is identifying the trade-offs between the various cost elements. The trade-off between the major tangible distribution costs of transport and warehousing is shown in Figure 5:17.

It must be recognised that the familiar concept demonstrated in Figure 5:17 represents only the consequence of good locations for any specific number of depots. An 'optimum' number of depots can be chosen, but if located in the wrong places can involve costs far higher than those from a well positioned higher or lower number of depots.

The trade-off between the tangible distribution costs and the less tangible costs of inadequate customer service is nearly always present in depot location studies, and must be considered, along with many other factors, when interpreting the results of the analysis.

Defining the distribution system

One of the common pitfalls when commissioning a distribution study is for the boundaries of the study to be too narrowly defined. We have seen the extent to which interaction occurs between different decision areas and cost elements in distribution. The implications of defining narrow boundaries are to ignore some of these trade-offs.

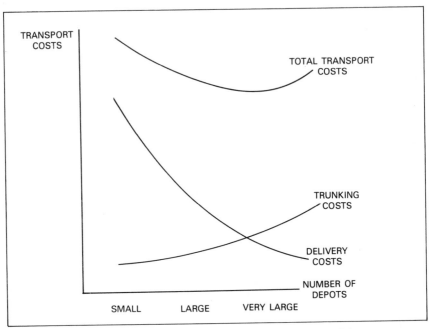

Figure 5:16   How total transport costs vary with the number of depots

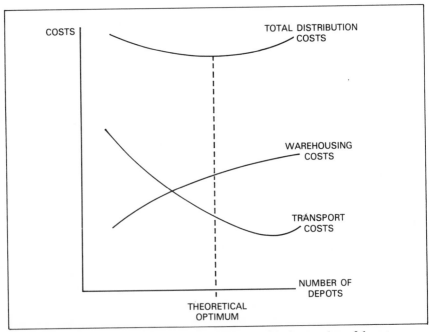

Figure 5:17   How total distribution costs vary with the number of depots

This can lead to cost increases outside the boundaries of the study that will erode and possibly exceed the apparent savings from the study.

The boundaries of the study need to be made wide enough to tackle adequately the problems being addressed by the study. This does not necessarily mean that every study must always be made as broad-based as possible, but it is important to choose the boundaries carefully.

The distribution centre manager of a company the author worked with was 'not interested in including trunking' because, unlike warehousing and delivery, it did not come under his budget. As a direct consequence, the company was losing-out on potential backloading opportunities for its delivery vehicles.

The distribution management of another company had, before consulting the author, carried out preliminary studies of moving from central to regional warehouses. They had ignored, in the study, the costs of supplying these warehouses because they 'didn't incur these costs, as suppliers will deliver anywhere'. Further examination by the author identified significant differences in supplier discounts between delivering to central warehouses as opposed to regional warehouses, which substantially affected the total economics of the system.

Many other examples can be quoted. The key to a successful study is not to accept any problem at its face value, nor to just 'carve off as much of the problem as can be managed in the time', but to recognise the full implications involved, and define the boundaries of the study, or the distribution system, as wide as are necessary to address the problem adequately. This does not of course rule out the 'back of an envelope' solution method. This is valid and essential in all management activities, so long as it is recognised that it is not a substitute for the very necessary strategic planning activity.

Tackling strategic decisions

Given the need to examine, or periodically re-examine, the distribution structure of a company, how should this complex task be accomplished? Such an analysis requires consideration of:

(a)   the current and likely future demands on the system, in terms of both the quantity and nature of sales, and the customer service requirements;

(b)   the network of facilities, including depots, that are best suited to meeting this requirement; and

(c)   the resulting resources and costs involved in operating these facilities and transport operations, together with the capital costs involved in developing the current facilities to meet future requirements.

This analysis can be complicated by the uncertainty in the forecast demands on the system, by the sheer number of alternatives to be evaluated, and by the number of calculations necessary to evaluate the operational and capital implications.

In determining the number, location and size of depots, assumptions need to be made about stocking policies, the level of warehouse technology used, direct delivery policies employed, and the nature and costs of trunking and delivery operations. Such assumptions can be represented in the cost relationships discussed earlier, and such an approach can reduce the number of calculations involved.

Collecting information for strategic planning

A substantial part of all strategic studies is the collection and analysis of data for use in the study. Many companies even today are not fully aware of the costs of their distribution operations, let alone how these costs might vary under different policies. Too often distribution management is not involved in, or even aware of, market projections. The information requirements will depend very much on the nature of any particular study, but in general will comprise:

(a)   existing and future demand, including customer service requirements;
(b)   geographical features affecting transport operations;
(c)   existing and potential future facility locations;
(d)   cost relationships for current and possible future types of facilities;
(e)   cost relationships for current and potential future types of transport;
(f)   constraints and limitations on the use of facilities and transport modes.

Demand information

It is unnecessary to represent explicitly every single customer. On the other hand total demand must be broken down in a way that meaningfully reflects the transport implication of alternative depot locations. In practice demand is aggregated into zones, centred on major geographical areas. Often the representation of all company product lines as a single 'product' will suffice. However, where certain line items may be made only in certain factories, or where different line items require substantially different handling, storage and transport methods, or result in significantly different costs, then product groupings need to be defined for the purpose of the analysis.

Where a range of drop-size categories is employed in the distribution operations, and where these significantly affect delivery costs, demand may need to be expressed in a number of drop-size categories, for example:

    – less than 100 kg
    – 100 kg to 500 kg
    – over 500 kg

Demand may vary significantly over the year. In this case information may be required to analyse the various demand seasons (for example, summer/winter).

Demand is often changing, year by year. Recent demand figures are normally essential for validation of the analysis method, but alternative forecasts of future demand will also be necessary.

Customer service requirements may vary between customers and products. They are necessary to derive realistic stocking policies, and it is also useful to consider the minimum delivery frequencies to particular demand centres.

Geographical features

The analysis will require a full set of transport costs for every transport link likely to be used. Tariffs are often inadequate for this purpose because of the sheer volume of data or because of the difficulty of interpreting how they might change in the longer-term under different assumptions. The alternative is to collect information representing the implications on transport operations and costs of the area geography. This information can in some cases be extracted, for example, from an existing road data base. In other cases distances and driving times can be derived from information representing how crow flight distances can be adjusted to reflect the road network, and major barriers and hazards such as rivers, mountains, and major conurbations.

Facility locations

The analysis will need to consider current and potential future locations of depots and other facilities. This data can often be restricted to a list of possible locations, such as major towns.

Facility costs

Cost information for current operations, and for possible future facilities (for example a new fully automatic warehouse), needs to be collected to derive the cost relationships discussed earlier.

Transport costs

Information is needed to derive the cost relationships discussed earlier, both for transport modes already in use, and for possible future transport methods to be employed (for example, the commissioning of bulk trains, or a change in vehicle size).

Distribution constraints

Capacity or handling constraints for factories, depots and transport modes need to be fully identified, for both current and future operations. Future investment may remove some of these constraints (for example, the installation of bulk handling facilities at depots).

Analysing alternative depot structures

We have seen that depot location decisions cannot be taken in isolation. The consequences of these decisions are far-reaching, and generally provide the opportunity for reviewing policies relating to the replenishment of goods and the use of different modes of transport through the distribution systems. Given assumptions relating to such policies, examination of the depot structure yields three interdependent results:

(a)   the number of depots in the system;
(b)   the locations of those depots;
(c)   the sizes of those depots.

The proposed sizes of the depots will be a direct result of the proposed number and locations of depots, together with the policies for using those depots.

The analysis can therefore be carried through in the following steps:

(a)   select locations for a specified number of depots;
(b)   allocate the flows through these depots according to specified assignment, or allocation, policies;
(c)   calculate the flows through each of the depots and for each transport link;
(d)   cost the depot and transport flows;
(e)   interpret the resulting operating and marketing implications.

The resulting operational improvements set against a current structure can then be regarded as a return on the capital investment required to implement the proposed structure.

The search for a best solution

It can be seen that 'optimisation' or the search for a 'best solution', is possible in three distinct elements of the analysis:

– in determining the optimum number of depots;
– in determining the optimum locations for these depots;
– in determining the best allocations of flows through these depots.

Optimum number of depots.   We saw in Figure 5:17 how the trade-offs in distribution costs can be represented by the way that total distribution costs vary with the number of depots in the system. The theoretical optimum will be the least cost solution. In practice the choice will also depend upon operating and marketing considerations, but will generally be close to the optimum as shown in Figure 5:18.

Optimum locations of depots.   The curve in Figure 5:18 represents the costs for the best locations of any particular number of depots. The theoretically optimum location of a depot will be the one that minimises the warehousing and transport costs associated with the goods flowing through that depot, given the customer allocations to that depot. The possible depot locations may be regarded either as an infinite set (assuming the depot could be located literally at any geographical point), or as comprising a feasible set (assuming that only certain locations, for example large towns, would be suitable practical choices).

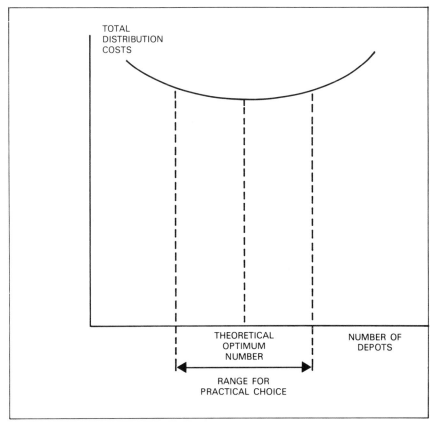

Figure 5:18   Practical interpretation of theoretical optimum number of depots

The feasible set approach is regarded as more pragmatic, as the solutions are readily interpreted. The infinite set approach is equally valid, however, as the effects on cost of changing a suggested location from, for example, a lake to a nearby practical site, are usually small, as illustrated in Figure 5:19.

Optimal allocations.   The allocations of customers to depots (or to factories for direct delivery of large quantities) and of depots to factories, are made on the basis of decision rules reflecting company replenishment policies. To achieve truly theoretically optimal allocations can require the use of mathematical programming techniques. In practice these decision rules can normally be based upon one of the following (not necessarily all different in practice):

(a)   allocation to the nearest depot or factory;
(b)   allocation based upon cheapest total costs (trunking and delivery transport, and also possibly warehousing costs);
(c)   allocations based upon customer service requirements;
(d)   allocations based upon current operations.

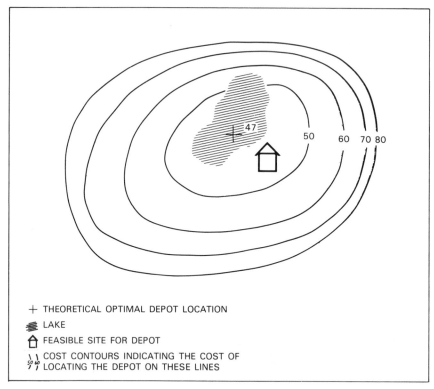

Figure 5:19   Practical interpretation of optimal depot location

It can be seen from these alternatives that the theoretically optimum allocation is not necessarily the best in practice. A comparison of the costs resulting from the application of different allocation policies can often be useful in costing out the implications of, for example, conceding to customer preferences.

The role of computers

Clearly the calculations in such analyses are laborious, repetitive and time-consuming, and may consume many man-weeks of clerical effort to evaluate even one possible depot structure. It is often necessary to evaluate many alternative depot structures, each under different assumptions relating to allocation policies, demand levels and costs.

The use of computers, as demonstrated in the next chapter, can help in reducing this workload and in increasing the number of alternatives that can be evaluated, yielding a better chance of finding optimal or near-optimal solutions. Computer techniques can in some cases also be used to suggest optimal or near-optimal solutions, although these still require careful practical interpretation owing to the assumptions necessary in using such solution techniques.

6

Computer techniques for siting depots

Alan G. Waller

Single depot location case

For the special case of a single depot, the problems of depot size and the allocation decisions of customers to warehouses do not arise, and the analysis is simplified. A brief study of some of the techniques for location of a single depot is useful in understanding the more general problem of multiple depot location.

Representing the costs

The key cost influencing the location of a single depot will be the final delivery cost. The depot will be of a size that can handle the total throughput, and therefore the throughput costs will not generally vary greatly for different locations. Under the simple assumption that transport is a fixed cost per tonne-km, we can represent the final delivery component H by:

$$H = \Sigma \alpha \, w_j \, d_j$$

where: H is the transport cost
α is the cost per tonne-km
w_j is the tonnes at demand point j
d_j is the distance from the depot to customer j

This representation assumes that costs just vary simply in direct proportion to the tonnes carried and distance travelled, and ignores, for example, loading and unloading costs. If trunking costs are important, then factories or suppliers can be represented by adding them into the above representation as large 'customers', with a different value of α, as the cost per tonne-km for trunking is likely to be less than for delivery.

If we simply want to minimise this total cost to find an 'optimum' location for the depot, then we want to find the values of d_j that give the lowest total cost. Unfortunately even in this simple case this is not as easy as it might appear.

Clerical evaluation

If we have just a few feasible locations, then we can evaluate the costs for each of these and select the cheapest as the theoretical optimum. If, however, we have a large number of possible locations, or if we regard the possible number as infinite for the purpose of analysis, then manual methods of evaluation are inadequate.

Centre-of-gravity method

One creative method of solution devised in the 1930s is the centre-of-gravity, or ton-centre, method. This draws on the analogy between the centre of least cost for depot location, and the centre of gravity as derived in physics. This analogy reflects the 'trade-offs' in the centre being drawn in opposing directions because of the influence of the different weights.

The concept is illustrated in Figure 6:1, representing a cut-out map of the sales area, with weights at each sales location representing the demand at that location. The point where the cut-out can be balanced is the centre-of-gravity.

The point representing the centre-of-gravity can be represented mathematically by:

$$X = \frac{\Sigma \, x_j w_j}{\Sigma \, w_j}$$

$$Y = \frac{\Sigma \, y_j w_j}{\Sigma \, w_j}$$

where X and Y are the Cartesian co-ordinates of the centre of gravity, and x_j and y_j are the Cartesian co-ordinates of customer j.

Unfortunately, this centre of gravity is not the same point as that of minimum delivery cost H. The simple example in Figure 6:2 makes this clear. The centre of gravity would result in transporting 20 tonnes over 10 km, and 10 tonnes over 20 km, in other words a total of 400 tonne-km. The least cost of H would be incurred if the depot were coincident with the largest customer, as this would involve transporting 10 tonnes over 30 km, or 300 tonne-km in all.

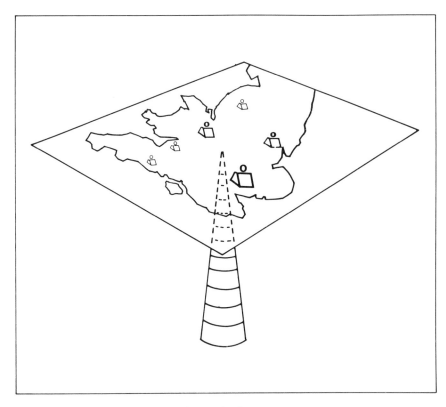

Figure 6:1   The centre of gravity method

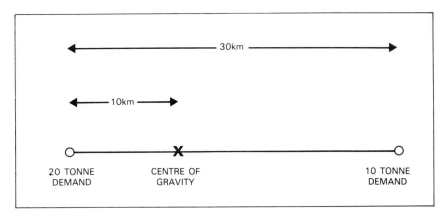

Figure 6:2   Simple two-customer example

Weights and strings method

Another ingenious attempt to solve this problem is termed the 'weights and strings' or 'mechanical analogue' method, and is illustrated in Figure 6:3. This represents a map pasted on to a table, with holes drilled at each demand location. Weights proportional to the demand are strung through each hole, and attached to a single small ring. If the friction of the strings through the holes is insignificant, then the ring will always settle in a unique position for which the potential energy of all the weights in the system is at a minimum.

   Unfortunately this method again does not produce a solution which minimises the total cost *H*. This can be easily seen by examining the effect of moving a customer further away from the position of the ring, in line with the direction of the string to that customer. The position of the ring will not change, whereas the cost of serving that customer would be increased, and so to minimise *H* the depot should in theory be moved in the direction of that customer.

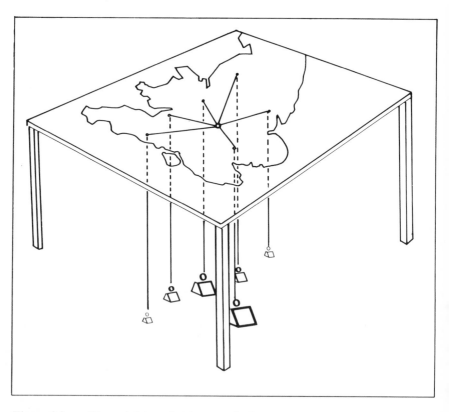

Figure 6:3   The weights and strings method

Computer-assisted solutions

The analogue methods described above are useful in their visual impact and ease of understanding, but they are cumbersome in use and do not produce costs showing the implications of alternative depot locations. More practical and flexible methods rely generally on the use of computers, and can be equally well applied to multi-depot networks.

Multiple depot location

The additional complications when more than one depot is involved concern the decisions on how many depots there should be, and the allocation decisions, that is the allocation of customers to depots (the determination of delivery territories) and of depots to factories. One approach is to divide up the delivery area into individual territories, for a particular number of depots, and then regard the problem as comprising single depot locations in each territory.

Although this considerably simplifies the problem, the approach ignores the interaction across the territories: for example, following the relocation of depots within predetermined territories, the territorial boundaries themselves may well then require re-examining, and following that the depot locations should again be reconsidered.

Representing the costs

If we take the final delivery cost H for all depots (and add on to these the trunking costs if not already considered), together with the warehousing costs, then we can describe the total distribution costs as

$$T = \Sigma H_i + \Sigma W_i$$

where T is the total distribution cost

H_i is the total transport cost associated with trunking to and delivery
from depot i

W_i is the warehousing cost associated with running depot i

Under the simple assumption that transport is a fixed cost per tonne-km, we can represent H_i by:

$$H_i = \Sigma \alpha w_j d_{ij}$$

where: H_i is the transport cost associated with depot i

α is the cost per tonne-km (with different values for factory trunking and
customer delivery)

w_j is the tonnes at demand point j

d_{ij} is the distance from depot i to customer j.

If we assume further that the warehousing cost relationship is simply a fixed and variable pattern, then W_i is represented by:

$$W_i = A + B T_i$$

where: W_i is the warehousing cost for depot i
   A is the fixed cost
   B is the variable cost per tonne
   T_i is the tonnage throughput of depot i

Even under these assumptions, there is no easy way of finding the best values of d_{ij}, or more precisely the depot locations that determine d_{ij}. The techniques developed are many and diverse, and a selection of them are briefly discussed below.

Clerical evaluation

As with single depot locations, manual evaluation is feasible only if one or two options and sets of assumptions are to be considered. Even then the work is extremely time-consuming, tedious and prone to error.

Analogue methods

Although the 'centre of gravity' and 'weights and strings' methods described earlier are generally inappropriate for multiple depot location, analogue models have been applied – for example, the representation of the distribution system using electrical circuits. One major disadvantage is the absence of cost evaluation.

Mathematical programming

Linear programming is an operational research technique used for finding an optimal solution to a well defined problem. The relationships between the variables are expressed as equations, and must be linear (that is, capable of graphical representation using straight lines), and the method will find the values of these variables that provide an optimum value of some quantified objective (for example, it will minimise total costs), under a set of quantified constraints (for example, the capacity of a depot).

One particularly useful method in the field of mathematical programming is the transportation method. This can be used to derive optimal allocations of goods from, for example, factories to depots and depots to customers. Unfortunately the technique as developed by Baumol and Wolfe for application to the multi-depot location problem has been shown to yield too many depots in the solution. This is because of the difficulty of apportioning the fixed element of the depot cost in deriving a cost per unit of throughput.

If the relationships between variables are not simple linear ones, and in distribution we have seen that this is often the case, or if the objective of the analysis is not easily expressed in a single quantified statement, then the techniques of non-linear programming, with multiple or weighted objective functions, can be used but are more difficult to apply and to interpret.

Heuristic methods

A number of interesting approaches have been developed using what are called heuristic methods. 'Heuristic' means the use of rules of thumb which can often not formally be proved to be correct but which nevertheless seem to yield results in practice.

An example of the use of heuristics is the method derived by Lawrence and Pengilly. This comprises an iterative, or repetitive, procedure for searching for improved depot locations, and one step of the procedure is illustrated in Figure 6:4.

Given a depot location, the procedure tries out the effect of relocating the depot at each of the four corners of a square with the existing depot at the centre, and with the size of the square determined by inputting a distance a. The total costs are evaluated at each of the four corners, and if the cheapest of these is cheaper than the current location, then the depot position is changed to that location, and the procedure repeated a number of times until no further improvement can be made. The

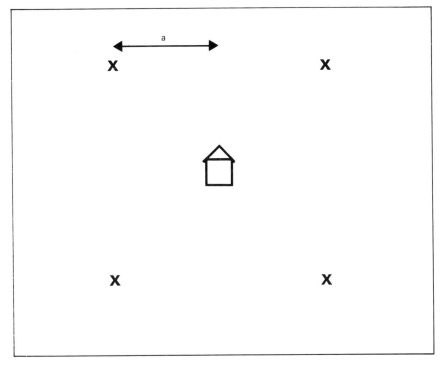

Figure 6:4   Searching heuristically for improved depot location

step size *a* is then halved and the procedure repeated. This process is continued until the step size becomes so small that further use of the procedure would not in practice materially change the position of the depot. This heuristic procedure is carried out for all the depots in the system. The method suffers the disadvantage of all methods that assume an infinite number of potential locations, namely that an optimal solution is not guaranteed. It does, however, enable non-linear cost relationships to be used.

Numeric analytic method

This method is based upon the use of the mathematics of differential calculus in attempting to derive conditions that ensure a minimum value of the total cost function, which are subsequently used in an iterative fashion in searching for an optimal solution. It is well described by Eilon, Watson-Gandy and Christofides, and its main disadvantages lie in the restrictions on the nature of the cost relationships that can be represented (although these can be non-linear), and in the problems of identifying truly optimal solutions.

Simulation

Simulation is one of the most widely used of Operational Research techniques. The power of simulation lies in the ability to represent complex situations and cost relationships. The drawback is that it does not attempt to suggest optimal solutions, but merely evaluates the alternatives presented. It can be argued that this is not necessarily a major drawback, as the search for theoretically optimal solutions often results in oversimplification of the real-life problem, ignoring the many factors such as customer service that cannot be adequately represented in a computer model, and leading to difficulties in interpreting and implementing these so-called 'optimal' solutions. When the power and flexibility of the computer simulation approach are combined with the experience and knowledge of the distribution specialist, it has been shown that high quality, practical solutions, capable of implementation, can be rapidly achieved.

Trends in modelling approaches

Developments in the practical application of computer modelling techniques to depot location problems have tended over the years to move away from optimisation techniques towards a greater emphasis on the use of simulation. These developments have occurred partly because of the difficulty of representing realistically the complex distribution networks and complex cost relationships that occur in practice, for solution by these optimising techniques. A second reason behind this trend is a certain disenchantment of managers with the use of the computer as a 'black box', where information is fed in and a solution comes out with little understanding of how that solution is derived and upon what assumptions it is based. The greater accessibility of computers and their increased processing speeds, coupled with the growth in interactive computing, have enabled simulation techniques to be developed and used to produce solutions under the guidance and full control of the computer user; and with far greater involvement and understanding of managers.

A simple package model

A number of ready programmed computer package models are available which employ the techniques discussed earlier. One such program the author has been involved in developing and using is CODIP (Coopers and Lybrand Distribution Program). The CODIP approach has been developed for application in a number of distribution studies in the UK, Continental Europe and North America. CODIP is essentially an interactive system used generally in a descriptive, or simulation, mode, although it also employs a heuristic similar to that developed by Lawrence and Pengilly and described in the previous chapter.

One of the key features of the CODIP approach is the treatment of costs. These are represented in a very general form and can be changed readily to match different applications. The simplest version, CODIP I, is shown below as a case study application.

CODIP I model flowchart

A flowchart showing the basic elements of the computer model is shown in Figure 6:5. An important consideration when developing CODIP was to develop a system that encourages, by the interactive nature of the program, the close involvement of distribution planners and distribution managers, in order that their experience and ideas are fully utilised in the analysis.

CODIP case study

The case study concerns a company manufacturing goods mainly for industrial consumers in Belgium, France, Holland, Italy, Luxembourg and West Germany.

Currently, the company has one factory in Rotterdam but is proposing to build another at Verdun in Northern France. To support an expected expansion of 50 per cent in demand over the next five years, the company plans to build or lease some eight warehouses in various locations in Europe. This proposed distribution structure, together with aggregated demand data, is shown in Figure 6:6.

Basic data is collected and entered in the specified form into the CODIP data files. The model is then used to cost out the proposed distribution structure. Part of the computer printout is shown in Figure 6:7.

Further runs of the model can then be made under different depot structures, different cost and future demand assumptions. The interactive nature of CODIP enables alterations to be evaluated rapidly from the computer terminal, and

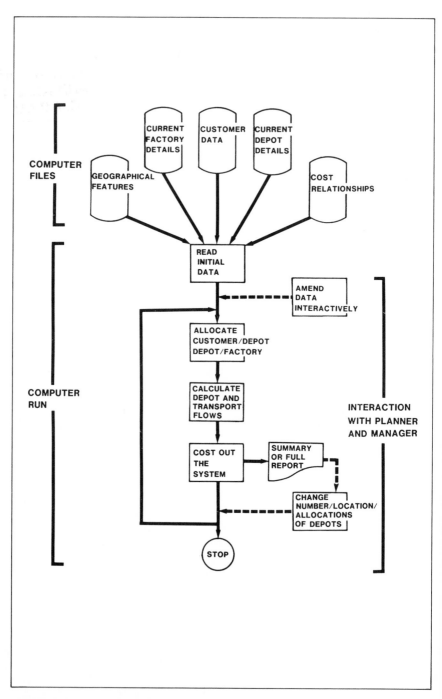

Figure 6:5　　CODIP I flowchart

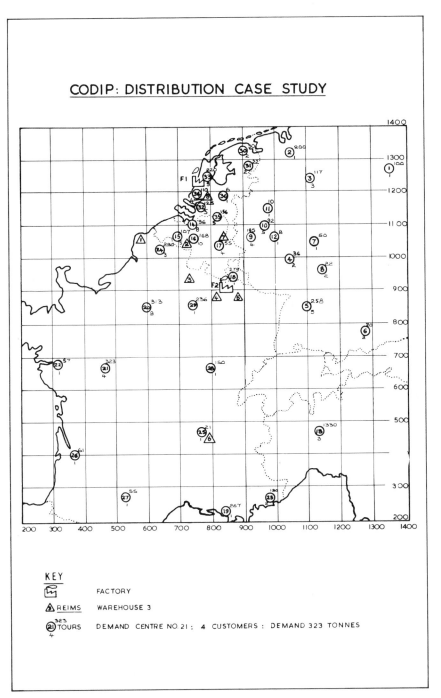

CODIP: DISTRIBUTION CASE STUDY

KEY

FACTORY

△ REIMS   WAREHOUSE 3

㉑ TOURS   DEMAND CENTRE NO. 21 : 4 CUSTOMERS : DEMAND 323 TONNES

Figure 6:6   Map of distribution and demand network

```
      FULL  FACTORY  DETAILS
FACT      NAME      XMAP YMAP  PRODN  CAP/TY
  1  ROTTERDAM...  750 1180  2508.  8000.
  2  VERDUN......  825  875  3560.  8000.

  ALL                        6068. 16000.


     WAREHOUSE   ALLOCATIONS
FACTORY            WAREHOUSE        W/HSE THRU/PT
NO.     NAME       NO.    NAME      SUPPLIED FR FACT
 1 ROTTERDAM...     1 CALAIS......       57.
                    2 MONS........      565.
                    7 MASTRICHT...      617.
                    8 ROTTERDAM...     1269.
 2 VERDUN......     3 REIMS.......      313.
                    4 VERDUN......      987.
                    5 METZ........      336.
                    6 LYON........     1924.

     FULL WAREHOUSE DETAILS     AND          COSTS
W/H    NAME      XMAP YMAP THRPT  CAP   DELIVY   W/HOUS   TRUNKG   SUMCOS
 1 CALAIS......  580 1080   57. 7000.  23537.  101425.   2186.  127148.
 2 MONS........  710 1020  565. 7000.  30464.  114125.  19966.  164555.
 3 REIMS.......  730  940  313. 7000.  33718.  107825.   9611.  151154.
 4 VERDUN......  825  875  987. 7000. 145267.  124675.      0.  269942.
 5 METZ........  880  880  336. 7000.  88570.  108400.   8446.  205416.
 6 LYON........  770  485 1924. 7000. 426090.  148100. 108954.  683144.
 7 MASTRICHT...  850 1060  617. 7000. 137257.  115425.  21303.  273985.
 8 ROTTERDAM...  750 1180 1269. 7000. 153216.  131725.      0.  284941.

 ALL                      6068.56000.1038119.  951700. 170465.2160284.

     DEMAND ALLOCATIONS
 W/H        CUSTOMERS

  1         22

  2         15   16   24

  3         20

  4         18   21   28   29

  5          4    5    6    8

  6         13   19   23   25   26   27

  7          1    3    7    9   10   11   12   17

  8          2   14   30   31   32   33   34   35   36
```

Figure 6:7   CODIP I output for initial structure

experience has shown that with interactive computing and well designed reports, the user can move rapidly towards optimum solutions.

The computer printout for an alternative depot structure is shown for the case study in Figure 6:8. This demonstrates potential cost reductions of some 25 per cent in utilising a depot structure which in addition provides better market access. The computer model results need, as always, to be fully integrated in the context of the distribution study with due regard to operational, political, marketing and other considerations, but nevertheless provide a useful tool for exploring improvements to the distribution system. More comprehensive models, such as CODIP II, are available to handle more complex distribution systems and are capable of representing several product groups and transport modes within the computer system.

```
      FULL  FACTORY  DETAILS
FACT    NAME       XMAP YMAP  PRODN  CAP/TY
  1  ROTTERDAM...   750 1180  2509.  8000.
  2  VERDUN......   825  875  3559.  8000.

ALL                           6068.  16000.

    WAREHOUSE    ALLOCATIONS
FACTORY          WAREHOUSE       W/HSE THRU/PT
NO.    NAME      NO.   NAME      SUPPLIED FR FACT
  1 ROTTERDAM...   8 ROTTERDAM...     1689.
                 10 GERMANY           820.
  2 VERDUN......   4 VERDUN......    1236.
                  6 LYON........      516.
                  9 MILANO           1807.

     FULL WAREHOUSE DETAILS     AND         COSTS
W/H    NAME      XMAP YMAP THRPT  CAP   DELIVY   W/HOUS   TRUNKG   SUMCOS
 4 VERDUN......   825  875 1236. 7000. 147053. 130900.      0.  277953.
 6 LYON........   595  585  516. 7000.  93000. 112900.  28082.  233982.
 8 ROTTERDAM...   750 1180 1689. 7000. 179996. 142225.      0.  322221.
 9 MILANO        1130  480 1807. 7000. 149284. 145175. 120006.  414465.
10 GERMANY       1000 1100  820. 7000. 132815. 120500.  36417.  289733.

ALL                        6068.35000. 702149. 651700. 184505. 1538354.

     DEMAND ALLOCATIONS
 W/H      CUSTOMERS

  4        5  18  20  28  29

  6       21  22  25  26  27

  8       14  15  16  17  24  30  31  32  33  34  35  36


  9        6  13  19  23

 10        1   2   3   4   7   8   9  10  11  12
```

Figure 6:8   CODIP I output for improved structure

All general models, or packages, because they are designed for wide applicability, are limited in their ability to represent particular company's operations with complete accuracy. The advantage of using such models is the speed of implementation, as the program development and testing has been completed before any particular study commences.

Custom-built systems

We have seen that package models are often incapable of representing particular company complexities to a sufficient level of accuracy. An alternative approach is to develop 'custom-built' computer systems designed to fit precisely the operations and costs of particular companies.

The author has worked in one such development for a multi-national company distributing from Italy over the whole of Western Europe. For this company, the complexity of the product flow, shown in Figure 6:9, together with the need to represent a large number of product groups, drop-size categories, transport methods and complex cost relationships, ruled out the possibility of employing an 'off the shelf' package. Instead, a comprehensive suite of programs was developed, using the CODIP philosophy, that accurately represented the company's total European distribution systems, under both current and alternative distribution structures, policies, demands and costs. This involved many man-months of program development, but the end result was a model that was used not only for distribution strategic planning, but also in assisting the location decision for a new factory, in assessing alternative production policies following a major fire, in evaluating an increase in pallet size, and in assisting operational and financial planning and control.

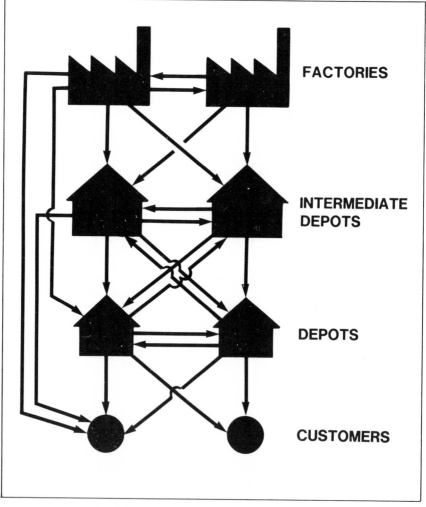

Figure 6:9   Possible complexity of product flows

A modelling system

It is clear from the previous sections that in the choice between using an 'off the shelf' package and developing a 'tailor-made' system there is a trade-off between speed of implementation, as a result of general applicability, and accuracy of representation. This is shown diagrammatically in Figure 6:10.

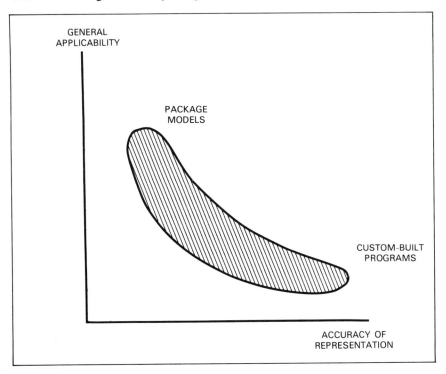

Figure 6:10   Choice of computer system

A modelling system is a way of getting the best of both worlds in this trade-off situation, as it enables the user to construct an accurate and detailed representation of particular distribution systems without the need for extensive model development. The author has been involved with an international consortium in the development of such a modelling system DSS (Distribution Strategy Simulator). The requirements of DSS were that it should:

(a)   be capable of representing complex distribution networks;
(b)   be capable of alternative and detailed demand representation;
(c)   be capable of realistic, and therefore complex, cost representation;
(d)   provide full user control over solutions produced by the computer model;
(e)   yield comprehensive but manageable reports;
(f)   be widely transportable on to popular mini and mainframe computers.

DSS satisfies these requirements by:

(a)   enabling the user to define his own facilities and build-up his own distribution structures;

(b)   handling alternative demand levels representing seasonal variations, or alternative demand forecasts, simultaneously within the system, and enabling these to be analysed and printed alongside each other for comparison;

(c)   representing demand at any level of detail specified by the user, in terms of product groups and drop-size categories;

(d)   enabling the user to specify the detailed resource implications in using a distribution system, and to describe any shape of cost relationships involved in using these resources;

(e)   providing full interactive facilities for data entry and amendment, guidance of model solutions, and report selection;

(f)   being capable of being run from remote or local terminals, and being written in a common language, Fortran, with versions available for PDP II and IBM 370 computers.

A flowchart of the DSS system is shown in Figure 6:11.

The availability of such modelling systems enables companies to take advantage of comprehensive software that is fully developed and tested, which when implemented will provide an ongoing tool for the analysis of distribution and related decisions.

Key stages of a study

A study involving the use of computer models for distribution strategic planning entails a number of relatively discrete stages, whether undertaken by company personnel or with outside help. These can be described broadly as:

1   Familiarisation.
2   Data collection.
3   Policy evaluation.
4   Policy implementation.
5   Performance monitoring.

Familiarisation

This will involve primarily gaining a detailed understanding of the company's distribution operations, and of the production, financial and marketing constraints. The boundaries of the study and detailed requirements of the analysis need to be fully determined, together with the availability and suitability of data. The method of analysis, including the choice of computer model, needs to be examined at this stage.

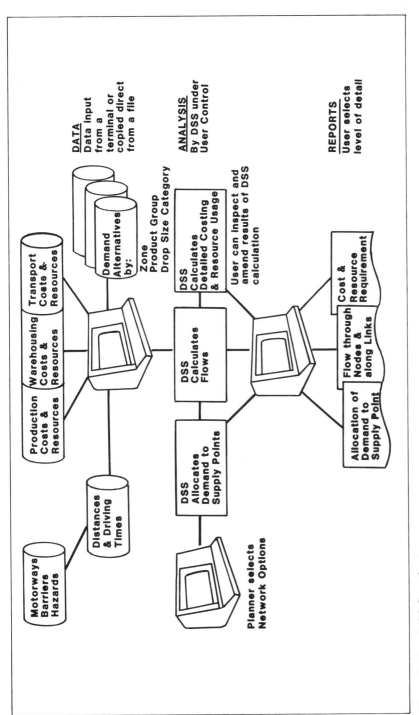

Figure 6:11   DSS flowchart

95

Data collection

Information as described earlier needs to be collected and analysed, and prepared for use in the subsequent analysis. The data finally used is inevitably a compromise between what is ideally required for the analysis, and what is able to be collected cost-effectively. The author was involved in one major European study where the actual content and timing of the data collection exercise were discussed and agreed at a two-day meeting in Germany of distribution staff from throughout the company's European operations. This was essential for that particular study, in order to achieve the right balance between data accuracy and data collection costs. This stage may also include the development and testing of the computer model to be employed in the analysis.

Policy evaluation

In this stage, the data is entered into the computer model, which is then used initially to represent current or recent operations, serving both to establish current operating costs and also to validate the computer model. The computer model is then used to explore possible future alternatives in terms of depot structures and distribution policies, under various assumptions relating to demand levels, costs and constraints. It is essential that company management at all levels is closely involved throughout the study, and this is particularly important in the Policy Evaluation stage, where company distribution, financial and marketing expertise is essential in arriving at sound, practical and acceptable recommendations.

Policy implementation

This may involve not only the implementation of recommendations relating to, for example, depot closure and expansion plans, and changes in transport policies, but also the improvement of information systems, which is an area where weaknesses are very often uncovered during the distribution study.

Performance monitoring

Distribution costs need to be kept continually under scrutiny, and distribution policies regularly reviewed. In many cases the ongoing use of the computer model is justified to help in these tasks, and can play an important role in the distribution management information system.

Further reading

R. H. Ballou, *Business Logistics Management,* Englewood Cliffs, N.J.: Prentice-Hall Inc.

W. J. Baumol and P. Wolfe, 'A Warehouse Location Problem', *Operations Research,* March–April 1958, Vol. 6.

D. W. Beattie, 'Improving the Structure of a Distribution System', *Operational Research Quarterly,* Vol. 24, No. 3, pp. 353–64.

S. Eilon, C. D. T. Watson-Gandy and N. Christofides, *Distribution Management: Mathematical Modelling and Practical Analysis,* London: Charles Griffin.

B. M. Khumawala and D. C. Whybark, 'A Comparison of Some Recent Warehouse Location Techniques', *The Logistics Review,* Vol. 7, No. 31, pp. 3–19.

B. M. Khumawala and D. C. Whybark, 'An Update on Warehouse Location Techniques', *The Logistics and Transportation Review,* Vol. 9, No. 3.

R. M. Lawrence and P. J. Pengilly, 'The Number and Location of Depots Required for Handling Products for Distribution to Retail Stores in South-East England', *Operational Research Quarterly,* Vol. 20, No. 1, pp. 22–32.

G. K. Rand, 'Methodological Choices in Depot Location Studies', *Operational Research Quarterly,* Vol. 27, No. 1, pp. 241–9.

H. N. Shycon and R. B. Maffei, 'Simulation Tool for Better Distribution', *Harvard Business Review,* November–December, 1960.

H. M. Wagner, *Principles of Operations Research,* Englewood Cliffs, N. J., Prentice-Hall, Inc.

A. G. Waller, 'Cutting Freight Costs', *Professional Administration,* September 1978, pp. 26–7.

7

Materials handling system design and warehouse operation

Ken Firth

Although materials handling principles and techniques associated with modern warehousing systems can be traced back over more than 100 years it is, perhaps, only since the late sixties that their true cost and profit implications have become more fully understood. In addition, warehousing systems have been subjected to more thorough analysis and have become more integrated with the distribution systems they serve. This chapter looks at the major components which contribute to efficient warehouse operation.

Why are warehouses necessary?

There are three reasons for having warehouse facilities:

1   To provide an adequate buffer storage against inequalities caused by unpredictable variations in supply and demand. This may be to guard against loss of production, to ensure batches of economic size, to provide marketing back-up by maintaining availability of spares and adequate service levels, and on occasions to provide a speculative hedge against anticipated inflation.
2   To safeguard stock from damage, deterioration and unauthorised removal by providing an environment which is appropriate to the materials being stored.
3   To record accurately receipts, stockholding and despatches, and to provide an efficient communicational interface with all appropriate parts of the system being served.

Less well recognised is that an efficient system can present an image, which, if properly exploited, can greatly enhance a company's prestige. This benefit alone has often been the determining factor in the choice of a mechanised system rather than a more labour-intensive approach which in a conventional accounting sense appears more cost-effective. The important single fact to remember is that the warehouse must provide all its functions on the basis of least cost to the total system which it serves, over the whole term of its anticipated working life.

Distribution costs have been increasing due to such factors as rising fuel prices, disproportionate increases in driver's pay relative to other workers, the dispersion of markets from city centres and the proliferation of product ranges. This has meant that warehouse operation costs have reduced relative to other parts of the distribution cost equation, although in most companies it still represents 20–40 per cent of total distribution cost.

The warehouse represents a significant cost and one clearly worthy of careful consideration, a fact which, perhaps, in the United Kingdom is not given the same prominence as in other parts of the world where total distribution costs are intrinsically of a higher order. Thus it may be seen that in countries such as Japan, Germany, USA, and Sweden much greater attention is paid to making sure that the warehouse integrates with the total distribution system in both a cost and operational sense. The danger in the United Kingdom is that the application of modern warehouse systems and technology will be ignored whilst operating costs still remain relatively favourable. It is not, however, possible to conceive that such relative economic advantage will remain forever, and the question arises whether many companies will be able to respond to the task of improving their warehouse requirements to the new standards when change is finally forced upon industry.

Warehouse operating functions

There are four functions in any warehouse operation: receiving, storage, order picking (or selection), and despatch. This simple list may be elaborated upon (Figure 7:1) although it should be recognised that not all the aspects shown in the chart need necessarily exist in every store or warehousing system. However the chart does serve to emphasise the importance of good communication in warehousing systems and the need above all to have accurate management information readily available.

Warehousing costs

To assist in the understanding of warehousing operation it is helpful to analyse the costs of the different functions for a typical warehouse under the headings: building, labour, equipment, and administration. Figure 7:2 shows a typical set of figures produced by the National Materials Handling Centre in respect of a conventionally operated grocery distribution warehouse.

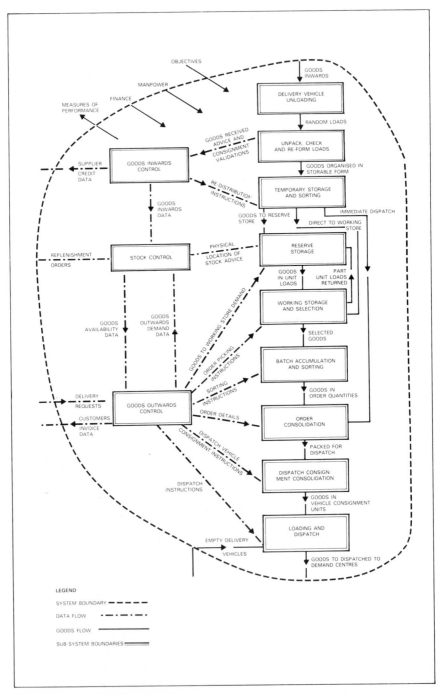

Figure 7:1   Warehouse system flows

	Building	Labour	Equipment	Administration
Receiving	0.42	0.40	0.15	0.55
Storage	1.68	0.47	0.60	0.20
Order Picking	0.78	1.44	0.55	1.80
Despatch	0.48	0.47	0.10	0.51
Total	3.36	2.78	1.40	3.06

Figure 7:2   Unit cost (pence per case output) for warehouse of 100,000 cases per week

Such figures should not be regarded as a norm for other warehousing operations but simply to emphasise that buildings and labour form a significant part of total cost, and as a guide to where savings may be made. What is certain is that once established both building and labour costs tend to be fixed in the long term and this means that when an opportunity arises to design or redesign a warehouse system the possibility of making economies through better warehouse operation and layout should not be overlooked.

Auditing warehousing operations

A natural corollary to understanding warehouse cost structure is that of knowing whether one's own operation is performing to a reasonable standard. In extreme circumstances this may be obvious, either good or bad, but all systems have a tendency to deteriorate over time and warehousing, with its dependence upon external factors (over which it may have little influence) is no exception. The commonly used method of assessing warehouse efficiency is by means of internal audit and some useful techniques have developed in recent years. Such audits may be carried out on either an intermittent or a continuous basis, dependent upon the needs and resources of the business. The actual physical process of carrying out an audit of a materials handling system frequently reveals shortcomings which have arisen and, because of operational necessity, have either been ignored or overlooked. The more subtle aspect of systems drift can be determined through repetition of the audit at given intervals and comparison with past performance. Attempts have been made in the past at external comparison which, although desirable from the operating manager's viewpoint, tend to be easier said than done. It is particularly difficult to find a group of warehouses which is reasonably comparable – even within the same organisation – and although relatively successful attempts at comparison have been made in the past the longevity of such exercises tends to be limited.

Selecting the right warehousing system

As shown earlier, warehouse operating structure remains much the same regardless of type, but the diversity and range of products which have to be stored, coupled with a wide variety of operating and design constraints, create a complex problem for the warehouse designer. This is made all the more difficult by the fact that warehouse operating conditions can be highly dynamic and this may cause the designer to opt for flexible solutions rather than the ones which appear to be least costly at the design stage.

The following are some of the factors which have to be taken into account when considering how best to operate a warehouse system – all of which place constraints upon the designer.

Product characteristics and handling class.
Range of products to be stored and handled.
Stockholding characteristics and stock location.
Throughput and stock turnover.
Equipment alternatives for storage and handling (including existing).
Building and site constraints.
Labour availability and quality.
Standards and synthetics.
Costs.
Legislation.
Insurance.
Safety.
Security.
Interface with other parts of the system.
Accounting conventions.
Capital available.
Time available.

This list should not be considered as exhaustive but rather as an indicator of the kind of information which needs to be considered. Thorough analysis of all relevant data should lead to the preparation of an operating statement which, when universally agreed, acts as a guide to the various design phases.

It is unusual, and probably unwise, to opt for a single warehouse design from the outset. There are many different ways of laying out and operating a warehouse and it is conventional for warehouse designers to design, cost, and evaluate several likely alternatives before a decision is reached. The least-cost sub-system may not be the final choice because a least operating cost warehouse system may lead to diseconomies elsewhere in the business.

Fundamentally the process of warehouse design is a combination of knowledge of basic materials handling systems, basic warehousing systems and layouts (see Chapter 8), the different types and costs of building, and the equipment which is available to carry out the required tasks.

Principles of materials handling

The use of unit-load techniques

Virtually all modern warehouse operations are dependent upon unit-load applications. A unit-load may be defined as the assembly of individual packages, usually of a like kind, to permit convenient composite movement. This definition includes both mechanical and manual movement.

The objective behind the creation of unit-loads is to form as large a unit as is compatible with safe and effective operation of the system, as early in the movement cycle as possible, and retain it intact for as long as is practicable. This has the effect of minimising the amount of movement, and the types of storage and holding media required. This process is assisted by working to modular sizes, preferably I.S.O. standards. The principal advantages of load untilisation are ease and speed of handling, better use of space – particularly headroom, protection of products, and minimisation of use of, and injury to, labour. In addition the technique aids both inventory control and stock location.

Making good use of the cube available

As may be seen from Figure 7:1, warehouse space can be an expensive commodity and the provision of 1 pallet space for a year can easily cost £50. This fact explains why so much effort has been put into making better use of the warehouse cube through improvements in the fork-lift truck and its close associate the automatic stacker crane. Thus we have situations where free-path fork-lift trucks are lifting 1.5 tonne loads to heights of 12 metres in gangways only 1.5 metres wide, whilst stacker cranes are now lifting to heights in excess of 30 metres.

There are considerable benefits in terms of cost per cubic metre when a conventional steel portal frame building can be built to accept 12 metre high racking (compared with only 6 metre high racking) although the equipment cost is initially higher and more expensive to operate. The trade-off lies in the markedly reduced building cost. Over 12 metres the advantage is usually that of better land utilisation particularly where land is scarce or expensive – this explains why the Japanese, with land values in excess of £2,000 per square metre, are so eager to make use of such facilities.

Minimisation of movement

Movement by definition adds to cost, and excessive movement within a warehouse results in unnecessary cost.

There is a variety of techniques associated with the limiting of movement within warehouses: for example, by determining the throughput levels of individual products and locating the most popular appropriately; by separating out order selection stocks from other stocks; by batching orders awaiting selection; by the use of goods to picker systems; and by departmentalisation and zoning. Over-enthusiasm should be avoided in attempts to minimise movement because in some circumstances this may lead to congestion in gangways with the consequent slowing down of the system and danger to personnel.

Controlling the direction of flow

It is desirable, whether movement be of goods, people or vehicular traffic, inside or outside the building, that flow is controlled in a smooth and uninterrupted manner with a minimum of cross-over points or areas of high traffic density.

There are two major types of flow within warehouse systems: 'U' flow, where input and output is normally on a single face of the building and 'through flow', where input and output are at opposite ends of the building. Whilst it is difficult to generalise, 'U' flow is frequently associated with goods received into and out of the warehouse by road transport whilst 'through flow' is often seen when a warehouse is directly attached to a manufacturing facility.

Care should be taken with the use of conveyors in warehouses because the positioning of a conveyor down the centre line of a building can be a serious hindrance to personnel and vehicular movement. Traffic flows and parking areas associated with the warehouse should also be carefully located, leaving adequate access and separating vehicular from pedestrian traffic.

Safety and security

The hazards and injuries experienced by personnel in carrying out even the most mundane materials handling tasks are well known and well documented. Back injuries caused by incorrect manual handling are the single largest source of loss of working effort. The introduction and implementation of the Health and Safety at Work Act serves to emphasise this point but no amount of legislation is a substitute for sound design, and safe operation.

However, design is but one aspect, for even with sound design materials handling equipment can be extremely unforgiving if not handled correctly. Adequate operator training is an essential adjunct to good design.

Product security, particularly where the value of the goods is high, must also be taken into account. Fork-lift truck drivers may double the cost of their truck by the damage they inflict on the products which they are paid to move and store. It is unlikely that the problem will be eradicated completely but careful attention to gangway widths, racking tolerances, and adequate stacking of loads can go far in alleviating this problem. There is, at the present, a move towards the automation of fork-lift trucks which may well result in the elimination of the need for a driver, but whether this will result in savings remains to be determined.

Important storage and warehousing techniques

The majority of storage and warehousing systems may be classified under three general headings as follows:

1   Palletised unit-load systems.
2   Small components systems.
3   Long load systems.

As may be imagined, there are considerable variations in the kinds of equipment used to meet these requirements. This chapter concentrates on man-rider or manually controlled equipment as opposed to automated systems which are considered in Chapter 8.

Palletised unit-load systems

Reserve storage areas

The main determinants in selecting alternatives for palletised reserve storage areas, assuming the unit-load design is known, are stock profile, throughput rate and building constraints – particularly the headroom available.

There are two basic techniques – (i) block storage, and (ii) individual pallet access storage, and in each case the location systems available are random or fixed access. In the case of 'block storage' random access would be by row whilst with 'individual pallet access' fixed location systems are comparatively rare.

Block storage

(a) *With a fixed location system:*   The fundamental principle of block storage (Figure 7:3) is the stacking of like products in rows two or more pallets deep (back to back) up to a maximum which is compatible with the operating and safety characteristics of the system. In this way the relationship between area of gangway and area occupied by stock should be maximised. The success of this arrangement depends upon whether there is a sufficient number of pallets for each line item to form the depth of row required and the degree of stock rotation needed. In practice it is unusual to achieve better than 70 per cent utilisation of available pallet spaces with block stacking systems (with the significant exception of powered mobile systems). The allocation of specific products to a fixed location within the system is usually associated with a low range of products and in particular a low variation between maximum and minimum stock. The reasoning behind this statement is that a low product range permits warehousemen to memorise quickly where products are, and because a fixed location system is based upon the warehousing of the maximum stock of every line item in the system at any time, there can be considerable wastage of space when there is a great variation between maximum and minimum stockholdings.

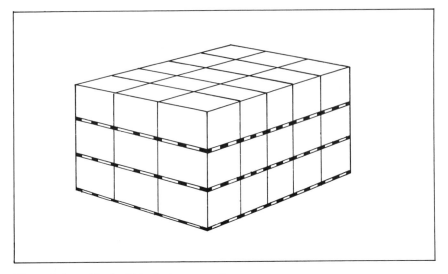

Figure 7:3   Typical block storage system

(b) *With random location by row:*   Where a palletised reserve storage profile (Figures 7:4–7:11) is block stackable but at the same time has a big variation between maximum and minimum stock the solution is to randomise the location system by row. This means that the warehouse floor area required can be based upon the average stock at peak holding of the aggregate of all pallets held in the system, plus a margin, taking into account wastage caused by having input and output lanes for each line item. This can be refined even further in the case of pallet live storage systems where the randomisation can be by individual storage lane rather than by row. The disadvantage is that some form of recording system or analogue board is required to maintain both stock rotation and location information.

Individual pallet access

As the description implies, every pallet within the store is individually accessible which automatically necessitates the use of some form of single or double entry pallet rack system. In turn it is almost certainly necessary to install a location system – these days usually based on variants of the 2-ticket system with a validity check. The advantage of racking systems of this type is that they can take advantage of head-room available and in particular make use of equipment such as high-lift reach trucks, narrow aisle stackers, and stacker cranes so that the usage of ground and building area is minimised. The utilisation of space in such racking is high – often as much as 95 per cent of the spaces made available. The adoption of fixed-location in pallet racking in reserve areas is rare because of the wastage of pallet spaces when any individual line item is at minimum stock level.

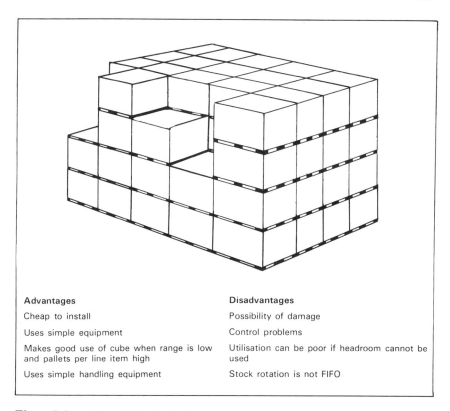

Advantages	Disadvantages
Cheap to install	Possibility of damage
Uses simple equipment	Control problems
Makes good use of cube when range is low and pallets per line item high	Utilisation can be poor if headroom cannot be used
Uses simple handling equipment	Stock rotation is not FIFO

Figure 7:4   Simple block stacking

Order selection with palletised unit loads

The operational objective of any order selection system is to provide a means of converting the form of products as held in the warehouse to a form required by the client, at the level of service demanded and at least total systems cost. This involves the presentation of a full range of products to the order-picker in as small an area as possible to minimise movement, but in quantities which will not involve excessive replenishment activity or the intermediate breaking down of unit loads. Additionally the whole procedure must look to the minimisation of the use of labour, through simplifying the clerical procedures involved and eliminating unnecessary down-time. The individual requirements are often not mutually compatible and inevitably 'trade-offs' have to be taken into account.

The basic techniques are the following:

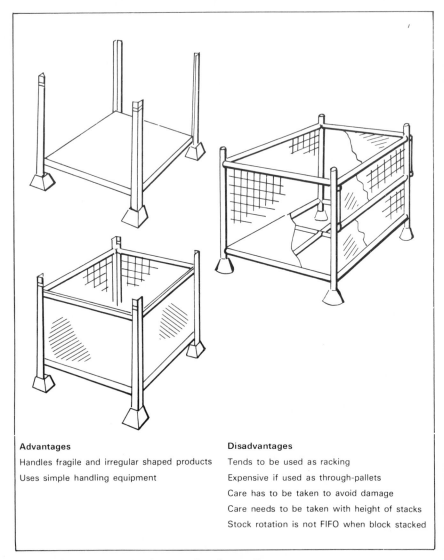

Advantages	Disadvantages
Handles fragile and irregular shaped products	Tends to be used as racking
Uses simple handling equipment	Expensive if used as through-pallets
	Care has to be taken to avoid damage
	Care needs to be taken with height of stacks
	Stock rotation is not FIFO when block stacked

Figure 7:5   Post pallets/cage pallets/box pallets

1   *Minimisation of Movement*
        Methods of separating forward from reserve stock
        Popularity storage
        Batching
        Zoning or Departmentalisation
        Fixed or Random Access
        Goods to Picker or Picker to Goods

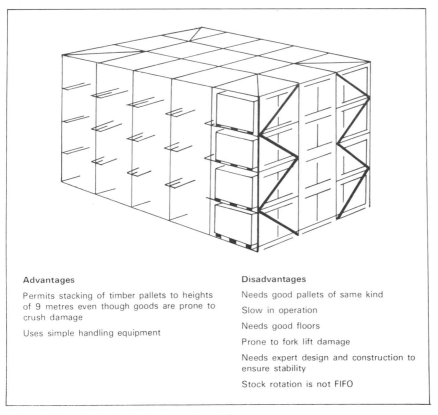

Advantages	Disadvantages
Permits stacking of timber pallets to heights of 9 metres even though goods are prone to crush damage	Needs good pallets of same kind
	Slow in operation
Uses simple handling equipment	Needs good floors
	Prone to fork lift damage
	Needs expert design and construction to ensure stability
	Stock rotation is not FIFO

Figure 7:6   Drive-in/drive through racking

2   *Simplifying Clerical Procedures*
    Provide the operative with the minimum of information to do the job accurately
    Eliminate ancillary clerical task – stock cards, etc.
    Provide clearly printed instructions
    Provide good lighting
    Provide the selector with adequate equipment to do the job e.g. simple mobile desk
    Devise procedures which minimise time taken in training
3   *Eliminate Ineffective Time*
    Cut out waiting time for instructions
    Cut out wasteful checking procedures
    Introduce incentive schemes
    Ensure correct work balance
    Schedule transport effectively
    Eliminate visits to stock-out locations

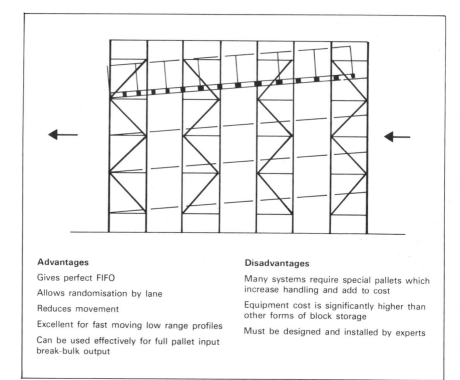

Advantages

Gives perfect FIFO

Allows randomisation by lane

Reduces movement

Excellent for fast moving low range profiles

Can be used effectively for full pallet input break-bulk output

Disadvantages

Many systems require special pallets which increase handling and add to cost

Equipment cost is significantly higher than other forms of block storage

Must be designed and installed by experts

Figure 7:7   Pallet live storage – gravity feed

4   *Order Selection System Alternatives*

The variations in approach and method to solving carton picking problems are too numerous to mention in detail; Figures 7:12–7:15 represent some of the more popular techniques.

Many systems using base location order picking have been coming under pressure because of the proliferation of stock. This has led to the use of 2nd level order-pickers, which in some circumstances can carry two roll-cage pallets. This method has the advantage of halving the distances travelled at the expense of order-picking equipment and a somewhat reduced rate of order-picking.

Small components storage and order selection

The process of storing and handling small components has vast potential for improvement in many present-day companies (Figures 7:16–7:20). This potential can be realised by concentrating upon the reduction of personnel movement within

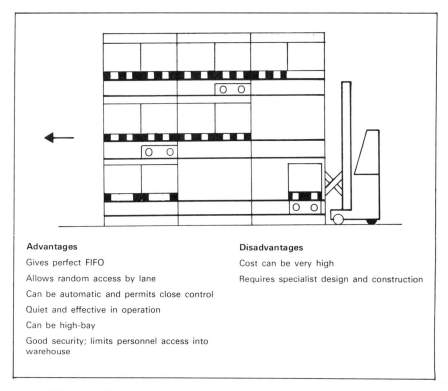

Advantages

Gives perfect FIFO

Allows random access by lane

Can be automatic and permits close control

Quiet and effective in operation

Can be high-bay

Good security; limits personnel access into warehouse

Disadvantages

Cost can be very high

Requires specialist design and construction

Figure 7:8   Pallet live storage – powered

the store, the compression of cube by making use of modern techniques, and in particular the use of dedicated real-time computer systems which give instant information on stock availability and location together with order processing and inventory control facility. The writer has seen an outstanding example of the latter process operated by a market trader selling electrical components – many larger and more prestigious organisations could follow this lead to their advantage.

A large number of small components installations depend upon the use of binning or shelving to hold their stock which, although an advance on many of the ramshackle pieces of equipment which have been adapted for the purpose, still leaves something to be desired in many systems. The reason is that most of the systems mentioned depend upon allocating space for storage upon the basis of the maximum stock for every line item held. The consequence is that the average installation looks less than half full even though the stock-keeper may be complaining about shortage of space. One answer is to employ a tote-box system where the stock of each line item is divided between an appropriate number of modular-sized boxes. In this way only the boxes actually being picked are partially empty with the full boxes being held in reserve. The penalty is the need to move boxes to forward stock as boxes become exhausted and the need to maintain a control system.

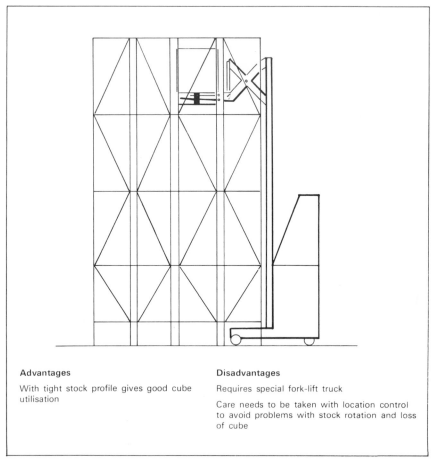

Advantages	Disadvantages
With tight stock profile gives good cube utilisation	Requires special fork-lift truck
	Care needs to be taken with location control to avoid problems with stock rotation and loss of cube

Figure 7:9   Double-deep system

Long load systems

This application area has been a relatively neglected aspect of storage and handling systems. A possible reason is that such techniques are usually associated with manufacturing engineering and this particular part of British industry is by no means distinguished in its approach to materials handling problems. There is a strong case for improvement, and if the manufacturing engineering industry can ultimately be persuaded that materials handling can offer important benefits and save costs the sector should prove lucrative to equipment suppliers.

Bar-rack techniques of the pigeon hole and cantilever pattern employing man-power and overhead craneage are well known, but neither system can be described as efficient in terms of either space or labour saving. The method depicted in Figure 7:21 makes use of specialised equipment to take advantage of the headroom available.

Advantages
Permits individual pallet access

Space utilisation is good with narrow aisle applications particularly between 8 and 12 m

Limits personnel access into warehouse

Easy to operate

Cost per unit of throughput can be low if correctly designed

Disadvantages
Floor tolerances have to be tight

Movement media has high initial cost and can be expensive to maintain

Usually requires feeder trucks

Needs location control system

Needs either rail or wire in floor guidance system

Source: Barlow Handling Limited

Figure 7:10   Narrow aisle high rack stacked and adjustable pallet racking

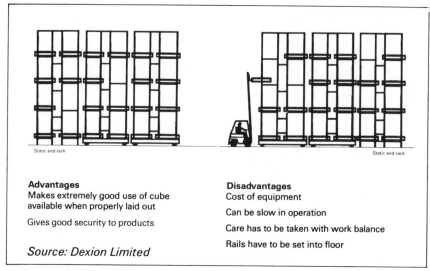

Advantages
Makes extremely good use of cube available when properly laid out

Gives good security to products

Source: Dexion Limited

Disadvantages
Cost of equipment

Can be slow in operation

Care has to be taken with work balance

Rails have to be set into floor

Figure 7:11   APR on powered mobile bases

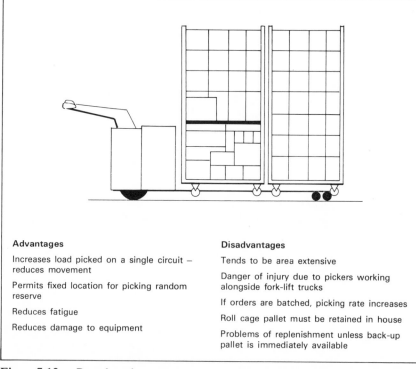

Advantages

Increases load picked on a single circuit — reduces movement

Permits fixed location for picking random reserve

Reduces fatigue

Reduces damage to equipment

Disadvantages

Tends to be area extensive

Danger of injury due to pickers working alongside fork-lift trucks

If orders are batched, picking rate increases

Roll cage pallet must be retained in house

Problems of replenishment unless back-up pallet is immediately available

Figure 7:12   Base location order selection into roll cage pallets transported in pairs by power pallet truck (up to 200 cases per man-hour assuming individual carton picking)

Figure 7:13   Second-level order picking machine   *Source: Rolatruc Limited*

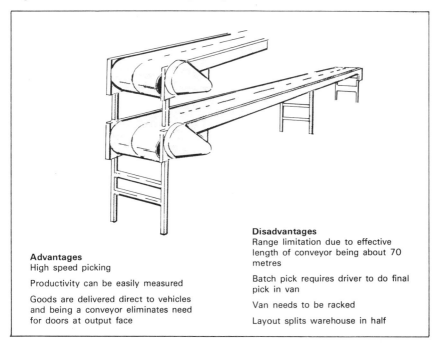

Advantages
High speed picking

Productivity can be easily measured

Goods are delivered direct to vehicles
and being a conveyor eliminates need
for doors at output face

Disadvantages
Range limitation due to effective
length of conveyor being about 70
metres

Batch pick requires driver to do final
pick in van

Van needs to be racked

Layout splits warehouse in half

Figure 7:14   Carton picking from pallet to flat belt conveyor and then direct to
vehicles (circa 600 cartons per man-hour)

Figure 7:15   Machine-assisted picking device (circa 300 cases per man-hour)
Source: Rolatruc Limited

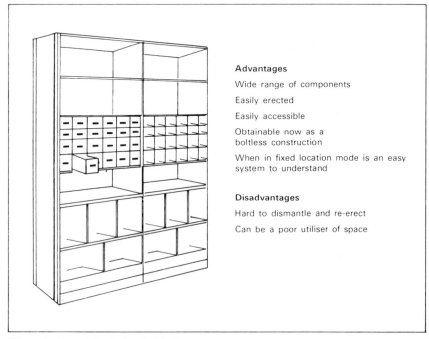

Advantages

Wide range of components

Easily erected

Easily accessible

Obtainable now as a
boltless construction

When in fixed location mode is an easy
system to understand

Disadvantages

Hard to dismantle and re-erect

Can be a poor utiliser of space

Figure 7:16   Binning – single tier

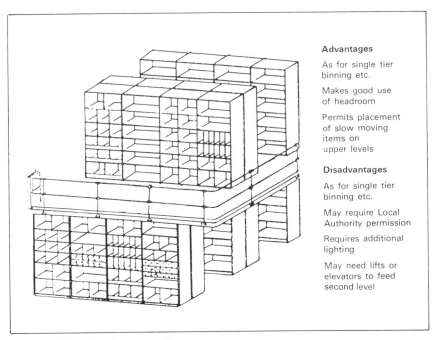

Advantages

As for single tier binning etc.

Makes good use of headroom

Permits placement of slow moving items on upper levels

Disadvantages

As for single tier binning etc.

May require Local Authority permission

Requires additional lighting

May need lifts or elevators to feed second level

Figure 7:17   Binning – two tier

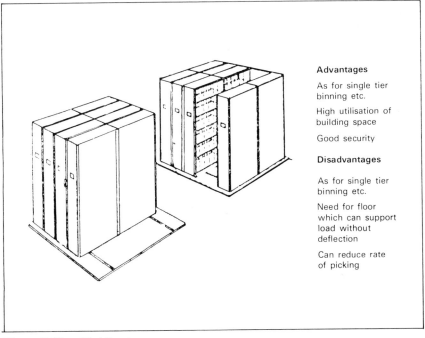

Advantages

As for single tier binning etc.

High utilisation of building space

Good security

Disadvantages

As for single tier binning etc.

Need for floor which can support load without deflection

Can reduce rate of picking

Figure 7:18   Mobile storage

Advantages
Works well in 2m to 6m lift range

Makes good use of space

Is effective in high-range low rate of
pick per line item situations

Free-roving capability is effective in
multi-aisle application

Disadvantages
Work-balance problems with
multi-machine applications

Needs careful handling and training

Limited access at low level

Source: Crown Controls Limited

Figure 7:19   High level order picking (free path)

Advantages
Effective in 5m to 12m range

Makes good use of space

Effective in high-range low rate of pick per line situations

Easy to operate

Mains supply powered

Disadvantages
Work-balance problems with multi-machine applications

Usually fixed to a single aisle, which favours long aisle lengths

Limited access at low level

Source: British Monorail Limited

Figure 7:20   High level order picking (fixed path)

Advantages
Gives good access to individual items
provided they can be manhandled

Makes good use of headroom

Makes better use of building volume

Makes limited use of manpower when
compared with craneage and slinging

Disadvantages
Side loaders need considerable space
at end of aisle

Can be slow when compared with
mechanised systems

Source: Cleco Kane

Figure 7:21   Cantilever racking with side loader/order picker

Load/unload facilities

The facilities provided for loading and unloading depend on factors such as product characteristics, quantities received and despatched, mode of transportation and additional requirements imposed by security, quality control and remodularisation. The choices are essentially between raised or level dock, through flow or 'U' flow, and the number of docks to be provided. In addition the necessary area of dock and marshalling space has to be calculated and experience suggests it is wiser to be generous in the allocation of space for this activity because a cramped loading dock leads to error and a slow-down in the operations.

Raised or level docks

The determining factor here is vehicle type. Generally it is usual to employ raised docks in conjunction with end-loaded vans and level docks with flat-vehicles, but many exceptions to this generalisation exist.

'U' flow/through-flow warehousing

'U' flow implies the placing of both receiving and despatch docks upon the same face of the building, and has the following advantages providing that the flow rates experienced are not so great as to cause congestion or confusion.

1   The docks may be allocated to receiving or despatch as pressure demands.
2   Building expansion can take place on three sides.
3   Vehicle parking and manoeuvring facilities are shared.
4   Personnel and equipment can be shared.
5   Control and security.
6   Environmental problems are simplified.

Through-flow, implying despatch and receipt at opposite ends of the building, or alternatively on adjacent sides of the building, is acceptable under certain conditions, viz:

1   In warehouses where the goods vehicle runs through the centre of the warehouse and can be progressively loaded e.g., builders merchants.
2   Where receiving is linked directly to a manufacturing resources.
3   Where the road transport used is of a different type e.g., 15 metre truckers at input and 6 tonne delivery vans at output; or where the transport mode is different as with rail and road systems in the same warehouse.

The number of loading bays

By the use of activity sampling and operations research together with the use of simulation programs such as HOCUS or GPSS it is possible to establish with reasonable accuracy the number of loading docks required. The application of such techniques has more relevance in systems having in excess of five or six loading bays because the tendency with smaller systems is to install as many loading bays as will fit into the side of the building on the grounds that they add little to the cost but provide the maximum possible safeguard against the possibility of delayed turn around.

Load/unload equipment

The range of load/unload equipment is extensive and it is not practical to do justice to the range in this chapter. The objective is clearly to decrease turn around time and the man-power associated with the activity. Efforts are now being made abroad to mechanise the process of loading box-vehicles, albeit without conspicuous success but the fact that time and energy is being spent on the design of such systems suggests that before too long a break-through might be made. It is, however, only too easy to sub-optimise the total system by introducing mechanical handling aids. For instance, it is still usually more economical to hand-ball goods into containers on long-haul rather than to use pallets, on the basis that palletisation can reduce container carrying capacity by as much as 20 per cent and also the cost of pallets has to be taken into account.

The advent of the computer on to the loading dock opens many possibilities in terms of rapid identification and recording of the receipt and despatch of goods and also the speeding up of quality control procedures. Coupled with coding and routing techniques, the possibility of reducing the labour requirement for sorting and clerical duties is considerable. The state-of-the-art is such that the Department of Defence in the USA are considering the introduction of coding at the manufacturing stage of all the many hundreds of thousands of different items required to keep that establishment working. It is conceivable that by simply passing a reading device over the coded component it will be possible to carry out a full audit trail back to the source of manufacture. The implications for the aircraft industry are clearly enormous.

Administration and control

The principles of administration – to identify and record what is received, to locate stock and record by line item, to organise and record withdrawals from stock and despatch – are easy to understand. It is the sheer volume of transactions undertaken in modern warehousing which causes organisational and administrative complexity. Little wonder that in many warehousing systems stocks are lost or misplaced. Part of the trouble in the past has been the employment of staff who are inadequate in themselves, inadequately trained and often not provided with either the right system or right equipment to carry out the job in hand.

The advent of the real-time dedicated computer offers an opportunity to change the image of warehousing. It is not necessary to provide a mechanised system to complement the computer. However, it is the ability of the computer to cope systematically and accurately with large volumes of data which is likely to make the task of warehouse management so much easier, provided of course, that the data base is in itself accurate. Warehousing is by its very nature management intensive and many hours have been spent in the past trying to find answers to what appear to be relatively simple questions such as how much stock and where. The small computer with its display screen can answer such questions accurately in a fraction of the time previously taken, and leaves executives free to involve themselves in management. What is more, the operation of information input and retrieval can be left to relatively low-grade staff provided that the system is adequately designed and well maintained. Although the cost of software is increasing, a number of packages are now becoming available on the market which will go part of the way towards alleviating the problem. Couple this with the fall in price of hardware and increasing power and we have a tool which no warehouse manager should be without.

Fire control and insurance

Increasing attention worldwide is being paid to the problems of fires in warehouses and the consequential losses which can be incurred by having large volumes of valuable stock in a single compartment. This has resulted from a series of large fires in block-stacked 'high-pile' systems and in one in particular where a very large quantity of post and cage pallets was involved. The problems of maintaining the reliability of sprinkler systems are considerable and even when they are correctly maintained there are many people who believe that their speed of response to an actual outbreak of fire is inadequate. A consequence of this latter problem is that a great deal of work is being done on devising effective 'high-speed' systems although their rate of acceptance is proving a slow and somewhat ponderous process.

Conclusion

The foregoing can only go part way towards indicating the complexity of modern warehouse operation. It is true to say that the area has not received its fair share of research and development funding in the past. Although the transport cost element has continued to dominate the distribution scene, it may yet prove difficult to make big economies in that area and ultimately, just as our Japanese colleagues have demonstrated, economies may be achieved in the warehouse operation element thereby helping to alleviate the problems of ever increasing final costs. Certainly there is a greater need than ever for the introduction of formal training of warehouse operators, warehouse designers, and distribution specialists so that the potential for cost savings in warehouse operation may be finally realised.

8

Warehouse design and layout

Ken Firth

The invention of the fork-lift truck in the United States of America in the 1920s and their development and use throughout the world since that time has had a profound effect upon warehouse layout and construction. The prime effect has been to limit the construction of multi-storey warehouses to a mere handful in recent times – good examples being certain types of mail-order system with their use of extensive conveyor systems, and warehouses where land values are exceptionally high as in Japan or Hong Kong.

Whilst the fork-lift truck has not been the only influence upon layout, its flexibility and adaptability has made it the most significant contributor to change in terms of handling palletised loads. The bulk of the effort has been to concentrate upon designing machines which can operate in narrower and narrower gangways with the facility of increasing lift up to heights of about 12 metres. The next stage of this progression will be to develop driver assistance to a point where the drivers themselves will become superfluous.

The reasons why fork-lift trucks have been developed in this way are not hard to find. In the first place narrower gangways mean a better area utilisation of the space available, and greater height of lift up to 12 metres takes advantage of the fact that most warehouse buildings cost less per unit of volume as their height is increased to this point. It is interesting to note that the practical lifting capacity of fork-lift trucks seems to be reaching its limit at about the same height as stacker-crane systems come into their own.

When considering the layout of any store or warehouse it is important to take into account all the principles of materials handling and the constraints mentioned in the previous chapter because these can have a profound effect upon cost (Figure 8:1). It is relatively easy to demonstrate their effect by applying values to some of the more

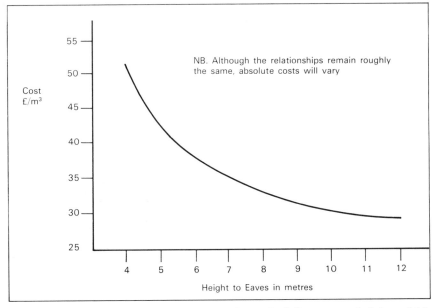

Figure 8:1   Cost curve for steel portal frame buildings up to heights of 12 metres

important parameters and by varying these demonstrating the effect upon the warehouse system.

Alternative approaches to the storage and order selection of palletised loads

For the purpose of simplicity let us ignore, at this stage, marshalling, goods receiving, despatch and ancillary areas, and concentrate upon the bulk storage and order-picking aspects. It is assumed that the requirements for 'other areas' will remain broadly similar regardless of layout.

Design parameters for a low product range system

In devising possible layouts against the parameters specified in Figure 8:2 it is important to consider both plan and elevation. In the example, the maximum stacking height (5.6 metres) fits in conventionally with the headroom available allowing for clearance and a single level of sprinklers. With only fifty products, the least of which has a minimum stock of sixteen pallets, it is pertinent to question whether a simple block stack will provide an answer to the bulk storage problem — thus requiring the least expenditure on equipment. Other solutions will probably operate under the

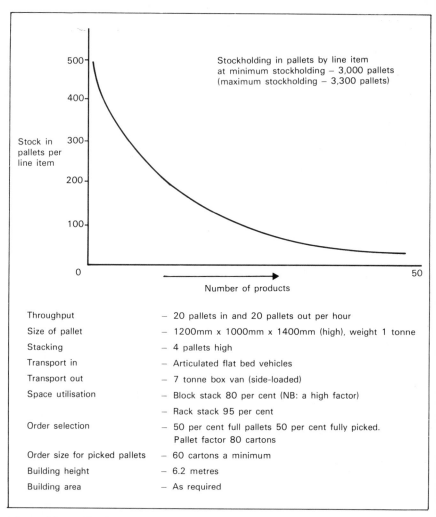

Figure 8:2   Design parameters

parameters laid down e.g., 'drive-in' racking, adjustable pallet racking, pallet live storage, and powered mobile storage, but in the context of this simple operating statement the economic relevance is doubtful. The most likely alternative with the absence of a stacking constraint and a limitation on height would be powered mobile storage if land and building values were exceptionally high. The tentative solution of simple block stacking, whilst answering the bulk storage problem neatly, and probably cheaply, means that order selection should be carried out in a separate area and the introduction of this part of the problem suggests that adjustable pallet racking with picking from base locations may be the answer. The approach to virtually any warehouse problem after assessing stockholding and throughput characteristics is a statement and appraisal of all likely alternatives.

Block storage layout with separate order picking

Using the basic data given in Figure 8:2 it is possible to determine whether a fixed or random location approach is correct for the layout. Fixed location, as the name implies, means that a fixed area is allocated to each product and this has to be based upon the maximum stock held for each individual line item. In the example, the difference between the sum of the maximum and minimum is only 300 pallets and with an average stockholding of 3,150 pallets represents only a small wastage of floor space if accommodation is allowed for 3,300 pallets (assuming 80 per cent utilisation, a total of 4,125 spaces would have to be provided). With a stockholding situation which has a much larger variation between maximum and minimum, say 3,300 pallets down to 2,000 pallets, a fixed location system might be inappropriate because of the space wastage. In this instance the warehouse would be normally laid out on the basis of average stockholding plus a margin say 10 per cent, i.e., 2,900 pallets (3,625 spaces at 80 per cent utilisation). This results in a considerable reduction in warehouse area compared to the 'fixed location' requirement, but has the penalty of requiring a record of stock location by row and age of stock. The big advantage of fixed location is the speed with which fork-lift truck drivers can learn the system (particularly if close control is kept on stock rotation), and the freedom from excessive administration.

The next step in preparing a block storage layout is to determine row length and height. The example already specifies four pallets high but the row length has to be assessed by a process of trial and error. This is done by estimating a reasonable length of row – not less than two pallets deep and usually not more than six. (This may be exceeded when large quantities of slow moving stock are held, but the level of damage tends to increase correspondingly.) More than one length of row may be employed but the greater the number of different lengths the greater the complexity of layout and operation. It is useful to consider the arrangement of rows in Figures 8:3 and 8:4 assuming the availability of a four way entry pallet.

The tolerances shown may be varied to suit operating systems but it is advisable to err on the side of generosity at the planning stage – in terms of both space and cost estimation.

It is sometimes advisable when considering alternatives to carry out a quick check to discover whether the pallet spaces required will actually fit into the building. This is done by calculating the space occupied by a single pallet and making due allowances for gangway requirements. With a direction of fork entry through the 48" face of the pallet the calculation would be as follows:

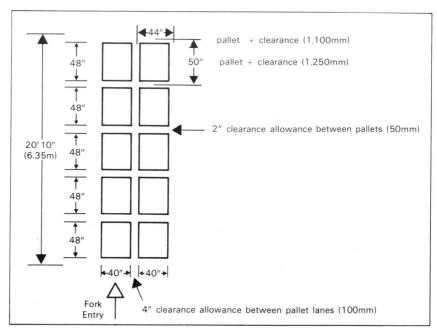

Figure 8:3   Fork entry through 40″ (1,000 mm) pallet dimension

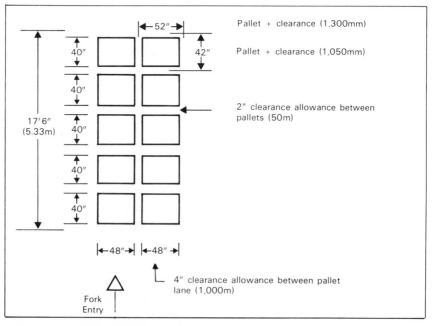

Figure 8:4   Fork entry through 48″ (1,200 mm) pallet dimension

Area occupied by a row of pallets (5 deep, 4 high)   = $6.929m^2$
1.5m x 5.33m

Gangway shared between two opposite rows (gangway 3m   = $1.950m^2$
wide) 1.3m x 1.5m

                                                             $8.879m^2$

Allowance for transverse gangways + 20 per cent $1.776m^2$

                                                        $10.655m^2$

Area occupied by a single pallet is $\dfrac{10.655m^2}{20}$ = $0.533m^2$

Area required to accommodate 3,300 pallets in fixed location
at 80 per cent utilisation in reserve block storage   = $2,198m^2$
(4125 x 0.533m²)

The calculation with fork entry through the 40″ face of
pallet yields the following results:

Area required to accommodate 3,300 pallets in fixed location
at 80 per cent utilisation in reserve block storage   = $2.134m^2$
(4,125 x 0.517m²)

The change in orientation of the pallets yields a theoretical saving of $64m^2$ which represents a building cost reduction of around £15,000 at 1980 prices. Other factors enter into the equation such as fixed building dimensions, right-angled stacking aisles of different types of fork-lift truck, the type of transport on which pallets are delivered and presentation of the pallet to the order-picker. The calculation will also show different results if different depths of block are used in the same installation.

Assuming that the building size will permit the storage of the pallet quantities required the correct layout is usually ascertained by making use of squared paper and templates. In the simple example quoted a minimum of 207 rows 5 deep and 4 pallets high have to be accommodated, which produces the layout in Figure 8:5.

Using a random location by row system, the area occupied would be of the order of $1,950m^2$, a building cost saving of around £50,000 at 1980 prices, which would have to be traded-off against the costs of operating a location control system.

The order picking area

The split between full pallet picks and part pallet picks places certain limitations upon the method of order picking and hence the layout. Output from bulk to the picking

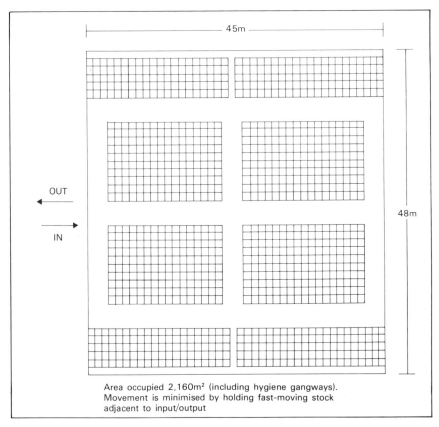

Figure 8:5   Simple block storage layout for 3,300 pallets in fixed location at 80 per cent utilisation (pallet spaces provided = 4,280)

area is at a rate of 10 pallets per hour (800 cartons per hour at level rates). In most picking situations the flow-rates vary to some extent throughout the day but as this example is being used to demonstrate picking layout the rate shown will suffice.

The objective in laying out a picking area is to place a full range of stock in such a way that walking is minimised – assuming that a 'picker to goods' technique is employed. In Figure 8:6 some 50 picking locations have to be sited, and sufficient stock held to avoid unnecessary stock-outs. It is virtually certain that 10 of the lines will represent 600 (total) cartons in the hour whilst the remaining 40 will represent only 200 cartons an hour. The number of order pickers employed at the best known order-picking rates, pallet-to-pallet, will be 4, but in view of the relatively low range, care has to be taken to separate the fast moving pallets from each other to avoid interference.

Figure 8:6 gives 2 pallets for each of 47 lines and 4 pallets for the 3 fastest movers. At an average turnover rate of 10 pallets per hour, a 1 truck operation is

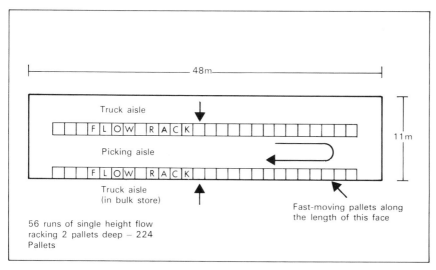

Figure 8:6   Order picking layout using pallet live storage (flow-through racking)

feasible. With this type of equipment it is possible to align the pallet flow in the 1,200 mm direction because the order-picker can step over the pallet to reach cartons at the back – this will eliminate the need to turn the pallet around when leaving the bulk storage. The pick on to a flat pallet would involve a 'U' walk of around 100 metres per picked pallet; a gangway of 3.6 metres is allowed to permit passing and avoid congestion. Whilst the order-pickers are separated effectively from the fork-lift truck operation, the warehouse in-feed and out-feed of full pallets is forced to the edge of the layout. A centre aisle through the centre of the picking area would be unacceptable.

An alternative solution to the order picking problem would be to run flat-belt conveyors 2 high (one above the other), down the centre of the order picking aisle, which would be only 2 metres wide including the conveyor. The conveyors may then be routed directly into the back of a retail delivery vehicle fitted with shelves. Batch picking from such a low range of stock can be operated at rates of 600 cartons per man-hour, but the approach requires a final sort by the driver of the vehicle. Care has to be taken with the disposal of empty pallets when using this technique. It should be remembered that when installing conveyors they have the disadvantage of isolating one part of the warehouse from the other if not carefully sited.

Drive-in, drive-through, and pallet live storage layouts (bulk storage)

A change in 2 or 3 of the design parameters as originally stated could result in a different equipment approach. If we assume that the products will not withstand a crush load exceeding 2 pallets high, and that headroom is increased to 11 metres, there is clearly going to be a severe wastage of the building cube. Although the rate of throughput will almost certainly be slower, per fork-lift truck used, a 'drive-in' or 'drive-through' approach is feasible. For preference the writer would make use of 'drive-in' equipment because it is inherently more stable than 'drive-through' at the heights being considered. An additional consideration is the type of fork-lift truck employed. In order to minimise aisle widths and also to ensure that the truck itself is sufficiently narrow to permit entry into the 'drive-in' aisle, the choice of a reach truck is almost mandatory at the heights mentioned. Alternatively, if the height available permitted stacking 5 or 6 pallets high, but the throughput was increased to 60 pallets in and 60 pallets out per hour, the use of pallet live storage might be considered with its inherent FIFO capacity. In this case the choice of fork-lift trucks is not so critical because the need for adequate gangways to cope with the higher rate of flow may permit the use of larger trucks, for instance a 'down-rated' 2 tonne counterbalanced machine.

Drive-in layout for 3,300 pallets at 80 per cent utilisation

Assuming a fixed location layout, the pallet spaces required will be 4,125 and the first aspect to be determined is how many pallets can be accommodated in 11 metres clear headroom, making due allowance for beam spacings, clearances, straddle legs of reach trucks (if operating in minimum aisle), and sprinklers to the appropriate FOC or NFPA rules. Such allowance calculations vary according to the types of equipment used, and the insurance hazard classification for high-piled risks. It is probably wise to contact one's insurance company in order to check their requirements because on occasion interpretation of rules has been a matter for some negotiation.

In our example (Figure 8:7) let us say that we can stack 6 pallets high with a lift of 9 metres being required. Whilst such a lift is high it is not outside the capacity of a modern reach truck, but the gangway requirements would be of the order of 3 metres. With a row length of 6 pallets deep the capacity of a row would be 30 pallets and this means that some 138 rows would be required, 70 less than the block storage layout but of course we have the penalty of having a somewhat wider row (1.5 metres) to allow for the racking structure. In this example the direction of entry into the pallet can be only one-way through the 1,200 mm face because although the truck can pick up a pallet only 1,000 mm wide it cannot enter the drive-in rack because the clear rack width will be less than the width of the truck. It should also be remembered that under present United Kingdom corporation tax rules an equipment orientated solution is more economical than a building orientated one providing the company is in a profit situation.

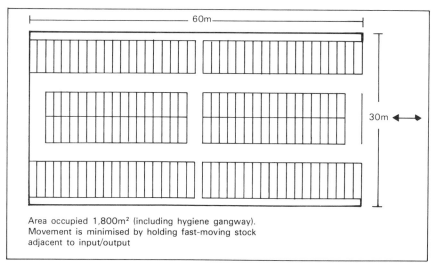

Area occupied 1,800m² (including hygiene gangway).
Movement is minimised by holding fast-moving stock
adjacent to input/output

Figure 8:7   Drive-in block storage layout for 3,300 pallets in fixed location at
80 per cent utilisation (pallet spaces 4,140)

Pallet live storage layout for 2,900 pallets in random access by lane

Gravity feed pallet live storage facilitates the use of random access by lane layout
because each lane can be accessed individually at the input and output ends. Thus a
total pallet requirement of 3,625 would be required. Assuming a headroom of 11
metres plus allowances for tolerances, sprinklers, slope, etc., it is likely that a total of
5 pallets high would be selected for this solution. However, within the limits of the
stock profile the lane lengths may be greatly increased. In our stock profile it is
possible to calculate that the smallest line item will have a stock of 16 pallets so a lane
length of 20 pallets would not be inappropriate as an initial approach. To minimise
the amount of live storage track required fork-entry would be through the 1,200 mm
face and the track length for 20 pallets x 1,000 mm would be of the order of 20.5
metres. Some 38 bays of live storage 5 high would be required in this configuration,
storing 3,800 pallets. This allows for wastage in the low stock line items. A typical
layout is indicated in Figure 8:8.

In this case the saving in building space compared with the drive-in racking
solution is 270 m², or around £70,000 at 1980 prices, but this has to be traded-off
against the considerably higher price of palletised live-storage equipment, some £20
per pallet space, which would fall somewhat short of the actual capital requirement.
Nevertheless the reduction in area makes site availability that much easier and the
speed of throughput would be considerably greater, provided that double handling is
not incurred through the use of slave pallets.

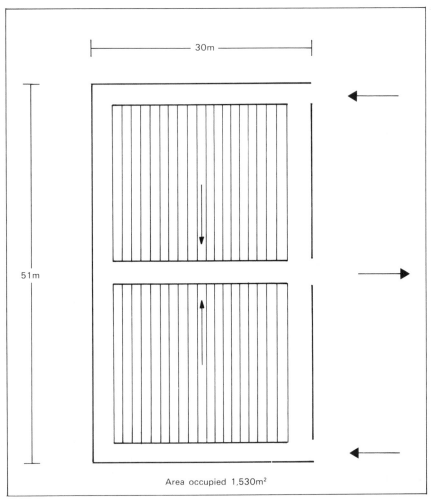

Figure 8:8   Pallet live storage layout for 2,900 pallets in random access storage

Individual random access pallet systems (bulk storage)

Using the design parameters laid down earlier but with an increase in range of products from 50 to 500 means that a block storage solution ceases to be practicable. The average number of pallets per line item is only 6.5 for 3,300 pallets. Possible solutions are:

– Adjustable pallet racking with reach or counterbalanced truck

(5 pallets high)

 – Adjustable pallet racking with 180° high-rack stacking trunk

(7 pallets high)
 – Powered mobile storage with reach or counterbalanced truck

(5 pallets high)

The pallet stacking heights, although selected arbitrarily here would have to be assessed in the light of equipment available and headroom.

The introduction of order-picking from 500 lines complicates the problem, and it is conventional to pick from base and possibly second level locations with the Adjustable Pallet Racking (5 pallets high), and the Powered Mobile Storage Systems (5 pallets high). In the case of the 180° High Rack Stacking System (7 pallets high) it is almost mandatory on safety grounds to separate the picking system when the bulk storage layout is constructed on a back-to-back rack basis; an alternative is single-entry racking with the order-picker and his equipment in alternate gangways to the High-Rack-Stack Truck.

As with simple block stacking it is possible to stack pallets either with the forks running through the 1,200 mm or 1,000 mm faces as shown in Figures 8:9 and 8:10 respectively.

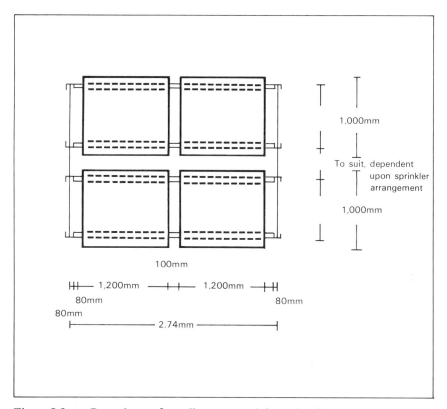

Figure 8:9   Beam layout for pallets accessed through 1,200 mm face

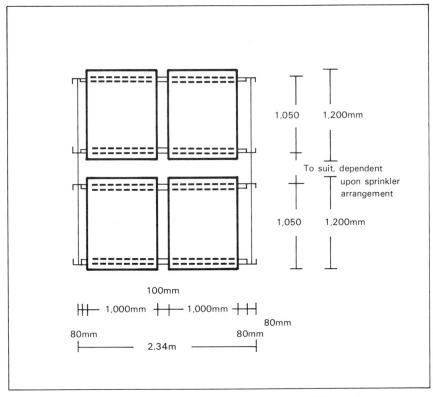

Figure 8:10   Beam layout for pallets accessed through 1,000 mm face

In bulk storage applications it is normal to expect that the access through the 1,000 mm face yields the most pallets per square metre, other factors being equal. This feature cannot always be relied upon due to the effect of fixed building dimensions. The choice of direction of entry may also depend upon the need to access pallets for order-picking, in which case picking through the 1,200 mm face is the normal solution. Where possible it is desirable to avoid the need for the fork-lift truck driver to turn the pallet around. (In the case of high-rack stacking where the delivery truck can access the 1,200 mm face, and the high-rack machine the 1,000 mm face, the problem of pallet turning need not arise.)

A comparison of Figure 8:11 with simple block storage shows the space penalty of having to operate a conventional truck system with random locations. Provided the truck aisle width can be maintained with the additional lift, the area can be reduced by some 275 m^2 if a 6 pallet high solution can be adopted. Picking can be easily carried out from base locations and would extend the area by some 200 m^2 assuming 550 additional locations.

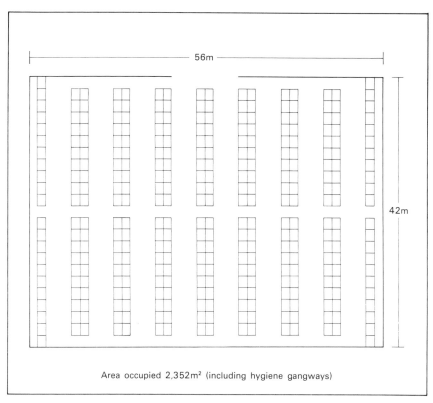

Area occupied 2,352m² (including hygiene gangways)

Figure 8:11   Typical layout for adjustable pallet racking (5 pallets high) using reach truck with access through 1,000 mm face for pallet for 2,900 pallets at 95 per cent utilisation (3,225 pallets)

Figure 8:12 illustrates dramatically the ability of high-rack stackers to save area (admittedly at the expense of feeder trucks and building headroom of up to 12 metres). The layout assumes the use of P and D stations and that rotation of the load in rack gangways is not a requirement. However, the inclusion of order-picking does present a layout problem which is demonstrated in Figure 8:13. Assume that an additional 550 order-picking spaces in a separated area have to be accommodated; the layout also assumes the use of second-level order picking equipment.

The area can, of course, be reduced if a multi-level order-picking solution is adopted but this will also slow down the operation considerably.

Another solution which has been used in conjunction with 180° high-rack stackers is the alternate single-entry layout approach as depicted in Figure 8:14. This represents a saving of some 238 m² over the double-entry racking approach and illustrates the importance of looking at likely alternatives. It also represents a reduction over the Adjustable Pallet Racking and Reach Truck Selection, but at the expense of increased height and more expensive handling and storage equipment.

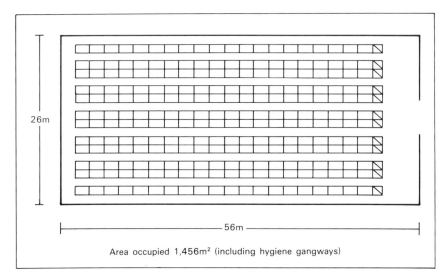

26m

56m

Area occupied 1,456m² (including hygiene gangways)

Figure 8:12   Typical layout for adjustable pallet racking (7 pallets high) using
               180° high-rack stacker with access through 1,000 mm face of
               pallet for 2,900 pallets at 95 per cent utilisation (3,225 pallets)

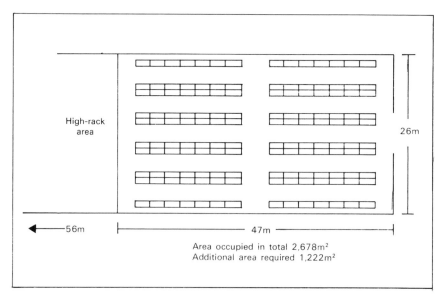

High-rack
area

26m

56m   47m

Area occupied in total 2,678m²
Additional area required 1,222m²

Figure 8:13   Additional layout for second-level order picking layout in
               conjunction with 180° high-rack stacking layout (550 picking
               pallets)

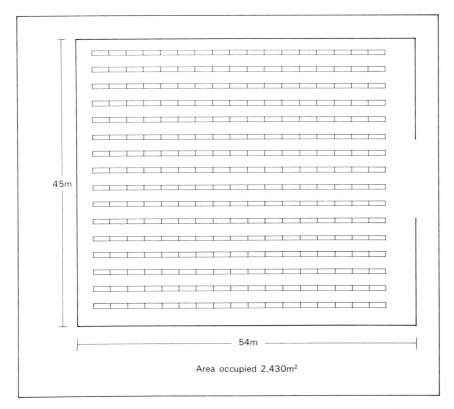

45m

54m

Area occupied 2,430m²

Figure 8:14   Layout for combined 180° high-rack stacking using adjustable pallet racking (7 pallets high) with access through 1,200 mm face for 2,900 pallets at 95 per cent utilisation (3,225 pallets) and incorporating 550 additional pallets in base-locations only for order-picking

Goods receiving and despatch areas

It is probably true to say that receiving and despatch areas in warehousing receive less attention from the layout planner than other functions within the warehouse system. The reason for this is not difficult to find because receiving and despatch are functions over which warehouse operators have little control, and this leads to the need for a flexible approach. In turn the designer concludes that the safest solution is to leave more than adequate space in the marshalling area to cover any emergency. It is certainly preferable to be generous in allowing operating space in these areas because congestion leads to error, bottlenecks, and failures in communication which affect the system and reduce customer service.

The factors which have to be considered when looking at goods receiving and despatch are as follows:

Types and sizes of vehicle.
Means of access on to site.
Traffic flow around the site.
Manoeuvring and picking areas for all types of vehicle on site.
Space requirements for marshalling, checking and quality control.
Product characteristics and throughput.
Unit-load characteristics and throughput.
The environment.
The number of load/unload bays required.
Control and administration.
Security and safety of personnel.

This is a formidable list and it is not difficult to imagine the possible permutations of loading bay design when all these variables are taken into account. As it is impossible to illustrate every facet of this aspect of design we will look at just one example (Figure 8:15) and draw from this as many points of interest as possible.

The layout represents a warehousing system which can accept a considerable amount of traffic of two distinctly different types. Incoming traffic comprises 15 metre box-van articulated trunkers which have (with the odd exception) a platform height of 1.35 metres. Variations due to compression of springs under load, etc., are taken care of by dock levellers. The provision of a scissor lift takes care of non-standard height vehicles. In the event of flat platform vehicles having to be unloaded it may be necessary to install a ramp which would permit exit from the warehouse by counterbalanced trucks. The second type of vehicle is of a box-van rigid retail delivery type, with a lower platform height, and in this case it is assumed that the natural slope of the ground on the site is downwards from right to left on the plan. The building is located so that the loading bays are not facing into the prevailing wind. The access to the site is from a one-way street giving ample clearance for two vehicles on either side of the gatehouse and the minimum of cross-flow. Traffic circulation in the United Kingdom around the site should be in a clockwise direction to facilitate the reversing of vehicles into loading docks. Ample accommodation for accumulation is allowed and clearance for reversing and pulling out in the case of 15 m vehicles is 35 metres and retail delivery vehicles 22 metres. The traffic office is sited so as to be able to see all traffic movement in and out of the warehouse and conveniently placed for a communicational link with the gatehouse.

There are two approaches to the assessment of the number of loading docks required. The first is to install as many loading docks as possible on the building face on the basis that they are not expensive to install in terms of building cost and if not used can be easily adapted to warehousing space. The alternative is to carry out activity sampling of arrivals and departures of vehicles and then through the use of simulation techniques assess the number of docks and parking spaces required. The trade-off is between the cost of the simulation study and the potential saving in loading docks. It is probably fair to say that of the many faults found with speculative warehousing, the attempts by developers to get as much building on site as is possible

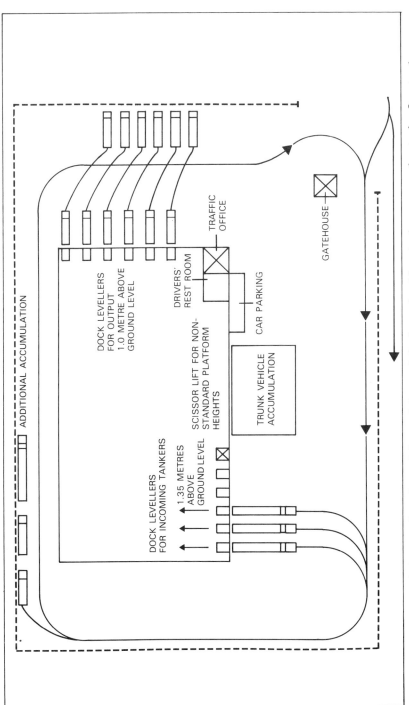

Figure 8:15   Schematic layout of goods receiving and despatch for incoming 15 metre box vans and outgoing 8 metre box vans

141

is the worst because of the delays caused by shunting vehicles into inadequate load/unload bays.

Ancillary areas

The layout of warehouses is not confined to the three main areas but also includes the installation of offices, maintenance areas and, in the case of electric-powered trucks, battery charging areas. Of the many warehouses that the writer has visited in the United Kingdom there is a general tendency not to provide sufficient space for the job in hand, particularly with maintenance and battery charging. In addition the methods of handling heavy pieces of equipment leave much to be desired. Whilst it is not possible in the context of this chapter to go into any detail it is important that warehouse designers of the future devote more time and attention to developing these parts of the warehouse system.

Choice of building structure

This chapter has so far concentrated upon illustrating different approaches to warehouse layout and design with the objective of arriving at a building structure which occupies the smallest possible area compatible with efficient operation. The same general procedure may be applied to small parts systems, although the equipment used and tolerances which apply are different. The important fact to remember is that the warehouse designer should produce a workable operating layout and, in the case of a greenfield site, fit a building around that layout in the most economical manner. It is most unwise when one has the opportunity of designing upon a greenfield site to let the building designer, whoever he may be, have the first go, because of all the constraints which exist in warehouse design those of building are the worst! By all means liaise with the architect at each phase of the design approach but do not go firm on the building until the warehousing system has been thoroughly appraised.

The warehouse systems designer, once satisfied with his own approach, must then provide the architect with a detailed brief which specifies the operating characteristics of the system and its requirements. This will include all critical dimensions, types of equipment, personnel and environmental aspects and it is then the responsibility of the architect to provide details of alternative building structures which will meet those requirements, as well as an estimate of the building costs. In effect the architect should be provided with a performance specification against which he should quote with the full backing of his professional competence. It is for the architect to recommend the most suitable type of building structure for the operation in hand – not the warehouse systems designer; equally, it is incumbent upon architects not to get involved in warehouse layout unless they are thoroughly acquainted with the techniques which are available.

Conclusion

In this chapter we have been able to consider just a few of the possible layouts which are available, and to show how building and equipment characteristics can affect the choice. The big problem for present day warehouse designers is the magnitude of the choice and the number of potentially viable alternatives which are available. Using traditional techniques it is impossible in most instances to study all possible variations, so the real skill in warehouse design is making the near optimum choice from intuitive experience. The fact that the design parameters for the warehouse will have almost certainly changed for indeterminable reasons by the time the warehouse is built and operating is, of course, in the designer's favour. The advent of the computer in cheaper and more powerful forms is permitting their use in the approach to warehouse problems, and certainly the existence of inter-active programs in the United States is a well established practice. In this regard there are two types, the first of which gives a read-out of dimensions of buildings, rack dimensions, fork-lift truck requirements, and costs within bounds specified by the designer. The second uses a visual display and graph plotter to produce an actual representation of the layout. The layout may be modified by means of a light pen and the selected solution is then printed out. The availability of such techniques will greatly speed up the work of the designer and it is hoped enable him to produce cheaper solutions, although it is difficult to conceive that the designer's function will entirely be replaced by such equipment.

9

Automated and mechanised warehouses

Ken Firth

The term automatic warehouse has been a much used, perhaps over used, phrase in the English language since the introduction of the 'automatic stacker crane' 20 years ago. There are in fact, few, if any, fully automated systems which, by implication, eschew all human activity except for the input of information, monitoring and control. Many warehouses are partially automated or mechanised and it is the objective of this chapter to explore the developments which have occurred and the equipment which is now available rather than consider a precise semantic definition of automatic as opposed to mechanisation.

The conventional objectives behind the introduction of such warehouse systems are as follows:

1   To gain financial advantage through cost reduction in the use of land, labour, transport, and stock holding.
2   To improve customer relations through the provision of speedier and more accurate service.
3   To obtain better control.

There are, however, other benefits which at the time of systems cost evaluation are intangible and difficult for accountants to quantify in conventional terms. Typical of these are improved worker morale and co-operation through being associated with a successful system, prestige with clients and customers by virtue of operating an advanced system, and better inter-departmental relations through improved control. In addition the strict disciplines which have to be imposed upon the warehouse operation tend to carry over into other areas of the manufacturing and distribution system, particularly in the areas of packaging and product rationalisation.

The conditions which favour automation and mechanisation are:

1   A high level of sustained throughput without major fluctuation due to seasonal or other changes
2   Low product range
3   High individual order lots
4   High product value or profitability
5   High labour costs
6   High transportation costs
7   The availability of article numbering systems
8   Market stability over time and in particular product size stability
9   High land costs or shortage of land
10 Unit load and product modularity
11 Round the clock operation.

This does not mean to say that it is not possible or even wise to design and construct a system in the absence of several of these criteria, just that it might be that little bit harder to arrive at a favourable justification.

In addition it is virtually certain that this initial capital investment will be higher than a non-mechanised approach and also that the amount of time spent upon investigating the system, detailing, preparing and implementing the design will be that much longer. A period of three years from conception of the idea to commissioning is not unknown, and some systems have as many as 30 man-years design time in their preparation.

It is true to say that quite a number of the earlier automated systems took longer to become established than anticipated, or were distinctly unsuccessful, and this led to a certain amount of scepticism amongst potential users. The reasons for this were manifold, but typical among them were over-ambitious design, inadequate understanding of the problems, and above all an unpreparedness to establish and maintain disciplines of operation and equipment maintenance by users. Whilst it would be unwise to claim that systems unreliability is a thing of the past it is certainly true to say that there are now in existence well established suppliers who can provide turn-key operations which will work effectively and with a high degree of reliability after only a short period of initial commissioning. An important contribution to a successful project of this kind is that both supplier and user dedicate themselves equally to the success of the project right through the construction and implementation phase, and also that there is acceptance from the outset that on such major projects some design changes will have to be introduced during construction. It is little short of lunacy for a potential user to place an order and then expect the supplier to be totally responsible for providing a working article ready for use at the appointed time. Equally a supplier must take the user's maintenance staff into his confidence from the outset and ensure that they are fully trained during the construction phase, even to the extent of involving them on the construction itself. Anyone contemplating the installation and operation of an automatic warehouse would be well advised to study the Japanese approach, because it is in the area of organisation and dedication to making systems work rather than to high technology that Japan has had such spectacular success.

Categories of automated and mechanised warehouse

It is possible to determine several distinct areas of mechanisation in warehousing, each having its own particular characteristics and also variations within each group.
The major groups are:

1   Automatic storage and retrieval units for full pallets, using random pallet access, bulk storage or long-load techniques.
2   Automatic storage and retrieval units incorporating man-rider picking facilities.
3   Automatic storage and retrieval units for small components.
4   High speed high throughput order-picking equipment for both cartons and regular shaped small items.
5   Wire in-floor guidance and control of both 'free-path' order picking machines and fork-lift trucks (counterbalanced and high-rack stackers).
6   Sorting conveyors using scanning devices and coding techniques.

In addition to the above list there is also a variety of equipment for specialised purposes, such as mail-order which although of great interest to the materials handling engineer has too little application potential to be discussed here.

A distinct feature of modern projects is the move away from the fully integrated automatic warehouse with all its functions controlled by a monolithic main frame computer. The preferred approach is the separation of physical activity and control of the main operating functions with a considerable amount of flexibility at the operating interfaces. The reasons are not very hard to find. The concept of the integrated distribution machine involved the monitoring and operational control of many thousands of simultaneous activities in a high throughput warehouse, and whilst the computer was up to this task in both the hardware and software terms, the electro-mechanical devices which were present in very large numbers had not the same degree of reliability. Furthermore a problem in one area could cause delays elsewhere and time lost was difficult to regain. Finally, the centralisation of control and computer maintenance was left to a relatively few specialised personnel which opened up possibilities of disruption due to people leaving or internal disagreement. The new approach is to isolate each function so that it may be controlled and operated independently of other parts of the system, but inter-communication is retained via distributed mini or micro computers. This may even be extended to direct communication with the company main-frame or in the extreme with other organisations' computing devices. This means that one has to provide space for buffer shorage between functions and also build-in sufficient flexibility within each operating system to catch up on back-log due to temporary failure. We are really applying the philosophy of distributed computer systems one stage further. The advantage should be enhanced control where it is required, namely, in the hands of the operational staff.

Automatic storage and retrieval systems for full pallets

Variants of the Full Pallet Automatic Storage and Retrieval System, as depicted in Figure 9:1, are by no means new to the materials handling engineer, but it is possible to detect one or two significant trends in recent times. In the first place nearly all equipment produced today is rail-mounted on the floor; the systems using rack-mounted devices were subject to many problems caused by rack movement under load. There is also increased usage of relatively standard pallet racking equipment up to heights of around 18 metres, confined by a fairly conventional warehouse building. Although roof-on-rack structures have been built with the latter type of racking, there is fairly general acceptance that structural sections are more appropriate to the problem, especially so when 'roof-on-rack' or 'rack-clad' warehouses are frequently found in the 20–30 metres height range. A significant development in the United States, and taken up with enthusiasm in Japan, is the design and construction of stacker cranes in the 8–10 metres height range, handling unit loads up to 1 tonne and as little as 150 kg. Such machines are modular in their design which permits simplification in their construction and a consequent reduction in their cost. It is pleasing to note that United Kingdom companies are now involved in the supply of such systems.

Further significant developments have occurred with input/output devices, in particular, the use of 'Cartrac' equipment in the United States of America and Japan. Also of interest is the fact that in certain situations, an input and output has been located at both ends of the system thereby taking advantage of the control and optimising capabilities of the modern computer. Finally, the computer itself has been used on-board cranes as a replacement for the logic devices previously employed. The advantage is twofold; a reduction in cost through being able to use an off the peg microprocessor as opposed to an individually designed unit, and the increased flexibility offered by the capability of being able to re-program the computer as required.

One factor which is disturbing in relation to the construction of Automatic Storage and Retrieval Systems is the potentially increased number of restrictions which are being placed upon them by both local authorities and insurers. A possible reason for this is that these organisations have some difficulty in differentiating between an automatic storage and retrieval system employing a minimum of staff, and a high-rack warehouse which can have large numbers of personnel. It is, frankly, very difficult to find evidence of fires which have occurred in an automatic system. An additional problem in this area is the confusing advice given to companies by local fire officers, which may well be diametrically opposed to that of the insurers. One instance will suffice to demonstrate the point: a fire officer insisted upon sheet steel cladding down the spine of the racking and horizontal baffles beneath specified pallet levels. Should a fire occur in this situation there will be a tendency for flames to spread horizontally and also bridge the gangway rather than rise rapidly in a vertical direction which is the preference of both insurers and sprinkler manufacturers. There is clearly a need for the Home Office and insurers to get together and establish a nationally acceptable approach to such issues.

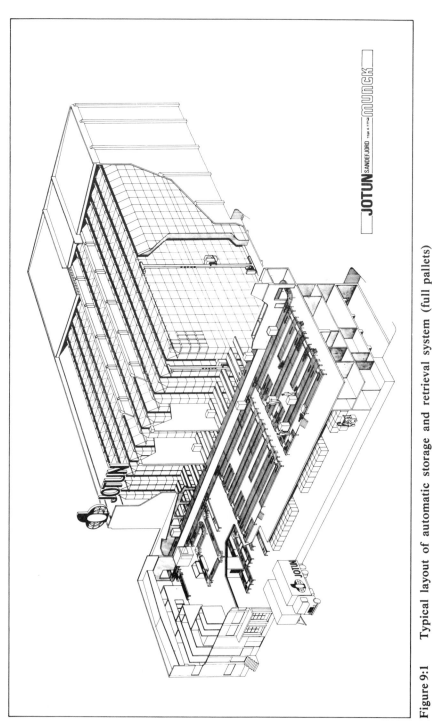

Figure 9:1   Typical layout of automatic storage and retrieval system (full pallets)

Automatic storage and retrieval systems for full pallet system – random access

The automatic warehouse operated by Nippon Paints at their distribution centre just outside Tokyo is an interesting example of the use of automatic equipment in what is, relatively speaking, a small warehouse holding only 2,240 pallets (see Figure 9:2).

The system comprises 2 rows of single-entry adjustable pallet racking, and 6 runs of double-entry pallet racking 35 metres long but only 8.9 metres high. The installation, supplied by Kawatesu-Interlake, is served by 2 punch-card controlled stacker cranes each with its own semi-automatic transfer car which permits aisle to aisle transfer. A fairly unusual feature is that the transfer cars accommodate both in-feed and out-feed P and D stations. On the in-feed side a simple wheeled transport is used, and on the out-feed a skate-wheel conveyor accumulator for 3 or 4 pallets. Delivery to and from the transfer cars is by counterbalanced fork-lift truck. Transfer of the cranes is smooth and quick and the car is positively locked to a fixture in the floor once it has arrived at the station, thus ensuring accurate crane-feed.

The system is installed within a conventional warehouse and was designed to operate cheaply and efficiently with only 30 per cent of the manpower used in a conventional system. The racking and cranes were installed and commissioned within four weeks of work commencing, and maintenance is undertaken by sub-contractors who specialise in this kind of equipment. Total pay-back was estimated at 2–3 years and the total cost of building cranes and racking was remarkably low by European standards. One of the reasons for this is that the approach to safety in Japan is of a different order to that in the United Kingdom; Japanese workers are expected to adopt a responsible attitude at all times, thus many safety devices which in the United Kingdom are considered mandatory are dispensed with.

Automatic storage and retrieval system for full pallet system – block storage

The use of stacker cranes as in-feed/out-feed devices in conjunction with large blocks of either gravity feed or powered live storage racking systems is not new; one of the earliest the writer can recall was at Potters of Darwin in the mid-1960s. Of course the number of applications is limited because there are not all that many stock profiles suited to the approach.

So far as automatic storage and retrieval is concerned there has been a distinct tendency towards the use of powered live storage systems or power assisted gravity systems because of the need to locate the pallet precisely at both the start and end of the storage lanes, thereby obviating the danger of damage to goods and stacker crane due to minor misalignment. One system of powered live storage pioneered by Construction Mills K in France has been taken up enthusiastically in the United States and Japan, and has been used in cold-storage and brewery applications. A variant of this equipment, manufactured by Mitsubushi Heavy Industries, has been installed by Whitbread at their brewery at Salmesbury, near Preston, Lancashire, for handling pallets of canned beer. A mass-loading device for handling 10 pallets at a time onto vehicles has also been installed.

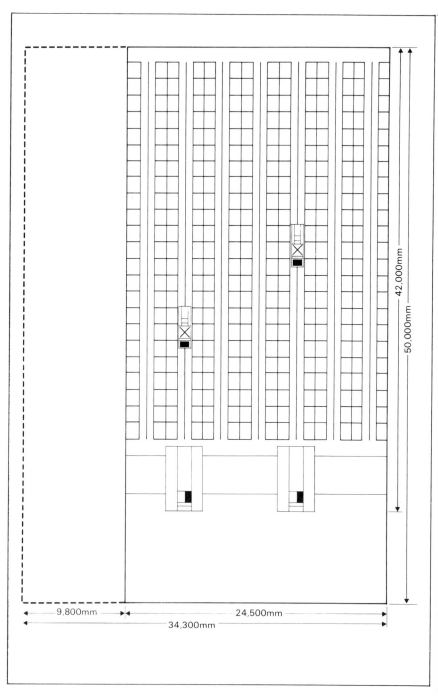

Figure 9:2   Plan view of warehouse of Nippon Paints, near Tokyo

American know-how has been used by the Japanese breweries Kirin and Suntory for the mass handling of beer using powered live storage techniques, and the Suntory brewery at Musashino has replaced a conventional warehouse employing 30 fork-lift truck drivers with an automatic warehouse of the same throughput and stockholding (see Figure 9:3). The warehouse has been installed on an area only half the size of a conventional unit and 3 men operate the system 3 times as quickly as the 30 fork-lift truck drivers; at peak performance a vehicle of 12 pallets is loaded every 2½ minutes. The capital cost of the system is 30 per cent more than that of a conventional system, but the operating cost is so reduced that pay-back is less than four years if the cost of land is taken into account. The system design implementation was Tsubaki Tramrail, a licensee of Cleveland Tramrail.

Automatic storage and retrieval systems – long load techniques

There have been a number of fairly recent developments in the handling of long loads – up to 6 metres for such products as bar-handling, aluminium extrusion handling and carpet handling. There are three approaches.

Pigeon-hole racking with machine retrieval

The layouts for this type of automatic storage and retrieval system usually comprise 2 opposed pigeon-hole bar-racks up to 6 metres deep each side with a central gangway slightly wider than the length of the largest bar or carpet. Product is stored in cassettes each of which can be withdrawn from its fixed location in the bar-racking by a large stacker crane which can automatically locate on the correct pigeon-hole and withdraw the cassette onto its platform for removal and delivery. There is quite a number of variants of such designs, pioneered by British Monorail in the United Kingdom and Hans Fehr in Switzerland, which range from the fully automatic to the man aboard versions; the latter permit the extraction of individual bars from a platform on the machine. An interesting example of this technology may be seen at the engineering works of Hans Fehr AG in Zurich (see Figure 9:4).

Cantilever racking with stacker crane placement and retrieval

An example of this approach may be seen at Toyo Linoleum Company, Itami City, Japan, where carpets in widths between 2 and 5 metres are manufactured, handled and stored in a cantilever racking system served by 3 Sumitono Heavy Industries stacker cranes 22 metres high.

The carpets are stored, 4 at a time, in specially designed unit loads which are fed to the cranes by transporter cars at the ground floor level. The computer controlled cranes place the unit loads away in the optimal position for storage according to the width of carpet and a record of the precise amount of carpet in store

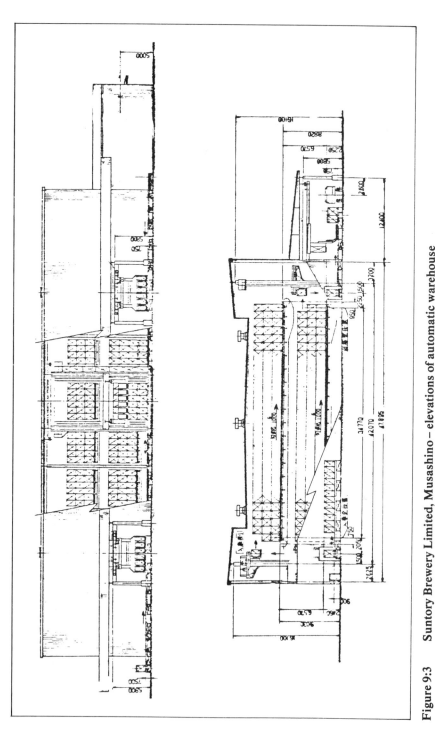

Figure 9:3 Suntory Brewery Limited, Musashino – elevations of automatic warehouse

152

Source: Hans Fehr AG, Zurich

Figure 9:4   High-bay warehouse with 3,500 bar pallet positions. Saws are fed
with material from this store

is held in the main frame together with the stock locations.

The handling process is complicated by virtue of the fact that the carpets have
to be cut to length on a cutting floor at first floor level. This problem is solved by the
cranes delivering the pallets to first floor level and a fork-lift truck driver withdrawing
the correct carpet for delivery to the cutter by means of boom truck, the pallet being
held at the output station whilst this operation is completed. After cutting, the carpet
is returned to its pallet, which is in turn placed on the cantilever racking by the stacker
crane and the stock record is automatically updated. The cost of the system, which
copes with 300,000 m^2 of carpet per month, was £800,000 in 1974. A total of 25
people, including cutters and up to 6 fork-lift truck drivers, operate the warehouse.

Cantilever racking with overhead gantry devices

Two West German companies, Remmert and Mehne, store long load cassettes in
cantilever racking but use a completely different handling technique (see Figure 9:5).
Runs of cantilever racking are laid out side by side with a gangway only slightly wider
than the cassettes used in the system. Parallel rails are run along the top of the racking

at right angles to the lengths of run and a variant of overhead travelling crane is mounted upon the rails. At the input station at one end of the racking the crane is loaded at ground level with a cassette and this is housed above the level of the racks so that the crane can be run to the appropriate gangway and the cassette then lowered to level. The operation is completed by feeding the cassette onto the cantilever racking, either by means of a roller mechanism or by using the overhead crane trolley and flip over forks. The process is necessarily somewhat slower in throughput than stacker cranes but is very economical for high volume low throughput situations.

Figure 9:5   Side elevation of long-load installation by Friedrich Remmert GmbH

Automatic storage and retrieval systems with man-rider picking facility

This type of facility is still comparatively rare, but situations arise, such as in high-volume small components warehouses, where throughputs are of a sufficiently high order to justify storage in unit loads and yet pick by individual item. In such circumstances the warehouse control is usually by computer and the instructions to the order-picker are via on-board line-printer or visual display unit (VDU). An early version of such a system was installed at Boots Limited, Nottingham, but big improvements have been made since then and there are now systems in existence where as many as 28 cranes are operated simultaneously by computer, each inter-connected to the output marshalling area by a series of inter-linked conveyors down which the picked merchandise can be despatched. In this way maximum use can be made of headroom, up to 20 metres high. But whether or not such systems are truly viable in view of the large amount of computer back up required, and the complexity and cost of the storage and handling equipment is still open to question. It is also questionable whether the degree of isolation imposed upon the order-picker can be regarded as a suitable working environment.

Automatic storage and retrieval of small components

The use of 'goods-to-picker techniques', so far as cartons are concerned, has not been overly successful in terms of cost per unit of throughput compared with more conventional approaches. On the other hand there have emerged in the United States, and to a lesser degree in West Germany, some excellent retrieval units for small components which, although having high capital cost, show promise of high productivity which is extremely advantageous when labour costs and product value are high.

There are two types, the first being based upon a miniature stacker crane as used in the 'Supreme' system featured in Figure 9:6.

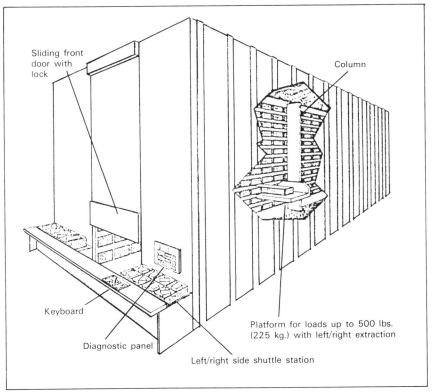

Figure 9:6   Schematic of the 'Supreme' system of automatic storage and retrieval of small components

The advantages which accrue include the ability to make use of headroom up to 12 metres, to condense stock, to safeguard stock by keeping unauthorised personnel out of the area, and to provide a good working environment. The picking rate achievable with such equipment depends upon a variety of factors, such as the length and height of the equipment, the speed of the machine, the packing factor of the products held and the system of operation. However, the fact that the operator can carry out picking tasks whilst the machine is placing away and retrieving boxes means that the labour should be better utilised than in picker-to-goods situations where walking time can amount to 80 per cent of the total time spent.

The second type of system is the carousel which can be supplied in both horizontal and vertical forms, as depicted in Figure 9:7.

Again, the order picker is located in one position and it is possible to achieve high productivity with the correct system design. In general horizontal carousels are associated with relatively light loads of about 500 kg per metre run whilst vertical carousels are capable of loadings up to 750 kg on each shelf level – up to 2.5 metres. It must be stressed that this is a broad generalisation and that heavy and light duty versions of both types of carousel are available. Care must be taken to avoid an operator being trapped in the mechanism, but this problem is well known to the manufacturers. Properly designed and installed, a high level of reliability is to be expected from this kind of equipment and in the United Kingdom horizontal carousels are currently enjoying a good deal of success.

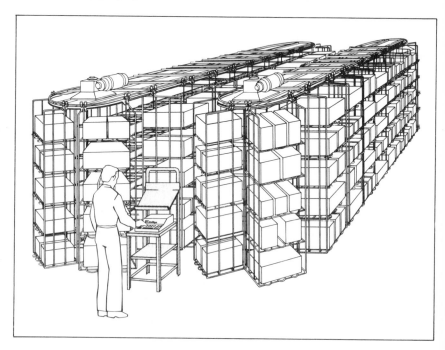

Figure 9:7 Carousel storage and retrieval system (a) Horizontal

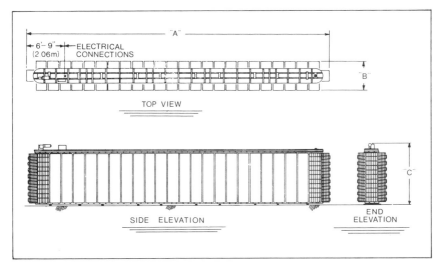

Figure 9:7   continued (b) Section

Figure 9:7   continued (c) Vertical

High speed carton and small item picking systems

The name S.I. Handling Inc. of the United States has long been associated with this area of automation and the company has been responsible for the major developments which have taken place. Although the principle of having chutes of product which can be fed to take-away conveyors is basic to both carton and small-item handling the approaches are sufficiently different to justify independent description.

The carton handling system known as 'Ordermatic' (Figure 9:8) has application where continuous carton picking rates are in excess of 3,000 per hour from as many as 3,000 different line items. The application is highly appropriate to frozen food order picking as well as ambient temperature order-picking. The principle of operation is that the slides in single-sided or opposing banks, usually 5 high, are loaded with product designated to each lane. This operation is controlled by computer which monitors stockholding and nominates product to be brought forward to the loading face. Delivery to the load face can be handled by a variety of methods.

The cartons slide under gravity to the bottom of the chute where they are restrained by an escapement which, when activated by computer, releases a carton at the right moment onto a slider bed, at the bottom of which is a chain conveyor with 'dogs' at 1.25 metre centres. The release of cartons occurs simultaneously along the length of the conveyors at each of the 5 levels (10 conveyors in all if double banked), and the flows are integrated onto a single take-away conveyor with the cartons in correct order sequence at precisely 1.25 metre centres. This activity is continuously monitored by photo electric cells and other sensors. A continuous stream of up to 10,000 cartons per hour is too great a flow to be handled by a single team of men at the end of the conveyor so the flow has to be split into manhandleable lots by means of diverters or luffing conveyors directed to the correct loading points. This is achieved by actually mixing orders on the integrating conveyor into lots of about 30 cartons at a time and then splitting the flow into queues which can be handled comfortably by the loaders. The most appropriate technique is to direct the flows into the back of the vehicle by means of telescopic conveyor, and clearly large individual order lots – preferably a van load to a single drop – are advantageous to the system. There are however many instances where the order lots have been broken down to roll-container sizes, which increases the complexity of conveying at the output face. Although most systems of this kind are confined to the United States a very advanced version of this equipment is now being operated in the United Kingdom and further installations are anticipated in Europe before too long a time elapses.

The 'Itematic' system for small regular shaped or cylindrical components (see Figure 9:9) operates on a very similar principle, except that instead of individual take-away conveyors at each picking level there is a single horizontal belt conveyor which can be elevated or lowered on command from the computer. Above the conveyors is a picking head which can be traversed across the picking face of the module and individually accesses each line item, again under computer control. The flow of products generated is directed via belt conveyors and diverters in order lots to packing benches where speeds of packing as high as 1,500 items per person hour have been achieved. This is done by placing the items into carton trays, together with the advice note and address label, obtained from a line-printer situated by the packing bench, and then passing the package through a shrink wrap tunnel. Machine speeds of 12,000 items an hour are attainable on pharmaceutical products.

Figure 9:8   Ordermatic carton handling system

Figure 9:9   View of SI Itematic
              Picking head releases item on to take-away conveyor in foreground

Wire-in-floor guidance system

The concept of wire-in-floor guidance of electrically powered vehicles is by no means
new and 10 years ago we witnessed the advent of computer controlled man rider order
picking machines which were very advanced, perhaps too advanced for their time.
Certainly there seems to have been a step backwards to simpler concepts and there
has been a lot of development of 'bolt-on' devices for conventional fork-lift trucks and
high-rack stackers. The developments in this area have been largely in the United
States, but we are now beginning to see some advances occurring in Europe and
Japan. The new stage in the development of wire-in-floor devices is the driverless
machine and this is being pioneered by Komatsu in Japan who claim to have more
than a dozen working installations, one of which is in Sweden. The West German
company Wagner have also introduced a high-rack driverless stacker. Greatest
development can be expected in this area as it is the fork-lift truck industry's counter
to the automatic stacker crane. Such systems already incorporate very sophisticated
sensing devices for identifying and locating unit loads and rapid advances should be
expected in the near future.

Coding, scanning and sorting

The advent of article numbering systems and their use with electronic point-of-sale equipment has pointed the way to other potential use in warehouses. Certainly the existence of public warehouses in the United States, with many clients and as a consequence many identification and sorting problems, has led to wholesale associations setting up advisory services which encourage their manufacturing customers to introduce article numbering. The rate of progress in Europe is, as yet, not spectacular but there are signs of increasing potential in this area, and with sort rates of between 3,000 and 6,000 cartons an hour being feasible, with error rates of only 0.003 per cent, the advantages to be gained are enormous. Typical of the sorting conveyors (Figure 9:10) employed are tilt band, tilt tray or tilt slat machines plus a considerable range of diverters including swinging arms, pushers, raising chains and raising skate wheels, etc.

Mechanisation of goods despatch area

As may be expected, the mechanisation of despatch and input have been left until last by the Materials Handling Engineers because these present the most difficult and intractable problems. To date the only real success has been associated with the 'mass loading' of pallets, notably in breweries in Japan and also in the United Kingdom (Figure 9:11). The method used has been to assemble pallets in slugs of up to 6 wide by 2 deep on to conveyors running longitudinally by the side of a flat vehicle and then loading the 12 pallets by means of an overhead crane fitted with 6 pairs of double length forks.

The problem of trying to load pairs of pallets semi-automatically into the back of a box van also has been undertaken by a Japanese company, Kao Soap. Their method involves lifting two pallets at a time from conveyors using a turret device which rotates through 180° and then bodily pushes the pallets into the back of the vehicle by means of an hydraulic pusher device. This approach could not be described as entirely successful so far, but the designers are confident that modifications envisaged will solve the problem.

Conclusion

The pressures to increase the degree of automation and mechanisation are rising steadily throughout the world, unhappily not so fast in the United Kingdom as elsewhere. There is clearly a need to persuade distribution management that to combat cost increases in transportation, and combat competition from abroad, they must seek to improve their warehousing methods before it is too late.

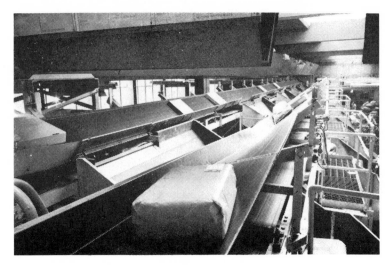

Tilt band conveyor

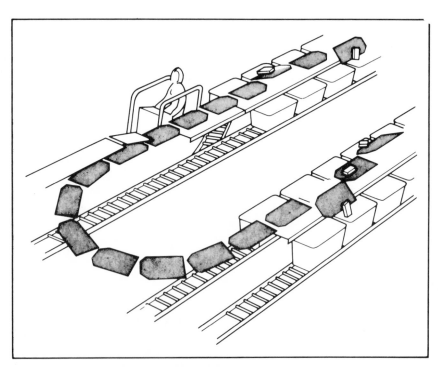

Tilt tray conveyor

Figure 9:10   Two types of sorting conveyor

Figure 9:11   Mass loading of pallets. Kirin Brewery, Japan (Tsubaki Tramrail)

PART THREE

Inventory

Overview

As Ray rightly points out in Chapter 10, in the current times of high inflation the proportion of total distribution costs accounted for by the inventory element is extremely high. Despite this, the distribution executive very often does not manage or control the size of such inventories; at best he supervises their disposition. In companies where this state of affairs exists, and they are the majority, a potentially significant source of cost saving is being lost. However, there are signs that this failure is now being redressed with the recent advent of the Distribution Requirements Planning (DRP) concept.

Ray's treatment of the inventory subject in Chapter 10 is pitched at the practitioner in an attempt to facilitate the best possible management practices within the constraints stated above. Ray concludes by exploring and illuminating the various key interfaces between the inventory element and other elements in the distribution mix. Included in this coverage is the all-important inventory-sales forecasting interface which many companies get hopelessly wrong, and suffer financially as a result.

10

Inventory Management

David L. Ray

The objective of this chapter is to examine inventory management as a key function in the business logistics chain; we explore the trade-off relationships with other logistic areas, illustrate the high costs involved in carrying stock, and the parameters within which inventory control should be exercised.

The physical distribution management 'mix'

The distribution manager is usually responsible for some of the main cost centre budgets which involve inventories, namely warehousing and transportation. He is not responsible for determining the size, depth or location of these inventories – merely for housing them and distributing them in the most cost effective manner possible within given constraints. The major scope for optimising distribution cost is thus lost unless the inventory manager is working within the distribution function and is adopting a total PDM approach (Figure 10:1).

Those distribution managers not determining and directing the shape of their logistic channels, but wishing to do so, need a clear understanding of the inventory management role if they wish to fully control the highly expensive assets at their disposal.

We start by looking at the very basics – the types and classes of inventory as summarised in Figure 10:2, and when each is used.

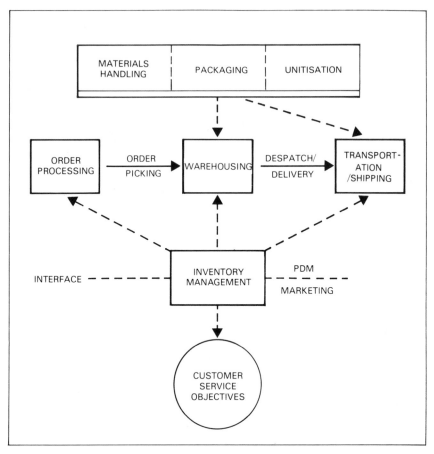

Figure 10:1   The physical distribution management mix

MATERIAL TYPES	RAW MATERIALS COMPONENTS AND FUEL STOCK	WORK IN PROGRESS STOCK	FINISHED GOODS STOCK
CLASS TYPES	WORKING (CYCLE) STOCK	SAFETY (BUFFER) STOCK	SPECULATIVE STOCK

Figure 10:2   Types and classes of inventory

Stock (material) types

Industrial and commercial stocks are held in three forms as follows:

(i) *Raw materials, components and fuel.* These are the ingredients stored in advance of industrial and production processes without which the operation could not function.

(ii) *Work in progress.* Stock consists of the conversion of raw materials and components into some semi-finished state, awaiting further processing packaging, or operation. It is normal for such stocks to exist between a chain of processes, but extra large stocks soon appear if bottlenecks develop, or machinery further up the processing chain breaks down.

(iii) *Finished goods.* Stocks exist at the end of the manufacturing/conversion processes in the factory warehouse and further up the distribution chain in wholesaling and retailing outlets.

In the UK, finished goods stocks have been about double work-in-progress and raw material stocks taken together, and the combination of the three have been so large as to equate with 35–43 per cent of GDP in terms of value. Total stocks in the UK at the end of 1979 were worth 58,252m at book value (37 per cent of GDP). Broken down into the three categories (and excluding £11,469m 'other industries' stock which remained unclassified) the following picture emerges:

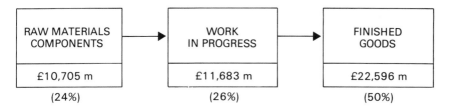

Stock classes[1]

Once again, industrial and commercial stocks come in three classes, within the form of material types described above.

(i) *Working (cycle) stock.* Working stock is that stock which is equated with actual demand, e.g. average monthly sales of an item = 10,000 units, working stock required = 10,000 units. In practice, demand is rarely constant. Thus in a production environment, 'cycle stock' or 'lot-size inventory' refers to the amount of stock produced in a typical run, and as production rates are generally much greater than demand rates (for economy of production), stocks peak at the end of a production run.

(ii) *Safety (buffer) stock.* Stock required to meet fluctuations and the uncertainty in demand is usually referred to as 'safety stock' or 'buffer stock', but sometimes as 'fluctuation inventory'.

In many industries and trades there are seasonal factors which produce peaks and troughs in demand, and even in situations where there is little or no seasonality, there may be random or irregular demand which is sometimes described as 'splash demand'.

(iii) *Speculative stock.* Speculative stock is stock held 'speculatively' against a future contingency, generally involving changes in demand or supply conditions. If demand for the finished goods has fallen flat, production of finished stock might continue against a speculation, or a forecast that future demand will in fact materialise.

Sometimes raw materials or components are forward-purchased on a speculative basis (e.g. coffee, cocoa), because of fear of shortages in supply or that increased demand will lead to significant price rises.

Costs of inventory[1]

Inventory is extremely expensive to keep on the shelf. Unfortunately many companies have failed to measure the total cost of stockholding, for if they had, it is unlikely that stock levels nationwide would be much more than half the total level they are today. However, the 17 per cent MLR, leading to a cost of finance ranging between 18 per cent and 21 per cent in the UK at the time of writing (and part of the current government's monetary strategy to drive inflation out of the economic system) has led to a large destocking programme by all sectors of industry, and slashed prices to the short-term benefit of the consumer.

The following basic costs categories cover the cost of stockholding:

Finance	Cost of working capital
Storage	Storemen's wages
	Materials handling equipment ⎫
	Storage racking ⎬ hire charge or depreciation
	Heating, lighting, water ⎭
	Insurance of stock and building
	Rent
	Rates
	Repairs and maintenance
Stock losses	Shrinkage
	Deterioration
	Depreciation
	Obsolescence

The total cost of carrying inventory, as a percentage of the stock value, obviously varies from industry to industry. But an approximate figure of around 35 per cent per annum, with current cost of finance at 18 per cent, would not be an untypical figure for many manufacturing industries in 1980.

Imagine a business where goods are wholesaled by the manufacturer at 30 per cent gross margin, and he has a stockholding cost of 35 per cent. On some ranges he is achieving a stockturn of twice a year and on others a dismal once a year. The cost of stockholding immediately reduces the gross margin on the faster moving lines to 12½ per cent and the slower items are already showing a loss of 5 per cent. In practice, frequent price rises are producing sufficient 'holding gains' or 'stock profits' to allow many to survive their appalling stockturn performance.

Reasons for carrying stock

Because of the high costs of holding inventory, companies need to inspect the reasons for holding stock; at the very least policies should be adopted to minimise the quantities of stock held.

Some of the main reasons for stockholding are listed below:

(i) *Cost of purchasing.* Cost of order raising: if goods were bought in as required (often daily), a large and expensive purchasing department would be needed to raise and process purchase orders, i.e. an expensive administration feature.

Quantity discounts: most suppliers offer attractive quantity discounts for bulk buying, and are passing on some of their own savings in lower unit costs of packaging, handling, delivery, etc., and of course inventory costs.

The purchasing executive should be attempting to minimise the total costs to the company of the cost of order raising together with that of quantity discounts by calculating an Economic Order Quantity (EOQ) for the goods concerned.

(ii) *Variability of demand.* In practice the only demand that is ever constant is average demand, so if stock-outs are to be largely avoided, then safety stocks need to be carried to cover most or all of the large demands experienced, whether due to seasonality, random demand or whatever.

(iii) *Variability of supply.* Suppliers' delivery time from receipt of order to goods arriving is known as 'lead time'. These are not normally constant and may vary by days, weeks, or even months.

To allow for this variation, additional safety stocks have to be carried if raw material stocks for manufacture, or finished goods for customers are to be assured to pre-set stock availability levels. If the supplier's industrial relations scene is poor, or past record bad, some companies may carry large stocks in an attempt to outlast the longest of strikes. Others, more fortunate, 'dual source' and switch orders between suppliers as necessary.

(iv) *Speculation.* Stocks are sometimes bought speculatively against changing conditions in either supply or demand, e.g. price rises, shortages due to natural conditions, industrial action, sudden demand changes, etc.

(v) *Work in progress.* Where a series of industrial processes is involved it is often unavoidable that semi-finished stocks appear at stages between these processes, each of which has its own speed of production and economy of scale.

(vi)   *Economies of production.*   Often economies of production and low unit costs are achieved at the expense of long production runs and short-term inventory peaks. However, in the light of the high costs of holding stock, the trade-off between production economies and stockholding cost may need redefining and adjusting.

(vii) *Costs of not holding stock.*   Whilst there is a high cost of holding stock, there may be an equally high cost of being out of stock.

The cost of raw material shortages may be as extreme as a whole production line out of use and labour standing by idle.

The cost of finished goods shortages may be the profit lost on the sale of the stock which would have been made, or the cost of a lost customer if the stock-out caused the customer to take his business elsewhere. Hence stocks should be carried to the level where the additional cost of holding stock is balanced by the cost of lost sales for not carrying higher stocks. This equilibrium is discussed by Ray and Millman[2] as a means of setting customer service levels.

Inventory and other elements of the distribution mix

So far we have referred to the different types of inventory, the costs of holding it and the costs of not holding it. In practice it is very difficult to avoid carrying stocks at all; the best solution is to attempt to minimise the amount of stock necessary to provide acceptable customer service levels. In this section we look at the effects of finished inventory on other logistical areas. (Most of the same arguments can be applied to raw material stocks with the factory as the customer.)

Inventory and order processing

Inadequate stocks of finished goods can lead to expensive order processing and affect a variety of cost areas. In a situation of low stocks the following main effects would be felt:

(a)   Lots of part-order deliveries, leading to low customer satisfaction and high unit-cost transportation with second or third deliveries being made to complete the order.

(b)   Progress chasing in the factory or with the suppliers concerned, followed by expensive expediting to keep customers happy.

(c)   Additional costs of invoicing/delivery note/advice-note paper-work caused by the raising of part orders.

(d)   Higher picking costs in the warehouse.

(e)   Higher administration costs in the sales ledger section.

(f)   Distortion of demand patterns if system measures number of deliveries per item instead of number of initial demands, or forecasting system is based on past demand and takes no account of demand not immediately satisfied.

(g) The probability that a certain proportion of orders will be cancelled with the ensuing loss of gross margin, plus the possibility that some customers might transfer their business to a competitor. (This largely depends on the state of competition, brand loyalty, and customer loyalty.)

However, it is wrong to assume that systems are failing purely because stock-outs occur and part deliveries have to be made. If no stock-outs occurred it would strongly suggest that stock levels are too high unless the business has unusually smooth demand. The reason for this is that to provide increased stock availability at the higher levels of service is disproportionately expensive.

For example, to increase stock availability from 95 to 97 per cent, we would have to increase safety stock by 14 per cent if demand was normally distributed. Yet, it is very unlikely that customers could distinguish, at this high level of stock availability, between the 95 per cent and the 97 per cent service.

If you are concerned about the adequacy of stock levels in your company, and no routine systems are yet available for measuring stock availability, then the first step to quickly assess your performance is as follows:

Take a sizeable batch of completed customer orders – say 100, or minimum equivalent to at least one day's throughput. Count the number of these orders which were completed in full on receipt and you have your first effective measure of customer service:

$$\text{e.g. 85 out of 100 orders met in full, service level} = \frac{85 \times 100}{100}$$

$$= 85 \text{ per cent}$$

This gives a good indication of the number of split orders for picking, transportation, second invoicing, etc. However, in itself this is only a very crude measure of stock availability, and takes no account of the partial completeness of the remaining orders. Suppose the above 100 orders have an average of 5 line-items per order and the total number of lines completed from stock first time was 450, then another customer service measure is obtained as follows:

$$\frac{\text{number of line items met in a given period}}{\text{number of line items ordered in a given period}} \times 100 \text{ per cent}$$

$$= \frac{450}{500} \times 100 = 90 \text{ per cent}$$

The second measure gives a better indication of stock availability, but the first a better guide to the cost effects in other logistic areas.

Inventory and warehousing

The decision as to where to locate finished goods is one of fundamental importance to manufacturers, wholesalers, and retailers; it also crucially affects the shape and size of the distribution channel in terms of numbers and sizes of both warehouses and transport fleet, and is absolutely fundamental in determining a large part of total distribution costs. Warehousing of stock is extremely expensive and is made more so by management errors as follows:

(a) Warehouse(s) larger than necessary, due to carrying dead stock, obsolete lines, slow-moving lines which should be kept back at a central depot, and too much safety stock.

(b) Too many warehouses. Typically wholesalers and manufacturers have been guilty of this, but much depends on the nature of the business. In industries where the industrial consumer or retailer are serviced regularly and are not concerned at all where stocks originate from, providing the service given is reliable, there is often scope for depot rationalisation and effective cost savings. (It follows that some additional transport costs may ensue from depot rationalisation, but not enough to negate the rationalisation programme.)

We have also seen from the previous section, that labour costs may be inordinately high due to excessive picking costs where low stocks result in too many part deliveries, and excessive handling and booking in of receipts due to uneconomic order quantities placed by purchasing.

By sorting out the abovementioned issues (with his inventory specialist and agreement with marketing personnel), the distribution manager is essentially engaged in shaping or reshaping his distribution chain, not just managing a 'fait accompli' in whatever form he was given it.

The following decisions need to be made:

–   What is my trading stock range (elimination of dead stock and obsolete items)?
–   If there are field depots, how much of the total trading range needs to be held there? (Fast and medium moving lines held at all field depots, being approximately 20 per cent of range; the 80 per cent slow-moving tail might well be held back at a larger central depot.)
–   Are all my field depots necessary? (Are they there for historical reasons only; can some of them be eliminated?)
–   Are my service level targets too high? (Is a lot of warehouse space taken up unnecessarily by safety stocks which are too high?)

Defining a stock range and what's held where

The starting point for those who have not already categorised their stock range could be as follows, in 'ABCD' categories:

'A' items: fast moving lines providing: 65–75 per cent of sales
'B' items: medium moving lines providing: 5–15 per cent of sales
'C' items: slow moving lines providing: 10–30 per cent of sales
'D' items: non-moving lines providing: no sales at all

Measuring sales over a useful time span (say 6 months to a year or whatever is most appropriate), we would expect Pareto's Law to apply, i.e. an 80/20 relationship or similar, where the top 20 per cent of stock lines ('A' and 'B' items) provide 80 per cent of all sales, and a large range of 'C' items (80 per cent of range) contribute only 20 per cent. But to categorise sales as above we need to know what criteria to apply (Figure 10:3).

Criteria:	When to use
1 Sales value:	When whole range sells at reasonably similar speeds and mark-ups and sales values.
2 Profit contribution:	When whole range sells at similar speed, but mark-up varies widely.
3 Sales frequency:	When stock range sells at widely different turnover rates, but similar gross margins.
4 Sales frequency/ profit contribution joint ranking:	Where stock range sells at varied speeds and mark-ups.
5 Sales frequency/ sales value joint ranking:	Where stock range sells at widely different frequency and large variations in sales price per item.

Figure 10:3   ABC categorisation criteria

Stock range	Where to hold	How much to hold
'A' items	all stocking points	high stock availability minimum – 90 per cent +
'B' items	most/all stocking points	good stock availability 85–90 per cent availability
'C' items	restricted stocking points	lower stock availability say, 70–80 per cent availability
'D' items	no stocking points	remove from all locations; sell if possible for scrap or disposal prices

Figure 10:4   Stocking guidelines

Figure 10:4 is only a rough guide and has to be geared to the competitive conditions experienced by the trading organisation concerned. In most cases one would not expect to provide 'A' item stock availability above 97–98 per cent. 'B' items can usually be afforded in all stock locations, but where a large number of stocking points exist, effectively diluting 'C' item demand to insignificant proportions, it is wise to only carry 'C' items at one central depot if at all possible. There are also obvious examples of 'complementary demand' where one should ensure that despite the above guidelines complementary items would not be separately located, e.g. cigarettes and cigarette lighters; if demand for the latter is low, at least a few lighters should be available at the very small chain tobacconist. Additionally, there are instances when 'C' items, although not in frequent demand, are nevertheless 'critical items' which have to be stocked to 100 per cent availability.

In these circumstances, it is vital for the company to measure the cost of stockholding incurred, and recoup this cost as a 'premium' for having available a rarely demanded item at an instant's notice.

Inventory and number of stock locations

The greater the number of warehouses the greater the proportion of safety stocks to be carried; the poorer the stockturn as demand patterns deteriorate the higher the unit costs in the smaller warehouses. In total, then, a high price paid for operating a number of branch warehouses unnecessarily. Some industries live on trade from the nearby vicinity and cannot avoid a local presence, but others can, particularly with improved road networks, yet they continue to administer out-moded distribution networks unrevised for a generation.

The first point to appreciate is the relationship between safety stocks and working stocks; the more concentrated the depot network the less need for safety stocks. For example, a distribution outlet sells a fast moving line at an average rate of 100 units per week, stocks are replenished from the H.Q. central depot on a weekly basis, and the computer calculates a replenishment based on a normal distribution to give 95 per cent stock availability.

The standard deviation (measuring weekly variation in demand) is 60 units, so the stock for this item is topped up each week to 199 units; i.e. approximately 50 per cent working stock, 50 per cent safety stock. This situation is repeated over 30 branches distributing throughout the United Kingdom giving a total stockholding of 5,970 units in field warehouses at the topping up stage, and an average stock level of 4,470. But, when the depot network is rationalised to 6 larger outlets, averaging sales of 500 units per week now having a standard deviation of 90 units per week, the total stockholding per unit at the replenishment stage becomes 648 units per depot.

Total field stocks have reduced from 5,970 to 3,888 at the topping up stage and average stocks have fallen from 4,470 to 2,388, i.e. almost halving the total stockholding.

It can be seen that the savings in depot rationalisation accrue because of the significantly large reduction in safety stocks that take place. There is a simple rule for calculating these safety stock savings called the 'square root law' of locations.

The 'square root law' of locations

The 'square root law' is a simple rule of thumb which can be used to estimate the effects on inventory levels when consideration is given to centralising, rationalising, or conversely de-centralising stockholding locations.

It is not a new technique and references to it can be found back as far as 1962.[3]

The square root law asserts that *THE TOTAL INVENTORY IN A SYSTEM* is proportional to the *SQUARE ROOT* of the *NUMBER of LOCATIONS* at which a product is stocked.

The square root law can be and has been proved mathematically by Maister.[4]

The importance of the law is that it shows the savings in inventory which are achievable by centralisation, e.g. a wholesale distributor delivering out of ten field warehouses can reduce his stocks by over 68 per cent by using one centralised warehouse. Large savings are made on the cost of holding stock, but a premium must be paid for speedier transport if the same level of customer service is to be maintained. An example of the technique is thus:

SQUARE ROOT LAW OF LOCATIONS : CALCULATION EXAMPLE

We are reducing stock from 20 branches into 5 regional depots:

Calculation : $\sqrt{20} = 4.472 \qquad \sqrt{5} = 2.236$

$$\text{Reduction in Stockholding} = 1 - \left(\frac{\sqrt{5}}{\sqrt{20}}\right) \times 100\%$$

$$= 1 - \left(\frac{2.236}{4.472}\right) \times 100\% \ = 1 - (0.50) \times 100\% = 50\%$$

And for those who don't want to do the calculations a simple ready-reckoner chart is shown in Figure 10:5.

Existing no. of stocking points	'New' numbers of stocking points						
	1	2	3	4	5	10	15
1	–	(29)	(42)	(50)	(55)	(68)	(74)
2	29	–	(18)	(29)	(37)	(55)	(63)
3	42	18	–	(13)	(23)	(45)	(55)
4	50	29	13	–	(11)	(37)	(48)
5	55	37	23	11	–	(29)	(42)
10	68	55	45	37	29	–	(18)
15	74	63	55	48	42	18	–
20	78	68	61	55	50	29	13

Figure 10:5   Percentage stock reduction achievable by stockholding concentration (using the square root law of locations)

Inventory and transportation

(i) *Transport and number of depot locations.*   The inventory management role has specific ramifications on the operation of transportation or the use of carriers.

By defining the number of stock location points, the parameters within which the transport fleet operates is being defined. If deliveries are made from a large number of field locations, a greater number of smaller vehicles will be needed as opposed to a smaller number of field depots which service customers from fewer but larger vehicles.

In the previous section we saw the possible savings from carrying reduced safety stocks in fewer depot locations. However, one of the off-setting costs will be higher transport costs as delivery areas increase in size and greater mileages have to be travelled.

Hence, when logistic changes are being planned it is important always to use a Total Costing Approach so that the trade-off effects of one distribution element on another is automatically measured.

Yet, normally the additional costs of transport will easily be out-weighed by the savings in warehouse costs and safety stock reductions. Providing new vehicles are correctly chosen, then:

(a)   fewer larger vehicles will be needed, offering economies of scale in numbers of drivers and unit costs.

(b)   larger delivery areas may provide better scope for transport scheduling with improved vehicle utilisation. These factors can go a long way in holding down the overall increase in transport cost, but some of the more remote customers could see an increase in delivery lead time and a reduction in delivery frequency.

It has also to be borne in mind when planning the distribution chain, that legal restrictions apply in many countries to driving hours and mileage travelled in a single day; e.g. the UK comes under EEC legislation which currently limits driving time to 9 hours a day (over 3.5 tonnes gross vehicle) and mileage to 281 miles (vehicles over 20 tonnes gross). With too few depots, such driving constraints can mean disproportionate increases in transport costs.

(ii) *Stock availability.*   Poor stock availability leads to part-order deliveries and uneconomical drop sizes. The resulting costs are easily highlighted when carriers are used who charge tariffs on the normal sliding scale.

Additional costs are just as real on 'own fleet' operations, but not always so obvious. Alternatively, if customers orders are held back until complete, unacceptable lead times can easily accrue. There is no real alternative to measuring and correcting stock availability levels.

(iii) *Stock ranges.*   When product ranges are proliferated unnecessarily by marketing decisions, this in itself can lead to more lines which may not always be in stock and smaller order quantities; hence more split deliveries and more part-pack quantities have to be delivered.

The first adds to the number of deliveries to be made, and both add to increased unit drop time, and collectively add unwittingly to the costs of transportation. Thus, it is important for the inventory manager to participate with marketing in decisions affecting stock range extensions, and to monitor ABC status of items so those at the end of their product life cycle are not retained indefinitely.

(iv) *Raw material stocks.* When delivery vehicles return empty, as they often do, consideration should be given to off-setting transport costs with 'back loads'. Raw material stocks offer a possible solution, particularly where the supplier uses a carrier to deliver his goods. Reduced prices for 'own collection' is the name of the game, but some suppliers concerned about own-fleet load utilisation will be less than keen about this option.

If such a programme is arranged between the transport, inventory and purchasing managers, the latter needs to keep a careful eye on the price being paid to ensure that the full 'with carriage' price is not reintroduced at some later stage.

Inventory and sales forecasting

Even when companies have rationalised their stock range, set realistic availability targets, and modified their depot network, all might be in vain if forecasts of stock requirements go astray.

The inventory manager builds up a system which estimates future demand and demand variability to provide a Total Stock Requirement at various points in time. Using for example, a 'variable order quantity – fixed order cycle' system, actual stock levels might be compared with required stock when the item hits re-order point and stocks topped up to meet the set stock availability target. Whatever the basic system used for stock control the essential features are:

(a)   estimating demand for the finished product (which obviously sets the requirements for raw material stocks, etc.), and
(b)   interpreting demand patterns to ascertain safety stock needs.

(i) *Estimating demand.* Many systems fall down on crude forecasting, typically where the only forecasts are made by ambitious or eternally optimistic salesmen who forecast 20%+ volume increases for the year ahead over and above what has been sold last year, and then proceed to divide by 12 to produce smooth monthly forecasts.

The inventory manager may well find that 'past demand' is his best guide to future sales and should provide his own independent forecasting system. He needs to ascertain the following:

(a)   from the marketing function
    - planned growth/contraction due to changes in pricing policy/competition/markets.
    - short-term changes in demand due to special promotions
    - planned introduction of new items/phasing out date for old items
(b)   from his own analysis of past demand, take into account the following:
    - seasonal variations
    - cyclical variations as caused by changes in business confidence/government policy/trade cycle (although this is becoming increasingly difficult)
    - irregular/random demand (sorting out one-off demand from repeat and regular business)
    - long term trends

By taking out, or allowing for as far as possible the above factors, a variety of past demand data periods can be experimented with to gauge which (if any) provide a realistic time series for estimating future demand, e.g. forecasting one month ahead, it might be found that using the average of the last 3 months' deseasonalised demand, re-seasonalised, produces a fairly accurate estimate, better than using 1, 2 or 4 months' demand in weighted on non-weighted variations.

Having found a reasonably sound means of forecasting the size of demand (working stock) in the short-term, we need to establish:

(ii) *The distribution pattern of demand.*   The distribution pattern of demand within the time-series observations (normally the replenishment lead time) needs examining, so that the safety stock can be calculated to provide the stock availability levels that are being targeted. Assume the wrong pattern and under/overstocking will result.

Statistical distributions are normally measured by two parameters – the mean of the distribution (average demand for the period) and the standard deviation (measuring the variability of demand or dispersion within the replenishment lead time).

It may be that different parts of the stock range selling with varying frequencies fit approximately to a variety of statistical distributions. By comparing past demand patterns to a statistical distribution and finding a reasonable fit, it is possible to estimate safety stock requirements to the probability levels required, provided that a similar pattern continues.

A few of the most commonly used probability distributions in business are:

(a)   Normal (gaussian) distribution – particularly useful at factory/production level, often providing an approximate fit when aggregating customer orders.
(b)   Poisson distribution – often useful at the wholesale/retail level.
(c)   Negative exponential distribution – also fits demand at retail and wholesale level, where the majority of orders are smaller than average size and a few are larger.

(d)   Gamma distribution – useful in some businesses where a single distribution is required to cover a stock range of varying sales frequencies. The distribution has no single characteristic shape, but varies between a normal distribution for faster moving lines to a negative exponential.

Conclusion

Inventory management is perhaps the key component in the business logistics arena, interfacing as it does with all the other main elements and embodying an area of high expense.

Without a full appraisal of inventory control and a planned inventory strategy the distribution practitioner can come nowhere near to applying the 'optimal cost' solution to physical distribution.

Notes and references

1   The terms 'inventory' and 'stock' are here used interchangeably.
2   D. Ray and S. Millman (Monograph), 'Optimal Inventories via Customer Service Objectives', *International Journal of Physical Distribution and Materials Management,* Spring 1978, Vol. 9, No. 7.
3   M. K. Starr and D. W. Miller, *Inventory Control: Theory and Practice,* Englewood Cliffs, N. J.: Prentice-Hall, 1962, pp. 162–4.
4   D. H. Maister, 'Centralisation of Inventories and the "Square Root Law" ', *International Journal of Physical Distribution,* 1975, Vol. 6, No. 3.

PART FOUR

Transportation

Overview

This section offers a wide coverage of transport-related topics beginning with a chapter on each of the three most common modes of transport.

Woodward considers the advantages of road freighting in Chapter 11 and follows this up with some useful detail on the categories (by weight and/or axle numbers) of vehicles currently in service. In Chapter 12, Bushell reviews the role of rail freight and discusses the key developments of the 1970s, including Freightliner, Speedlink, ferry services and the TOPS system of tracing railway wagons and locomotives.

Air freighting is covered by Ross in Chapter 13 and great emphasis is placed on the necessity to undertake trade-off analyses of the type mentioned in Chapter 1, in order to gain a fair comparison for the air mode. Among the other topics covered in this chapter are freight rates, the value-weight equation, and the relatively recent application of total distribution cost computer models to the task of air freight marketing. Slater explains the significance of the choice of transport mode in Chapter 14 and outlines the factors which affect this choice. Various methods for making the selection are offered along a spectrum which stretches from simple to sophisticated. In the end, however, Slater concedes that the final selection will depend upon management's skill to determine and quantify the significant options.

Slater continues in Chapter 15 by detailing the techniques and methods available to the distribution manager for the purpose of routing and scheduling his vehicle fleet on a day-to-day basis along either fixed or variable routes. Various operational research type methods are also reviewed.

Finally, in Chapter 16, Rawnsley covers packaging, unitisation, and containers to round off a comprehensive treatment of the transportation topic.

11

Road freighting

Frank H. Woodward

One of the ingredients of an efficient distribution service is the choice of the correct method of transport, or a mix of more than one method. On practical as well as economic grounds no company should decide to employ road transport without first giving consideration to the available alternatives. Many arguments can be put forward showing the advantages of using each different mode of transport, whether it be air or inland waterway, rail freight or parcel post, or even by encouraging customers to collect goods from a factory or warehouse by offering a discount. In each case the objective of keeping transport costs to a minimum must be balanced against both the customer service requirements and the trade-offs with storage, handling, packaging or other cost elements within the total distribution cost.

In developing a transport plan, the range of choices available can be embodied within the answers to five questions:

1   Does the distribution of the product need vehicles?
    Liquids and gases can be distributed by pipelines, some products can be moved between plants by conveyors, and some circumstances lend themselves best to direct customer collection.
2   If vehicles are needed, should they be road vehicles?
    The possibility that rail services, aircraft or waterways may give the customer a faster, more reliable, or more economic service needs to be explored.
3   If road vehicles are needed, are the services of the haulier more efficient than a company operating its own fleet?
4   If a company is to operate its own fleet of road vehicles:
    (a)   should they be owned, leased, or on contract hire?
    (b)   how many are required, what types are needed and where are they to be based?

Advantages of road freighting

For inland transport, the movement of goods by road has unquestionably become the most used method in the UK. Figure 11:1 shows the tonnage and ton-mileage over the period 1967–77, indicating a steady increase in the road proportion.

Year	Tons (millions)	% Road total of all freight movements
1967	1625	89.0
1972	1603	90.2
1975	1577	90.2
1976	1492	89.6
1977	1538	90.5

Source: Department of Transport

Figure 11:1   Estimated tonnage and road freight proportion of all freight carried by road goods vehicles in Great Britain, 1967–77

In 1967 road movements represented 89 per cent of the total tonnage of inland freight, and by 1977 this rose to over 90 per cent. Over the same period the quantity carried by rail movements decreased from 201 million tons to 169 million tons, a reduction of approximately 16 per cent. It seems likely that this general trend will continue in the future and certainly that road transport will continue to be the main artery for feeding factories, warehouses and retail outlets. This is because it has certain inherent advantages.

Through-movement

One of the main advantages of moving goods by road is the possibility of making through-movements, from consignor to consignee. This removes the necessity of trans-shipment, so speeding up the operation, eliminating the cost of double handling and reducing the risk of loss by theft.

Flexibility

Another major advantage of road freighting is its flexibility. Whether the operation is carried out by a professional haulier or on own account, it is more easily controlled, and routes and loading routines are more easily changed, than in any other form of transport. The capital investment in providing the means of movement by road is also lower than for any of the other modes. An investment of as little as £4,000 can give an operator the means of moving up to 1½ tons anywhere in the UK, or within Europe; he can arrange his own schedules, operate night and day, assemble a multi-drop delivery, and at all times be in complete control of the movement.

Fast turnround

The use of articulated vehicles – that is, tractor units with detachable semitrailers – and the rapid development of the demountable body (Figure 11:2) on both rigid trucks and trailers, contribute to the advantages of road freighting, particularly where the process of loading and discharging is lengthy in relation to the in-transit time.

This enables relatively inexpensive trailers and demountable bodies to be used as standing storage during unloading and loading, while the more expensive tractor unit or rigid vehicle is kept fully employed. To secure maximum benefit from operating articulated outfits, each tractor should have a minimum of three semitrailers: one at each end of a route and one in transit. Many companies today have even adapted manufacturing areas so that trailers and demounted bodies can be loaded at the end of production lines; others even load the trailers or bodies several weeks before delivery is required, and use this equipment as a mobile warehouse for storage of the product.

One way to increase transport productivity even further would be to introduce legislation permitting a tractor to be coupled to two semitrailers – known in the United States as 'double-bottoms'. (Special dispensation has been given to operate

Figure 11:2   Demountable bodies
Where loads can be assembled ready for delivery by returning trucks, the use of demountable bodies will have financial advantages. Photo shows a demountable box body fitted to a Dodge 'G13' Commando

'double-bottom' outfits within the United Kingdom, but the restrictions placed on the operations and the requirement for special braking devices has ruled out any changeover to such vehicles.)

The first step in the development of such a combination has already been taken by the use of a dolly towbar attachment behind a rigid vehicle, which makes it possible to use a semitrailer as if it were a drawbar trailer. The drawbar operation gives an operator the facility to 'drop' the trailer en route, and then proceed to another delivery point with the rigid vehicle. After the latter delivery, the driver can call back and pick up the empty or reloaded drawbar trailer before returning to base. Since 1970, when legislation removed the need for a second man in the cab of a drawbar-trailer outfit, industrial companies and hauliers have been able to take advantage of increased volume and platform area on vehicles; they are, however, still restricted to the legal maximum of 32,520 kg for the gross train weight.

Vulnerability to industrial action

In the delicate field of industrial relations, the consignor will understandably have more confidence that his arrangements will not be interfered with by the industrial action of third parties if the movements are carried out by road, where they are under his control from door to door. This is equally true whether the movement is made by his own vehicles or by a road haulier, since the latter will be keen to maintain a good service, and can always be replaced by a competitor. Experience has shown, unfortunately, that movements of goods in the hands of third parties such as British Rail tend to be more vulnerable to industrial action, and when stoppages do occur in any part of that large organisation, it can be a major problem to find alternative means of transport at short notice.

European operations

The growth of the roll-on/roll-off (RO/RO) services linking Britain to the mainland of Europe along the entire coastline from Scandinavia to Spain has provided the advantage of easy through-routes by road freight without the need for intermediate handling. The RO/RO ships are specially designed to allow the largest vehicles to drive on board and drive off again at the port of destination. Driver accommodation is excellent, first-class catering is provided, and every effort is made to ensure an easy passage through the Customs facilities. The 'Through EEC Movement' documents ('T' forms) give an operator the opportunity of sealing his vehicles before leaving the UK, travelling across frontiers with the minimum of procedures, and having all the import documentation carried out at the final delivery point.

Types of vehicle used in road freighting

One major UK commercial vehicle manufacturer lists no less than 200 different models of vehicle in its sales brochure, and this does not take into account the many options available on individual models, which can include different axle ratios, gearboxes, and engines. This great variety of choice means that for virtually every specific use a vehicle is available which precisely meets the need. In general, goods vehicles can be grouped into the following broad classes:

Vans under 1,500 kg gross vehicle weight (GVW).   These are usually referred to as 6-cwt, 8-cwt, or 10-cwt vans, these being their respective payloads (the maximum gross vehicle weight (GVW) less the unladen weight). Such vehicles are mainly used for small parcels traffic, for urgent deliveries, for specialised services such as transporting computer tapes and distributing newspapers.

Vehicles not exceeding 3,500 kg GVW.   These may be either box vans, or flat trucks, and are again generally referred to by their maximum permitted payload, which may be 18 cwt, 22 cwt, 25 cwt, 30 cwt, or 35 cwt (914, 1,118, 1,270, 1,524, or 1,778 kg). They are used in many types of transport operations, ranging from express parcel deliveries to air-freight collection services, and from the distribution of parcel post to High-Street shop deliveries. The key point is that under the 1968 Transport Act, a user of this type of vehicle does not need an operator's licence and yet is free to carry goods for hire and reward. In the six years up to 1978 the number of vehicles in this class increased by over 11 per cent (see Figure 11:3).

Figure 11:3   Vehicle not exceeding 3½ tons GVW
              A twin-tyred rear-axle Luton van of 3.32 tons GVW, typical of this
              class of vehicle, for which no operator's licence is required

Vehicles not exceeding 7,500 kg GVW.   Legislation is again responsible for the popularity of this class of vehicle. The driver of a vehicle under 7,500 kg GVW does not have to hold a heavy goods vehicle (HGV) licence. The range of vehicles available is very wide and includes box vans, flat and drop-side trucks, refrigerated vehicles, local-authority vehicles, and tippers. All are based on the 4 x 2 configuration (4 wheels, of which 2 are driven), and can be seen in almost every type of road freight operation (Figure 11:4).

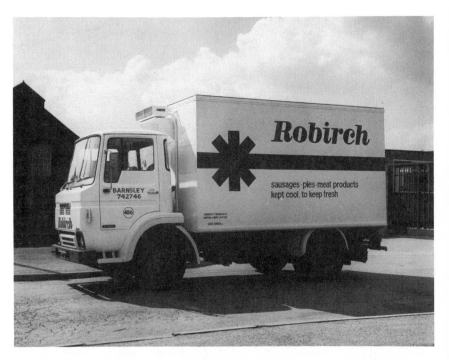

Figure 11:4   Dodge Commando 'G75', having insulated body with cooling equipment (non-fridge) for shop to shop delivery of chilled meat products. No HGV driving licence is needed

Two-axle medium-to-heavy vehicles.   These vehicles can vary from a gross vehicle weight of 8,000 kg to the maximum permitted on two axles of 16,257 kg (Figure 11:5). Various wheelbases are available, from 3,048 mm to 5,740 mm. A wide variety of products can be carried on this type of vehicle, and the types of body used include box vans, refrigerated vehicles, flat and drop-side trucks, tippers, 'tilt' vehicles, tankers, and 4 x 4 construction-site vehicles. Handling equipment in the form of tail lifts and vehicle cranes can be fitted in order to speed up loading and unloading.

Figure 11:5   Ford D1314 specially designed for carrying telephone racks
                The truck carries a 'mounted crane' in the centre of two flat platforms,
                the forward area having 4.5 metres of platform length with another 4
                metres to the rear

Multi-axle heavy vehicles. This is a more specialised type of vehicle, and variations include:

1   Six-wheelers. These usually range from approximately 12,000 kg GVW to 24,385 kg GVW, and can have 6 x 2 (single drive bogey) or 6 x 4 (double drive bogies). The use of the smaller six-wheelers has proved advantageous in High-Street deliveries, especially in the soft drink and brewery business (Figures 11:6 and 11:7). The six-wheel configuration enables smaller wheels to be used, so that the platform height can be reduced without the need for wheel boxes, and embarrassment when carrying palletised traffic. A large vehicle of this type is shown in Figure 11:8.

2   Eight-wheelers. This type of vehicle is available both in 8 x 2 and 8 x 4 form, and although some vehicles of this type are used on haulage activities, the more general use for them is as tippers for moving earth, sand, gravel, etc. The maximum permitted gross vehicle weights go up to 30,480 kg according to the axle spread and the type of tyre equipment.

Figure 11:6   Dodge Commando of Watney Mann, Norwich Brewery
               17″ wheels and a York trailing axle have enabled the platform
               height to be lowered without the need for wheel arch boxes

Figure 11:7   Dodge 100 series Commando 'G15' at 14.74 tonnes GVW
               A major factor in achieving the low loading height is the use of
               Dunlop SPIII low profile radial tyres 11/70R–22.5. The body is
               fitted with a Boalloy curtain-sided 'tautliner', giving an all round
               loading capacity, with all the advantages of a standard box van

Articulated vehicles.   A tractor plus semitrailer has a use in most types of transport operations, and the range of available models is very wide. One UK manufacturer produces a complete articulated outfit rated at as low as 1,016 kg gross combination weight (GCW), while at the heavier end of the scale the same manufacturer produces a 44,000 kg GCW tractor. At present (1980) the maximum permitted gross weight of an articulated outfit in the UK is 32,520 kg but this is dependent on the number of axles and on their spread, as follows:

1   Three axles: maximum permitted 24,390 kg. The only possible configuration is a two-axle tractor with a one-axle semitrailer.
2   Four or five axles: maximum permitted 32,520 kg. In this case the tractor may have either two or three axles, and the semitrailer may have one, two or three axles (Figure 11:9).

Figure 11:8   Articulated unit for urban delivery work
                Dodge 'Commando' G16 – 16 tonne gross train weight, specially designed to carry '10 ton' unit loads. The trailer platform is 7.7 metres long with a maximum platform height of a little over one metre for 'easy deliveries'

Within each of these there are many variations of maximum permitted gross weight according to the 'axle spread', which is measured between the rear axle of the tractor and the inner axle of the trailer. For details of these, reference should be made to the current Construction and Use Regulations.

Figure 11:9   Dodge C36 – 36 tonne gross train weight unit with Boalloy tautliner
               trailer
               Used for rapid trunking between depots and for supermarket deliveries.
               Until higher maximum operation weights are allowed, this outfit can
               only operate at 32,520 kg GTW within the United Kingdom

Drawbar-trailer outfits.   A rigid vehicle towing a two- or three-axle trailer is
referred to as a 'drawbar outfit'. As already mentioned, the front axle of the trailer can
be a detachable 'dolly' with a 'fifth-wheel' plate mounted on it, in combination with a
semitrailer. The main advantage of such a vehicle is that it gives increased platform
space, since the overall maximum length is set at 18 metres, 3 metres longer than the
current maximum length allowed for an articulated vehicle. The gross weight is still,
however, restricted to a maximum of 32,520 kg.

When a rigid vehicle is set up for towing a trailer, it is essential that a good-
quality coupling is used, and that a push-bar coupling is fitted to the front of the
vehicle so that the trailer can be 'nosed' into difficult and restricted loading areas.
Most 16,260 kg (16 ton) GVW vehicles are likely to be rated at a gross combination
weight of at least 28,450 kg (28 tons) and many are rated at 32,520 kg (32 ton)
GCW.

Dependence of particular industries on road transport

There are certain industries in which, even if it could be shown that movement of their goods by means other than road was cheaper, practical considerations tend to dictate the use of road freight. The reasons for this vary according to the type of industry.

The food industry.   The perishability of the product carried is generally the main consideration in this industry, applying mainly to fresh fish, meat, fruit, and vegetables. There is also a need for precise timing in arrival at wholesale markets. Refrigeration has helped partly to solve this problem, but apart from shipping, there has been little development in applying modern refrigeration techniques to railway stock or to aircraft. This leaves road freight as the main means of moving foodstuffs to the markets. The same considerations also apply to the horticultural industry.

   To achieve maximum flexibility of a vehicle used for delivering frozen and chilled food products, consideration should be given to incorporating into the vehicle design specification a facility to carry not only refrigerated goods but 'dry goods' as well (see Figure 11:10).

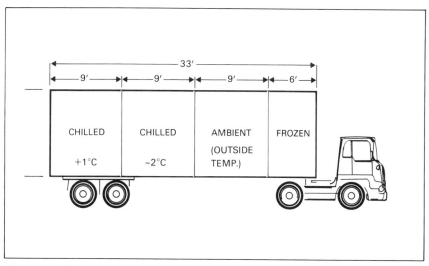

Figure 11:10   Proposed vehicle by 'BOC' to give higher utilisation

Fragile goods.   Industries concerned with the movement of fragile goods, such as radio and electrical equipment, precision instruments, glass and chinaware, have found by experience that damage is least when door-to-door road transport is employed (see Figure 11:11).

Figure 11:11   Dodge 'G13' Commando specially designed to give 'all round'
                loading and unloading capability and also fitted with Ratcliffe '30
                cwt' tail lift with platform almost 2 metres in depth
                Used for delivery of electrical and telecommunication equipment, and
                provides the driver with a facility to 'unload' without assistance at
                customers' premises

Bulk liquids and solids.   This category of products covers all those which are
conveyed in bulk tankers. They may be liquids like petroleum, edible oils, liquid
chemicals, alcoholic beverages, milk, sugar, syrup or molasses; or they may be dry
solids, like grain and flour, animal foodstuffs, sugar crystals, cement, sand and gravel,
and dry chemicals. The freighting of these products by road makes door-to-door or
tank-to-tank movements possible, and eliminates the need for intermediate storage
facilities. There is a trend in this type of industry to use Freightliners for movements
of tanks over the larger distances. Containers designed as tanks are now in use and
these can be carried by rail on the Freightliner network and transferred to road
vehicles for final delivery to the customer.

Company trains are also now used by the larger companies to move their
products to key distribution points, for subsequent onward transport by road. Special
grants are available to companies who are able to use 'Company Trains'.

Road transport for inter-operational movement

There are some industries in which road transport is regarded as a link in the chain of production. In the clothing and boot and shoe industry, it is common for raw materials or semifinished products to be despatched from one factory to another for additional processing, blending, or assembling, to leave the second factory as a marketable product, or even in some new form to be further processed at yet another factory. Road freighting, usually under the direct control of the manufacturing function is the only way to maintain production schedules. Other examples of industries heavily dependent upon an interplant road-freight activity include motor vehicle manufacturing, where chassis, press mouldings, component parts and finished vehicles are constantly being moved between plants and vehicle distribution compounds; and the newspaper industry, where a steady supply of paper (newsprint) is essential to feed the printing presses.

In all these cases, a true evaluation between road and rail freighting is not just a question of comparing relative costs, but of viewing the cost within the framework of the overall costs and service needs of the business as a whole.

Planning road-freight operations

In making cost comparisons between road and other methods of product movement, a company will need to consider a number of other matters connected with the road-freighting operation.

Owning, leasing or contract hire

One factor will be the availability of capital, and whether any capital released could be used for more profitable parts of the business. Any exclusive commitment to one alternative could be criticised, and the best compromise may be to skim the cream of regular traffic with company-owned vehicles and meet the balance by hiring, especially at peak periods. Vehicles may either be hired on a self-drive basis, which ensures the most complete day-to-day control of operations, or hired with driver.

Number and size of vehicles

In general, the larger the vehicle the lower the unit cost of movement, and at first sight there may be a natural tendency to go for the minimum number of maximum-capacity vehicles. However, this has to be balanced against the need to provide an adequate level of customer service, which may well mean the use of vehicles of less-than-maximum capacity. With increasing fuel costs the balance between the level of customer service and total distribution costs is even more important. Full loads should be the real aim of any distribution plan in order that the cost per unit of product or goods moved can be minimised.

Scheduled speeds

Now that the motorway network is almost complete, most transport schedules will include some travel on roads where the maximum speed limit is in excess of the 40 mph standard restriction. The present 60 mph maximum on motorways (even for drawbar outfits and articulated vehicles) enables average speeds of at least 45 mph to be maintained by the heaviest of modern trucks. This development has a direct bearing on road-freight operations and costs. But again a balance between 'speed' and 'increased fuel costs' must be maintained.

Length of journey

Since the 1968 Transport Act, attempts have been made to legislate 'maximum' distances for road haulage vehicles; 100 miles from base for over 16 ton GVW was a provision within the 1968 Act and 450 km (281 miles) is the maximum limit of a 20 tonne GVW articulated vehicle under EEC rules. All these have 'failed' in some way, and are today not needed due to the reduced 'driving hours' limitations for goods vehicles.

Since 1 January 1981 a driver of a goods vehicle operating under EEC National rules has been limited to driving his vehicle 8 hours each day and with a weekly limit of 48 hours, and 92 hours each consecutive two weeks. This in itself limits the 'miles' which can reasonably be covered each working day. A balance will have to be made between each type of road over which the vehicle is routed. Motorways will allow speeds up to 60 mph or an average of 40 miles in each hour of driving, whereas arterial trunk roads with a limit of 40 mph reduce the average distance to 28 miles each hour. *Routing* becomes all important if the maximum use of 'hours driven' and 'miles covered' is to be achieved.

Tachographs are required to be fitted to all goods vehicles to which the EEC National driving hours rules apply – generally vehicles in excess of 3,500 kg GVW – and with effect from 1 January 1982 all drivers of such vehicles had to use this instrument as the method of recording *hours of work and driving* instead of the previous written records. The tachograph will record *actual* driving periods and it will not be possible to 'avoid' compliance with the 'hours' rules.

Both the 'tachograph' and 'hours limitations' make the job of route planning an essential part of the Distribution Function.

Living with the lorry

The negative approaches of reducing the size of lorries; closing parts of the road network to goods vehicles; trying to force traffic on to the railways; and refusing to build new roads, may appear attractive because they can be carried out by administrative action and do not involve any direct investment of public money. But these policies would increase costs on the community, and, by themselves, would bring little, if any, environmental advantage.

This is an extract from Dr Clifford Sharp's study of road goods vehicles in the environment, *Living with the Lorry,* which was jointly commissioned by the Freight Transport Association and the Road Haulage Association, and published in 1973. The report points out that the real problem of providing a service in the consumer area is to balance the level of service to be given to customers with the inconvenience caused to customers by the delivery of his requirements into the consumer area. For example, stocking up a supermarket fully with a week's supply of goods can be done by using six maximum-size articulated vehicles which will block the whole street each Monday morning. The benefits to the consumer are a fully stocked shop and no traffic obstructions caused by deliveries for the rest of the week. The alternative is to have deliveries spread over the trading week, and have only one vehicle a day delivering to the shop. The result is less traffic obstruction on each Monday, but some traffic obstruction on the remaining days of the week, together with the possibility of having some goods not available on certain days.

If shops are to be stocked, road vehicles are the only way in which stock can be moved from the producer or warehouse to the shop shelves. Railway and other modes of transport may be used for part of the journey, but the *final* delivery to the point of sale can only be made by road vehicle (see Figure 11:12). The emotions over the presence of heavy lorries in towns and cities run high, but it needs to be understood

Figure 11:12   Dodge Commando 'G13' truck fitted with rear tail lift
Assembling loads into 'units' for one shop enables delivery time to be
cut down, thus reducing congestion in busy shopping streets

that if the shopping habits of the consumer are to require High-Street service, then the road delivery vehicle must be accepted by everyone who benefits from the supplies it brings into the shops.

On the other hand, this in no way justifies the goods vehicle virtually taking over the High Street at the expense of all other environmental considerations. The Heavy Commercial Vehicles (Control and Regulations) Act 1973 gives local authorities a statutory duty to survey their areas and, within a time schedule, to prepare plans for controlling the use of roads by heavy lorries. Some local authorities have already restricted the size of lorries which are permitted to pass through certain areas if not required to make a delivery. It is reasonably certain that, as plans for more controls are drawn up, some absolute restrictions will be placed on the size of lorries allowed into a town or city, even if they are making a delivery. Paris has successfully banned large lorries from its Blue Zone for some years and, although initially inconvenient to some distribution outlets, today the control is accepted and business activity does not seem to have been unduly inconvenienced.

Controlling the large vehicle

Many schemes are already established in towns and cities for segregating goods vehicles, especially the larger ones, from the area used by pedestrians and private cars. Coventry took advantage of its wartime destruction to rebuild the shopping centre and to establish rear-loading facilities and common loading and unloading areas behind blocks of shops. Stockholm has developed a system of taking the goods vehicles under the shopping areas, whereas in Swindon, Wiltshire, a shopping centre has been built with an unloading and parking area for goods-delivery vehicles on the top. Clearly there is room, indeed a need, in modern society for the large, maximum-length heavygoods vehicle, but it is against the interests of the community to allow such vehicles to operate without any control up and down every High Street. Designated routes for large vehicles are one obvious answer to this problem, and provided that operators, retailers, and consumers can arrive at an acceptable compromise which will necessarily cost the consumer something – then the emotional reactions aroused by the 'juggernauts' can, at least partially, be allayed.

Another answer to this problem would be for legislation to permit the free operation of the 'short-double' drawbar outfit – a special version of the 'double bottom' already mentioned (see Figure 11:13). This consists of a tractor and two semitrailers, which in total are still contained within the present maximum 32,520 kg gross limit, and within the present maximum length of 18 metres. It is already in use in America. The main advantage is the high load-space utilisation by the operator on the trunk route, while once it is in the delivery area the vehicle can be split into an articulated vehicle consisting of the tractor with one semitrailer of approximately 7.5 metres length. This gives an overall length of under 12 metres, which is also within the present maximum permitted length of a rigid vehicle.

For operating between depots on designated routes, greater productivity is achieved by the use of the 'turnpike twin' version of the double bottom, consisting of a tractor unit with two 12-metre semitrailers. With the cost of fuel oil now a major factor in transport costs, it is essential that maximum load utilisation is achieved. Allowing larger vehicles, and especially vehicles capable of moving a greater volume of goods, is one way of reducing the fuel requirement of the transport industry.

The ultimate would be the acceptance of 'road trains' made up of a maximum-weight tractor unit coupled up to three semitrailers. These would be limited to specified motorway routes, with transport operators pooling their resources and establishing motorway marshalling areas to handle the movements and group loads together.

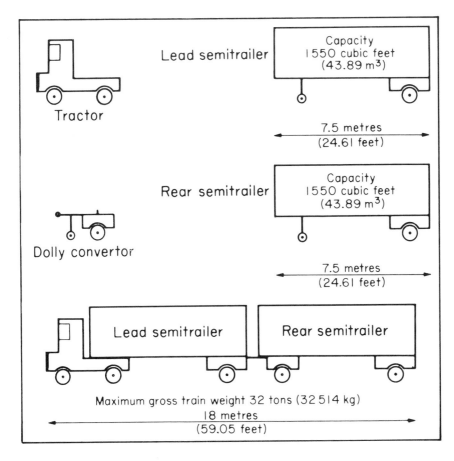

Figure 11:13   Short-double drawbar outfit

Conclusion

The advantages, both outright and relative, of road freighting which have been set out in this chapter are no more than general principles. The final conclusions in any individual situation are bound to be determined by the size and circumstances of each individual business and trade. Even though a firm may decide that road freighting is best, the final decision may in due course be in the hands of a licensing authority. That is all the more reason why the intending user of road-freight transport over longer distances should make every effort to be sure that he is on firm ground in making his decision.

12

Rail freighting

Chris Bushell

Fifty years ago, the railways were the main providers of transport in Britain. With development of the motor vehicle and rapid improvements in the road network, the proportion of total inland freight carried by rail diminished to 9.5 per cent in 1978 (the most recent figures available). Expressed in tonne-km terms, the railways' share rises to about 15 per cent, reflecting the greater average haul performed by rail compared with road transport.

Rail freight carriage fell from 208.7 million tonnes in 1970 to 169 million tonnes in 1979 due partly to the general industrial recession towards the end of the decade, and partly to withdrawal by British Rail from uneconomic flows of general merchandise which involve road cartage at each end of the rail haul. The cost of rail freight compared with road is still too high to permit a major attack on the lucrative general merchandise market, but new technology, modern equipment, aggressive marketing and above all improved staff productivity will all help to win new traffic.

Before considering the role of railways in the transport of freight today and in the immediate future, it is useful to look briefly at railway history and examine, in particular, the changes which have taken place in the industry since the Second World War, and the underlying reason for these changes.

Historical background

The railways were developed to their fullest extent when the horse and cart and canal barge were the only other means of moving goods around the country. In the early Victorian period, hundreds of individual companies sought to bring and extend the benefit of the new invention to all parts of Britain. There was no national plan, and the rail network grew, slowly at first, and then with increasing rapidity, into an overlarge, unwieldy and mainly unco-ordinated system. Many small companies failed, and amalgamation followed amalgamation. By the turn of the century the last main line had been completed and Britain, the inventor of the railway, found itself with a far more intricate network than it really required.

There was little to challenge the dominating position of the railways' near monopoly until the internal combustion engine, improved out of all recognition by the impetus and demands of four years of war, entered into peacetime competition from 1919 onwards. Road transport quickly began to eat into traditional railway traffic, taking the lucrative high-rated goods and leaving rail with lower-rated bulk traffic. The difficulties faced by the hundred-odd private companies had long been obvious, and the advantages of having them under a single management had been clearly demonstrated during the war.

Accordingly, in 1923, under the provisions of the 1921 Railways Act, they were regrouped into four main line systems known as the 'Big Four'. Substantial economies were envisaged, but in fact little was done to rationalise methods and patterns of operation, and the overlarge network with its duplicated routes and stations remained.

Fierce competition between rail and road continued unabated during the interwar years and no-one, it seems, really understood how the complementary nature of the two forms of transport could be welded into a unified national system. On the outbreak of war in 1939 the railways again came under government control and bore the brunt of the vast wartime transport requirements.

They emerged from the war intact but in poor physical shape, and at a relatively high level of activity. An abundance of freight traffic, thrown on to the railways largely because of petrol rationing and the limited road transport facilities, helped pay the way until 1952, but from then on British Railways, at that time in their fifth year of public ownership, failed to meet capital charges although still showing an operating surplus. This surplus disappeared in 1955 and the annual loss on operating account increased year by year thereafter.

The realisation that the railways were being run down for want of capital investment led to the decision in 1955 to embark on a comprehensive modernisation plan to bring them up to the standard of other advanced nations. The aim was to replace steam by diesel and electric traction, concentrate marshalling yards, mechanise freight handling and generally to modernise equipment. By these means it was expected that costs would be reduced, more traffic attracted, and the railways made to pay once again.

Five years later, against a background of declining traffic and mounting deficits, it had become apparent that the hoped-for fruits of the modernisation plan would not be realised. A substantial remodelling of the network was forecast, and subsequent investigations by the government resulted in the Transport Act of 1962, the main provisions of which separated railways from the other elements of nationalised transport, gave the newly-created British Railways Board a more realistic financial structure, and cleared the way for a complete reshaping of the railway network along commercial lines.

The Board's Reshaping Report, published in 1963 and forever after known as the 'Beeching Report' after the industrialist who had been brought in to manage the new BRB, threw fresh light on the problems facing the railways and pointed out the hard road to recovery. The thought underlying the whole report was that 'the railways should be used to meet that part of the total transport requirements of the country for which they offer the best available means, and that they should cease to do things for which they are ill-suited'. The report triggered an extensive programme of closures of uneconomic lines.

One of the report's principal proposals was for a 'Liner Train' service for the combined movement of containerised merchandise by road and rail, later to become known as the Freightliner service. Its early development and the state of rail freight generally, was radically affected by the provisions of the Transport Act of 1968, which set out new government thinking on the industry.

The role of rail freight

The 1968 Act set up a new publicly-owned authority, the National Freight Corporation, the aim of which was to provide integrated road and rail services, and in doing so to make the maximum possible economic use of rail. The NFC became responsible for two former rail subsidiaries, Freightliners Limited, and National Carriers Limited. These companies took over important sectors of railway activity, namely the high-capacity container business, and the nationwide distribution service for consignments of less-than-wagonload proportions, commonly known as sundries or smalls. All the companies' assets other than rail wagons were transferred to the NFC, but BR retained a 49 per cent interest in Freightliners Limited.

BR was left with full control of the greater part of its traffic, representing some 210 million tonnes. Some of this business, consisting of bulk commodities such as oil, was already carried in full trainloads on through runs. This is a very efficient method of operation, which becomes more productive where large and regular flows move in a predetermined pattern, and the company/bulk train network has expanded throughout the 1970s to account for 90 per cent of all rail freight by 1979.

On the debit side, some 120 million tonnes was being moved by traditional means in smaller units of one or more wagonloads. Wagonloads marshalling costs are high and extended transit times give poor utilisation of wagons. Consequently, a large amount of this traffic was carried at a loss. After some uncertainty in the early-1970s, BR now plans to stay in the wagonload business, but to do so successfully, it will need to improve efficiency by reducing still further the number of terminals and marshalling yards. A good start has been made with an express wagonload service known as Speedlink, aimed at less-than-trainload bulk flows and semi-finished products. Speedlink is to be the standard wagonload service of the future.

There were important advances in haulage of some commodities during the early-1970s, particularly aggregates and petroleum products, but there was no great upsurge in rail freight business. Two provisions of the 1974 Railways Act, implemented from 1 January 1975, opened up exciting prospects for rail freight growth at a time when public opinion was demanding more effective action to combat environmentally undesirable heavy freight movement by road. The 1974 Act transferred BR's track and signalling costs, hitherto charged against capital account, to the revenue account, a move which promised to reduce track costs for freight operations. Additionally, Clause 8 of the Act provided for government grants towards the cost of installation of private sidings and other facilities for rail freight haulage. This has been a strong incentive to manufacturers considering transfer of their traffic to rail, and had resulted in some 16 million tonnes of new business up to the end of 1979.

Important though these measures were in helping slim down the deficit on freight operations and in encouraging new bulk traffic, both 1974 and 1975 were difficult years which set the scene for performance right through to 1979. Recession and inflation bit hard in the following years, while in 1979 severe weather conditions, a shortage of motive power, and the effects of industrial disputes all took a heavy toll. Rail freight ended the 1970s with carryings at their lowest point ever, 169 million tonnes, and with prospects no better for the immediate future. One major achievement against this background was the reduction in the loss on freight operations of £60 million in the mid-1970s to break-even point at the end of 1979. Subsidies to rail freight had ceased by the end of 1978.

These gloomy statistics disguise a number of bright spots, particularly the success of Speedlink and train ferry services to the continent, and an encouraging 10 per cent increase in parcels business during 1979. Also highly significant to the overall picture was the return of Freightliners Limited to full railway ownership in 1978.

There can be little doubt that development of the high-capacity container and the equipment to handle it has been one of the most significant developments in general freight transport since the Second World War. In Britain, the railway was the first transport medium to adapt itself to the new pattern, and the Freightliner system will therefore be described in some detail later, following the other traffic groups.

Company trains and bulk traffic

For many years the movement of bulk commodities such as coal to public utilities and iron ore to steelworks in block trains has been a normal feature of railway operation. However, it is only in the past 20 years that the principle of the company or customer train has been extended to other products. The railways define a company train as one carrying traffic from one consignor to one consignee (or frequently between two plants operated by the consignor) in one through journey, normally without any intermediate marshalling (Figure 12:1).

In 1963, about 600 company trains were scheduled to run each week, but by 1977 the figure had grown to 825 per day. This included 200 'merry-go-round' trains

Figure 12:1   Typical BR company train: Foster Yeoman privately owned
hopper wagons discharging aggregates at Botley depot

from mine to power station, and 125 Freightliner trains. Company trains carry a very
wide range of products whose distribution pattern and general characteristics make
them suitable for this type of operation. Principal traffics are coal and coke,
aggregates, petroleum products and chemicals, raw materials and finished products
for the iron and steel industry. The main gains in the 1970s were in aggregates and
petroleum products, while in recent years an interesting development has been the
movement of domestic rubbish by container loaded on to block trains.

In several cases, large-scale movement has led to development of high-capacity
wagons and special-purpose loading and discharge terminals. Petroleum and
aggregates are prime examples of commodities for which industry has invested
heavily in private-owner wagons and mechanised terminals, while BR's heaviest
freight trains move iron ore from Port Talbot to the British Steel plant at Llanwern in
South Wales (Figure 12:2). There has also been considerable growth in the
movement of motor vehicle components between manufacturer's works, and in
completed cars from works to main distribution points.

Distribution of coal, coke and manufactured solid fuels accounted for about 55
per cent of freight tonnage in 1979, and almost half the total freight revenue. Coal and
steel movements taken together contributed 69 per cent of revenue, excluding parcels.
Other 1979 statistics include: iron and steel raw materials and products, 25 million
tonnes; petroleum products and chemicals, 21 million tonnes; aggregates and building

Figure 12:2   BR's heaviest trains haul iron ore to the British Steel plant at
               Llanwern in South Wales

materials, 19 million tonnes.

Although these are all bulk commodities, not all are moved in company trains. Increased emphasis has been placed on through movement of trains, concentration of domestic and industrial coal depots, and the merry-go-round system of feeding coal-fired power stations which is expanding all the time. In merry-go-round, trains of 32 tonne coal wagons with a total capacity of up to 1,400 tonnes move continuously between pit and power station. The wagons are unloaded automatically as specially geared locomotives haul the complete train at a steady ½ mph over reception hoppers at the power station (Figure 12:3). Up to 1979, 56 collieries had been equipped with rapid loading facilities, and nine more are being developed. In 1970, 20.6 million tonnes of coal was carried in merry-go-round trains, of which 33 per cent was from sites equipped with rapid loading facilities. By 1979, these figures had risen to 50 million tonnes and 63 per cent respectively, and the proportion of coal loaded through rapid-loading facilities continues to increase.

Wagonload freight

After a period of neglect while bulk traffic was burgeoning, it is now accepted that wagonload traffic, in less-than-train load quantities, constitutes a major growth area,

Figure 12:3   Power station coal on the move at ½ mile/h
              Merry-go-round train about to discharge its load at a major power
              station

and considerable attention has been paid to improving wagonload movement by the detailed replanning of services over trunk routes, and by the development of a computerised system, TOPS (Total Operations Processing System). This is designed to maintain a current index of all wagons, locomotives and traffic carried. It enables up-to-date information on any wagon to be available on request, furnishes regular reports on customers' traffic, and provides detailed or summarised information on which to plan train and traffic movement. All key locations – yards, depots and offices – are connected to a central computer through the railways' tele-communications network. General efficiency and wagon turnround time have been improved, while the system has also identified wagons that are surplus to requirements – assisting the process of slimming down the wagon fleet.

Establishment in 1977 of the Speedlink network of fast overnight trains was a significant move towards capturing more of the general merchandise traffic (Figure 12:4). Speedlink freight moves in modern air-braked wagons capable of 120 km/h; in 1979 there were 38 services, and carryings reached 3 million tonnes.

Whether for complete company trains or in wagonload quantities only, there is a growing tendency on the part of large companies to invest in their own specialised wagons made for particular types of traffic – oil, steel, cars, cement and liquid oxygen for example. By 1979 there were 18,676 privately owned wagons, mostly long wheelbase (15 feet or over) which can travel at 120 km/h.

Figure 12:4   Wagonload freight on the move at 120 km/h in a Speedlink train,
the fast overnight service tailored to penetrate the general
merchandise market

Of British Rail's own fleet the older short-wheelbase wagons (10 feet, limited to
70 km/h) are still in considerable use, constituting well over half the 1979 total wagon
fleet of 137,589. Replacement of these is going ahead, with 1,500 wagons built by BR
in 1979.

Rail express parcels

Freight carried by passenger train or similar service includes parcels, perishables,
newspapers, Post Office parcels and letter mails. As a group these traffics have
consistently shown a surplus over direct costs, and in fact parcels are, after coal and
coke, the biggest money-spinning freight traffic. In 1979, parcels income rose by £11
million to £130.8 million. Of this, nearly £41 million came from postal parcels and
letter mails.

The Rail Express Parcels Service provides a convenient method of distribution
for traders and manufacturers requiring express transits. With the growing volume of
station-to-station traffic the involvement in collection and delivery services has
declined but REPS still employs a road fleet of some 2,000 vehicles to ensure the
highest quality of service is maintained.

The station-to-station traffic Red Star service on nominated passenger trains continues its success, and carryings in 1979 amounted to 5.5 million packages. With the introduction of road transfers between terminal stations in London, Manchester and Glasgow, coupled with controlled rail transfer facilities at certain main line interchange points, the Red Star network is now very extensive. New, simplified scales of charges were introduced in 1980 for all sections of rail-carried parcels with the aim of bringing greater flexibility to the business and allowing REPS to be competitive in the market place. These new scales replaced a more complicated system which had been in operation since 1964. Rail has advantages over the Post Office parcels service in that there is virtually no restriction on package size and shape and the upper weight limitation of 100 kg (2 cwt) covers practically the whole of the market requirement for this type of service. Heavier packages are accepted by prior arrangement.

Traditionally parcels were conveyed in the guard's van or in vans attached to passenger trains. But the growth in traffic, especially in the mail order sector, and the need to segregate parcels from passengers, led to the increasing use of special parcels trains and to the introduction of a unit loading system. This employs a four-wheeled caged pallet known as the BRUTE (British Railways Universal Trolley Equipment) which was designed to accommodate traffic of irregular shape and size (see Figure 12:5). After sorting by destination at the originating station, parcels are stowed into BRUTES, which are in turn loaded into fixed-formation parcels trains working in circuit to serve specific railway operating areas. Progressive adoption of this system has resulted in economies in rolling stock and equipment, higher staff productivity, quicker transits and reduction of claims through loss, damage and delay.

Container traffic

Historical background

Containers of one kind or another have been used on railways for many years. In 1926 the London, Midland & Scottish Railway introduced the first of the containers which could be considered as the forerunners of the present Freightliner and ISO containers. From then on all four main-line companies designed and built containers of differing types and capacities. By the mid-1950s the railways owned some 30,000 containers of all categories. While most of these matched the demand of the times, progress was slow and their use was confined to a small segment of the available suitable traffic. The containers were small because they were related to the then current wagon sizes and their tare/payload ratios were too high. Moreover there was no attempt to concentrate on selected assembly and delivery points and thus take advantage of trainload working; road/rail transfer was slow and inefficient; shunting at marshalling yards and exchange points caused disturbance of loads and damage to contents; the time was not yet ripe for the road and rail industries to come together in the national interest.

Figure 12:5 A BRUTE (British Railways Universal Trolley Equipment)

Freightliner service

The circumstances leading to the Transport Act of 1962 provided ideal conditions for making a break with the past. The means had to be found to enable the railways to get back into the general merchandise market, and the high-capacity container system seemed a likely solution. Growth of road freight traffic had been grossly underestimated in the Modernisation Plan, and by the early 1960s the railways were losing traffic dramatically. The first comprehensive survey was made of non-railborne traffic, in an attempt to identify what proportion could be regarded as potential Freightliner business. Some 16 million tonnes were seen as being vulnerable to Freightliner competition, and on this basis it was decided to establish five prime routes which had been shown to carry the greatest quantity of potentially profitable traffic. These were London to Glasgow, Manchester and Liverpool; Glasgow to Manchester; and Glasgow to Liverpool. Total tonnage carried by road over these five routes was later estimated at 8 million tonnes, of which 80 per cent was suitable for transfer to Freightliner.

British Rail pioneered the Freightliner concept at a time when containerisation was in its infancy. There were no standard container sizes, and no standard loading equipment. Small-wheeled wagons had to be designed to allow passage through BR's restricted loading gauge of the 8 x 8 ft containers which were seen as the minimum viable size. Later appearance of the ISO standard 8 ft 6 in. high maritime containers forced a change, and work has been going on throughout the 1970s to give sufficient headroom on principal BR routes for these larger containers.

The first Freightliner train ran between London and Glasgow in November 1965, and traffic was swiftly attracted to the novel, highly-efficient and speedy transit system. Under the control of the National Freight Corporation between 1968 and 1978, Freightliners grew to become the world's largest overland container haulier.

Business reached a peak of 717,400 containers handled in 1976, falling to 713,000 and 695,200 in the succeeding two years. In 1979, however, saw a recovery to 707,000 containers.

In 1980 the company operated at 40 terminals, including 11 at ports and 4 privately owned, between which 200 Freightliner trains were operated every day (Figure 12:6). By this time, the market orientation of Freightliners had changed somewhat. Originally conceived as a domestic container service, Freightliner's business is now predominantly maritime, with deep sea movements accounting for 36 per cent of volume, European 15 per cent, and Irish 7 per cent. The remaining 42 per cent is domestic traffic, which is still seen as offering considerable opportunities for growth, possibly in a loose partnership with BR's own Speedlink wagonload service.

Freightliner operation is essentially simple. Loaded containers are brought to the Freightliner terminal by road from the sender's premises either by his own vehicles, by road haulier or by Freightliner's own vehicles. Transfer to stacking ground or direct on to the waiting container train is carried out in minutes by modern lifting equipment (see Figure 12:7). The train, consisting of up to 30 continuously coupled flat bogie wagons, each providing 18 m (59 feet) of container space, departs

Figure 12:6   Freightliner network of terminals totalled forty in mid-1980

Figure 12:7   Large-scale Freightliner operations at a major terminal, with various types of company and privately owned containers

according to a predetermined timetable direct to its destination, without passing through a marshalling yard, at a maximum speed of 120 km/h (75 mph) and a start-to-stop average of 80 km/h (50 mph). At the receiving point the reverse procedure takes place.

When full with loaded containers the maximum trailing load can be 1,050 tons for a twenty-wagon train with payloads up to between 900 and 950 tons. High speeds, punctuality and rapid transfer of containers all contribute to high utilisation of the wagon sets and, therefore, to unit costs lower than those for traditional wagons and trains. The trains are capable of carrying any combination of standard 2, 6, 9, and 12 m (10, 20, 30, and 40 feet) containers.

Freightliners are now equipped to deal with any containers conforming to the ISO standard specification and can handle other containers within the UK provided they conform to the design and construction requirements of the British Railways Board, which is an essential condition in the interests of safety. The fleet owned by Freightliners Limited was 7,000 in 1979 and included ISO box types, insulated, curtain-sided, steel-carrying and open containers, but privately owned containers carry over half of the traffic. Better control of container movement should be possible following commissioning of COPS, a real time computer-based control system similar to British Rail's TOPS. It is expected to improve throughput of containers at terminals by making more productive use of cranes, and will allow a reduction of about 10 per cent in the number of containers for the same annual volume.

The principal materials used in container construction today are light alloys or steel and resin-impregnated plywood to give high structural strength coupled with low tare weights. Special-purpose types are nearly all privately owned; many users find it more convenient to lease units especially when they are required to circulate internationally or are to be painted in company livery.

Terminal transfer equipment has progressed rapidly with the operational experience gained over the years. The earliest cranes to be used at the first five Freightliner terminals were Drott Travelifts, built under US licence in Britain. They were diesel-powered, hydraulically operated and fitted with pneumatic tyres. The working head, or grappler, consisted of a frame with four arms which could be automatically adjusted to lift standard sized containers from the bottom corners, with a time of transfer of two minutes for lifts up to 30 tons.

Later designs have been modified to give higher utilisation and greater reliability. They are now rail mounted and electrically operated and the larger versions span up to eleven rail tracks or roadways (Figure 12:8). (Because ISO requirements stipulate that containers should be capable of being lifted from the top corner castings, lifting frames now have the dual capacity to lift from both top and bottom.) An exciting prospect for the 1980s is the possibility of opening up entirely new markets served by smaller terminals. Freightliners is evaluating a rail-mounted unit which transfers containers from road to rail vehicles, from train to train, or to a platform or the ground. If proved successful, the Container Transfer Vehicle (CTV) (see Figure 12:9) could eliminate the need for costly overhead gantry cranes, and allow terminals to be set up in areas where it would have been uneconomical to install full-scale crane facilities. In rapidly expanding industrial areas, CTV could be used to set up a Freightliner terminal in a matter of days rather than months as at present, and would certainly help Freightliners' competitiveness with road hauliers.

Figure 12:8   Sophisticated lifting equipment is the key to quick and efficient
                transfer of containers from rail to road vehicles

Figure 12:9   Hope for the 1980s is the CTV (Container Transfer Vehicle), which could revolutionise Freightliner operations by cutting drastically the cost of setting up new terminals

13

Air freighting

David Ross

The air freight industry has come a long way since the 1920s and the commencement of scheduled international passenger services, along with the carriage of mail, diplomatic pouches and some small urgent packages. After the Second World War, the surplus of military aircraft available led to an increase in aircraft being used for commercial purposes. This growing civil aviation system began to consider the needs of all traffic – passenger, mail and freight. Many of the world's major airlines used pure freighter aircraft in support of their key freight flows on passenger aircraft. In 1948 the Berlin Airlift demonstrated to the whole world what could be achieved in a major civil emergency; the more farsighted saw the commercial applications.

The 1950s saw a rapid growth in airline development enabling air freight to increase at a spectacular rate. Aircraft sizes were increasing, the number of routes being operated were increasing, the whole expansion of the aviation industry was matched, and in some instances, overtaken by the demand for air freight capacity.

The development of the jet engine and the re-equipment by the major airlines effectively reduced the world in a way that seemed impossible only 10 or 20 years earlier. It was possible to carry passengers, mail and freight half way round the world in under two days. As a result of a significant demand for air freight capacity more and more carriers offered specialist freight services. The 1970s, with the advent of wide-bodied aircraft, provided the biggest single impetus to the air cargo industry.

Despite the significant increase in air freight, particularly since 1945, it is important to note that by the mid 1970s the proportion of international trade which moved by air was less than 1 per cent. In value terms, UK exports which moved by air represented approximately 17 per cent of our total exports, and for imports about 13½ per cent moved by air.

The airlines' dependence on air freight has increased significantly; air freight capacity is now an integral part of their aircraft procurement plans. However, although the number of pure freighter aircraft has increased substantially, most airlines regard them as 'back-up' on key routes. The level of business carried on passenger aircraft is still substantial and is likely to continue. In British Airways, some 80 per cent of freight (Figure 13:1) is carried on passenger aircraft. Freight represents approximately 12 per cent of BA's revenue but for some international airlines it is as much as one-third of the revenue contribution. BA's freight revenue is approximately £200 million in 1980-1 – a very significant business.

Figure 13:1   The British Airways 747 freighter aircraft

The role of air transport in physical distribution management

Until the mid 1950s it was generally assumed by airlines and shippers that air cargo was only really suitable for the carriage of emergency shipments. Shippers assumed that air cargo rates were far too high for planned distribution. In recent years, however, considerable thought has been given to the science of physical distribution in universities, industry and the transport industry. The airlines have not been slow to look at the role of air cargo in physical distribution management and have developed sophisticated computer programs in an effort to promote the benefits of using air cargo as part of a planned distribution strategy; the central concept in most of these programs is that of the potential 'trade-off' between the various elements in the distribution mix.

We are concerned specifically here with the part of the distribution chain which starts when goods have left the production line to being received by the consumer.

This involves warehousing, packing, transportation to port, movement from port of embarkation to port of arrival, then transportation from port of arrival to the consignee, inventory levels in the consignee's warehouse and final despatch to the ultimate consumer (where not the consignee). The choice of transport mode can be critical when competing in overseas markets and it is clear that, to compete on equal terms in these markets, an exporter will benefit from a fast form of transportation which gives him the facility of being able to deliver specific orders at least as quickly as a domestic producer in that market.

Customer service comes high on the list of factors leading to increased volume of sales. To an importer, 'on time' delivery is vital to the successful operation of his business. He cannot plan his activities either as a user of products purchased for consumption or for re-sale to consumers unless his goods arrive on time. Delivery delays are some of the main deterents to expansion of overseas sales. An exporter cannot always control the sequence of events leading to delays. Component suppliers can deliver late, labour disputes both external and internal can disrupt planned delivery schedules. Ideally, the exporter needs to have available a variety of transport modes to circumvent delay situations. Complete flexibility of choice to use air or sea transport and ensure 'on time' delivery should be a positive requirement of all exporters. Recognising the need for a mixed air/sea distribution is one thing; why do so few exporters and importers actively plan to use air cargo in a rational way? It should be part of an overall marketing plan for all of them.

Airlines have, until recently, contributed to the failure of industries engaged in international trade to use air cargo as a natural part of their distribution plans. Most promotional efforts have appealed either to the casual shipper of emergency items, the exporter of high value products or the agent and forwarder.

Conversely, too many exporters have looked no further than their warehouse door, selling on FOB terms and breathing a sigh of relief when the goods have left the warehouse door. It has been all too easy to adopt what looks at first glance to be the easy way out. Fortunately, times are changing and companies are now looking at the various facets of the distribution function and the interplay of all the various areas of responsibility involved. It is noticeable that several companies are now appointing distribution managers with corporate responsibility; but there are still many companies who leave the responsibility for efficient distribution to junior members of staff who have no real conception of what the distribution function entails.

However, there is no need to paint too dark a picture; there are clear indications that the importance of physical distribution management is being recognised and that selling in overseas markets on CIF terms is seen to allow companies to retain total control of the distribution function.

The total distribution cost concept

It has been traditional in exporting industries to place greatest importance on the price of a transport mode. In other words, whichever transport mode appeared to be cheapest was the one to be selected. The belief was that if pure transportation cost was marginal, then the customer was more likely to be satisfied with the transportation. It is well known that the slower surface modes cost correspondingly less than air, therefore surface tended to be chosen. Speed was sacrificed in favour of price. Who can measure the manifestations of this decision? Making speed a priority would have meant that the customer received his goods very quickly, which implies customer satisfaction, therefore he is more likely to re-order from a fast source of supply.

Traditionally, airlines have more frequent services to specific destinations than do surface carriers. Therefore there are no long delays waiting until a further service is available. Another important factor to consider is reliability. The airlines by necessity are highly conscious of serviceability, therefore a pool of aircraft is available from which a substitution can be made. In the case of a surface breakdown, waiting for spares can take time and create long delays (shipping lines, in fact, use airlines to maintain their serviceability).

Lastly, environment should be considered; the problems and hazards to which consignments are subjected while in transit. By air, goods are handled carefully on pallets or in airline containers and are less subject to bad handling. Goods are loaded under cover and the environment in which the goods are handled is generally very good, hence there is less likelihood of damage.

All these factors should be taken into account when considering a mode of transport and any allied benefits in terms of customer satisfaction.

Freight rates – the density effect

As already discussed, it has been traditional for a shipper to look at the difference between surface and air cost purely in terms of the freight rate charged, e.g. £60 per tonne by sea and £350 per tonne by air. It has, therefore, been easy for such a person to make a value judgement and come to the conclusion that surface rates are cheaper than air. However, it would pay a studious shipper to look a little further than this at the true cost of shipping by surface and air. Most distribution or shipping departments have long known whether a volume penalty will apply by either surface or air transportation, but in practice the two are not generally compared together.

There are two basic methods of applying freight rates; either per unit of weight or unit of volume. Sea freight rates are usually quoted per unit of volume, e.g. £50 per cubic metre. Air freight rates are quoted per unit of weight, e.g. £0.50 per kilo or £500 per metric tonne, and only when a consignment is very bulky in relation to its weight (in practice, more than 7 cubic metres per tonne), is it charged on volume.

This means that for high density goods (low volume per unit of weight) sea freight rates tend to be significantly lower than air. But for goods of average and low density, air freight is more competitive than is generally believed.

For example, assume a consignment of 1,000 kilos (one tonne) with a volume of *3 cubic metres* for which the quoted rates are:

    Sea £60 per cubic metre   Air £350 per tonne (£0.35 per kilo)

At these rates the comparative charges for the consignments are:

Sea	3 cubic metres at £60	=	£180
Air	1 tonne at £350	=	£350

However, take another consignment weighing 1 tonne but with a volume of 7 *cubic metres* at the same rates. Now the charges are:

Sea	7 cubic metres at £60	=	£420
Air	1 tonne at £350	=	£350

and air freight is suddenly much cheaper than sea. In both cases the quoted rates are the same and the weight of the consignment is the same. The all important factor that has affected the total charge is the density of the consignment.

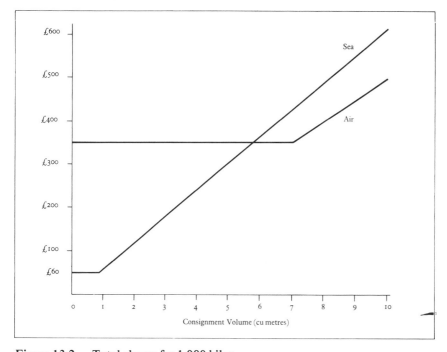

Figure 13:2   Total charge for 1,000 kilos

    The relationship between sea and air freight rates at differing densities is illustrated in Figures 13:2 and 13:3. Figure 13:2 compares the total charge for 1,000 kilos over a density range of 1 cubic metre/tonne to 10 cubic metres/tonne, and shows that as density decreases the difference between the air and surface charge gradually diminishes until at a density of 6 cubic metres/tonne and below air becomes cheaper than sea.

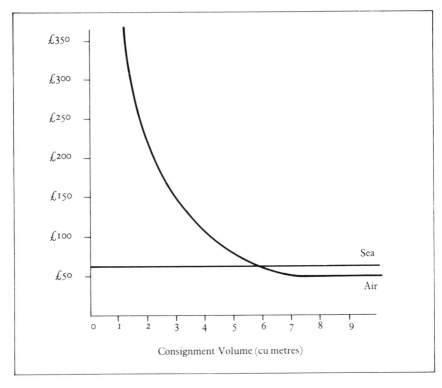

Figure 13:3   Rate per cubic metre

Figure 13:3 is based on the same information, but expresses the comparison in terms of a rate per cubic metre showing that as density falls the sea rate remains constant while the air rate falls until, once again, the air rate reaches a point below sea.

The point at which air becomes cheaper than surface depends upon the quoted rates and sometimes it will never be cheaper on a straightforward freight rate comparison. The important thing to remember is that sea freight can be very cheap if the goods are very dense but as density reduces (bulk increases in relation to a constant weight) the charge escalates rapidly. On the other hand, while air freight (when compared with sea) may be more expensive for goods of very high density, the charge remains constant for all densities down to 7 cubic metres per tonne (ex the UK only 5.5 cubic metres; except USA).

It would be useful at this juncture to have some idea of the type of product which could be shipped more advantageously by air. Below are shown a few examples of products which, because of their volume and weight characteristics, mean that the gap between air and surface costs is less than at first appeared.

	m^3/tonne
Ladies' shoes	6.643
Men's shoes	5.575
Computers varied	6.937
Colour TVs	6.855
Refrigerators	6.855
Spectrum analysers	6.371
Industrial cookers	6.239
Towels	6.932

It is also useful to know that the airlines do offer cheaper than normal rates on specific commodities; this can further lower the cost of shipping by air. These specific commodity rates may apply at varying breakpoints, e.g. 100 kilos, 500 kilos, 1,000 kilos, etc. Obviously the larger a consignment the more likely it is to qualify for a higher breakpoint and, therefore, a lower rate.

The value to weight equation

The traditional method of identifying potential traffic for air cargo has been to look at products of a high value. The reason for this has been that high value goods were said to be better able to bear a higher transport cost. In other words, transport cost represented a smaller percentage of invoice value if goods were of a higher value. However, the value to weight equation is valid for a different reason.

When the *Total Distribution Cost* concept is applied, any difference between surface and air pure transport cost can be offset by the release of capital 'tied up' on the high seas and 'tied up' in substantial inventories held to cover long transit times from a supplier. If one considers the amount of idle capital 'tied up' in high value goods in transit and in inventory, plus the lost benefits of opportunity cost of capital which this represents, one can appreciate that a transport mode which offers short transit times, and the opportunity to minimise inventory levels, becomes even more attractive the higher the value of the goods.

A simple example will serve to illustrate the point. Assume that a company holds 10 tonnes of stock to meet surface lead times and expected market demand. If the goods are worth £10 per kilo then the value of the inventory is £100,000. If, on the other hand, a company holds 10 tonnes of stock worth £1 per kilo then this represents a stock holding of £10,000. Clearly, while the weight of the stock is equal, the value of a given amount of stock varies considerably with the value per kilo.

It follows that if a faster mode of transport is used, the goods can be received from the supplier in a much shorter period of time, thus the necessity to hold the level of inventory previously required to meet slower lead times diminishes and a much smaller inventory level will suffice.

In the example quoted where goods are worth £10 per kilo, e.g. £100,000 of inventory, it may be possible to reduce this inventory by 50 per cent, e.g. £50,000. This will release £50,000 which can be invested at the opportunity cost, albeit short term investment or speculation, or ploughed back into another area of the organisation where the need for cash may be critical.

The same concept can be applied to capital 'tied up' in transit. It follows that if goods are moving, say, to India by surface, with an average door to door time of 90 days, then the value of the goods which are in transit, and therefore cannot be sold in the marketplace, represent capital 'tied up' and cannot be sold and converted into cash for increasing a company's cash flow. If a mode of transport with a shorter 'door to door' time is used, obviously the goods represent capital 'tied up' in transit for a much shorter period of time, they can then be sold and converted into cash more quickly and invested at the opportunity cost.

A simple example may serve to illustrate the point in question again using India as the destination:

Surface
£10,000 stock in transit for 90 days x 20 per cent (notional opportunity cost)
= £493.15
Air
£10,000 stock in transit for 7 days x 20 per cent (notional opportunity cost)
= £38.35

This shows simply that the lost opportunity cost of using surface is £454.80 on one shipment. Imagine the effect of this on a company which ships every week to India, e.g. £454.80 x 52 = £23,649.60 per annum. A not inconsiderable amount, particularly in view of the relatively small value of the consignment in question.

Illustrated here in simplified form are the basic factors involved in the *Total Distribution Cost* concept.

To reiterate the points made so far: it is important first of all to establish the real cost of transportation in volume to weight terms; second, it is important to offset any deficit in comparing air freight rates with surface, by reducing stock 'tied up' in transit and inventory to match shorter door to door and lead times. There are many more implications in terms of reduced need for warehousing space, less risk of obsolescence due to optimised stock levels, less risk of damage, reductions in packing costs and cheaper insurance. A crucial factor, which is inherent in the use of air transport, is the benefit in terms of marketing, e.g. having goods available in the marketplace when the customer wants them.

Development of the TDC computer model

For several years there have been attempts to market computer models which looked at total distribution costs. Initially, these models tended to be complex with many variables, some of which were difficult to quantify. In recent years, however, models have evolved which are less complex and produce information which is quantifiable and meaningful. British Airways has developed a model (Figure 13:4) which has met these criteria and has had notable success in analysing distribution systems. These models also perform a useful function from the airline marketing point of view. An airline is able, given the relevant data, to test various markets and establish what rates would convert traffic and assess whether these are viable from a costing point of view. Measuring these against the acceptable price in the marketplace, it is possible to test quickly whether there is potential for development within a specific industry or on a specific route.

Figure 13:4   An airline executive using a computer model to assist in developing a proposal for a potential air freight customer

If it were possible to establish this picture on all routes worldwide then the airlines would be greatly aided in their market development, marketing planning, forecasting and future capacity requirements.

The role of the cargo sales agent and freight forwarder

The comprehensive services provided by the airlines are supplemented by those of the air freight agents and air freight forwarders, often referred to as consolidators who are equally qualified to advise on air freight matters. With the great number of cargo sales agents and freight forwarder offices scattered across the world, in addition to airline offices, the shipping public has a large number of specialised air freight centres at its disposal.

There is a good deal of similarity between the services provided by cargo agents and freight forwarders. Many cargo sales agents are forwarders and vice versa. Both can handle cartage, packing, warehousing and the complete documentation that is involved in air shipment, including air waybills, export declarations, commercial and consular invoices, certificates of origin, bank documents, insurance, export licences, letters of credit and so on.

Cargo sales agents are appointed by the airlines to promote and sell air freight. They handle any size of shipment requiring immediate transport as an individual consignment to destination, and receive a standard rate of commission from the airlines for their services. Shippers who have not previously made use of air freight can consult the cargo agents handling their surface consignments. If the agents concerned also handle air freight, then they should be in a good position to advise on the relative merits of different forms of transport as they affect their customers' particular requirements.

The main difference between cargo sales agents and freight forwarders is that freight forwarders serve the shipping public by assembling small shipments into single large consignments which are passed on to an airline in the name of the freight forwarder as shipper. This involves receiving individual packages from different shippers and consolidating them, for subsequent despatch, but not necessarily by the first available service. Consolidated consignments are then disassembled at destination, or at a convenient intermediate point en route, and individual consignments reforwarded to destination. The compensation for the freight forwarder comes from his taking a percentage of the difference between the rate he charges the shipper and the quantity discount rate which he gets from the airline after consolidation. Consolidation is such an important activity of the freight forwarder that he is often referred to as a 'Consolidator'.

The volume discount offered by the airlines for large consignments permit freight forwarders and consolidators to offer attractive rates to the general shipping public, particularly for the despatch of small consignments. This means that freight forwarders are often in a position to quote lower than airlines rates, because of their ability to make use of these high breakpoint discounts by consolidating many smaller consignments from different shipping sources. It is the existence of the spread of rates established by the airlines for varying sizes of shipment, that enables the consolidator to accept shipments at rates that may be competitive with, or lower than, the applicable airline rates for consignments of the same size.

Freight forwarders also specialise in various ground operations that ensure speedy handling at shipment origin and destination. They advise on suitable packing, issue air waybills, prepare documentation and arrange for transport to and from airports. Freight forwarders also protect the shipper's cargo against loss or damage en route through the issue of their own House air waybill, representing the contract between shipper and freight forwarder; maintain their own facilities, such as trucks and warehouse space, both to expedite cargo to the consignee and for sub-contracting to other surface transport companies, usually trucking companies, where necessary. National associations of freight forwarders have been set up in a number of countries to maintain ethical practices and to establish liaison with the airlines with a view to providing the best possible service.

Shippers need not be located in the same city as freight forwarders to be able to make use of their consolidation services, as they often draw their shipments from surrounding cities and areas. Freight forwarders assemble shipments originating from different points at a single centralised point. The individual shipments of the consignment are then either delivered locally or reforwarded separately to their ultimate destination.

Cargo sales agents and freight forwarders can be considered as an extension of the airlines' selling effort. In the same way, they are always pleased to advise shippers on such matters as applicable freight rates for different commodities and weights, flight frequencies, arrival and departure times and pick-up and delivery costs – in short, on any matter pertaining to air freight.

The role of the International Air Transport Association

The majority of airlines operating scheduled cargo services are members of IATA. (See Figure 13:5 for IATA areas.) IATA is best known as the medium through which the airlines fix a common tariff. Less thought is given to the advantages of the system to shippers.

As IATA evolved over the years, the airlines themselves became increasingly concerned about the difficulties in reaching agreement on rates and realised that the system needed to be considerably more flexible. Therefore a body derived from member airlines was given the unenviable task of reviewing the whole structure and future of IATA. In October 1978 their recommendations came into force.

A two-tier structure has been devised; firstly, all member airlines operating scheduled international services can now join what is known as the Trade Association. Within the Trade Association two major decision making bodies have evolved – the Cargo Services Conference and the Cargo Agency Conference.

The Cargo Services Conference will be responsible for developing uniform standards of operation essential to the maintenance of an integrated air transport system: for example, the standardisation of air waybills, interchange of pallets and interline agreements. This arrangement will also permit non-IATA carriers to participate and benefit fully from the work of the Trade Association.

The Cargo Agency Conference will be responsible for appointing cargo agents

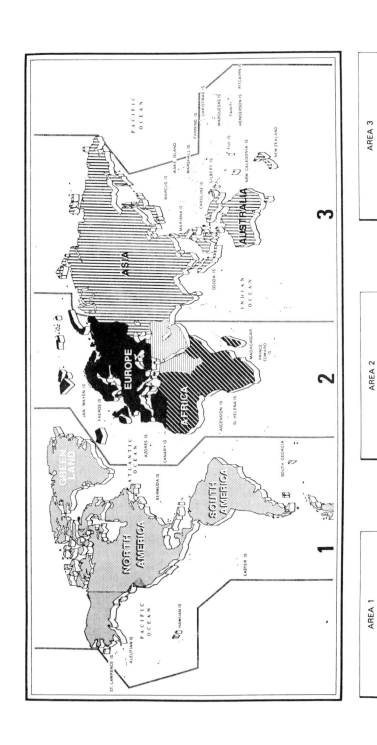

Figure 13:5   IATA areas

AREA 1

North, Central and South America and environs.

AREA 2

Europe   Middle East   Africa

AREA 3

Far East, Australia, New Zealand and Pacific Islands.

234

and ensuring that standards are maintained, as at present, through the cargo investigation panels and cargo registration and review boards. Secondly, in the area of tariff co-ordination activities, they will be responsible for the discussion of cargo rates and agency remuneration. Furthermore, to enable an airline to respond quickly to changes in the market, innovative rates may be introduced on routes between its home country and another country where it operates. Another important factor is that innovative rate filing cannot be vetoed.

Associated with these changes, the role of compliance is being reorientated away from the traditional punitive approach to a more realistic preventative one. This seeks to bring to an airline's attention any deviation from agreed rules and agreed standard practices, with a view to that company taking corrective action, not only in its own interests but also in the interest of maintaining a stable system around the world. Only when a serious malpractice is evident will IATA invoke previous compliance procedures. The response to the change has been most encouraging, with the majority of active members opting for continued participation in tariff co-ordination activities.

The airlines have developed an improved structure for working with the cargo agent. A joint IATA/FIATA Cargo Agency professional training programme has been developed and has proved to be an immense success.

Also a task force was set up to study the role of the cargo intermediary, e.g. freight forwarder. This has led to closer discussion in an effort to enhance the carrier/forwarder relationship and the future of the industry as a whole. As a result of regular meetings in the UK, British Airways has established a Cargo Consumer Council where agents and commercial companies meet with British Airways Cargo management.

In the area of cargo rates the advent of 747s and other wide-bodied aircraft, plus the rapid changes which took place during the 1970s, placed considerable pressure on carriers because shippers had access to more cargo space than ever before. As a result, new rating structures were introduced. Historically, world markets, oneway traffic flows and government controls have all contributed to a pot-pourri of rates. Many rates which could have been used for developing new cargoes by air were vetoed by smaller airlines, simply because they were not able to participate in the carriage themselves. This has now changed and innovative rates can be introduced under the new IATA structure by a carrier without fear of veto.

The air cargo tariff

Historically, air cargo rates were arbitrarily set in 1945 without a basis of real knowledge of the future technological growth of aircraft or of future airline costs. The first rate structure was based on taking a one-way passenger fare and dividing it by 100 to produce the basic kilo cost of cargo. A second level at 45+ kilos was given a 25 per cent rebate. Cargo was not important enough in the first post-war years to justify more than a limited interest to men rebuilding airlines from scratch. Aircraft were uneconomic adaptations of wartime forebears and it would have been surprising had anyone had any conception of the true costs of carrying cargo in the long-term.

On this unpromising tariff basis, cargo languished for several years. Its only virtue was its simplicity. Successive attempts to respond to introduction of new aircraft types with their increasing hold capacity for cargo produced a few more layers of tariff and a welter of rules and regulations to counter the anomalies arising yearly.

Within the airlines grew a new profession of tariff specialists, linked to a similar growth of people within IATA. The growth of airlines to their present size, with every developing country waving an airline flag, made universal agreement on any tariff matter an endless compromise.

Certainly, there will be a flow of air cargo at almost any rates due to the inability of manufacturers to meet delivery dates or emergency requirements. This is hardly the long-term base of business that airlines can rely on for their future well-being. It can be argued that the traffic on which one should base future revenue is the cargo which is economically planned for air movement. This requires a rate which is attractive to the user as a part of a rational distribution plan.

The current position is that the industry has inherited a massive tariff with thousands of different rates spread throughout the world, governed by the International Air Transport Association. Certain rates were introduced as and when necessary to meet the demands of potential regular shippers with substantial traffic. These rates were introduced with the blessing of IATA and are known as specific commodity rates.

There have been attempts to classify demand for air cargo and, broadly speaking, it was found that there were three main classifications:

1 *Immediate arrival date.* Goods such as ships' spares which are wanted immediately where price is not a significant factor; e.g. £500 spent on sending an urgent consignment to re-start a production line, to overcome penalty clauses or make a ship seaworthy, is insignificant in relation to the substantial losses incurred if that piece of equipment takes longer to reach its destination.

2 *Arrival date required in 4 days.* Into this category fall rush orders, e.g. to top up inventory when there has been an unexpected run on demand in the market place.

3 *Arrival date required within 5/14 days.* Into this category fall stock orders with a reasonable degree of urgency, generally with a higher degree of urgency than the surface modes of transportation can offer.

It was presumed that Category 1 traffic would continue to bear higher freight rates; Category 2 would bear a relatively high price, while Category 3 traffic appeared to have the largest potential for development, in other words, a growth market. It would allow the airlines some flexibility in that they could hold the traffic to a point in time when it is more convenient from their point of view to ship the goods, i.e. when the demand for capacity is at a lower point. It could also allow the airlines to be more flexible in the level of rate they desire.

The future

During the 1950s and 60s the air cargo industry developed at a substantial rate. Confident predictions were made that in the 1980s revenue from cargo would exceed revenue from passengers in many airlines. Since the early 1970s, with the Middle East oil crisis in 1973, the rate of growth has slowed. However, there is no need to paint too dark a picture as the airlines in their innovative way are looking at ways of improving their long-term viability. We have already discussed the development of the market in making sure that commercial companies are fully aware of the benefits offered by air cargo in terms of increased cash flow, market penetration, etc.

The airlines are also looking at other avenues of development; for example, the door-to-door concept of operation where goods are collected by the airline from the consignors in specific areas and transported by road to a nodal point, flying these goods the major part of the journey and again delivery by road for clearance on the consignee's premises. In other words, they will be developing a total transport concept by making a greater commitment to road transport. This is even more pertinent now that larger intermodal containers are carried on freighters by many of the larger airlines.

Moves are afoot to speed up documentation and communication through the inception of a communications system linking all airlines and agents, so that goods can be cleared before reaching their destination and can be located at any given time within the system on a worldwide basis.

Airlines have already diversified into the agency business to secure for themselves a greater share of the market and bring to bear a further influence on the market place. There are some airlines involved in air/sea operations in an attempt to offer the best of both worlds in terms of price and speed. These operations involve moving goods part of their journey by sea and the rest by air. The idea of using airships for the transportation of goods is now being looked at as a more serious possibility, particularly in view of the fuel problems now being experienced in most parts of the world.

One thing is certain: despite short-term economic setbacks, the airlines will continue to innovate and are steadily increasing their share of the world cargo market.

14

Choice of the transport mode

A. G. Slater

It is difficult for the Transport Manager to identify and quantify those factors which influence the selection of the transport requirements, particularly when transport costs may be traded-off against other component costs within the distribution system. When the requirements have been identified and defined, then these have to be matched with the characteristics offered by each transport mode, where many of the attributes may be difficult to measure and compare.

However, in the final analysis, if a company operates a profit maximisation philosophy, then every transport factor must be identified and defined in terms of cost. Subject to the basic constraints of customer service level requirements and labour preference, the choice of the transport mode should be a financial one either minimising the operating cost or maximising the after tax return upon capital.

In order to be able to identify the 'optimum' transport mode, it will be necessary to:

– identify the significance of the choice by determining the impact of transport on the distribution system,
– identify the factors which determine the choice of the transport mode,
– identify a method of choice,
– subsequent feedback that the choice is correct.

Further complications occur if the impact of potential changes are calculated, since the operating environment is dynamic and even the fundamental requirements of the transport mode may change over time, and it is then impossible to obtain the optimum transport mode for more than a short period.

The significance of the choice

In order to identify the significance of the choice of the transport mode, it is necessary to be able to determine the impact of transport upon the distribution system. This could be achieved by an analysis of existing transport cost, realisation of the profit leverage effect and analysis of the impact of transport upon the other elements of the distribution system.

Transport costs

Transport cost varies from 2 per cent (machinery) to 40 per cent (food) of the recommended selling price of products, depending upon the nature of the product range and its market. However, the average transport cost is between 5 per cent and 6 per cent of the recommended retail price of the product. The productivity boom of the early 1960s, when containerisation and mechanical handling devices were introduced, is now over, and the unit costs of transport are currently rising. Total road transport operating costs are increasing at a net annual figure of approximately 31 per cent with labour and maintenance charges showing the latest increases. Current trends are not likely to be easily curbed, although wage restraint may have brought the increase in operating costs down to below an increase of 25 per cent per annum. The majority of transport costs rise by a minimum of 12 per cent per annum and there seems to be an abundance of surcharges to further increase the total price.

Transport is a cost which tends to be rising more rapidly than most, and it is therefore important that the correct operational method is adopted in order to avoid incurring high costs unnecessarily.

Profit leverage

Transport represents a direct cost added to the price of the product and any reduction in transport costs would lead to an increase in profit (assuming that the price remains constant). The impact of reducing transport costs is shown by the profit leverage effect in two ways:

> Assuming that a company has a 10 per cent profit margin on sales turnover and prices do not change, then
> 1 A cost reduction in transport expense of   £100,000
>   is equivalent to an increase in sales turnover of   £1,000,000
> 2 If transport costs are estimated at 20 per cent of total costs, a 1 per cent reduction in total transport costs would give a 2 per cent increase in profits.

Distribution systems

Transport cannot be considered alone because it offers a service which moves product from one location to another and at each terminal, capital and labour facilities exist. Throughout the movement process, the product will need to be monitored with documentation in order that its approximate location is known.

Transport, therefore, is a process or system which transfers the product between two or more locations; and the form or forms of transport used must be compatible, not only with the terminal systems at both ends, but also the operating environment through which the movement takes place. Sufficient information should be generated to enable this movement to take place and enable the producer, customer, haulier, government agencies, financial institutions and other relevant groups to monitor the progress at all times.

Factors which affect the choice of the transport mode

There are numerous individual factors which determine the choice of the transport mode. However, these factors could be divided into three distinct groups:

1 *Operation factors* – covering the operating environment, the product, the company and its customers.
2 *Characteristics of each alternative mode of transport* – identifying the features of each alternative mode of transport.
3 *Channel situation* – covering the alternative approaches to the total distribution system.

Operational factors

The operational factors which have a bearing upon the transport mode include:

– national   ⎫
– international   ⎬ operating characteristics (see Figure 14:1)
                             ⎭
– characteristics of alternative transport modes (see Figure 14:2)

and combined together, these factors give rise to the potential customer service level and operating costs (see Figure 14:3).

Each operational factor should be considered in terms of its potential impact upon the transport operation, and the important factors clearly identified. Four important areas should be analysed (see Figure 14:4):

– Customer characteristics.
– Environmental characteristics.
– Product characteristics.
– Company characteristics.

The risk of change for each factor should also be considered over the maximum time span of any capital committed or likely to be committed, to provide or support the transport mode.

National	International
Bureaucratic system	National economic conditions
Operating infra-structure	(inflation, value of currency)
Legal system (control on movement	Taxation and export incentives (tax
and marketing)	advantages and grants)
Level of technology	Barriers to trade (import quotas, and
Local labour costs, availability, skills	customs duty)
and productivity	Export controls and licensing
Relative costs, availability and	Conditions of trade (penalty clauses)
quality of service support	Cultural system and national
requirements (particularly at the	practices
terminal facilities)	Development of communications
Availability of local capital, the	system
credit situation, and interest rates	Availability of international banking
	services

Figure 14:1   National and international operating characteristics

Characteristics of alternative transport modes

It is important to determine accurately the operating characteristics of each available transport mode, to establish whether it would suitably match the important operating factors. The important features are:

Useful load   – physical capability and maximum load as a percentage of gross weight

Density   – cargo density (weight per cubic unit)

Overheads   – fixed costs as a percentage of total cost (as an indicator or risk for price increases and support requirements)

Productivity   – Calculated in ton miles per direct man hour.

Figure 14:2 indicates these features for a specified variety of each transport mode. It is significant to note that:

–   the 12 ton lorry offers the highest useful load,
–   the cargo vessel offers the highest density,
–   the freight train has the highest overheads,
–   the cargo aircraft has the highest productivity.

Each mode of transport also has its own individual characteristics which affect the preparation of product before movement (e.g. packaging for sea freight must be more substantial than for air freight). These characteristics are particularly important when considering inter-continental traffic utilising more than one mode of transport.

Channel strategy

The choice of the transport mode is not merely a choice between one form or type of transport, but between a system or process of transportation between the

	Useful load	Density	Overheads	Productivity
	Maximum load as % of gross weight	Cargo density lb/cu. ft	Fixed costs as % of total costs	Ton miles per direct man hour
1 Cargo aircraft (32 tons)	48	11	22	8,250
2 Cargo vessel (1,500 ton displacement)	69	42	30	6,000
3 Freight train (wagon 12 tons)	64	30	34	5,200
4 Lorry (12 tons 3 axle)	73	23	4	420

Figure 14:2   Characteristics of various transport modes

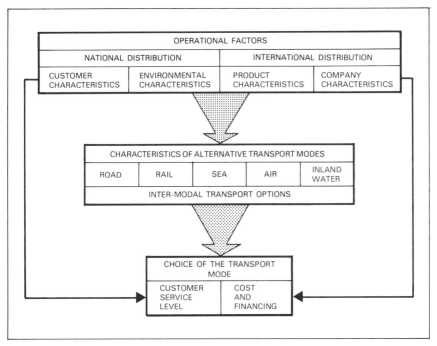

Figure 14:3   Operational factors which determine the transport mode

Customer characteristics	Environmental characteristics
Geographical situation/location	Infra-structure
Delivery point features	Distribution methods available/potential
Size of order (drop size ratio/annual turnover)	Law and taxation
Return loads	Availability of labour, capital and operational requirements
Product utility/service level requirement	Technology
Credit rating	Climatic conditions
Competitors' rating	
After sales service requirements	
Elasticity of demand/product alternatives	
Type of sale (FOB/CIF)	
Product knowledge	

Product characteristics	Company characteristics
Size/shape	Manufacturing locations
Weight	Warehouse locations
Value	Marketing centres
Fragile nature	Financial situation
Obsolescence/deterioration	Market dispersion and segmentation policy
Danger (toxic)	(Existing delivery system)

Figure 14:4   Operational factors affecting the choice of the transport mode

manufacturer or seller and the customer or buyer. This process involves separate sectors (e.g. production line to warehouse), material handling interfaces at each terminal facility and documentation which is processed to support the product.

The complete marketing channel must be defined and each sector where movement takes place clearly established (see Figure 14:5). Each sector should be analysed separately for transport requirements, in accordance with the terminal customer characteristics, the volume of product moved and the operating environment between the stages of the channel. Each sector of movement throughout the channel may require separate transport methods and it is important that all the operating characteristics for each sector are clearly identified (see Figure 14:6). The important factors to consider when analysing the transport requirements of each sector are:

1 *Control*
   – Ownership
     Security (documentation and product)
     Financial standing
     Information processing systems
2 *Product movement*
   – Mechanical handling interfaces
     Stock levels required at each terminal
     Packaging
     Safety (for product, capital and manpower)
3 *Marketing factors*
   – Variations in service level requirements
4 *Labour factors*
   – Training requirements turnover
5 *Risk factors*
   – Potential changes
     Inter-type competition
     Government influence
     Profit potential

The major influence upon the choice of the transport mode may be the ability of the transport concern to match or adapt the requirements of two parts of the marketing channel to maximise the use of the transport offered.

Specialisation of transport modes is created by the impact of channel costs which are incurred either before or after transportation – where the introduction of specialisation reduces the mechanical handling costs, packaging costs, etc., during the terminal function. Only rarely will specialisation of the transport mode be introduced purely to maximise the movement of transit costs.

Objective assessment

The objective by which the transport mode should be chosen depends upon whether the company is using revenue or capital to buy the transport. In the case of *revenue,*

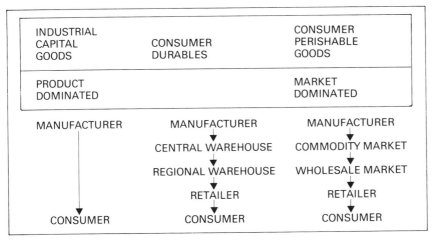

Figure 14:5   Type of channel

minimum cost throughout the transport process should be the objective, and in the case of *capital*, maximum after tax return upon capital should be the target; since both of these objectives give the shareholders maximum return.

In certain cases both capital and revenue expenditure will be included in the operation; under these circumstances, the combination of the minimum revenue expenditure and maximum after tax capital return could be calculated by determining the net cash flow after tax for the life of the capital asset. The criteria for choice will then become the maximum discounted return or minimum discount cost in terms of net cash flow, calculated with a discount rate equivalent to the cost of capital.

Although these criteria for assessment are relatively simple, complications could be added by identifying the need to calculate:

–   all revenue expenditure incurred by the utilisation of a particular transport mode (e.g. packaging)
–   all capital expenditure incurred by the utilisation of a particular transport mode (e.g. mechanical equipment at the terminals)
–   the risk associated with any capital asset with a life of over two years, where the asset may need to be modified to meet changing operating or environmental characteristics.

Even when a method of assessment has been determined, the degree to which calculations are taken becomes an important factor to ensure that a correct decision is made.

One basic rule is that any capital or revenue cost incurred, in order to operate a particular transport mode, should be taken into account in the calculation. Similarly, any significant risk incurred by capital assets which may be reasonably calculated should be accounted for in the financial calculations based upon the probability of occurrence.

CHANNEL	FACTORS	IMPORTANT OPERATING CHARACTERISTICS			
MANUFACTURER	(1) CONTROL	Ownership	Documentation (information processing)	Security (documentation product)	Credit worthiness
CENTRAL WAREHOUSE	(2) PRODUCT MOVEMENT	Mechanical handling interfaces	Variations in stock holding	Product marketing and packaging	Safety (product labour)
REGIONAL WAREHOUSE	(3) MARKETING	Variations in service level	Advertising and promotion policy		
RETAILER	(4) LABOUR RELATED	Labour training	Labour turn-over		
CUSTOMER	(5) RISK	Potential changes	Inter-type competition	Profit potential	Government influence

Figure 14:6   Characteristics of the marketing channel

A further rule is that where possible trade-off analysis should be used to assess the impact of each transport mode upon other functions in the business system; and to indicate the impact of changes upon the distribution system as a whole.

Method of selection

The selection procedure for the choice of the transport mode could vary from the simple decision either to identify one feasible method of distribution or to follow the competitors' procedures, to the complex decision which calculates every cost incurred and produces an optimum solution. There are four potential selection methods:

1 *Judgement.* Where the Transport Manager identifies the important factors affecting the transport problem, and identifies a transport mode from a short list of alternatives, which are considered to be available, in order that the most important features of the transport requirements are satisfied. The shortcomings of this particular selection method are numerous: factors other than transport matters are ignored, and transport is considered as a service rather than part of the distribution system; a complete list of alternative transport methods may not be considered; and costs are not important because the decision is made upon operational ability.

2 *Cost trade-off.* Where the impact of transport is calculated in relation to its immediate terminal activities and the total cost of the distribution system optimised. This approach acknowledges the existence of trade-offs within the numerous alternative approaches in an attempt to assess the situation to minimise total costs.

3 *Distribution models.* Which identify and explain the inter-relationships between the components of the distribution system at various levels of daily/weekly/ monthly demand. These models could be built to examine the impact of alternative transport modes and methods, as either the demand changes or the components in the system change. The models are a logical and mathematical attempt to simulate operating practice and conditions. The major shortfall of model building lies in the ability of the operations research analyst accurately to calculate the operational algorithm (mathematical inter-relationships) – otherwise errors will be compounded.

If the three methods are combined a *systematic* selection procedure could be identified using the best features of each system and eliminating all the shortfalls.

4 *Systematic selection.* Based upon analysis of all the factors affecting the transport problem with the selection of the most important. The calculations of effect of transport upon the distribution system leading to cost trade-off analysis to minimise the cost. Finally operations analysis to experiment with the planned system to validate the calculations and check that the inter-relationships with other areas have been calculated correctly.

Systematic selection

A systematic selection procedure to determine the transport mode would be based upon four inter-related stages (see Figure 14:7)

1 Environmental analysis – Identifying the characteristics within the operating environment
2 Channel strategy   – Identifying alternative channel selections and interfaces between each transport sector
3 Trade-off analysis   – Comparative and financial analysis of all potential alternatives
4 Operational analysis   – System operating test, validation of assumptions and continuous monitoring of results.

Each of these stages may also be sub-divided into separate stages with particularly defined questions.

Environmental analysis

1 Customer Characteristics – should be analysed to identify:

   – delivery point features, to determine the size and nature of the vehicles/ equipment to be used
   – size of order and annual turnover, to identify number and volume of trips annually
   – service level requirements, that is, the customers' expected order to receipt time
   – type of sale required for international transactions
   – after sales service requirements
   – seasonal trends in sales by product.

   This analysis should aim to give sufficient idea of the total annual sales volumes, any seasonal trend in sales and the delivery service expected by the customer. This should now be compared with customers requirements from competitors to identify any significant differences together with the reasons for these variations.

2 Environmental Characteristics – should be analysed to identify:

   – distribution features in the infra-structure
   – law and taxation of the countries in which operations take place
   – climatic conditions.

   This analysis will aim to determine the major opportunities and constraints within the operating environment.

3 Product Characteristics – should be analysed to identify the particularly important distribution features of each product.

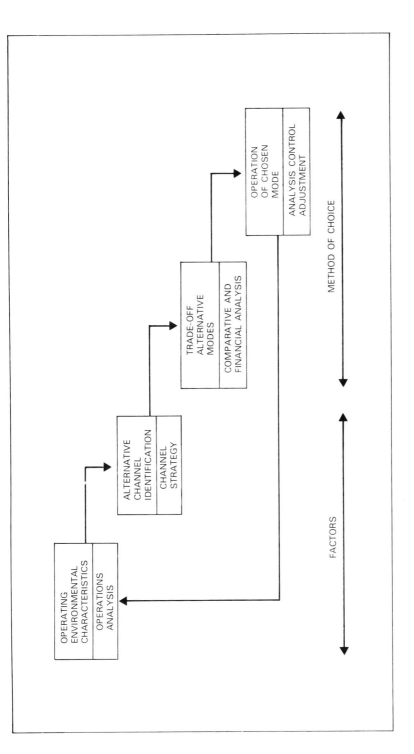

Figure 14:7   Choice of the transport mode

249

4   Company Characteristics – should be analysed to identify:
     - potential manufacturing locations of each product
     - potential warehouse locations for each product
     - location of marketing centres
     - target customer service level and important distribution features in the company marketing policy
     - analysis of any existing delivery system.

This analysis should give a clear situation of the existing facilities to meet the marketing requirements and any shortfalls or potential failures should be highlighted.

From this type of environmental analysis, it should be possible to match the customer's requirements with the constraints imposed by the environment, the product and the company's existing operating system. Opportunities, vulnerabilities and problems should be highlighted in order that they may be exploited and solved in the process of selecting the transport mode.

Channel strategy

From a combination of the customer characteristics and existing company operations, it should be possible to identify the existing marketing channel and any proposed alteration. From an analysis of the marketing channel each transport segment could be identified (i.e. each stage between terminal activities) and a definition made of the annual volumes through each segment, together with the terminal facilities at the ends of each segment.

The product characteristics and environmental characteristics could now be matched to each sector. In this way a profile is built up of the transport requirements for each sector of the marketing channel giving:

-    volume (annual throughput)
-    service level required
-    length of sector, environmental characteristics
-    products carried
-    terminal facilities available.

It is now possible to match the available transport modes to the profile of the requirements identified for each sector.

Trade-off analysis

The next stage of the selection procedure is to identify each transport mode available for each sector of the marketing channel (see Figures 14:8 and 14:9). The problem then becomes one of choosing that mode of transport which meets the profile required for each sector of the marketing channel for the lowest cost in the case of revenue expenditure or the highest after tax return upon capital employed in the case of capital expenditure.

The main opportunities for trade-off are between various capital and labour options which fall into three categories (see Figure 14:10):

1   Volume of capital to quantity of labour input – e.g. the question of whether mechanical handling devices are used to move the product from one place to another or whether labour is used.
2   Capital type or labour type options – e.g. whether a particular make of vehicle is bought or whether the transport fleet is operated from the source of supply or market place, depending upon the characteristics of the labour market.
3   Source of finance or source of labour options (see Figure 14:11), e.g. whether to use hired transport, leased transport or to buy vehicles and whether to hire labour from third parties or use company payroll employees.

These combinations of options only begin to introduce the complexity of choosing the transport mode because each category of trade-off could also be considered for various types of trade-off. The types of trade-off are defined by the effect they have upon other functions within the marketing channel. There are three types of trade-off to consider: horizontal, vertical and lateral (see Figure 14:12):

1   *Horizontal trade-offs* occur between various transport modes or types to undertake the same task (e.g. air or sea freight comparisons).
2   *Vertical trade-offs* occur between independent elements of the distribution system (e.g. whether to use full pallet loads of product in a transport container rather than loose boxes, to gain mechanical handling advantages at each terminal facility).
3   *Lateral trade-offs* occur where a third party will incur additional costs to reduce the total costs of the distribution channel (e.g. the manufacturer of whisky bottles dispatches the bottles to the distillery in the same carton as they leave the distillery, thereby eliminating additional packaging costs in the distillery; even though empty bottles could be packaged cheaper, the cartons would not be suitable when the bottles were full).

After various options have been considered and costs established, the cheapest option meeting the profile of requirements will be selected

Operations analysis

After the initial selection, it may be necessary to produce a physical test situation to ensure that the costs are adequate and close to those stated in the analysis. Once the system is fully operational, it is essential to monitor the progress, to compare it with the forecast results and determine whether there are any significant changes in a month-to-month basis. This could be achieved by a monthly analysis of the operating costs, calculating trends, comparative data and significant ratios (see Figure 14:13). Any significant deviation should either be explained by changes in the customer, environmental or product characteristics (identified by the ratios); otherwise the transport operation will be responsible. Once the fault has been identified, then a decision should be made to correct the fault or reconsider the choice of the transport mode.

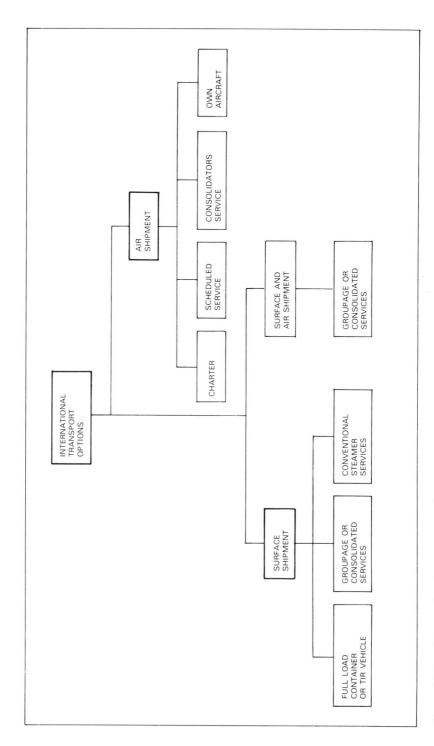

Figure 14:8   International transport options

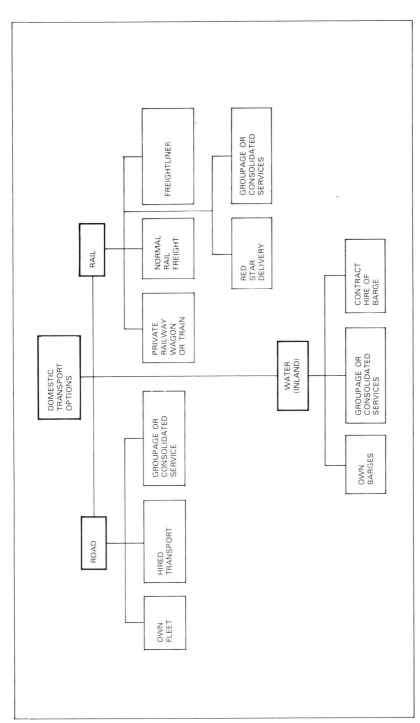

Figure 14:9   Domestic transport options

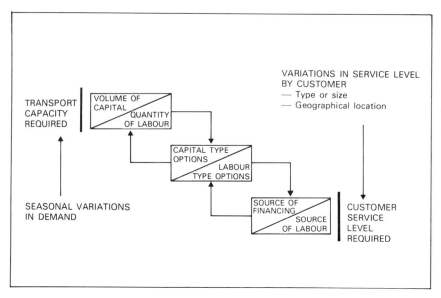

Figure 14:10   The main cost trade-off options

Capital					
Bought		Leased		Hired	
Bought Capital Internal Labour	Bought Capital Hired Labour	Leased Capital Internal Labour	Leased Capital Hired Labour	Hired Capital Internal Labour	Hired Capital Hired Labour
Internal				Hired	
Labour					

Figure 14:11   Alternative sources of finance and labour

A significant part of the operational analysis may be to test alternative operations, and this is particularly useful if considerable seasonal variations occur or a company considers that there is a risk in operating their own fleet. Under these circumstances, it is possible to use company owned transport for the majority of the demand and hired/contract transport to meet seasonal demands or unusual transport requirements. The difficulty in this type of policy, is to determine how much should be company operations and how much hired. It could safely be assumed that company operations should cover the minimum demand levels and hired or contract operations should cover all above minimum, so that maximum use is made of company owned capital. However, it should be remembered that in the event of utilising a specialised fleet of company owned vehicles, it is impossible to hire and

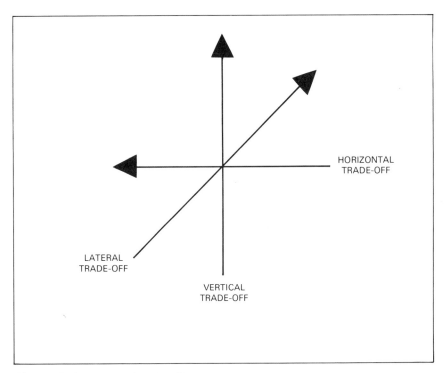

Figure 14:12   Types of trade-off

extremely difficult to change the operating mode; and in these cases, it may be necessary to capitalise up to maximum demand or just below and accept a slight deterioration in service level at peak times.

Financial analysis

The important feature of the whole selection process is the financial analysis at the comparative analysis and trade-off stage. The financial analysis may be undertaken at one of three levels:

1   Simple freight cost or transport cost comparison – suitable for inter-type trade-off (e.g. one make of vehicle compared with another of similar characteristics).

2   Detailed cost comparison – including all the direct costs associated with that mode of transport. For example, for a sea and air freight comparison, then the following direct costs would need to be determined for each mode: packaging costs, transport costs to and from the port, trans-shipment costs, dock dues and taxes, insurance costs and customs duties.

Distribution costs   Business:

Transport   Period:

Trends   £000's

Actual this period	Operating costs		Previous year	Moving annual totals to P(−8)	P(−4)	This period
	Wages and expenses	(1)				
	Fuel and oil costs	(2)				
	Depreciation	(3)				
	Maintenance costs	(4)				
	Insurance costs	(5)				
	Warehousing costs	(6)				
	Administrative overhead	(7)				
	Total cost	(8)				

Comparative data		This period	Previous year	Year to date	Same period last year
(9) Number of vehicles	Number				
(10) Total vehicle capacity	Tons				
(11) Total working days available	Days				
(12) Total working days lost	Days				
(13) Total delivery cap available	Tons				
(14) Total tonnage delivered	Tons				
(15) Total number of journeys	Number				
(16) Total miles clocked	Miles				
(17) Total number of drops	Number				
(18) Total hours worked (clocked)	Hours				
(19) Overtime hours worked	Hours				
(20) Number of employees	Number				
(21) Value of goods delivered	£000s				

£

Costs	This period	Year to date		Ratios	This period	Year to date
Total costs:				(31) Miles per drop		
(22) – to deliveries				(32) Weight per drop (tons)		
(23) – per employee				(33) Miles per journey		
Transport costs:				(34) Miles per day		
(24) – per drop				(35) Weight per journey (tons)		
(25) – per journey						
(26) – per mile				(36) Deliveries per day (£)		
(27) – per ton				(37) Deliveries per journey (£)		
Administrative cost:						
(28) – per journey						
(29) – per ton				(38) % Load capacity		
Warehouse cost:				(39) % Vehicle days lost		
(30) – per ton				(40) % Overtime worked		

Figure 14:13   Monthly operating costs analysis

3   Complex cost comparison – including both direct and indirect costs, the latter sometimes being significant where the transit time is significant. Thus for a sea and air freight comparison, the following indirect costs may be considered: administrative costs, depreciation on capital, sales lost through transit time and any penalty clause costs incurred.

The financial analysis of each alternative mode of transport is not easy because of the complexity of determining how deep to undertake the analysis and which factors to include in the comparison. Sometimes even having determined a factor which should be considered, it is not always easy to calculate an appropriate figure; this is particularly true for indirect costs, e.g. sales lost figures.

Improving the choice over time

Throughout the life of any capital assets, there will be a number of changes and it is important to monitor these changes in order to adapt the choice of the transport mode to the new circumstances, or change the transport mode if necessary. The main areas which should be monitored include:

technology	–	particularly of transport and mechanical handling systems, in order to change or adapt quickly if cheaper or better alternatives appear
environment	–	the operating environment should be continually monitored to ensure that the system does not infringe laws and maximises upon all available opportunities
volumes carried	–	particularly if they are moving up or down dramatically, to ensure that the correct volume of capital is being utilised
competitors	–	to ensure that the correct customer service level is being maintained.

It should be remembered that once the choice of the transport mode is made, it is not a simple procedure to change, particularly if a large quantity of capital is employed in vehicles and mechanical handling equipment.

Conclusion

The choice of the transport mode is a complex decision involving many factors and one which offers many opportunities. The final selection will depend upon management's skill to determine and quantify the significant options available; and this will be achieved only by a thorough and systematic approach to the problem.

As prices rise and transport becomes identified as a significant cost, then there will be pressure upon management to improve both the method of selection of the transport mode and justify that selection in a rational and defined manner.

15

Load planning

A. G. Slater

Load planning is a method or technique used to match existing customer orders with vehicles and available manpower, by the generation of routes or schedules for vehicles. The efficiency of these routes or schedules determines the operating cost for the transport fleet and the potential customer service level offered by the company.

It is possible that efficient vehicle load planning may minimise the variable operating costs by providing a minimum total mileage, and a maximum operating time, for the minimum number of vehicles on the road. On a cumulative basis, the limitation of the total daily number of vehicles on the road may lead to a reduction in the total fleet strength and thereby reduce the fixed operating costs incurred, particularly depreciation, manpower, insurance and road tax.

If the total transport costs are analysed, it becomes apparent that route planning has a direct effect upon many costs. The significant effect, however, is upon the main cost-centres in a transport operation; particularly fuel, labour costs, routine maintenance and vehicle depreciation. It is possible that even small changes in the load planning methods or operating practices may lead to significant changes in the total transport costs, particularly if fixed costs may be reduced in response to improved load planning techniques.

The load planning problem

The load planning problem could be defined as one of determining the routes and schedules on a day-to-day basis for a number of vehicles from one or more depots to supply customers orders to an acceptable customer service level, and at an acceptable cost to the company.

To solve this problem it is assumed that:

1   The vehicles have a limited physical capacity which cannot be exceeded by the sum of orders to be delivered.
2   The length of any one vehicle route, or combination of routes for the one vehicle, must be low enough to supply all the customers on the route within a specified legal working day for the driver or combination of drivers employed. A vehicle may be allocated schedules for two or more days, but legal requirements for the driver's working day must be considered.
3   All deliveries could feasibly be possible within each customer's earliest and latest delivery time.
4   The vehicle will be physically capable of executing the delivery in an economic manner and one which is acceptable to both the driver and customer.
5   All back loads are scheduled so that the physical capacity of the vehicle cannot be exceeded, and in a manner which allows the driver to work the load.
6   All route restrictions are taken into consideration.

Many factors and constraints need to be considered when undertaking a load planning exercise; the main ones are listed in Figure 15:1 and fall broadly under the six headings of:

- Manpower characteristics
- Vehicle characteristics
- Customer characteristics
- Company characteristics
- Environment characteristics
- Routing and scheduling methods

The important objectives of load planning are customer service, minimum cost and efficient operation. The way in which all these operational factors combine to direct and constrain the load planning routine is shown in Figure 15:2.

To achieve the objective it is possible to consider a number of potential aims for the load planning system:

- High customer service level
- Minimum mileage to minimise variable costs
- Minimum vehicles to minimise fixed costs

Any combination of these is also feasible, however, in the final analysis, load planners generally fail to achieve any of these aims, but settle upon what amounts to an acceptable distribution of orders amongst the available fleet which is likely to be successfully delivered by the drivers concerned. This human consideration of knowing what resources are available, together with what it is possible to achieve, finally results in the aim being a load plan which is marginally acceptable. The failures of the operating system are recognised by management, but accepted because it is difficult to generate substantial improvements without extensive effort or considerable business risk.

Manpower characteristics

Number of men
Type of licence held
Training level
Union operating restrictions
   (driving speeds)
Hours of work
Shift pattern
Rota pattern (job allocation)

Vehicle characteristics

Number of vehicles
Type of vehicle (mix in fleet)
Maintenance/repair
   requirements
Carrying capacity (weight/cube)
Height/width

Customer characteristics

Order pattern
Locations (in relation to depot)
Delivery point features
Opening/closing times
   (for deliveries/collections)
Day/night delivery
Return load availability

Company characteristics

Customer service policy
Running speed and operating
   policy
Vehicle load capacity policy
Product characteristics
Depot locations
Return load policy
Management operation target
   levels

**Environmental
characteristics**

Road pattern/road works
Weather, climate conditions
Legal restrictions

Routing and scheduling

Technique adopted
Legal requirements

Figure 15:1   Operating factors affecting load planning

Development of load planning

Load planning may develop from some very simple beginnings to a complex process including computer applications (see Figure 15:3). Each development has its particular advantages and disadvantages.

Initial load planning for a small fleet has often been carried out by the Transport Foreman or Supervisor, who planned the day's work for each driver drawing on his understanding of the driver's capability and knowledge. When the task became large enough for one or more people to be employed full time on load planning, then traditionally, ex-drivers were employed. Their loads would be based upon delivery experience in the area and would result in what they considered to be a fair day's work for each individual, often calculated by set speed and number of calls per hour. Although the routing would be excellent, giving minimum mileage and

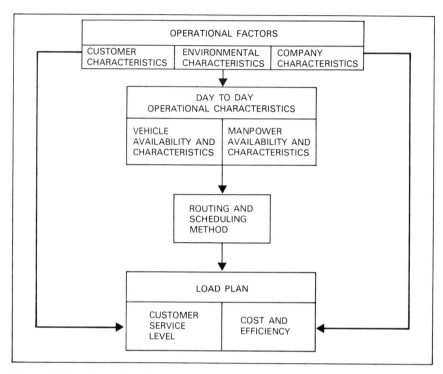

Figure 15:2   Operating factors which determine load planning

maximum probability of delivery or collection, the vehicle would not be loaded to maximum capacity and the driver's time would not be fully occupied. This identifies the first operational problem of being able to maximise the load and the driver's time, together with a minimum mileage and a high probability of achieving delivery.

To solve the operational problem and achieve a result closer to the optimum, new Organisation and Methods techniques were devised, leading to a potential for using general clerical effort to implement the manual O and M techniques. The clerical or mathematical approach to load planning improves utilisation of vehicle capacity and driver's time. It is possible that an industrial relations problem is generated because the scheduling emphasis is based upon a mathematical approach to achieving set targets for vehicle utilisation, rather than a knowledge of the geographical area and the customer's individual needs.

When the emphasis upon load building, in terms of the vehicle capacity and driver's time, grew to a system of routine calculations it was determined that this analysis could be performed by a computer. Standard 'packages' have been developed to take away the routine clerical calculation effort, but these leave a load planning solution which has excellent vehicle and driver utilisation but poor routes. The industrial relations problem is likely to increase, as drivers are presented with machine calculations and poor routes. It is extremely difficult to cater for individual

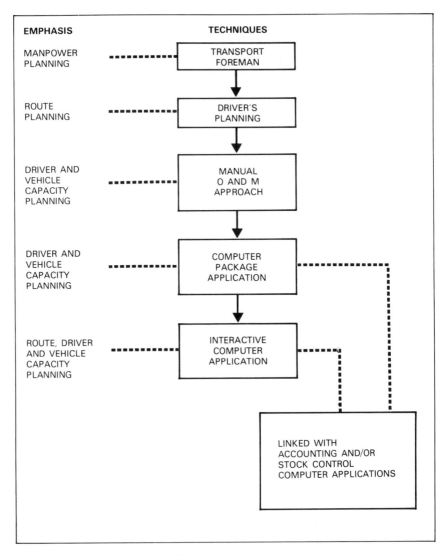

Figure 15:3   Development of load planning

customer needs, and customer service may suffer.

To improve the routing, interactive computer scheduling has been developed with a generation of mini- and microcomputers. Interactive scheduling is that in which the load planner/or scheduler is able to change parameters in the calculation routine and build in any necessary constraints or changes as the scheduling process is being undertaken. The scheduler's knowledge of the area is combined with the computer's ability to calculate rapidly, producing planned loads to variable parameters, which are normally acceptable to both drivers and management.

Alternative load planning methods

The alternative methods of load planning operated on a day-to-day basis may be largely determined by the customer demand pattern and the customer service level objectives established by the company. Two basic categories of load planning occur:

1 Fixed routes.
2 Variable routes.

The *fixed route* system is one in which vehicles have a regular delivery route for each day, and customer orders are matched to those routes. Fixed routes can limit the delivery areas to particular days of the week but give a high level of customer service because the customer knows which day, and often what time, the vehicle will arrive. This system, however, may not be particularly efficient because the vehicles will not be filled to capacity or, conversely, orders may exceed the vehicle capacity and be left until the next trip; moreover, the real-life last-minute changes of urgent orders, drivers sick or vehicle breakdowns undermine the complete system, particularly if sufficient vehicles or drivers are not available.

The *variable route* system is an attempt to generate routes to meet the customer order pattern, and has the advantage of being able to change with fluctuations in day-to-day demand. The main advantages of variable routes are that vehicle capacity and drivers time may be utilised efficiently, and that the number of vehicles on the road each day will be limited to the orders taken; therefore total mileage and variable operating costs will be minimised. The major disadvantage is that the customer may not know the day or time of delivery, particularly if total orders exceed the fleet carrying capacity and an order back-log is generated.

In some cases it is possible to mix these two methods by having *variable* routes in *fixed* geographical areas, thereby gaining the advantages of both systems.

Construction of a load plan

A vehicle load is constructed by assuming that:

1 vehicle capacity is limited (cube and weight);
2 the driver's time is limited;
3 each order has a location for which there is an established driving time to and from the depot or to the next customer;
4 each order has a specific quantity of goods for which there is an established time to deliver/collect at the customer's premises.

An individual vehicle load is calculated by taking one order and:

– establishing the time from the depot to the customer;
– adding the time taken to deliver at the customer's premises;
– checking that the total time available to the driver is not exceeded;
– checking that the vehicle is not over capacity . . .

... then adding the next order in geographical proximity and:

- establishing the time taken from the first customer;
- adding the time taken to deliver at the customer's premises;
- checking that the total time available to the driver is not exceeded;
- checking that the vehicle is not over capacity.

This procedure continues until one of the restrictions is nearly reached, then efforts are made to add a final order which completes the available driver's time or fully loads the vehicle. The planning procedure is followed until either all orders are allocated or all available vehicles are fully loaded.

If a vehicle is full to its weight capacity, the load planner has the additional problem of determining whether the vehicle could be loaded within the axle weight limits and should provide a loading diagram which achieves an effective distribution of the load.

Three types of route are normally generated (see Figure 15:4) these are:

1   *Arc* or *circumferential* routes, which link customers in an arc shape at various distances from the depot.
2   *Area* routes, which link customers in concentrated areas.
3   *Radial* routes, which link customers along radial patterns to and from the depot.

The type of route generated will depend upon a number of factors:

- the technique used to build up the schedule;
- the geographical characteristics of the area and route patterns;
- the size of product orders in relation to the vehicle capacity.

Each type of route has different characteristics, the most important being that *arc* routes generate high mileages because the distance between the depot and the first and last calls is significantly higher than in the other two types of routes.

The construction of loads should also take into account the possibility of undertaking multi-trips or overnight trips. These are used when loads are constructed which have reached either the physical vehicle capacity or driver's time constraints without fully utilising the other constraint. Thus a load with a physical capacity constraint may form the basis of a multi-trip because a second load could be computed to complete the driver's available time. Similarly a load which completes the driver's time but does not fully utilise the capacity constraint may have additional orders added to meet the capacity constraint and the driver may be allocated two or more working days to complete the delivery.

Theoretical approaches

Load planning is considered by operations research scientists to be a 'quantitative problem' which has an optimum solution depending upon the specific aim and weighting given to each influencing factor. There are a number of theoretical

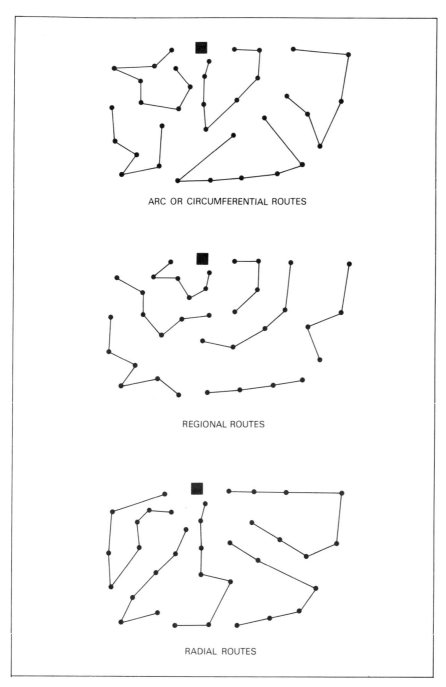

ARC OR CIRCUMFERENTIAL ROUTES

REGIONAL ROUTES

RADIAL ROUTES

Figure 15:4 Types of route

approaches which may form the basis for manual or computer load planning methods.[1]

Savings method

The *savings method* first introduced by Clarke and Wright[2] in 1963 is the best known method of vehicle routing and forms the basis of both manual and computer load planning systems. The savings method is best described by a simple example (see Figure 15:5). Assume two delivery points A and B are serviced from the depot O and the distances between OA and OB and AB are *a*, *b* and *x* respectively; then if we assume that two vehicles cover the delivery points A and B so that one vehicle goes to each customer, then the total distance covered is $2a + 2b$. If, however, only one delivery vehicle is used then the round trip is made linking A and B together, and the total distance covered is $a + b + x$. The saving achieved by linking A and B together is $(2a + 2b) - (a + b + x) = a + b - x$. More generally the savings formula is related as:

$$S_{ij} = d_{oi} + d_{oj} - d_{ij}$$

where: S_{ij} = distance saving by linking together any two delivery points *i* and *j*
              d_{oi} = distance between depot O and delivery point *i*
              d_{oj} = distance between depot O and delivery point *j*
              d_{ij} = distance between the two delivery points *i* and *j*

For problems larger than two depots, it is necessary to generate a 'savings matrix' based upon a distance matrix which relates the distances between all customers, each customer and the depot. The first link which is selected is the one which offers the highest saving (shown on the savings matrix) given two orders. The sum of these orders is tested to determine whether they meet the vehicle capacity and driver's time constraints; if not further orders are obtained. Additional orders are added to the initial pair by selection of the next highest saving (shown on the savings matrix) linking another customer with one of the two already selected, assuming that when the additional customer is added the vehicle capacity and driver's time constraints are not reached (see example Figure 15:6). The process continues until all the customers orders are scheduled or all the vehicles are fully utilised.

There are some notable features of the savings method:

1   The savings from linking two customers together will not be negative (if straight line distance calculations are used).
2   The savings property is additive, that is, the savings achieved by linking a third customer are added to the savings of the first two customers.
3   The closer together the customers, and the further away from the depot customers become, the greater the savings achieved by linking customers.
4   *Arc* type routes will provide greater savings than other types, but total mileage may be higher than *area* or *radial* routes because the start and finish points may be further from the depot.

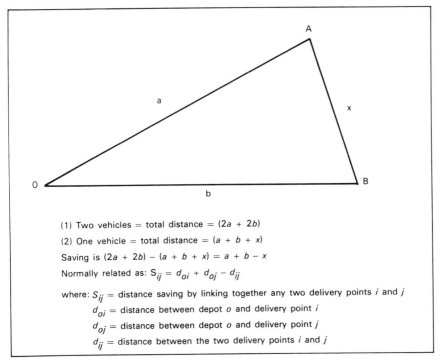

(1) Two vehicles = total distance = $(2a + 2b)$

(2) One vehicle = total distance = $(a + b + x)$

Saving is $(2a + 2b) - (a + b + x) = a + b - x$

Normally related as: $S_{ij} = d_{oi} + d_{oj} - d_{ij}$

where: S_{ij} = distance saving by linking together any two delivery points i and j

d_{oi} = distance between depot o and delivery point i

d_{oj} = distance between depot o and delivery point j

d_{ij} = distance between the two delivery points i and j

Figure 15:5   The savings method

5   If the total demand (the sum of the orders) is greater than the maximum fleet capacity, then some deliveries will be multi-trip (see Figure 15:6) particularly those near the depot. Sometimes both total vehicle capacity and driver's time are overloaded, in which case orders will be unallocated, but affected orders will be those in close proximity to the depot.

6   It is extremely difficult to plan both deliveries and collections (unless these are made at the same point on a full-for-empty basis) because the method works on distance NOT order category.

7   The method could be based upon time rather than distance, which is particularly useful if there are variable driving speeds for different categories of road.

8   The total number of vehicles required is calculated and it is not possible to limit the total vehicles available. If the method produces a requirement for more vehicles than are available, orders have to be taken off (producing a back-log) to provide a solution.

3–Optimal method

The major limitation of the savings method is that the number of vehicles needed for the final solution is beyond the parameters of that method, and it may be necessary to

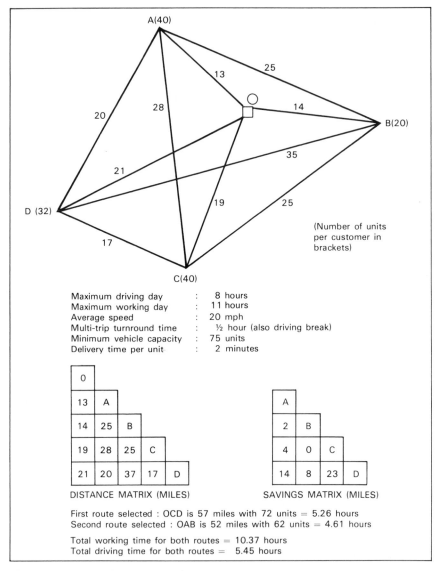

Maximum driving day   :   8 hours
Maximum working day   :   11 hours
Average speed   :   20 mph
Multi-trip turnround time   :   ½ hour (also driving break)
Minimum vehicle capacity   :   75 units
Delivery time per unit   :   2 minutes

0
13	A
14	25	B
19	28	25	C
21	20	37	17	D

DISTANCE MATRIX (MILES)

A
2	B
4	0	C
14	8	23	D

SAVINGS MATRIX (MILES)

First route selected : OCD is 57 miles with 72 units = 5.26 hours
Second route selected : OAB is 52 miles with 62 units = 4.61 hours

Total working time for both routes = 10.37 hours
Total driving time for both routes = 5.45 hours

Figure 15:6   Calculations: savings method

establish routes for a limited number of vehicles. In 1969 N. Christofides[3] developed the *3–Optimal* method of route planning to solve this problem.

The method is based upon the principle that the established route configuration is optimal and any attempt to replace any of the links will generate a sub-optimal situation. The method starts by randomly selecting a route, then systematically analysing each route by determining whether any 3 links could be removed and replaced by another 3 to obtain a more effective solution. If so the new links are substituted and the process continued until the optimal solution determined.

It is possible to minimise the total mileage by adopting the 3–Optimal method since *area* routes are generally produced. It is also possible to solve the 3–Optimal method for limited numbers of vehicles, because orders are analysed to meet vehicle or driver's time constraints. The significant drawback, however, is that the method is essentially heuristic and cannot be operated without computer assistance.

Operations research methods

A number of complex OR techniques have been developed which achieve marginal improvements over the savings method or 3–Optimal method. These include a generalised savings model developed by Mole and Jameson[4] in 1976 and a method known as a heuristic tree search algorithm which combines a number of calculation methods to determine the optimum solution.[5] All complex OR techniques require computer assistance and the calculation principles may not easily be understood by distribution managers or load planners, which substantially limits their value.

Operational methods

Current load planning practices include a number of both manual and computer based systems, which are refined by individual companies to meet the needs of individual depot management.

Manual methods

Two basic manual load planning techniques are noteworthy: firstly, 'SDS' or Simplified Delivery Service and, secondly, 'TRANSIT' or Timebased Routing and Scheduling of Industrial Transport; TRANSIT has been slightly modified into a third system known as 'BOX'.

SDS – Simplified Delivery System. The SDS load planning system is based upon dividing the geographical territory to be covered by a depot into sub-areas, each of which are numbered with a two character code – one alpha and one numeric. The alpha codes follow the main routes, normally radiating away from the depot, and the numeric codes provide convenient sizes of sub-areas arranged by the geographical features (e.g., hills) or by a potential cluster of customers. Each customer is referred to by its SDS sub-area code. The load planner works from an array of pigeon holes, one for each sub-area, into which the orders are initially placed – loads are built up starting at the most remote sub-area and working into the depot following the established alpha patterns. Only when close to the depot does the load planner cross alpha boundaries and mix loads with different alpha characters (Figure 15:7).

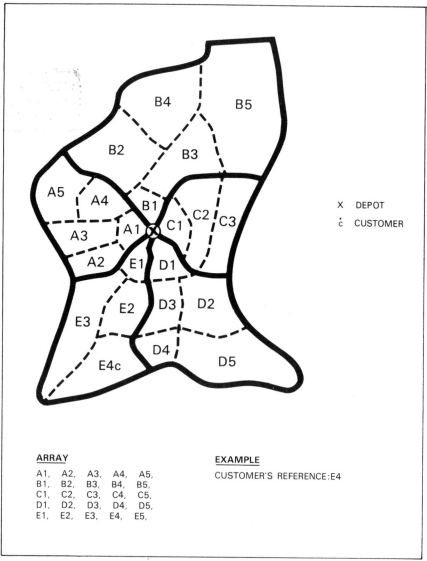

Figure 15:7   SDS – Simplified Delivery Service

The original system does not include driving times to/from the sub-area or within each area, but sometimes these are added. The main advantage of SDS is that it is possible to accurately reflect geographical features (e.g. canals) which produces excellent routes which are acceptable to both management and drivers. The whole system depends upon what is the locally accepted concept of 'a fair day's work', and relies heavily on the load planner allocating work load evenly amongst the available vehicles.

TRANSIT – Timebased Routing and Scheduling of Industrial Transport.
TRANSIT is also based upon a map, but the delivery area is broken down into 10-kilometre squares (taken from the National Grid System). Each customer's location is given an accurate grid reference; and each 10-kilometre square is allocated a driving time from the depot and a driving time within that square (see Figure 15:8). The load planner then undertakes a systematic process:

- Sorts orders in the 10-kilometre pigeon holes.
- Identifies the most remote 10-kilometre square from the depot.
- Re-sorts all those orders into a 10 x 10 matrix (so sub-dividing into 1-kilometre squares).
- Starts to build up a load from the furthest 1-kilometre square.
- As the orders are selected the total time is calculated, by starting with the driving time to the 10-kilometre square, adding the call time, time to off-load/re-load, and the driving time to the next customer. A similar cumulative check is made on the vehicle carrying capacity.
- The load planner moves from one 10-kilometre square to the next about the depot axis.

Box scheduling uses exactly the same process, but relies upon 5-kilometre squares instead of 10, and eliminates the need for re-sorting the orders into 1-kilometre squares.

The main advantage of TRANSIT/Box methods is that timings are good and vehicles are allocated a full day's work. The routes produced, however, are not as good as with SDS and often show peculiar patterns unless certain boundary constraints are created to develop a pattern similar to the SDS sub-areas.

In general, manual methods work adequately and are accepted by the drivers. This acceptance, however, is all too often because the load planner bends the rules to match the loads with the drivers, favouring certain drivers for certain light loads and others with heavy loads – realistically there is no sense in a load planner generating a load for a driver whom he knows is incapable or unwilling to complete the deliveries; the object is to achieve delivery or collection.

The major failing of manual methods is that they are not by nature 'efficient'. The load planner is working under pressure when compiling the loads and is bound by human nature to make the task as easy as possible, leading to a tendency to plan the loads to the available vehicles. In one experiment, a normal day's loads were generated by the load planner working in normal conditions, requiring 27 vehicles; the next week exactly the same orders were re-scheduled by the load planners in less time, in an experimental atmosphere of no pressure and 24 vehicles were required – an 11 per cent improvement. Further experiments indicated that manual load planning may vary enormously, not only from load planner to load planner, but even an individual will produce a wide variety of performances from day to day.

The main advantage of manual methods is that management and drivers may easily check to determine whether the load planner has produced a reasonable load which may be achieved within the working day. Although it takes a long time, it is practical to change loads in the event of vehicle failure, drivers sick or the late arrival of an urgent order.

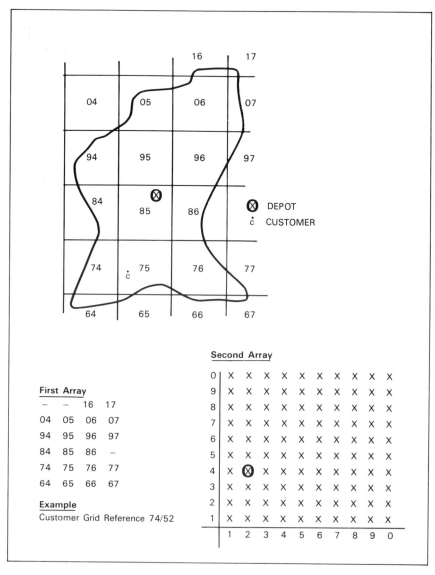

Figure 15:8   TRANSIT – Timebased Routing and Scheduling of Industrial Transport

Computer methods

The combination of 'manual' and 'theoretical' load planning models has led to the development of a number of computer-based load planning systems. There are two forms of system available: the general 'package' program often tailored for a particular customer, and the special purpose-built and developed load planning system for an individual company requirement.

The majority of computer manufacturers and large computer businesses offer standard packages; for example IBM's 'VSPX', Scicon offer BRSL 'PATHFINDER' and a new inter-active system called 'VAN-PLAN'. As a result of the operations research interest, Imperial College, London University, offer a system called 'VERSA', and Wren and Holliday[6] at Leeds University have developed a package called 'TRAVELLER' which uses a facility of scheduling orders from more than one depot. All these systems are highly technical, relying upon a large amount of data input and complex algorithms. (See Figure 15:9 for characteristics offered by computer load planning packages.)

In order to match other computer based business systems (e.g. sales forecasting, stock control, invoicing, or order entry), some companies have developed computer based load planning as part of other systems. The majority of these systems often rely heavily upon crude calculation ratios and planning data and, therefore, may produce a relatively inefficient result. Some individual systems, however, are capable of matching both computer packages and manual systems, particularly those which are developed to reflect the advantages of the manual systems. Some of these individual systems have developed to the stage where the load planner may interface with the machine (known as inter-active) to change parameters as necessary and build up loads on a load by load pattern.

The main advantages of computer load planning are:

- Speed of calculations.
- Accuracy of calculations (which if based upon a manual system represent the load planner's 'best effort' each time).
- Potential to interface with other computer based systems (e.g. invoicing, stock control).

The main disadvantages of computer applications are:

- Original hardware based upon mainframe applications give a slow turnround and the costs are high – this may have been changed with the advent of the mini- and microcomputer.
- The practical aspect of computer systems was that management found it difficult to re-apply when last minute orders needed scheduling, vehicles broke down or drivers were absent.
- Early computer systems were based upon a map which calculated distance in straight lines. This has now been revised[7] but it is difficult to build into the file structure physical boundaries over which routes should not be constructed.

	Company	Product	Program Characteristics						
			Variable road speeds	Alternative vehicle types	Access constraints	Collections and deliveries	Delivery restrictions	Maintenance scheduling	Monitoring costs
1.	ANALYTICAL SYSTEMS	ROUTEMASTER	*	*	*	*	*		
2.	DIPS	DIPS	*	*	*	*	*		
3.	FCS – Fleet Plan Limited	FLEETPLAN						*	*
4.	HOBNOB LIMITED	ALPA	*		*		*		
5.	ICL	VEHICLE-ROUTEMASTER	*	*	*	*	*		
6.	LUCS	VERSA	*	*	*	*	*	*	*
7.	PACTEL	PARAGON	*	*	*				
8.	SCICON	(a) PATHFINDER	*	*	*	*	*		
		(b) VAN-PLAN	*	*	*	*	*		
9.	SYNERGY LOGISTICS	VEHICLE SCHEDULING ROUTE MODULE	*	*	*	*	*	*	*

Note: Constant changes are made and table indicates the position in early 1980

Figure 15:9 Characteristics of computer load planning package

- Poor input coding of customers' exact location.
- Unacceptable routes being developed in built up areas because of the inaccuracy of the map file and calculation method in the algorithm.
- Both management and drivers tend to be suspicious of computer methods because they are difficult to understand (presented by operations research specialists not distribution managers) and while errors in loads are simple to spot, they are difficult to correct.

The weakest link of computer load planning is not really the packages themselves, but the way in which they are used by management. With the introduction of the VDU and the mini/micro computer it is now possible for a load planner to actually use a computer package for building up loads. This has the effect of using the computer for storage of information and difficult calculation routines, and the load planner's knowledge of customers and feasible routes, to produce a fleet schedule. This form of inter-active load planning combines the advantages of both manual and computer systems and produces good loads in terms of low mileage, high driver time utilisation and excellent routes, all at relatively low cost. The difficulty is that the hardware must be available, and that drivers must be convinced that the computer merely assists the load planner rather than generates the load, otherwise industrial relations problems are inevitable.

Applications of load planning

Both manual and computer load planning is useful to the distribution manager in three applications (see Figure 15:10): the *strategic* planning of the fleet and its operations; the *tactical* planning of period scheduling; and the *operations*, or day-to-day, load planning.

Strategic planning.   Load planning may be used to assess the effect upon the delivery process of particular changes in the system, e.g.:

- depot location;
- use of different types of vehicles;
- imposition or relaxation of certain driver's restrictive practices;
- changes in the length of the working day;
- changes in order pattern or customer's opening hours.

These studies may be done manually but are completed at lower cost if undertaken on a computer using a 'package' program.

Tactical planning.   To determine period schedules which form the basis of a 'milk round' or 'fixed route' schedule. This is particularly useful if there are seasonal changes in demand, or certain road works are expected to delay vehicles on one route for a considerable period.

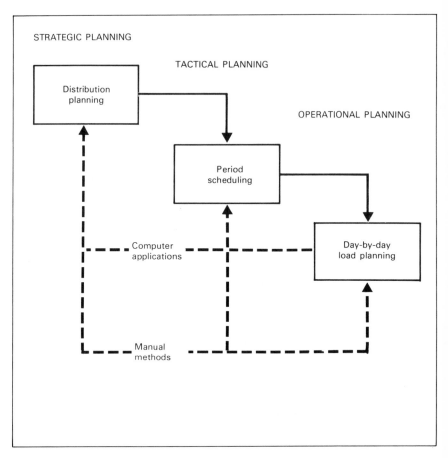

Figure 15:10   Application of load planning

Operations planning.   The establishment of day-to-day routes and schedules which are planned each day in response to customer demand and vehicle/driver availability.

Conclusion

Load planning has developed in the last decade, from manual simple rule of thumb methods, to reach the stage of complex interactive computer systems. The speed of developing new load planning systems will be severely constrained by the unions, because drivers will be reluctant to accept the fact of a 'black box' generating, quantifying and checking their day's work – particularly if the computer systems are more efficient than manual ones. Technically, there are now only a few drawbacks to computer systems, all of which may be overcome; but emotionally, management will have to direct considerable effort towards convincing drivers that computer applications should be introduced. Once established the future of load planning will be in the redesign and development of computer applications.

Notes and references

1   For a description of the development of load planning at Cadbury Schweppes, see J. Mowat, 'The Cadbury Schweppes Approach to Load Planning', a paper presented to the OR Society Conference, York University (October 1978).

2   G. Clark and J. W. Wright, 'Scheduling of Vehicles from a Central Depot to a Number of Delivery Points', *Operations Research,* 1964, Vol. II, pp. 568–81.

3   N. Christofides, 'Modern Methods of Vehicle Scheduling', *Freight Management,* November 1979, pp. 53–6.

4   R. H. Mole and S. R. Jameson, 'A Sequential Route Building Algorithm Employing a General Savings Criterion', *Operational Research Quarterly,* 1976, Vol. 27, pp. 503–11.

5   C. D. T. Watson-Gandy, 'Advances in Distribution', a paper given at the OR Society Conference, York University (October 1978).

6   A. Wren and A. Holliday, 'Computer Scheduling of Vehicles from One or More Depots to a Number of Delivery Points', *Operational Research Quarterly,* 1972, Vol. 23, pp. 333–44.

7   R. A. Fildes and J. B. Westwood, 'The Development of Linear Distance Functions for Distribution Analysis', *Journal of the Operations Research Society,* June 1978, Vol. 29, No. 6, pp. 585–92.

16

Containers, unitisation and packaging

A. Rawnsley

From a very early stage of man's development it has been obvious that a variety of commodities can be carried more easily by putting them onto a tray, into a sack or indeed into any suitable receptacle with a low tare weight of its own. This is the concept of unitisation; whereas three white mice could prove difficult to transport individually, six mice in a shoe box would be no problem.

It was also apparent in those early days that meat wrapped in leaves or children wrapped in furs survived longer and maintained their condition better than the exposed article. So packaging was discovered.

Notice that if the transport of the six mice is considered in terms of packaging and not just simple unitisation then the difficulties may begin to build up. It may be found that journey time is long enough for the mice to gnaw through the box or climatic conditions are such as to harm the health of the mice or allow their escape through rain-softened cardboard.

Functions of packaging

Packaging fulfils three basic functions, either singly or in combination. These are containment, protection and identification (or communication). As far as physical distribution is concerned they are all important, but the following rather more specific reasons for packaging are worth bearing in mind:

1   To protect goods against breakage, contamination or distortion.
2   To reduce the cube, and thereby cut freight costs.
3   To facilitate handling.

4   To facilitate storage.
5   To group goods into a convenient unit for distribution.
6   To reduce opportunities for pilfering.

Other considerations may occur, not least of which is the ultimate appearance of the goods in the marketplace, an extremely important factor but beyond the scope of this discussion, except in so far as marketing considerations impinge on purely physical distribution problems.

Basic considerations for packaging policy

The best solution to any one of the packaging problems listed above will not necessarily represent an ideal answer to the others. For example, the packaging material needed to prevent any breakage of particular articles under any circumstances might make the resultant package heavier and larger than necessary, and too difficult to handle. Similarly an extreme preoccupation with preventing spoilage could cost more than paying for the spoiled fraction. Packaging is a question of economics, and the first consideration must always be whether or not to package and to what extent to protect, to contain or to communicate. The following factors need to be evaluated:

1   The duration and type of transit involved, and the strains it will impose.
2   The fragility or perishability of the goods to be transported.
3   The handling and stacking methods which will be employed at each change in mode of transport.
4   The sensitivity of the goods to environment and to the other goods with which they are likely to come into contact.
5   The unit value of the goods and the extent to which packaging can be afforded.
6   The extent to which the goods have to be packaged for other reasons (such as marketing requirements) and the opportunities and constraints this imposes.
7   The likelihood of the goods contaminating other goods in transit.
8   The need for identification.
9   The desirability of not having to break down the package for ultimate consignment.
10   The desirability of separate items arriving together at the ultimate destination.
11   Border documentation and inspection requirements.
12   The need to prevent pilfering.
13   Limitations imposed by doors, hatches, cranes, etc.
14   Statutory requirements – for example, BR packaging regulations, IATA rules.
15   Insurance requirement.

A complementary consideration must be the types of materials which will achieve the desired operating specification, and their costs. These will include paper and board, wood, textiles, metals, felts, wickerwork, plastics and glass, in numerous permutations.

The distribution problem caused by irregular packages

When one considers the possible shapes and sizes of goods that are to be transported, the variety of packaging materials available and the possible combinations of factors affecting package selection, it is not surprising that the transport system has to deal with an almost infinite assortment of packages. Each consignor will tend to choose the type and shape of packing which best suits his own operations. The traditional pattern of freight transport has evolved around the requirement that all shapes, sizes, densities and materials have to be handled and transported. The warehouse, the cargo ship, the van, the boxcar, the derrick and the docker are all responses to the problem of not knowing what might come next, and they all help to provide the elastic-sided system required. The flexibility of the system is its strength and its weakness. Its strength is obvious: it can cope with anything, but its versatility is ensured at the price of loss of specialisation. Ordinary cargo ships are designed to carry almost everything, and so are not particularly good at carrying any one thing. A crane which can lift a tank is wasting its strength on a Mini, and a boxcar which could swallow 500 cases of canned beans is not operating to the limit when carrying 500 feather pillows.

The first goods to command their own specialised forms of transport were the bulk commodities, such as grain and oil, which originate from one point and effectively terminate at another, are homogeneous, and are usually under a single ownership. This homogeneity made possible the introduction of specialised handling machinery, and the continuity of traffic permitted the construction of purpose-built carriers. This suggests that the problem with packages might be resolvable if uniformity were introduced.

Pallets for unitisation

The pallet represents the major attempt to unify dry-cargo loads. At its simplest it is a flat tray upon which several articles can be placed, which can then be handled as one article. Its essential features in the context of freight transport are that it should be rigid and sturdy enough to support its load and constructed so as to allow mechanised handling.

It has been estimated that in Britain alone 12 to 14 million pallets are produced each year, and well over ten times that number are turned out in the USA. They range from the platform of planks, held together by wooden battens, through cardboard and plastics to heavy-duty metal pallets designed to carry several tons.

Although palletisation is now so well established the design of pallets is still an active area of innovation as possibilities in combining materials in construction are explored and the pallet requirements for distinct categories of consignment are met. Although severe increases in the price of timber have brought demands for greater use of disposable pallets and non-timber returnables, they have not wrought as much real change as might have been expected. The timber pallet remains typical.

Disposable pallets can now be had for only 20 per cent of the price of the conventional timber returnable item. Typically, 70 per cent of disposables are of light wooden construction and the remainder are of board or plastic composition.

Private National pallet exchange pools are operated in Britain by GKN Chep, and in Australia by Brambles Industries, but only limited private exchange systems operate in the USA. The UK scheme was started in 1975 and operates through a network of depots. Customer companies are provided with the pallet service which allows them to hire and de-hire GKN Chep's distinctive blue pallets, exchange them with other companies, or have other companies return them to the depot. This system, which avoids losses and repair costs for pallets, was immediately popular with the food and drink industries. Currently, there are 17 depots nationally, serving 700 clients, and 2 million pallets in circulation. Additions to the pool are being made at the rate of some 450,000 units per annum, and the expansion into Europe is already well under way. Chep Europe was established in 1978 as a three-way equal partnership between GKN, Brambles Industries and Banque Bruxelles Lambert, and now has 33 depots. Five of these depots are in Benelux and 11 in France.

Although disposable pallets were advocated to overcome the lack of pallet exchange schemes, they still fall far short of the importance that was forecast for them a few years ago.

Metal strapping or binder twine, nets, plastics film or more elaborate restraining devices are used to secure the articles to the pallets. In some cases no fastening is needed, if the shape and weight of the packages provide adequate stability.

The fork truck and the pallet have developed in line; in the UK the first important use of the two was by the American armed forces in the second half of the Second World War. The combination has proved formidable. Road vehicles, railcars and ships have been modified to accommodate them, and the pattern of intermodal changes at the dockside has to a large extent been revolutionised.

To appreciate the nature of the improvement brought about by palletisation it is as well to recollect the traditional procedure involved in sending goods overseas. The goods are packed at the factory according to the consignor's estimate of their value and fragility, and so on. The quantity bulked together is determined by the size of the order and by weight and volume considerations, usually related to the manner in which the package will have to be handled or stored at source. The goods are loaded into general-purpose haulage vehicles and are discharged ultimately at a dockside warehouse, where they are stacked and documented for shipment. When the ship arrives the goods are unstacked, transferred to the quayside, assembled, lifted by crane, lowered into the hold, disassembled and stowed. At the sea terminal the reverse procedure occurs, and the goods finish up in another warehouse until they commence the next part of the journey.

Repeated handling of individual pieces of traditional international freighting (studies have indicated 26 times as normal) certainly entails higher risks than are encountered in more refined methods. Furthermore, such cumbersome loading and discharge procedures ensure that the ship spends up to 50 per cent of its working life in harbour. A further consequence is that extensive and costly warehousing facilities are required at each end of the sea route, since the load must be ready for the ship.

Effects of palletisation

The most obvious benefits resulting from the use of pallets are a reduction in the time and labour needed to load and unload vehicles, and an improved utilisation of warehouse space. These benefits were recognised in factories some time before pallets gained much acceptance for sea freight. For these benefits to be fully achieved for sea freight, some changes are necessary. Depositing pallets at the bottom of the hold is only half a solution. The other half is to provide access to the ship's hold for fork trucks through the side of the ship. This eliminates the up, over and down crane manipulation and permits more frequent transfers, since fork trucks are cheaper than cranes and do not interfere with each other's operation to the same extent. The increased rapidity of loading and stacking shortens the turnround time in port and thus improves the utilisation of the most expensive piece of capital equipment in the system – the ship.

The move towards palletisation has also given rise to other benefits: individual packages can be assembled in the plant onto a pallet, and hand-operated pallet trucks, which are cheap and can be used by unskilled labour, move the pallets to store or to road or rail vehicles; the vehicles are loaded more rapidly and pallet loads can be arranged to contain a single order for a customer. It has been found that damage in transit can be appreciably reduced and delivery times cut by this means. Perhaps the most telling benefit is a relative reduction in delivery costs, which, when added to the savings on internal handling costs, add up to a substantial incentive to examine the pallet system.

As with all things, however, there are drawbacks. One of the most apparent is the lack of uniformity and standardisation in pallet construction. In 1969 it was estimated that around fifteen hundred varieties of pallet were in current use. Since then efforts towards standardisation have worked towards reduction, but there has been a counter-movement in the adoption of palletisation for many small, rather specialised applications. Nevertheless the problem of lack of uniformity could be overstated. Between 35 and 40 per cent of United Kingdom pallet production is of timber 1.0 x 1.2 m units and there has been a significant move towards metrication generally. Around 90 per cent of production is now made to metric dimensions.

The current British Standard BS 2629:1967 (Pallets for material handling for through transit) adopts the International Standards Organisation (ISO) recommended pallet sizes for through transit of 1.0 x 1.2 m (39⅜ x 47¼ inches) in preference to the previously preferred Imperial size of 40 x 48 inches.

Development of true pallet pools has been very slow. Two well known arrangements, between Continental railway systems and between some United Kingdom food manufacturers, appear to be more in the nature of agreements to collect and return partners' pallets.

Where loads consist of fairly solid single-sized packages which stack like building blocks, some attempts are being made to solve pallet problems by dispensing with the pallets altogether while retaining pallet-type handling operations. In one system the lower packages of the stack are strapped around channels which allow the entry of fork truck tines. A bonus beyond the saving of at least some of the direct cost would come from the utilisation of much of the space normally occupied by the pallet. Shrink wrapping, in so far as it is load-stabilising, may be an aid to palletless utilisation in some cases.

Shrink wrapping

Pallet wrapping using plastics film and shrink wrapping in particular (although stretch wrapping may now offer a lower-cost but more limited alternative) has become significant quite recently. Shrink film (polyethylene) is common, is placed around and subjected to heat, causing the film to contract drastically. The source of heat can range from a hand held 'gun' to a permanently installed infrared heat tunnel.

Shrink wrapping offers a number of real advantages: better load stability; weather protection (though some materials particularly vulnerable to damage by moisture may need the inclusion of desiccants as protection against under-film condensation); lower associated labour costs; better product visibility and identification; maintenance of cleanliness; greater security, since pilferage is immediately visible; unitisation of odd lots and, in some instances, the chance of increasing the pallet load by reducing the need for shock-absorbing materials like corrugated board between fragile items, since the items of a shrink-wrapped load are pressed together tightly.

Shrink wrapping is being used on a surprisingly wide variety of pallet loads, including bottled beer, steel tubes, and furniture. Such consignments may travel as individual pallet units or palletised in containers. Containers are the next logical stage where the limitations of the flat pallet alone become serious – for example their unstackability where load tops are uneven, or the product being carried has poor load-bearing qualities.

The container revolution

Railways in the United Kingdom and abroad have used containers for many years to transport special commodities or packages. But containerisation until the past decade or so was largely confined to domestic routes. The new development was the widespread adoption of large, multipurpose containers of standard size with standard fittings, which are truly international and intermodal, that is, they can be conveyed by road, rail or sea, though not yet generally by air economically. The first commercial service was started in the United States in 1957 by Matson Lines, while Sealand had a van-trailer/sea service as early as 1952.

Essentially containers are boxes 8 feet high by 8 feet wide by 10, 20, 30 or 40 feet long (2.4 x 2.4 x 2.9, 6.0, 9.1 or 12.2 m) the dimensions and essential features being covered by British Standards and ISO Series 1 recommendations G68–1979 (freight containers – external dimensions and ratings) 1894–1975 (General Purpose Series I freight containers – minimum internal dimensions). Important size exceptions are the ISO Designation 1AA container, which is 8 feet 6 inches (2.6 m) high, and the 35-foot-long unit used by Sealand.

Containers are currently produced in a variety of materials, including steel, aluminium, plywood and glass-reinforced plastics. Early designs concentrated on features desirable from the point of view of sea-freight requirements but the latest designs are equally concerned with the need for containers to be handled by several types of ground equipment. In addition to top-corner lifting fittings, most containers now have reinforced lifting points underneath to facilitate fork-lift and straddle-lift handling. The attractiveness of the various materials from which containers can be constructed may vary somewhat with planned usage. On the short sea routes between the United Kingdom and the mainland of Europe there is a tendency to favour steel for its strength against very frequent handling whereas on long sea hauls the lightness of aluminium may more than compensate for its higher cost. Special cargoes require special features, so there are insulated, or insulated and refrigerated containers.

Such units are built to ISO recommendations and are compatible with standard general-purpose (GPF) containers. Bulk powder and bulk liquid transport has not been overlooked, and units are available with dimensions compatible with British Standards (BS) and ISO containers. This can be achieved by mounting a tank, of material and type dictated by the requirements of the traffic, within a framework which conforms with the lifting and stacking requirements of GPF containers. Discharge points are within the 8-foot-square cross-section. Containers are also available with side doors or end doors, or no door but with one wall of weatherproof sheeting. There are fractional-height containers without roofs, full-height containers without roofs, collapsible containers, containers with removable pillars, removable ends, and so on. This diversity makes it easier to select the right container for the job from the consignor's point of view, but if carried to extremes could negate one of the most important benefits of containerisation – interchangeability.

Basic considerations for container policy

As with packaging the consignor of goods by container is faced with several choices, the first of which is whether to lease or buy. In arriving at a decision he should take the following into consideration:

1   The initial cost of the containers, provision for their depreciation.
2   The annual provision necessary for maintenance and repair.
3   The cost of insurance.
4   The cost of storing and handling.
5   The costs of managing a fleet of containers.
6   The volume and stability of the freight flow.
7   The cost of returning empty containers where no return load is available.

These factors have to be assessed in terms of the return on the capital to be employed, this return being equal to the lowest-price leasing contract which would otherwise have to be entered into. Leases take a variety of forms ranging from the 'trip' lease, which may be for a return journey or place to place, to the 'lifetime' lease where the container is rented, at much lower rates, for its nominal life which may be nine to ten years. In this latter arrangement the lessee is responsible for maintenance.

Leasing of containers began early and it is now a very significant practice; one of the largest leasing companies has some 80,000 'TEU' (twenty-foot equivalent units). Leasing companies often face difficulty in ensuring container availability in particular ports, and geographical factors are considered in pricing contracts. A lessee wanting to offload his leased containers in a port where container demand is high is likely to get better rates than one wishing to relinquish containers where a surplus exists.

The questions of construction material, tare weight, or whether to lease or buy are not the only ones to be considered in the light of the nature of the goods to be carried and their destinations. Ease of maintenance, security, handling characteristics and method of loading are also major considerations.

Loading containers

As far as the consignor is concerned, the container is partly a form of packaging, while for the haulier it is entirely a package. However, except in special circumstances such as the shipment of wine in a bulk-liquid container, it is not the only form of packaging required. This is particularly true where the consignor has insufficient volume to fill a container himself and transports his goods initially to a forwarding agent for assembly into full loads – groupage. The essential features of packaging may also have to be retained to meet the distribution requirements of the consignee.

The consignor is still faced, or his forwarding agent is, with the problem of loading and unloading ('stuffing' and 'unstuffing') the big boxes. If this is not organised sensibly, many of the benefits of reduced pilfering and reduced intermediate handling can be lost. Container loads are often now made up with palletised goods but vigilance is needed to avoid damage to the cargo resulting from loose stowage.

Specially designed container-loading fork trucks are available. These have a low profile and are lighter than normal so as not to exceed permitted container floor loadings (see Figure 16:1).

Moving containers

By road

Transporting a container from factory to dock presents few problems. The first link is usually the road haulier, and one large or two small containers constitute a load which is stable, uniform and quickly transferable. The main snag in practice is that the container – the commonest is 20 feet long and loaded up to 15 tons – has to be put

Figure 16:1   Container loading by fork truck
Specially designed to load ISO containers, this Lansing Bagnall unit
is fitted with a mast of low collapsible height

onto the road vehicle, and lifting cranes of suitable capacity are not always available in smaller companies. There are several alternatives to a direct lifting crane:

1   A fork truck. Larger models than the usual factory model are required with reduced, but still good, manoeuvrability. They need not, of course, be used exclusively for container handling and their costs can be spread over a wider operation (see Figure 16:2).

2   A side-loader. This is essentially a side-loading fork truck which can operate in narrower aisles.

3   Portal frames. These are low-cost lifting gantries, with no facility for travel. The truck backs under the raised container.

Figure 16:2   Lancer Boss forklift truck handling containers

4   Leg system. The container is equipped with legs at each corner, and a jacking
    device. The container is raised to the height of the truck, the goods are put in the
    container then the truck backs under the raised container.
5   Self-loading devices. A special lorry with a built-in lifting mechanism is
    employed.
6   Hover-containers. An air-cushion is generated under the container, enabling it to
    be moved easily from a loading bank over a bridging plate on to a trailer or
    vehicle platform. This cannot, of course, be used with skeletal semitrailers.

A further alternative is provided by the Freightliner service of the National Freight
Corporation. Empty containers are transported to the consignor by semitrailer, and
do not have to be removed from the vehicles during filling.

    One hindrance to the free flow of container traffic in the UK is the legal limit on
gross (road) vehicle weight, affecting in particular 40-foot ISO containers.

Although a road haulier can take the container straight to the dock, this may prove increasingly uneconomic in the UK over long distances in the face of Freightliner developments. The Freightliner system grew essentially out of earlier rail container systems but the radical improvement in terms of method and equipment was a response to the loss of business from railways to road. Freightliners carry containers, the majority being to ISO standards, on high-speed, specially built wagons running in fixed-formation trains over medium and long distances. Containers are accumulated in train-load quantities at strategically sited terminals designed for rapid transfer between road and rail or ship. Freightliners have so far confined their own containers to Britain and Ireland (the Republic and Northern Ireland) but the organisation acts on an agency basis for 'Intercontainer' (International Company for Transport by Transcontainer) and it forwards traffic for overseas destinations in containers hired for the journey.

At port terminals

Major changes in cargo handling at docks have resulted from the introduction of containers. First there are changes in the terminal itself. Ample room is needed for assembling incoming and outgoing containers, at the rate of about an acre per hundred containers. As containers are weatherproof, this area need not be roofed, and from a distance may look like a caravan park. Inland container clearance centres have also been established since the assembly and distribution of containers does not necessarily have to be done on the quayside, and such centres can be a way of mitigating the effects of port congestion and so reducing overall journey time.

A second major change is in the handling equipment. The conventional derrick is not designed to move containers around, so new equipment such as that described below has had to be installed at container terminals.

1   Straddle carriers. These come in several forms but consist essentially of a self-powered mobile portal frame, with four-wheel steering. They lift and transfer containers, and some varieties can stack them up to three units high (see Figure 16:3).

2   Side-loaders. These are powerful lift trucks with the forks at the side.

3   Overhead travelling cranes. These can be rail-mounted at ground level or elevated. They straddle the container road/rail discharge point and part of the assembly area.

4   Container cranes. There are several types, but a common feature is a horizontal member capable of reaching amidships on berthed vessels. Containers are fed to the crane on rail tracks or roadways running between their legs, lifted and traversed until they are over the ship (see Figure 16:4).

Not all ports are equipped with the newer types of loading crane, and derricks and slewing jib cranes have been fitted with spreaders, to give four-corner lifting. Likewise ship-borne derricks can be modified where they are of satisfactory lifting power and reach, but in these cases the container must be brought to the crane, and sometimes

Figure 16:3   Straddle carrier – a Ferranti VC 835 van carrier
This is an eight-wheeled machine with a payload capacity of 35 tons under lift frames. It can stack standard 20ft long containers up to three high, 40ft long containers up to two high, and is also available as a long wheel-base version capable of stacking 40ft containers up to three high

Figure 16:4   Container cranes capable of reaching amidships on berthed
               vessels
               Three Stothert and Pitt transporters in service at Clydeport

the ship has to be moved as well. An example of a shipboard lift is shown in Figure
16:5.

Cellular ships

The most fundamental change has been in the design of the ship. With a present world
fleet of 600 fully cellular deep-sea container ships (with a carrying capacity of over
750,000 TEU) it is worth recollecting that the first purpose-built container ship was
only commissioned in 1968. The 1,200 container vessels then forecast have not been
achieved, but the fleet doubled by 1979. The emphasis, however, is still on ship
utilisation, and hence rapid turnround.

Impact of containerisation

Some of the arguments, sometimes contradictory, for and against containerisation in
general are listed in Figure 16:6. These will no doubt continue. Meanwhile, although

Figure 16:5   Shipboard container lift in action
The container is being lifted direct from the road vehicle onto a ship
by means of a container lift fitted to the vessel itself

in international deep-sea containerised trade the North America/Europe routes will predominate in terms of containership employment, container systems are being taken up increasingly in the rest of the world. Currently worldwide growth in container trade is estimated to be running at 15 per cent per annum.

At present, in countries which were involved in the beginnings of containerisation, the first cycle for containers and handling equipment has started. This is the time for reconsideration, and perhaps innovation. Whatever developments are seen, the majority are likely to be centred around the container box system as described above.

Roll-on/roll-off ferries

The expense of container-lifting equipment and the problems associated with handling containers at manufacturers' plants have been noted. Likewise, the container system demands transfer equipment at every stage where there is a change of transport mode. The question arises: Need the container ever leave the truck? The answer is: Not always.

The movement of goods across short sea routes by train ferry is old-established, but of more recent origin is the road ferry. The impetus again comes from the desire to speed the turnround of high-cost ships and to eliminate intermediate handling. The idea is achieved when a lorry is loaded at the manufacturer's works, driven onto a ship and driven off at the end of the voyage direct to the consignee, using the ship as a moving bridge. However, this is by no means a problem-free solution. A lorry, to the haulier, is the capital with which he earns profits, and it is out of action on a ferry. The most expensive part is the engine and transmission; this need never go out of service if it is used in the form of a tractive unit with semitrailer or drawbar trailer. The trailer is rolled onto the ship and rolled off at the terminal. A compatible tractive unit must be available at the right time to take the trailer on its next stage.

Even without the tractor a trailer has a lower effective payload than a container, due to the weight of the running gear and the volume under the frame which cannot be utilised. Until the late 1960s this led to the belief that the place of the RO-RO ship was, for cost reasons, strictly limited to the short sea routes where it first made its mark, but since then events have shown that there is also a demand for ocean-going RO-RO capacity, and over 100 such ships are now operational on routes between Europe, North America, Australia, New Zealand and Japan. The majority of these ships in fact combine RO-RO capacity with a substantial container-carrying ability and so provide a versatile intermodal system between continents. One cost-reducing innovation that has helped to widen the field of application for RO-RO services has been the ship-borne angled ramp that allows a vessel to be independent of expensive, and perhaps underutilised, dockside ramp facilities.

In recent years, RO-RO vessels have come into their own in situations where traditional port facilities have been greatly overloaded. During the rapid development of Saudi Arabia, for example, where the infrastructure was not growing fast enough to

Benefits claimed

1 Door-to-door shipment times reduced

2 Freight costs reduced

3 Intermediate handling of packages eliminated:
   (a) Reducing damage
   (b) Reducing pilfering
   (c) Making domestic packaging sufficient

4 Boring and degrading tasks at the docks vastly reduced

5 Better utilisation of expensive capital equipment, through uniformity of cargo

6 High labour productivity

7 Warehousing and inventory costs reduced

8 Inland terminals for sea freight possible

9 Shorter training required for operatives

10 Shorter delays in intermodal transfers

11 Less danger of mis-routing

12 Loading and sealing at shipper's plant

13 Environmental control simplified (insulation/refrigeration)

14 Grouping of interrelated components possible

15 Fewer documents involved

Possible drawbacks

1 Heavy capital investment is involved in ships, containers, terminal facilities and equipment

2 Not all cargo is suited to containerisation

3 The system needs a high load factor to be economic

4 The average traditional consignment is significantly less than a twenty foot container-load

5 Some goods must therefore be packaged well enough for transport to the container groupage point and for the last leg of their journey after the container has been unloaded

6 There is a danger of lack of standardisation

7 There is the problem of return loads

8 There may be high breakages if goods are not properly stowed in containers

9 There is the possibility of higher insurance rates. Liability is difficult to establish where there are several carriers and no intermediate inspections

10 Increasing dependence on fewer sea carriers, with possible monopolies

11 Proper equipment may not be available at plants to handle containers

12 Those who pay for the system may not be the main beneficiaries

13 Air freight does not yet fit into the system

14 Theft may actually be easier in some cases

Figure 16:6   Summary of benefits and drawbacks of containerisation

keep pace with the demand, RO-RO vessels showed their ability to land their cargo of trailers using shipborne ramps. This method of handling is being copied by many developing countries and has thus assured the RO-RO idea a permanent position in intermodal transport.

Barge carriers

The first ocean voyage of a barge carrier, in 1969, was reported in some places as if it signified the beginning of the end for international container box traffic whereas in reality the carried barge and the container box are in most respects complementary. The inventor of the Lash (lighter aboard ship) system, Jerome Goldman, regards the Lash barge itself as a large container (capacity up to 380 tons, compared with a container box capacity which seldom exceeds 20 tons) which can be floated. The rationale behind barge carriers is the profitable carriage of cargoes not really suitable for normal containerisation. A tacit acknowledgement of this is the emergence of dual-purpose barge-carrier/container-carrier ships. Delta Lash ships have complete flexibility to carry either 80 barges or 1,740 TEU of containers, or any combination in between.

Lash system

Numerically, this is by far the most important of the barge-carrying systems, with some 20 ships in service. Nearly 2,000 Lash barges have been built, but it has been found that the Lash concept is only viable in areas which have shallow water facilities. Hence there is a move to convert some vessels back to straightforward container carriers.

The system of Lykes Line uses much larger barges than does the Lash, each one capable of carrying around twice as much cargo. Seabee ships use a 2,000 ton shipboard submersible barge elevator, and now five ships of this type (over 35,000 d.w.t.) are in service. The barges are of three types: hopper, flat deck and refrigerator, and are used on the New Orleans to London, and North European services. The latest vessels have been built for Russia and further new buildings are likely.

Baco system

Developed by owners, Rhein Maas und See, to overcome the congested conditions of West African ports, particularly Lagos, this new system incorporates opening bow sections, to allow 12 rectangular steel barges, each carrying 800 tonnes, to float in and out. Two mother ships are in operation with a third in prospect. They carry a total of 21,000 tons, with conventional containers making up the balance. Three sets of barges will operate; one set loading/unloading at each destination and the third set in transit. Like the Seabee system, hopper, flat deck and refrigerator barges are available. (See Figure 16:7.)

Figure 16:7   Baco barge being Pushed into Baco Liner 1

Recent developments in barge carriers include SPLASH and Condock ships. Both these vessels feature some container capacity with a submersible deck (to a depth of 3.5 m for SPLASH and 2.3 m for Condock) to allow barges to be floated in. Once in position, the ship's ballast tanks are pumped dry and the barges are secured. SPLASH (self-propelled Lash) vessels are used to feed the mother ships. Three vessels are already in operation.

The Condock design is universal, in that Lash, Baco, and, with a little modification, Seabee barges can be carried. With watertight, heavyduty, hatch covers, Condock can also double as a RO-RO vessel. A promising future is claimed for this class of ship.

Importance of barge carriers

In the sense that barge-containers are waterborne throughout, the systems are not intermodal, but in being able to load and discharge at inland and coastal locations not open to normal shipping they have the ability to substitute for some intermodal traffic.

Public concern over energy problems and environmental pollution appears to favour the increased use of river estuaries and inland waterways for freight movement. Barge carriers allow such traffic to be international without trans-shipment.

Although barge carriers should, conceptually, be totally independent of ports, they have been slow to exploit this attribute. Indeed, the Lash and Baco experiences are at the opposite ends of the spectrum, and it is difficult to foresee the worldwide future for such systems. There is a strong possibility that they will never gain universal acceptance, and will be confined to specialised opportunities only.

Air cargo and standardisation

For some years, airlines had no real problems with freight, and the volume was slight. By 1979, volume had grown to an estimated 27.7 billion tonne-kilometres and had become significant in operating economics. The introduction of wide-bodied passenger aircraft with large freight holds checked a movement towards all-freight aircraft. Recent orders for Boeing 747s have shown a preference (80 per cent) for the 'Combi' version which incorporates dual passenger and freight capacities. With increasing fuel prices, airlines are facing stagnant passenger demand, but increasing freight traffic. Growth of freight volume during the 1970s was running at 9 to 10 per cent per annum, and is expected to continue in the 7 to 8 per cent region in the early eighties.

Airlines have been active promoters of the use of many kinds of ULDs (unit load devices) such as pallets, pallet/net assemblies and 'igloos', partly to avoid damage to aircraft but also to accommodate, as far as possible, the cargo to fuselage curvature and to raise efficiency by facilitating ground handling, both on the apron and in the terminal.

This led at one time to a great proliferation of designs, including ones approved by IATA (International Air Transport Association) as each airline sought to solve its problems in its own way. Now, however, IATA recognition extends to only 36 ULDs. Twelve of these are 'standard aircraft' units: they range from 4.53 m³ (160 cubic feet) to 36.25 m³ (1,280 cubic feet) external volume, some being intended for particular routes only. These ULDs interface with aircraft loading and restraint systems. A further 24, classed as 'standard non-aircraft' units are divided equally into metric and non-metric units. The metric units range from 1.821 m³ (64.31 cubic feet) to 10.671 m³ (376.84 cubic feet) and the non-metric from 63.44 cubic feet (1.796 m³) to 376.81 cubic feet (10.670 m³) external volume.

Progress towards air-intermodalisation

At present intermodal despatches of international freight to include movement by air are not significant in total freight movement but neither are they rare or new. The 'Flying Fish' service pioneered by Manchester Liners and Air Canada is now operating worldwide in conjunction with major operators. Any combination of land/sea/air movements can be arranged. Seaboard World Airlines also carry 8 x 8 x 20 foot containers on their Boeing 747F all-freight service between London and New York, but these are not the standard ISO containers described earlier. The only regular air service for these heavy steel containers is believed to be operated by Aeroflot with their Il-76 aircraft on the Europe to Japan route via Moscow.

Proposals for an aviation equivalent of the skeletal trailer or railway flatcar have been put forward by Lockheed-Georgia Co. (see Figure 16:8). Passengers would travel in a pressurised module containing all the usual facilities, and cargo would be in intermodal containers covered by a fairing.

If all-freight container air services with some intermodality are a success and expand significantly there will be increasing pressure towards making large air-freight containers interchangeable with others and vice versa; perhaps leading eventually, from a standards viewpoint, to a unification of containerisation generally. If this does happen it is likely to be a long process but some future edition of this book might well note the present time as the period when containerisation in its most familiar form began at last to sprout wings.

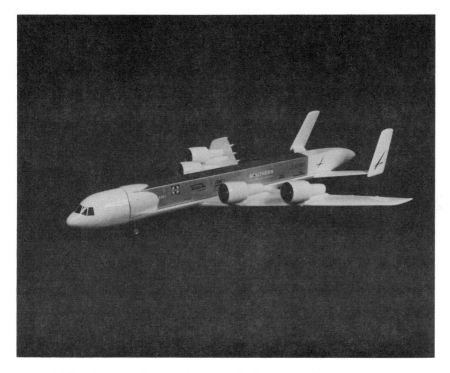

Figure 16:8   An aviation equivalent of the semitrailer; as proposed by
Lockheed Georgia Co.

Further reading

Cargo Ships, London, MacGregor Publications, 1979.

'Containers, Pallets or Lash?' in *The Economics of General Cargo Shipping,* London, Economist Intelligence Unit, 1973.

H. P. Drewry, *The Advance of Deepsea, fully Cellular Container Shipping,* London, H. P. Drewry [Shipping consultants] Ltd., 1978.

Fairplay Guide to RO-RO Shipping 1980, The, London, Fairplay Publications Ltd.

P. Finlay (ed.), *Jane's Freight Containers,* London, Jane's Yearbooks, Jane's Publishing Company, 1980.

Freight Industry Yearbook 1980, Surbiton, Surrey, England, Transport and Distribution Press Ltd., 1980.

R. F. Gibney (ed.), *Containerization International Year Book 1980,* London, National Magazine Co. Ltd., 1980.

Globe World Directory for Land, Sea and Air Traffic, 1979, Oslo, Globe Directories, 1979.

RO-RO 80 Proceedings, Rickmansworth, Herts, England, BML Business Meetings Ltd., 1980.

G. Van den Burg, *Containerization and Other Unit Transport,* London, Hutchinson Benham Ltd., 1975.

Bibliography compiled with the assistance of Containerization International.

In addition, many transport and freight journals publish articles on containerisation, packaging and palletisation, including, in the United Kingdom: *British Shipper, Cargo Systems, The Dock and Harbour Authority Freight Management, Freight News Weekly, Containerization International, Materials Handling News, Freight, Freight Forwarding,* and *International Freighting Weekly. Distribution Worldwide* and *Air Transport World* are published in the USA but circulate also in the UK.

PART FIVE

Fleet Management

Overview

Operating a road vehicle fleet, whether on line-haul or local delivery activities, or both, is a complex task. The planning involved starts early, in fact at the vehicle design and selection stage, as indicated by Woodward in Chapter 17. Sizing the body, choosing construction materials, deciding which materials handling aids to fit, are just a few of the considerations which must be covered. Woodward provides a comprehensive checklist of the items which a fleet operator should find useful in the pre-purchase stage.

Kelly, in Chapter 18, focuses on the financial aspects of vehicle purchasing, e.g. the different methods of financing available, the impact of taxation and depreciation, etc.

In Chapter 19, Harper gives a detailed account of the issues involved in vehicle maintenance right down to the types of documentation and records which should ideally be kept on each vehicle's operational performance. He also emphasises the need for proper workshop facilities and properly trained workshop staff if best results are to be achieved.

Finally, Wilson tackles the knotty question of security in Chapter 20 and gives some very practical advice to fleet operators, which, if followed, should reduce their losses through theft and consequently reduce insurance premiums.

17

Delivery vehicle design

Frank H. Woodward

Definitions

'Delivery vehicle' is such a general term that any attempt to define a specific design criterion, to apply to all vehicles within the distribution function of industry, would not only be useless for some types of operations but misleading to most. Every vehicle in use is a 'delivery vehicle' – being used to transport people or goods to destinations or point of use. 'Goods' may be solid, liquid or gas; packed, loose or bulk; boxed, barrels or bottled; pallets or unit loads. So many variations are required that the 'ideal delivery vehicle' simply does not exist.

The vehicle and the product

The first essential in considering the type of body required for a vehicle is to keep the product and production line in mind. Whether it be the mass production of everyday commodities, or the production of single pieces of large engineering plant, the vehicle body must be designed to carry a product safely, efficiently, economically and without damage. The distribution of a product is just as much a part of production as are the departments which actually make the goods. The machines manufacturing the goods will have been planned and designed to produce the goods in the most economical way. Similarly the vehicles, which are the tools of distribution, must also be planned to give the most economic return. Distribution management must remain aware of the company production programme and should be familiar with all the various products made. By knowing the production plan and any product weaknesses, it is then possible to fit the vehicle plan to the distribution needs. Any company fleet, whether box vans or flat trucks, should always be planned and vehicles designed around the needs of product distribution. Once it has been decided that a custom-built vehicle is needed the following are the main points to be considered.

Type of chassis

The make of vehicle will decide the type of chassis and, generally, fleet operators prefer to keep vehicles as standard as possible. Do not accept a body to fit a chassis. If the type of operation requires a definite body length, then make the chassis fit the required body length. There are many types of chassis extensions available and vehicle manufacturers have extended their warranties to cover such modifications. A number of manufacturers, through their 'special vehicle order' department, will also supply different lengths of chassis to suit the buyer's requirements.

Size of body

This is the most important decision to be made. If the body is too small or too large, the design will be economically wrong. The production programme should be balanced against the delivery requirement and this will indicate a load factor requirement from which the most effective size, or range of sizes, of vehicle can be determined. As an example, consider the use of a pallet size 1,200 mm x 1,000 mm. To obtain a maximum use of the floor area of a vehicle, the width should be approximately 2.3 m and the length should be designed to take an exact number of pallets. Figure 17:1 shows a typical floor layout of pallets on a 6-metre body. It can be seen that maximum use has been made of the floor area and that had the floor length been 6.5 m then this additional 0.5 m would have been wasted if loads had been palletised. Furthermore, the additional space would have allowed some movement of the load in the vehicle, which would add a risk of damage.

Body design

Custom-built bodies do not mean elaborate bodies. A special body can be of the simplest design – for example, a flat platform truck designed to carry an exact number of wooden cases of definite and regular dimensions is a special body. Care should be taken in designing a vehicle body not to make the vehicle so specialised that it is not able to carry other goods. 'Flexibility' is an important ingredient in vehicle design – in developing a fleet of vehicles for distribution use within the 'own account' section of the transport industry, a change of product must always be planned for, and when this happens the vehicles used to carry the previous product must continue to carry the new product.

Choice of materials

The load to be carried is the deciding factor in choice of materials. A box van carrying

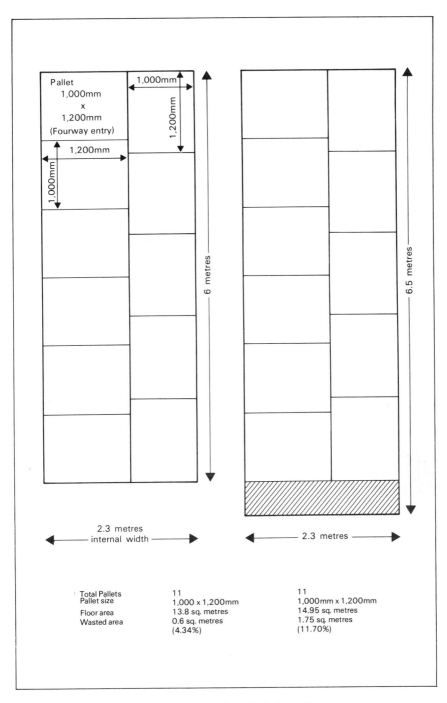

Total Pallets	11	11
Pallet size	1,000 x 1,200mm	1,000mm x 1,200mm
Floor area	13.8 sq. metres	14.95 sq. metres
Wasted area	0.6 sq. metres	1.75 sq. metres
	(4.34%)	(11.70%)

Figure 17:1   Planning the floor area of a vehicle for pallets

products stacked on the floor of the vehicle needs only a body capable of acting as a cover, because the main weight of the load is taken on the floor of the vehicle and on the chassis members. On the other hand, if loads are suspended from the roof of the van, as in the case of the clothing industry and in meat haulage (see Figure 17:2) then the body frame will be taking most of the weight. One of the advantages of having a custom-built body is that it is possible to select the right material, whether timber, steel, alloy or plastic. These materials can be intermixed throughout the body construction in order to achieve strength with lightness. Care must be taken when using alloy and steel, as without sealing at the joints and rivets, corrosion will take place very quickly. The use of plastic panels has been developed by some coach builders, and these can be obtained with the paint impregnated during the process of moulding the panel. The main problem with using plastic panels is in carrying out major repair work to the body. This is a specialised task and cannot be undertaken with the same ease as pop-riveting an alloy panel to make good accident repair damage. Fibreglass translucent roof panels and complete translucent roofs are ways of bringing more light into a box van and this material has proved extremely successful.

Figure 17:2   A specially designed vehicle to carry heavy carcases of beef
               The strength of this vehicle has to be built into the roof to carry the
               suspended load

What will it cost to have a special body built, and what increased return can be expected? Taking as an example a box van with steel framing alloy or steel panelling, translucent panels in the roof, unlined, with lashing rails, and a roller shutter door, a standard body would cost approximately 30 per cent less than a similar specification for a custom-built vehicle. The increased cost for a custom-built body may seem excessive and unnecessary, but taking the cost of the vehicle chassis into consideration, the total vehicle costs would increase by only 20 per cent. It is possible to obtain standard bodies at lower prices, but it must be understood that one only gets what one pays for. Cheaper bodies will have hardboard panels and roof, wooden roller shutter, and possibly the floor timbers will not be as well seasoned. In the long term, the most economic body is the one which gives the longest life and remains a credit to the organisation whose goods it carries.

One point often overlooked is that custom-built bodies may be more difficult to dispose of. The more elaborate the design, the more difficult this task may be. Depreciation can be heavy, but by keeping the design simple and as near to a standard design as posible, while still incorporating all the extra features required, this problem can be largely overcome. In deciding on whether to purchase a standard body or having one specially designed, always consider the use to which the vehicle is

Figure 17:3   Custom-built delivery van with GVW under 3,500 kg
This van is used for a sales delivery round, but can be quickly adapted
as a general delivery vehicle

to be put. What goods is it to carry? What changes in the company production are likely to take place? Is the company distribution pattern likely to change? What national freight changes are likely? What new transport legislation can be expected? Plan well ahead and review the circumstances each time a new vehicle is purchased. Do not hesitate to change previous decisions if circumstances alter. Remember that when a vehicle is purchased it will still be in use in five, six or seven years' time, and even then it must still be of good design and able to carry the company's product safely, efficiently, economically and without damage.

Handling aids

There are many types of handling aid which can be used to assist in the loading and unloading of the vehicle. From the simple sack truck to the powered pallet truck, and from the manually operated demountable body to the more sophisticated and expensive overhead crane to handle fully loaded containers. The primary objective of providing a handling aid with a vehicle is to load or unload that vehicle with the minimum effort and in the minimum time.

Securing the load

Although devices for restricting the movement of a load when carried on a vehicle are generally accepted as necessary to prevent damage, this equipment can also be classified as a handling aid. A van driver who at every delivery point has to sort through his parcels to find the correct ones for that particular customer, is wasting not only time, but effort. Containing the parcels in pallet cages, strapping one customer's order to a pallet, or even placing all the items for one customer in a single cardboard box, will assist the driver in effecting a quick delivery. The interior of a box vehicle can be designed to provide equipment to prevent the loads moving. Tie rails, shoring bars and inflatable dunnage bags are examples of this equipment.

Interior fitments

In designing custom-built vehicle bodies, ensure that the interior fittings are suitable for the product to be carried. Do not accept old ideas, always be on the lookout for new systems and ways to overcome the loading and unloading problems, as well as the storage and security of the goods carried. By having a custom-built body, loading aids can be built into the vehicle instead of having to carry out expensive modifications to standard bodies. Such aids as tail lifts, vehicle cranes, and special tracking for handling palletised loads reduces the time for loading and unloading, and in the long term can repay the additional cost.

Access to the load

Having easy access to the load is another form of handling aid. For small-parcel deliveries, a small door in the side of a box vehicle will provide plenty of room for a driver to enter the vehicle without having to take time and effort in opening the rear doors. Where access has to be from the rear, building into the design a well-balanced and easily opened roller shutter will reduce the effort needed by the driver in making a delivery. The choice between roller shutter and hinged rear doors will depend upon the type of operation.

When designing a vehicle it must be realised that in the case of delivery vehicles the main unloading areas will be in the 'High Streets'. Platform height of a vehicle is another important area of design which may cause unloading problems. When side access is good, it can be a great waste of time and effort if the vehicle platform is so high that the vanman has to climb up onto it in order to reach the goods. Ideally, the platform should be at waist height, so that he can reach the entire load standing beside the vehicle either on one side or the other.

Figure 17:4   Ford 1010 box van fitted with side door to enable driver to enter van without having to open rear doors
Note also 'airvane' slats at front of body which reduce drag and increase mpg fuel return

The difficulty in lowering the platform height lies in the fact that it is largely dictated by the size of the wheel and tyre required to carry the vehicle and its payload. This problem has been solved very simply by adding a third axle to what would normally have been a four-wheeler. This is illustrated in Figure 17:5. The same result can also be achieved by employing a three-axle twin-steer chassis.

Figure 17:5   A 6-ton vehicle
                Low platform height makes for greater efficiency in loading and
                unloading for increased vehicle stability

Moving the load inside the vehicle

A 9-metre box van will hold approximately 800 packages of a size 2 x 1 x 1 ft. If one person was required to unload this vehicle, package by package, by moving the packages only to the rear of the vehicle, he would be required to walk over two and a quarter miles! This illustrates the effort and time which can be wasted by not having the correct handling aids on a vehicle to enable unloading with the minimum of time and effort. The following are some of the many ways of making the task easier and, in building a vehicle for delivery work, most of the aids available can be built into the design.

Use of a pallet truck

A completely flat floor area, with no wheel arches, will assist in the use of a pallet truck. Using one-piece marine plyboard will also be effective in preventing the movement of the pallet truck from cutting up normal flooring.

Wheeled cage pallets

Again, a flat and ridge-free floor will assist the movement of wheeled cage pallets.

Rollers

Rollers built into the floor of the vehicle will enable loads on normal pallets, or on pallet boards, to be moved easily inside the vehicle. Care must be taken to provide a method of stopping the movement of the load on the rollers when the vehicle is moving, and this can be done either by retracting the rollers below the level of the floor, or by having a brake or chock system built into the design.

'Joloda'

This is a patented method of moving goods on pallets or pallet boards by using special channels built into the floor of a vehicle. A special trolley conveyor fits into the channel under the pallet and load, and, by a jack action, lifts the load which can then be moved along the vehicle. This retractable protable fork-lift conveyor is used in pairs (Figures 17:6, 17:7) and is capable of lifting and moving up to 1½ ton from the tailboard of the vehicle to the headboard and vice versa. One of the previous problems in using 'Joloda' in delivery vehicles has been overcome. It was found that the open

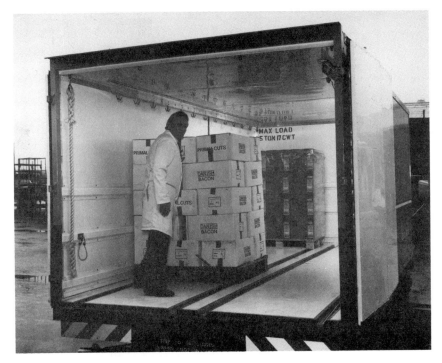

Figure 17:6   Joloda equipment used in an insulated van
The 'skate' can be seen under the pallet
(Reproduced by kind permission of Joloda Limited)

Figure 17:7   Joloda equipment specially designed for use with pallet cages
                 The 'skates' can be seen with the extended pieces lifted under the
                 cage
                 (Reproduced by kind permission of Joloda Limited)

tracking built into the floor of the vehicle was a potential hazard when people were
working in the vehicle, especially if using a hand pallet truck. A new 'flipover' track is
now available wherein, when the equipment is not being used, the whole of the open
track is covered by simply turning over the track to become 'flush' with the vehicle
floor.

Overhead conveyor rail

Those industries whose product is hung in the vehicle can benefit from the fitting of an
overhead conveyor rail inside a vehicle which, if required, can be powered from the
engine of the vehicle in the same way as tipping gear or tailgate equipment.
      This type of overhead rail can be connected to the factory production line so
that a continuous movement from manufacture or warehouse to inside the vehicle is
possible, thereby reducing loading effort to a minimum.

Moving the load on and off the vehicle

Few problems arise in loading a vehicle, mainly because this takes place at company premises and the provision of facilities is the direct responsibility of the company operating the vehicle. Loading by fork-lift truck, or from dock level, straight into a vehicle presents little difficulty, and no matter whether a company is engaged in heavy engineering or in High Street distribution, the loading facilities at the factory or warehouse are usually adequate for that particular product. Delivering to customers' premises present different problems. An engineering company commissioned to produce, supply, and install a piece of plant weighing over two tons, for a company engaged in dry cleaning, could not expect the customer to have a fork-lift truck of their own capable of unloading this equipment. The driver arriving at the customer's premises will need to have some means of unloading. This can be catered for when the vehicle is being built, and should form an extension of the facilities provided for moving the load inside the vehicle.

Tail lifts

The powered tail lift (Figures 17:8, 17:9) is the most widely used piece of equipment for moving heavy and bulky loads from the rear of the vehicle to ground level. Many types and variations are available, but in fitting a tail lift to the rear of a vehicle, care must be taken to ensure that extra strength is built into the rear frame and chassis, so as to withstand the additional weight and stresses caused by projecting heavy loads far outside the centre of gravity of the vehicle. The 'Joloda' tracking equipment mentioned previously can be built into any tail-lift platform. A number of companies engaged in town deliveries have fitted a small tail-lift facility to the side of their vehicles, and these have proved adequate for handling large items of equipment weighing up to 5 cwt. The advantages are many, but perhaps the main advantage to the driver making the delivery is that he is free from the road area behind his vehicle and does not present an additional road hazard.

Vehicle cranes

Many uses have been found for the vehicle crane mounted on a flat-bed vehicle, and many different types are available (Figure 17:10). Steel pipes, caged pallets, building and engineering plant, are just a few of the areas where the use of a vehicle-mounted crane has reduced the turnround time. In designing a vehicle to carry a crane, additional strength will be needed around the floor area, and the addition of extra chassis strengthening may be desirable.

Most truck manufacturers are now able to advise on fitting the various models of cranes available, and operators are recommended to consult the vehicle manufacturer concerned about the requirements of the hydraulic or air line fittings. Failure to conform to the recommendations may lead to a denial of warranty for a vehicle.

Figure 17:8   Low-profile loader from Anthony Loaders, specially designed to
                cater for wheeled pallets and to give a smooth vertical lift
                'Fingerlift' controlled lifting of the tailgate through an adjustable
                torsion bar assembly cuts operator fatigue
                (Reproduced by kind permission of Anthony Carrimore Limited)

Demountable bodies

An industrial fleet must be planned around a policy of flexibility so that the right type
of vehicle is available for the particular task to be carried out. The larger the fleet, the
more flexible it will be, but even with a factory requiring only a single vehicle a degree
of flexibility can be provided. In such a situation a decision has to be made on
whether a flat vehicle or a box van is needed. A solution to this problem is to provide
a demountable box container carried on a flat-bed truck. It will then be possible to use
this vehicle as a box or flat as needs arise.

The increase in use of the demountable or 'swap' body has also helped to cut
down the standing time of delivery vehicles. The demountable body can be loaded or
unloaded while the motive vehicle is out delivering another load. This type of vehicle
has been used in many types of operation, from the food delivery van to the coal
merchant, and from the refrigerated vehicle to the heating-oil supply-tanker. At the
present moment demountable bodies have a direct cost advantage in that when
assessing the weight for tax purposes, the weight of the demounted body is not

Figure 17:9   New type of rear lift designed by Wilsdon & Co. Ltd.
The lift platform is the rear floor of the van and gives every advantage
of a normal tail lift without having the problem of obstructing the rear
doors when not in use
(Reproduced by kind permission of Wilsdon & Co. Ltd.)

included. The only proviso is that the body must be 'in the habit of' being taken off the vehicle. A saving of over £120 per year per vehicle is possible with such an operation.

The swap body is not a new method of operation in the UK. Over fifty years ago a number of companies used this type of truck and uncoupled the bodies from the chassis by using push-through rods laterally across the rear and front of the body and then reversing between sloping ramps. The body lifted from the chassis and after being secured on the ramps the tractor unit simply moved away. Today the method of lifting the body from the chassis or flat bed is more sophisticated and may or may not need less effort on the part of the driver. There are various ways of removing the body:

Figure 17:10   The vehicle-mounted crane
This is one of the most versatile pieces of materials handling
equipment. It illustrates here how a large piece of plant can be taken
off a truck and placed right outside the customer's premises by the
driver of the truck
(Reproduced by kind permission of George Cohen Machinery
Limited – Hiab cranes)

1   Manually operated screw-type jacks placed at each corner of the body.
2   Power or hand operated hydraulic jacks fitted permanently to the outside of the
    body.
3   Electrically operated portable jacks which attach to the body and can lower the
    body down to ground level.
4   Power-operated lifting equipment fitted to the chassis of the vehicle. After lifting
    the body clear, legs drop down from the body and it is then lowered before the
    vehicle pulls away.

Manufacturers are now able to offer complete demountable systems (Figure 17:11)
adaptable to rigid vehicles from 6.0 tonne GVW through to semitrailer and drawbar
trailer outfits operating at the maximum gross permitted weights of those vehicles.
The flexibility of such a system provides an opportunity for an increased vehicle

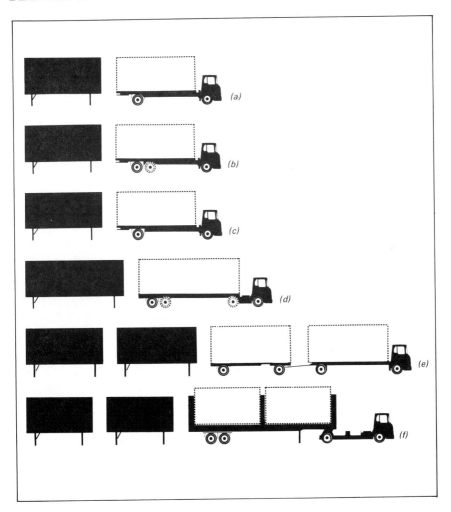

Figure 17:11   Six basic systems of demountable bodies

utilisation, which will produce a more economical operation. In adopting a fleet
policy based on a demountable operation, a decision will need to be taken on whether
the bodies are to be mounted on a skeletal chassis or on a flat-bed vehicle. For a large
fleet there is an advantage in having a system based on the skeletal type of fitting, in
that the weight of the vehicle as declared for tax purposes is kept to a minimum. On
the other hand, for a small operation, where the process of removing the body is not so
frequent, then carrying the box body on a flat bed will give a second vehicle available
for immediate use when the box is demounted.

Drawbar-trailer demountable bodywork

For several decades now the drawbar trailer (Figure 17:12) has been very little used, having been superseded by the articulated vehicle. But with the development of swap bodies there has been an increasing interest in drawbar units as one means of delivering goods using a single power unit. The cost advantage, if it takes the place of sending two vehicles over long distances to make deliveries, is evident.

On arrival in the destination area, the trailer can be parked while the van itself makes deliveries; the van then returns to the trailer, swaps the two demountable bodies, and makes the remaining deliveries from the trailer's body. Alternatively the drawbar configuration may be used only on the trunking leg of the journey, with a second chassis power unit, based at the destination point, being employed to take the trailer body out to make the deliveries.

Figure 17:12   A demountable body system
A Ford D1411 fitted with Dobson Type 41 hydraulic equipment

Refrigerated and insulated bodies

Demand for refrigerated and insulated van bodywork (Figure 17:13) is on the increase, particularly for frozen-food delivery services and the transport of fruit. Design work has produced bodies of composite construction, in which either glass reinforced plastics (GRP) or 6 mm plywood (usually of the Finnish type because its larger number of plies provides greater strength) is employed in conjunction with rigid polyurethane to provide thermal insulation.

In the case of refrigerated vehicles, whether using mechanical equipment or liquid nitrogen, there may be a need to incorporate into the internal design some provision for ensuring an adequate circulation of air around the load. This is so as to ensure an even temperature distribution.

Figure 17:13   Insulated and refrigerated body ATP Class C equipped with Petters plant and Ratcliff 1½ ton tail lift
Body constructed in GRP 'sandwich', three meat rails in roof
(Reproduced by kind permission of Massey International Coach Builders Limited)

Driver comfort

A new word has been added to the transport vocabulary, 'ergonomics'. This is the study of the human at work, with or without machine, in an environment. Applied to transport, this includes the comfort and safety of a driver in his cab, and the conditions to be met in handling his load on to and off the vehicle.

Items such as reclining seats, adjustable headrests and armrests, tinted glass, carpets, radio and tape players, VHF equipment, air-conditioning and sleeping facilities are now becoming standard. Instrumentation designed to give the driver a complete picture of running conditions of the vehicle will also feature in the cab design of the future. Warning lights advising failure in any of the vehicle systems, such as lighting, fuel, lubrication, coolant and braking systems, as well as indicating axle loading limits, will also be seen in future cab instrumentation.

In designing a vehicle body, the operator is able to incorporate features to minimise the effort required by a driver not only in the actual driving of the vehicle, but also in making his deliveries. The driver is the person who may have to load and unload the vehicle in the loading bays, or in most cases in the main streets of the cities and towns. Such considerations as ease of entry, adequate interior lighting, all help the driver to make his deliveries more easily. Prior to the Health and Safety at Work Act 1974, there was no real legislation to safeguard the conditions under which a truck driver was asked to work. The Act, in Part I, covers the health, safety and welfare of an employee in his environment. This affects all areas concerning transport operation, from the mechanical safety of the vehicle driven, to the 'in cab' conditions of that vehicle, and the effort required to handle the load at delivery areas. In selecting vehicles suitable for a particular operation, transport services management has now a direct responsibility to ensure that the aims of the Health and Safety at Work Act are adequately met.

Fuel costs

It is important to take into account fuel costs when evaluating the specification of a truck. Fuel consumption of any vehicle can be improved by reducing 'drag' as the vehicle passes through the air at normal road speeds. Fitments are available which, it is claimed, smooth out the airflow and reduce the drag on vehicles, especially those vehicles which carry high containers or boxes. Claims of improvement in mpg in excess of 10 per cent have been made, but it is important that any saving is not accompanied by other areas of increased cost. Fitting 'anti-drag shields' on the top of vehicle cabs in front of the load area will 'smooth out' the airflow, but the additional weight and strain on the cab roof could cause damage to the cab over a period of use. Fitting of aerodynamic 'slats' around the front and leading edges of the container or box is considered a better method (Figure 17:14). Using these 'slats', ensures that the area of vehicle which causes the drag always carries the anti-drag device, whereas fitting shields to the tractors of articulated outfits requires every tractor in the fleet to be fitted to give total maximum benefit. This may mean that in a mixed trailer fleet, tractors with anti-drag equipment fitted, will be coupled to flat-bed trailers with little or no effect on fuel consumption. There is also no advantage in vehicles which spend nearly all their operational activity stopping and starting around a set delivery area.

A vehicle plan

To obtain the maximum efficiency in any type of vehicle operation, and especially in the problems of distribution from factory and warehouse to customer outlets, a balance of improved productivity must be kept between the utilisation of the capital invested and the manpower employed. Relying on productivity schemes and bonus schemes in the form of payments to the labour force is only a very small part of the problem. Obtaining a higher work output from the vehicles by cutting down

Figure 17:14   A 'Roadline' 12 metre articulated outfit, fitted with a 'EUROPA
SPOILER' airfoil designed to remove drag by smoothing out the
air flow
(Reproduced by kind permission of Generation Trading Limited)

unproductive standing time will yield a much higher return. The cost of providing a
good quality tilt may be high, but set against the payment of a bonus for roping and
sheeting a vehicle, the cost over a number of years will be quite small. Any vehicle
plan needs to be built around the requirements of the product which has to be carried.
Vehicle design should be planned as an extension of the product line and the effort of
movement of the product from the point of manufacture to the shopping basket of the
consumer should always be under investigation. Vehicle size is dependent upon
product size and unit load size. The height of the vehicle must take into account the
unloading area, whether it be in the High Street or in the yard behind the shop. The
cab is an important feature in vehicle design and especially in those vehicles which
are subject to 'short stop' deliveries.

Climbing in and out of a cab can be very tiring, and no bonus scheme will
replace an easily accessible and comfortable cab. The total distribution area must be
considered in developing a vehicle plan. Trunk vehicles, delivery vehicles, fork-lift
trucks, electric vehicles, even the salesman's car and light van play a part in providing
the efficient movement of goods to the consumer areas.

18

Vehicle purchasing, replacement and costing

J. R. Kelly

Introduction

High interest rates, spiralling fuel costs and rapidly increasing prices for purchasing and maintaining vehicles have combined to focus the attention of management on the importance of distribution. No longer can this area be regarded as an unavoidable on-cost after goods have been produced and sold. The total distribution function can and must be managed professionally. Unfortunately, while operational techniques and standards are often high, the financial and cost factors relating to transport are either unknown or ignored. In certain ways this may be understandable. A fleet frequently grows at a rate greater than the controls required to manage it efficiently. The transition from a simple to a complex operation can be gradual and occur without management realising it. Also it is often thought that a company's normal financial management, through the medium of a profit-and-loss account and balance sheet, is adequate as a method of cost control. Yet once a decision has been taken to operate a fleet of vehicles, in preference to the other methods which are available to fulfil the transport stage of the distribution chain, such controls become wholly inadequate. The decision itself demands answers to a whole series of questions concerned with capital and revenue cost. In particular the potential operating costs of the fleet need to be compared with the costs of existing or alternative methods. The methods used to finance the purchase of the fleet, to depreciate its cost and to provide for its replacement are vital in the processes of decision and control.

It may seem naive to emphasise that the first step towards acquiring vehicles must be to analyse carefully the distribution task to be performed. Too often companies plunge into the acquisition of vehicles and drivers without carrying out the essential feasibility study thoroughly enough. To take one example, it is often sensible to purchase just enough vehicles to deliver the base load traffic and to contract out to third-party hauliers the seasonal traffic peaks.

Again, distribution is usually managed completely separately from the purchasing function. Yet, empty vehicles returning from making their final drop might be able to collect a load of components from a supplier.

Different methods of acquisition

Once the correct number and specification of vehicles to be purchased have been determined, the first financial problem is how to obtain the vehicles required. At first sight this is a simple issue. The vehicles can be bought outright from the manufacturer or distributor, involving a cash outlay. Alternatively the company can borrow the cash and pay interest on that borrowing. Other alternatives lie in getting another company to buy the fleet and then leasing back from them, or in becoming a party to a contract for hiring the vehicles. The competitiveness of these alternatives may be evaluated from quotations. The problem arises, however, when it is recognised that the right choice depends on the cash resources of the company, its capital structure and investment programme, and the influence of taxation. Thus a reduction in tax liability, the conservation of capital/cash resources, or the priority of other investment opportunities may be the important factors which prompt a company to make what may otherwise appear to be an illogical choice. In the first instance, therefore, the details of each method of securing a fleet must be understood if these problems of finance are to be properly interpreted.

Outright purchase

This is perhaps the most obvious method involving the straight allocation of cash funds to capital expense. The outlay is a net figure dependent on such factors as part exchange or trade-in agreements for existing vehicles, or fleet discount negotiations. Although modifications can be introduced, such as phasing of payment to the dealer, this method is absolute, conveying the ownership of the vehicles immediately and entirely to the buyer. It also means that, subject only to conditions contained within the purchasing agreement, such as a warranty on vehicle parts, the buyer assumes immediate responsibility for all overhead, standing and running costs of the vehicle, including repairs and maintenance. Even if a company has the necessary liquid resources for outright purchase, it is sensible to be at least aware of the opportunity cost of the capital used. The company may have other capital investment projects, the return on which will not be realised if the capital is spent on buying vehicles. Even in the absence of such projects, the company will be sacrificing the rate of return it is obtaining on its liquid funds.

Borrowing for outright purchase

The buyer can achieve the same end, and assume the same liabilities, by borrowing the necessary funds. In essence these facilities are merely a modification of straight purchase but adding the real – as opposed to notional – cost of borrowing the capital. In other words interest becomes payable. Although the date at which full title passes to the operator is a variable, facilities of bank loans, hire-purchase or borrowing from finance house (lease purchase) come within this group.

Leasing

Here is the first main alternative. Leasing a vehicle or fleet of vehicles means that ownership does not pass to the operator. The leasing company provides the cash or capital and, on the instructions of the operator, transfers such funds to the dealer in full settlement. According to the sum involved, the operator pays an amount, usually monthly, to the leasing company calculated rateably, that is so much per £1,000. As a result of the rapidly escalating cost of vehicles and the consequent inadequacy of depreciation provisions, leasing has been growing rapidly as a method of acquiring vehicles. Many commercial and industrial companies have set up leasing subsidiaries to take advantage of the benefits of deferring tax through writing off the whole cost of the vehicles in their accounts in Year 1. United Carriers and Marley are two cases in point.

There are two major varieties of leasing arrangements:

1   *Closed-end leases (leasing with guaranteed dealer buy-back).*   These leases, as their name implies, are for a fixed period duration and, since the supplier knows that he is going to receive a second-hand vehicle at a fixed date in the future, he will try to recover the full cost of the vehicle plus interest less the estimated residual value over that period. Thus the effective rate of interest can be higher, since the guaranteed residual value of the vehicle will be more conservative.

2   *Open-ended leases (full financial payout leasing).*   In this instance, capital cost and interest is amortised over a primary period. If the vehicle is retained after the primary period, then a nominal or peppercorn rental is charged during the secondary leasing period. At the end of either period, the vehicle may be returned to the lessor for disposal, or indeed disposed of by the lessee with the agreement of the lessors, who commonly return 95 per cent of the achieved selling price by way of a lease rebate. This can be an attractive facility in times of escalating vehicle prices.

In both options the rental figures quoted should take into account the fact of having given away the taxation benefit of the 100 per cent first year capital allowance. In addition, some leasing companies have favourable discount arrangements with vehicle manufacturers and these should be passed on to the lessee, who is unlikely to have the same negotiating power. Terms and Conditions may vary but the following is an example of an open-ended leasing contract for an articulated vehicle (at a time when MLR stood at 17 per cent):

Tractor Unit: Cash price: £22,500
          Less 15 per cent = £19,125
Monthly rentals calculated at £22.20 per £1,000
Monthly rental = £425
Total rental payable over 5 years is 60 at £425 = £25,500

Trailer Unit (40' flat)   £ 5,880
          Less 15 per cent = £ 5,000
Rental calculated at £22.20 per £1,000 per month
Monthly rental = £111
Total rental payable over 5 years: 60 at £111 = £6,660

Notes: 1   These rentals take account of a 100 per cent first year allowance on capital expenditure against taxation.
    2   In open-ended contracts, after the expiration of the five-year primary period, the secondary period rate would be at a peppercorn rental of roughly 1 month's primary period rental per annum.

Contract hire

The contract hire of vehicles is similar to closed end leasing, but with some important differences. Ownership again remains with the hiring company, but they undertake to provide, repair, maintain and replace the vehicles. An additional option, which has become popular in recent years, is the provision of drivers. Thus all costs can be included within an agreement with the advantage that budgeting is made much simpler. Contract hire agreements tend to be tailor-made for a particular client, but they are all normally based on a fixed standing charge plus a running charge per mile. Both these charges are usually reviewed at specified intervals and adjusted in line with some form of inflation index. The most often cited advantage of running contract hire vehicles is that a substantial proportion of fleet administration time and therefore cost is delegated to the hiring organisation. The main pitfall is that of defining the volume of traffic which is to be carried over the period of the contract, which is usually five years. There are many examples of companies signing contracts for too many vehicles and, in addition, of the wrong specification. Of course, reputable contract hire companies should assist their clients to ensure that this does not happen, since in the long run they will have a dissatisfied client. However, there are unscrupulous organisations around who are not averse to making a short-term killing. A checklist of points which should be considered before signing a contract hire agreement is set out on Figure 18:1. To quote a specific example, the author's company was recently called in to review the costs for a client who had signed a three-year contract hire agreement of which only one year had elapsed.

---

1 Period of contract
   – is it normal?
   – does it represent the worklife of the vehicles?

2 Livery and provision for repaint.

3 Detailed items to be provided, for example,
   – all repairs, including those incurred away from base
   – all tyres including replacements
   – tachograph fitting and maintenance

4 Specified vehicles or a specified number of a type.

5 Replacement vehicles
      conditions and delays – 24/28 hours

6 Drivers
   – conditions e.g. guarantees, etc.
   – replacements

7 Excess mileage charges.

8 Changes in cost.

9 Periodic payments
      in advance
      in arrears

10 Insurance and indemnities.

11 Potential for modifying fleet size.

Figure 18:1   Checklist for contract hire

The facts are these: a three-year contract was signed with the client specifying vehicles of greater than necessary horsepower (which caused premium capital costs and also premium running costs). The contract having been signed, legal opinion indicated no means of breaking the agreement without considerable damages for breach of contract and, in order to reduce operating cost, a longer term contract was negotiated. The result of this was a high operating cost in the first two to three years, leading to a more acceptable cost in the last two years, when comparing the costs of running four- to five-year-old vehicles with any acceptable alternative method of providing their replacement.

The contractor might reasonably have been expected to point out the premium costs involved in buying the specified vehicle: the client might reasonably have been expected to have obtained an alternative quotation: neither of these actions was taken and the result was as summarised in Table 18:1.

The essential difference between leasing and contract hire is that leasing is simply a financial method of providing a vehicle, whereas contract hire additionally transfers a significant proportion of fleet management activity and costs to the hiring organisation, who may be presumed in most cases to be able to offer a more

Table 18:1

Costs per vehicle (32 ton incl. driver)	Original agreement	Re-negotiated agreement	Competitor's quotation on vehicles of adequate specification
Standing (£pa)	23,500	18,500	16,464
Running (£/mile)	0.275	0.275	0.250
Average mileage (pa)	50,000	50,000	50,000
Assessed annual cost	37,250	32,250	28,964
Term of contract	3 years	5 years	5 years
Assessed fleet-cost (£pa)	782,250	677,250	608,244
Saving (£pa)	–	105,000 (13.4%)	174,006 (22.2%)

professional service. What must be emphasised most strongly is that, in both leasing and contract hire, it is up to the client company to utilise the acquired vehicles efficiently and make them earn their keep.

The major advantages stressed by the hiring company's marketing staff are:

1   Whilst the vehicle is physically under the control of the operator, the hiring company is responsible for all standing and running costs.
2   The hiring company arranges all maintenance and repairs and supplies replacement vehicles after accidents or breakdowns, ensuring peak availability at all times.
3   Administration of the fleet is reduced to one invoice per month. Accountancy and budgeting worries are things of the past. Total transport costs are known in advance and these costs are fully allowable against profits for tax purposes.

The emphasis is on relief from problems and the hiring company's assumption of responsibility. These are all undoubted advantages but they must be paid for. The problem is for the operator to assess each method in both cost and efficiency terms. It has to be accepted that some of the advantages of contract hire are difficult to cost, such as the availability of replacement vehicles or simplified accounting. Both leasing and contract hire are valuable services for the operator. The choice depends on a series of factors:

1   *Number of vehicles in the fleet.*   The smaller the fleet the more valid becomes contract hire. In such circumstances capital conservation may not be as important as the advantages of simplified transport budgets and guaranteed replacement.
2   *Location.*   The proximity or otherwise of the hiring company's maintenance centre is important. The operator who has access to good alternative maintenance facilities near to his base may prefer purchasing, or leasing, to contract hire.
3   *Vehicle design.*   The need for specialist vehicles can favour leasing. The contract hiring company, though prepared to enter contracts on such vehicles, tends to favour the standard type of vehicle.

4   *Cost.*   Considerable effort is made by leasing, hire-purchase and contract hire companies to prove their case in cost terms. The important point is that, over the life of the vehicle, all costs must be considered, including depreciation and their effect on company taxation. Secondly, the decision to buy, lease or hire depends in part on a series of estimates by the operator, particularly concerning operating costs, which he will or will not pay himself, depending on his decision.

Effect of taxation

The effect of taxation on this decision cannot be ignored. Under the UK tax system covering assessment of profits for tax purposes and capital allowances, all net expenditure on vehicles, including their capital cost, ranks for tax relief. Whilst it is not appropriate to delve too deeply here into the complexities of our tax law, it is important for the fleet manager to understand the basic points which affect his function:

1   The Inland Revenue gives allowances on capital expenditure during the life of the asset. For commercial motor vehicles an initial allowance is given in the first year of purchase.

2   Capital allowances on commercial vehicles tend to change occasionally but at the present time they are 100 per cent initial allowance. Because of this allowance, the amounts set aside for depreciation are not allowable.

3   Corporation tax is assessed at 52 per cent for larger companies. In terms of the flow of cash funds, the difference between comparative project costs is reduced by the tax element. Briefly, a company which pays out more for the use of an asset will thus reduce its profit and therefore its taxation liability.

4   To take account of the resale value of vehicles, there is a system of setting the sale proceeds against purchases to reflect net capital outlay.

5   In addition, all labour, standing and running costs are allowable. The same applies to any cost incurred through hire-purchase, leasing or contract hire agreements.

An interesting cosmetic advantage is sometimes put forward as a reason for leasing or contract hiring. The charges incurred are treated as revenue expenditure and are therefore tax deductible. By removing the capital cost from the balance sheet, the ratio of return on capital employed is improved and the debt-to-equity ratio is reduced. These factors are not wholly cosmetic, as the following example will demonstrate. A pharmaceutical company employed Davies & Robson to examine its distribution costs. It soon became apparent that there was no case in transport terms for the company to be running its own vehicles. However, the company was most reluctant to dispose of its vehicles, because its major client was the National Health Service, which has the right to demand that its suppliers do not make more than 20 per cent on their assets employed. The company therefore had no wish to improve its return on capital by reducing its capital employed.

Cost comparison of different methods

To answer the most important question of the different methods – what the eventual cost is likely to be – the final stage is to bring all this data together. The schedule in Figure 18:2 sets out the various costs under each of the methods discussed and is designed to illustrate the various cost centres as well as the influence of taxation. The schedule highlights the following points:

1   In terms of overall cost (that is, bringing together both the capital and revenue costs), vehicle operating costs are dominated by wage and running costs.
2   The effect of this is to pull into focus the relationship between capital or purchasing costs and pure operating costs. Thus, although the alternatives to outright purchase involve extra cost in the form of 'guarantee' costs, their importance in relative terms becomes less.
3   This is even more emphasised when taxation is taken into account. The point is that extra costs incurred are allowable for tax, thus reducing the difference between the costs of the various options.

No allowance has been made for opportunity costs in the outright purchase option, on the other hand depreciation is a charge which differs from the other items of expenditure in that it does not involve an actual cash payment. It is this most important subject, in the context of vehicle replacement policy, to which we must now turn our attention.

Vehicle replacement policy

The operator's replacement policy is a vital part of fleet management. It is unwise to operate a fleet without planning for replacement and creating reserve funds for this purpose. If this planning is neglected, then the picture of operating costs and profits will be seriously distorted. The factors involved are:

1   The life of a vehicle and the depreciation of its cost.
2   Future capital cost of replacement.
3   The timing of replacement.
4   The appraisal of investment.

Vehicle life

Without use, the theoretical life of a motor vehicle is long term. However, a vehicle is purchased for use, and it is the nature of this use and the costs incurred which determine vehicle life and, by implication, a replacement policy. The prime factor is cost but there are others:

1   Development in design of vehicles, i.e. obsolescence.
2   Legislation on construction and use of vehicles.

DATA Vehicle design 16 tonnes gross, 4 wheel rigid, flat platform *Initial capital cost* £16,000 including tyres *Estimated annual mileage* 35,000 mpa
Estimated life of vehicle 5 years *Residual value* £2,000 *Cost of tyres* £1,250 *Fuel cost per gallon* £1.20; Consumption 12 mpg

	OUTRIGHT PURCHASE	HIRE PURCHASE	LEASING	CONTRACT HIRE (without driver)
	£	£	£	£
TIME COSTS (a year)				
Depreciation	3,200	3,200	–	–
Licences	419	419	419	–
Insurance	400	400	400	–
Sheets and ropes	150	150	150	–
Overhead and administration	1,750	1,750	1,750	1,750
Hire purchase charges (averaged over 5 years)	–	4,560	–	–
Leasing charges (including 95% rebate on selling price)	–	–	3,884	–
Contract hire – standing charges	–	–	–	8,225
Total:	5,919	10,479	6,603	9,975
RUNNING COSTS (a mile)	p	p	p	p
Fuel	10.7	10.7	10.7	
Oil	0.3	0.3	0.3	
Maintenance and repairs	10.0	10.0	10.0	
Tyres	2.5	2.5	2.5	
Total per mile	23.5 8,225 (pa)	23.5 8,225 (pa)	23.5 8,225 (pa)	23.5 8,225 (pa)
TOTAL TIME AND RUNNING COSTS A YEAR	14,144	18,704	14,828	
WAGE COSTS (a year)				
Basic	4,350	4,350	4,350	4,350
Overtime, subsistence, pension and NHI	2,300	2,300	2,300	2,300
	6,650	6,650	6,650	6,650
TOTAL COST (a year)	£20,794 (59.4p a mile)	£25,354 (72.4p a mile)	£21,478 (61.4p a mile)	£24,850 (71p a mile)
Total cost over 5 years	103,970	126,770	107,390	124,250
Less resale price	2,000	2,000	–	–
Total net cost (5 years)	101,970	124,770	107,390	124,250
Less tax allowance capital allowances (or net capital outlay)	14,000	14,000	–	–
operating costs	87,970	110,770	107,390	124,250
	101,970	124,770	107,390	124,250
Tax relief at 52% on	53,024	64,880	55,843	64,610
FINAL COST	£48,946	£59,890	£51,549	£59,640

Cost is the major factor, simply because at a certain point it is cheaper to replace a vehicle than to continue to use and maintain it. Put another way, it is more economic to invest in new vehicles than to spend the equivalent funds on major repairs to existing vehicles. Cost in this case is related to both time and mileage. The longer a vehicle is in operation, the more it will cost to maintain; the more miles a vehicle covers, so will the cost of maintenance per mile increase. On the other hand the capital cost will decrease or the rate of depreciation will slow down. There is therefore an important relationship between maintenance cost and capital cost. The process of cutting the level of maintenance cost justifies the expenditure of capital resources – in other words the rate of return secured is sufficient to prompt capital investment. These then are the vital factors determining replacement policy. The first step is to quantify the trends of cost in time and mileage terms.

Maintenance

There is no doubt that the longer a vehicle is in operation in mileage terms or in time, the more it will cost to run, maintain and repair. The problem is to produce firm trend figures which could apply to all types of vehicle. It is always preferable for actual experience to replace estimates or theory, eliminating the host of variables such as quality of drivers, terrain on which the vehicle operates or the design of the vehicle itself. The data in Figure 18:3 illustrate the point about cost trend.

The figures reflect maintenance cost of a ten-year life and the effect of a major overhaul in year six. In this case the overhaul cost merely delayed, for one or two years, the continuous increase in cost. The conclusion must be that at a certain point there is a financial advantage in reverting to the low cost of the earlier years. Put another way, savings in maintenance cost can be achieved by investment in a replacement vehicle. It is vital to identify the point in time for that investment.

Depreciation

The offset factor which quantifies this is capital cost or depreciation. To depreciate an asset is to reduce profit by the cost of capital used in the business. Although many accountants might disagree, the layman may think of the objective of this procedure as being to build up a fund which is available for purchasing a replacement for the asset at the end of its useful life. The two most common methods of depreciation used in management accounts are reducing balance and straight line. The reducing balance method deducts a percentage, commonly 25 per cent for motor vehicles, on the written down annual value of the asset. Thus on a vehicle costing £16,000, depreciation would be £4,000 in the first year, £3,000 in the second year, £2,250 in the third year and so on. In the straight line method, the number of years of the useful life is divided into the initial value to obtain the annual depreciation amount. Thus with a vehicle costing £16,000 with a five-year life, the depreciation would be £3,200 per annum.

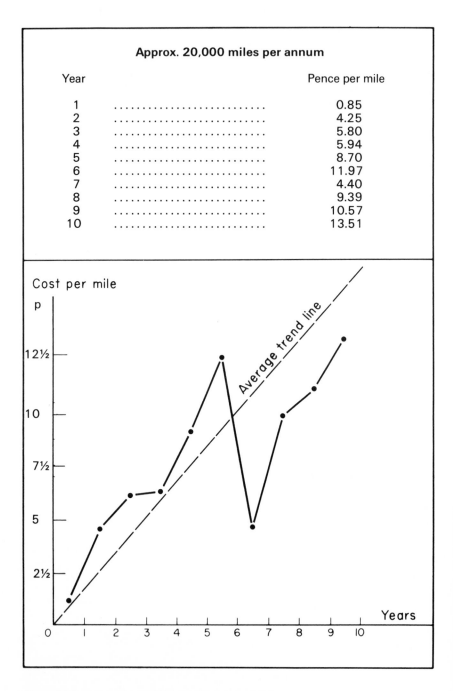

Approx. 20,000 miles per annum

Year		Pence per mile
1	....	0.85
2	....	4.25
3	....	5.80
4	....	5.94
5	....	8.70
6	....	11.97
7	....	4.40
8	....	9.39
9	....	10.57
10	....	13.51

Figure 18:3   Trend of vehicle maintenance costs

These methods, although in widespread use, have serious deficiencies in a period of inflation. The cost of vehicles has quadrupled over the last seven years. This means that companies have made inadequate provision for the replacement of their vehicles. They have, in effect, been overstating their profits by the amount that they have been 'spending' capital in real terms. This problem is somewhat mitigated by companies who possess a vehicle fleet whose age structure is spread evenly over the useful life of the vehicles.

Unfortunately, many companies have been hit by unanticipated capital demands, not only for vehicle replacement, but also for the many other assets due for replacement which have also increased in price as a result of inflation. In many instances, companies have been obliged to defer replacement decisions on vehicles and have thus distorted the age structure of the fleet and built up worse problems for the future. The accounting profession have eventually been forced to recognise these problems, and have agreed on current cost accounting procedures which reflect more accurately the real profitability of a company in inflationary periods.

Regardless of companies' current practice in their published accounts, it is prudent for them to make depreciation provisions based on the current replacement costs of vehicles. This procedure is open to the criticism that the replacement vehicle is quite likely to have an enhanced specification and so cannot be compared with the depreciating asset, but by and large it does seem to represent the best and simplest option available.

Schedule of costs

The data in the schedule in Figure 18:4 are designed to illustrate the points that have been made so far in this chapter. It is clearly not intended to reflect the effect of inflation on vital factors such as labour costs, cost of fuel, insurance and so on.

It has been assumed that all such costs remain static over the vehicle's life in order to focus attention on the complementary effect of depreciation cost and running cost. It is also assumed that maintenance costs will increase at a reasonably steady rate. This will not always be the case, as illustrated previously, but the average trend in maintenance will be upwards as time progresses.

If the figures for standing costs and running costs are plotted on a graph (Figure 18:5), it will be seen that they intersect between years 6 and 7. The major influences on these graphs are, of course, depreciation in the standing cost and maintenance on running costs. If we subtract depreciation from maintenance costs, we find that between year 5 and 6 the difference exceeds £4,000 for the first time. The indication is, therefore, that overall costs could be reduced at this time by investing in a replacement vehicle.

As any transport manager will tell you, the cost of time and money spent in the workshops is only part of the story. A vehicle off the road is not earning its keep and, with a demanding distribution task to carry out, the transport manager must either have spare vehicles available or resort to spot-hire of relief vehicles. Such costs have not been shown in this chapter for the purposes of simplicity of expression, but they

TIME COSTS	YEAR 1 £	2 £	3 £	4 £	5 £	6 £	7 £	8 £	9 £	10 £	11 £	12 £
Depreciation (25% on diminishing balance)	4,000	3,000	2,250	1,688	1,266	949	712	534	400	300	225	169
Licences	419	419	419	419	419	419	419	419	419	419	419	419
Insurance	400	400	400	400	400	400	400	400	400	400	400	400
Sheets and ropes	150	150	150	150	150	150	150	150	150	150	150	150
Overhead and administration	1,750	1,750	1,750	1,750	1,750	1,750	1,750	1,750	1,750	1,750	1,750	1,750
WAGE COSTS	6,650	6,650	6,650	6,650	6,650	6,650	6,650	6,650	6,650	6,650	6,650	6,650
	£13,369	£12,369	£11,619	£11,057	£10,635	£10,318	£10,081	£9,903	£9,769	£9,669	£9,594	£9,538
RUNNING COSTS (a mile)	p	p	p	p	p	p	p	p	p	p	p	p
Fuel	11.00	10.00	10.00	10.00	10.00	11.00	11.00	11.50	12.00	12.00	12.50	12.50
Oil	0.25	0.30	0.30	0.35	0.40	0.45	0.45	0.50	0.50	0.60	0.65	0.65
Maintenance and repairs	2.00	7.80	10.00	12.40	14.00	14.75	16.00	17.25	18.25	19.50	21.00	23.50
Tyres	2.50	2.50	2.50	2.50	2.50	2.50	2.50	2.50	2.50	2.50	2.50	2.50
	15.75	20.60	22.80	25.25	26.90	28.70	29.95	31.75	33.25	34.60	36.65	39.15
TOTAL RUNNING COSTS (annual mileage 35,000)	£5,513	£7,210	£7,980	£8,838	£9,415	£10,045	£10,483	£11,113	£11,638	£12,110	£12,828	£13,703
TOTAL ANNUAL COSTS	£18,882	£19,579	£19,599	£19,895	£20,050	£20,363	£20,564	£21,016	£21,407	£21,779	£22,422	£23,241
MAINTENANCE (total cost)	£ 700	£ 2,730	£ 3,500	£ 4,340	£ 4,900	£ 5,163	£ 5,600	£ 6,038	£ 6,388	£ 6,825	£ 7,350	£ 8,225
Maintenance minus depreciation	–£ 3,300	–£ 270	£ 1,250	£ 2,652	£ 3,634	£ 4,214	£ 4,888	£ 5,504	£ 5,988	£ 6,525	£ 7,125	£ 8,056

Figure 18:4 Vehicle costing – depreciation and running costs

are nonetheless real and should not be ignored in fleet costing. Indeed, what many companies do is to retain their replaced vehicles for one or two years as spares.

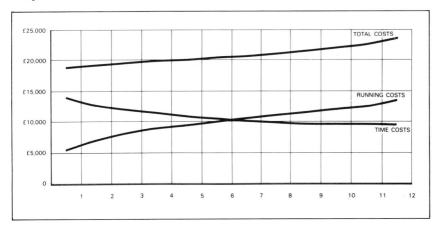

Figure 18:5   Running, time and total vehicle costs

Appraisal of investment

The factors involved in the replacement analysis are now quantified. The capital cost of replacement (and the various methods available), and also the trends in running costs, can be assessed. Savings will accrue in running costs if a new vehicle is introduced. Put another way, a return can be obtained on the capital investment required. The need is to time that investment so that the return is adequate to justify it.

Because of the exclusion of inflation effects, the depreciating balance method of inflation has been used.

Discounted cash flow

This investment appraisal technique has been much in vogue over the last few years, but the rates of inflation experienced recently have added a new dimension to the guessing game of financial forecasting and planning and it is becoming less widely used. Its important contribution is that it takes into account the time value of money (that is, that £100 today is worth more than £100 in five or ten years' time as a result of the use that can be made of that money in the interim). There are several steps to be taken in building up a DCF analysis:

1   Assess the required rate of return.
2   Calculate the net flow of cash during each year of the potential life of the asset (the vehicle).
3   Calculate the present value and yield of the investment.
4   Build up the DCF analysis and compare alternative projects.

For a simple example of DCF analysis, see Figure 18:6.

YEAR	0:	1:	2:	3:	4:	5:
(a) Initial purchase	–16,000					
(b) Lease cost saved		4,250	4,250	4,250	4,250	4,250
(c) Resale at end of life						1,940
(d) Net cash flow (not discounted)	–16,000	+4,250	+4,250	+4,250	+4,250	+6,190 = +7,190
(e) Present worth factor at 10% discount	1,000	0.909	0.826	0.751	0.683	0.621
(f) Discounted cash flow at 10% (d × e)	–16,000	+3,863	+3,511	+3,192	+2,903	+3,844 = +1,313
(g) Present worth factor at 15% discount	1,000	0.870	0.757	0.659	0.573	0.499
(h) Discounted cash flow at 15% (d × g)	–16,000	+3,698	+3,217	+2,801	+2,435	+3,089 = – 760

So the discount rate, which exactly balances discounted cash flows, lies between 10% and 15%. In fact it is 13%, as is shown below:

	0:	1:	2:	3:	4:	5:
(i) Present work factor at 13% discount	1,000	0.885	0.783	0.693	0.613	0.543
(j) Discounted cash flow at 13% (d × i)	–16,000	+3,761	+3,328	+2,945	+2,605	+3,361 = 0

So, in this simplified instance, if the company can earn more than 13% by using the £16,000 elsewhere, it should lease. Otherwise, it should purchase.

Figure 18:6   Example of discounted cash flow

The information required from the transport manager will be the calculated receipts and expenditure (giving net benefits) and the capital cost of the vehicles. Each course of action which could be taken is then evaluated by discounting the flow of cash to give a present value. The alternative with the greatest present value will be chosen. In the replacement context, such alternatives could be:

1   To continue using the existing fleet.
2   To replace with the same number and design of vehicles.
3   To replace with less vehicles of greater capacity or vice versa.
4   To purchase higher-quality (or indeed lower-quality) vehicles with a reflected effect on expected life and maintenance cost trends.

This kind of alternative series illustrates clearly the fundamental decisions involved in a policy of replacement.

Recording and controlling operating costs

Hitherto the various methods of purchasing and replacing vehicles have been examined, together with the implications on both capital and revenue cost. It is clear that total operating cost, and its break-down, are important in this context. Before looking at the process of costing itself, the first step is to identify the motives for costing. It is an obvious step but one which is often ignored. The two primary motives are:

1   To provide the data which are essential to permit effective management decisions to be taken.
2   To provide a control mechanism on vehicle or transport cost as an integral part of company profitability.

Within these broad definitions lie the reasons for costing – to create the ability to correct faults in the system; to prepare comparative data on alternative methods; to identify sources of economy within an existing system; to establish the timing of vehicle replacement, tyres, engines to determine the costs of providing various levels of service. The case for costing, and maintaining adequate records to do so, must therefore be accepted. There are three stages which make costing a meaningful exercise:

1   To estimate what costs will be incurred at given levels of activity (to budget ahead).
2   To record actual costs and highlight variances from budgeted cost levels.
3   To relate vehicle or transport costs to company operation.

For this chapter, budget and actual costs can be taken together. Budgetary control is dealt with in Chapter 22. Its importance cannot be over-emphasised as a vital part of the control process, but our interest here is in the form of costing. At least the layout for forecasting and recording of costs will be the same, if not the results.

The two basic factors in vehicle cost are time and mileage. Certain costs are incurred because of the time a vehicle is in operation and others incurred because of the mileage it covers. This provides a natural division for a cost breakdown:

Time costs	depreciation	overhead
	licence	administration
	insurance	gross wage costs
Mileage costs	fuel	maintenance and repairs
	oil	tyres.

This form of allocation and layout has been used in the hypothetical vehicle cost data in earlier sections but in the first instance the requirement is to introduce a practical and feasible system of costing and cost records. The salient features involved in building up such a system, although essentially adapted to the particular function of the vehicle – for example, bulk freighting or delivery, the nature of the company's products, sources of control – are:

1   To identify which of the costs are readily available (through a company accounting department for example) and which are capable of simple allocation on a departmental or vehicle basis.
2   To establish those cost centres where the problem of management control is accentuated (that is fuel purchasing, route mileage, subsistence).
3   To distinguish between the information which the fleet manager requires for management decisions and the data necessary in order to produce that information.

Following this through in sequence, the process could be:

1   To develop, in conjunction with the accounting department, a cost budget for fixed costs – depreciation, licence, insurance, overhead and administration.
       This would establish an essentially accurate section of cost for standard application throughout each cost period. The only changes to be introduced would be due to legislative or unforseeable fluctuations. This implies that a useful part of operating cost can be simplified and adjustments made infrequently.
2   To introduce a system for recording vehicle and cost activity which will provide the detail for summary costing of vehicles.
3   To establish a system for calculating, or picking up, gross wage and associated costs probably in conjunction with the wages department.
4   To bring the detail of fixed wage and running costs together to present a meaningful total costing of vehicle operation.
5   Finally, and most important:
       (*a*) To relate results to budget forecasts.
       (*b*) To produce management information relative to company activities (that is – distribution cost per product unit compared with forecast unit costs).

Since the appearance of earlier editions of this handbook, there has been a phenomenal reduction in the cost of computing. Due to the commitment of many companies to earlier generations of expensive mainframes, the potential of the new technology has so far been largely unappreciated and unexploited. What it opens up in particular is the prospect of the 'local' computer, serving in the distribution context, maybe, just a depot or the transport department.

The application of computers to vehicle costing has, of course, not gone unrecognised and indeed many excellent systems are available. The first main category of these are those sponsored by truck manufacturers. In this class, we find:

> FOCAS – Ford
> SAVE – British Leyland
> FIST – Mercedes

There are in addition two competing systems which have derived from the now defunct MAINSTEM suite of programs. These are:

> ABCAS – Allied Breweries
> FLEETPLAN – Fletcher Computer Services

The first class mentioned lays emphasis on providing the facility of comparisons against national averages, and of course the inter-make comparisons are of great interest to the sponsoring manufacturers.

The second class does not offer the comparative aspect, although ABCAS can provide a qualitative appraisal service from one of their senior engineers. FLEETPLAN, however, can offer an extremely varied range of analysis programs which to all intents and purposes amounts to a bespoke suite for each client. It has also met with the approval of the Freight Transport Association as meeting all necessary requirements from a costing system.

At present all these systems mentioned operate on a bureau basis with information supplied by operators. This may depend on existing documents used for vehicle costing and maintenance activities, or it may require special coding sheets to be submitted. There is obviously a pressing need for standardisation in nomenclature and codes for all vehicle costs. This has been recognised by the Institute of Road Transport Engineers, but there still seems to be some way to go before such a system – Vehicle Maintenance Recording System (VMRS) – receives widespread acceptance.

Although ABCAS have adapted their system to run on a Digico mini-computer, none of the other systems are available to run on a locally based computer. Certainly FOCAS and FLEETPLAN are working on providing direct access to their data bases from locally based terminals. International Computers Ltd have recently introduced a system called VEHICL based on a stand-alone minicomputer, but the all-in price is still relatively expensive. The market does seem to be wide open for a microcomputer based stand-alone system, which would provide both vehicle costing and computing power to transport departments, for such applications as load planning, picking lists, warehouse optimisation, maintenance scheduling, export documentation and so on.

However, whether the data is processed electronically or manually, the information input and output requirements are not greatly changed. What has changed is that the introduction of the tachograph opens up a new potential for capturing details of operating activities. Combined with optical scanning techniques, Lucas-Kienzle are already offering an analysis system based on computers. Other, perhaps cheaper alternatives are sure to follow.

Documents providing a basis for a vehicle costing system are set out in Figures 18:7 to 18:10. The fixed cost budget (Figure 18:7) offers a starting point. Variable costs are controlled on the vehicle journey record (Figure 18:8) and the vehicle operating cost sheet (Figure 18:9). Performance against target is recorded and evaluated, with analysis of departure from budget, on a management information sheet (Figure 18:10). These illustrations are merely an example of a method of isolating 'problem' costs and bringing total operating cost together. Their merit is that the results mean something and are simplified by the time the data are presented for management use. The emphasis is on expressing costs as per unit (i.e. per mile, per case, per ton), and on an analysed comparison with budget forecasts. There is a vital need for prompt information on these lines, on which effective management action can be taken to rectify an adverse trend and review the fundamental points of actual methods in use. Senior management can use the system to examine cost levels compared with alternatives and the effectiveness of management at every level.

Such a system can be developed to cover the whole operation of distribution. This point emphasises that any vehicle, transport or distribution costing system must be designed for the particular operation involved. However, if these points of emphasis are maintained, the system will be infinitely preferable to the production of a mass of data which merely confuses the issue and results in its being ignored by the fleet manager.

The costing system must be so organised that management personnel are not driven back to using purely instinctive judgement. The whole issue is complex and demands at least some detailed analysis.

Note

The author would like to acknowledge that this chapter draws extensively on the chapter of the same title which appeared in previous editions, written by the late S. L. Purvis.

Vehicle description _____ Registration number _____ Date of purchase _____ Capacity _____ Base _____

Month	Fixed costs		Wage and expense costs		Running costs			Total cost	Units carried and cost		Miles run	Cost per mile
	Standing	Overhead	Wages	Expenses	Fuel	Oil	Repairs and tyres		Product units	Costs unit cost		
January												
February												
March												
April												
May												
June												
July												
August												
September												
October												
November												
December												
Total												
Budget costs												
Variance												

Figure 18:7 Vehicle operating cost sheet

Management information				
	Month		Cumulative	
	Actual	Budget	Actual	Budget
Total units carried				
Total vehicle cost Trunking Delivery				
Unit cost Trunking Delivery				

Figure 18:8   Management information sheet for transport budgeting control

Vehicle description _____   Date of purchase _____
Registered number _____   Cost _____
Base _____

Depreciation

Written down value at _____
Depreciation for year _____
Depreciation per month/accounting period _____

Licence

Unladen weight
Licence cost for year
Licence cost per month/accounting period _____

Insurance

Total cost for year
Allocation cost per month/accounting period _____

Overhead

Total overhead cost per budget
Allocation cost per month/accounting period _____

Figure 18:9   Fixed cost budget

Registration number _____	Trip dates	Route
Based at _____	Start _____	From _____
	Finish _____	To _____
		Return _____

Mileage

Speedo—Finish _____

Start _____

Trip miles _____

Product carried

Type _____

Quantity _____

Units _____

Allocation

Trunking miles _____

Delivery miles _____

Total _____

Allocation

Trunking _____

Delivery _____

Total _____

Fuel intake

Company _____

External _____

Oil intake

Company _____

External _____

Trip expenses

Subsistence _____

Telephone _____

Parking _____

Other items _____

Total _____

Driver's signature _____   Date _____

Figure 18:10   Vehicle journey record

19

Vehicle maintenance

F. E. Harper

The transport engineering function has become increasingly important as vehicle maintenance, and its related operations, have become major factors in fleet efficiency and cost effectiveness. The requirements of the Road Traffic Act 1972 for annual testing of goods vehicles, and the sections of the Transport Act 1968 dealing with vehicle maintenance relating to the 'O' licence, created a situation where operators have to ensure that, at all times, their vehicles are in a fit and roadworthy condition and that their maintenance, inspection, and maintenance record systems meet the requirements laid down by these Acts.

The adequacy of any system depends, among other things, on the type of vehicles used, the work upon which they are engaged, and the mileages run. For these reasons, specific rules cannot be laid down, but intelligent adaptation of the principles set out in this chapter should meet the requirements.

Vehicle selection and replacement

One of the most important tasks facing the transport engineer is the correct selection of an additional, or replacement, vehicle for the particular job it is required to perform. It is therefore essential that both the operations and engineering departments work closely together to make certain that maximum efficiency is obtained at economical running costs in the vehicle operations, at the time the specification is prepared.

In theory, a vehicle being made of durable materials could last practically for ever. However, these are factors which determine vehicle life, and by implication, a replacement policy. The prime factor is costs, but there are others, namely:

(a)   Obsolescence in design and non-availability of spare parts.
(b)   Payload factors – unladen weight.
(c)   Speed factors.
(d)   Image of the company – an old vehicle can give a poor image.
(e)   Legislation requirements.
(f)   Basic economics of maintenance – change before a major overhaul is due.
(g)   Accessibility to customers and own premises.
(h)   Change of policy from rigid to articulated operation.

The second-hand market for commercial vehicles also has an effect on the replacement policy, as the market price is usually poor with the steepest drop in the first two years. Sales values of the average make of vehicle are as follows:

Year	Percentage of list price
1	55
2	40
3	25
4	15
5	5

After five years vehicles are worth little more than scrap value because of the obsolescence factor. Selling a vehicle just after a costly overhaul does not add considerably to its resale value.

There are certain definite points which must be given most careful consideration before the final choice is made, especially in the heavier and more specialised range. These generally can be classified as follows:

Rigid or articulated	–	many considerations regarding load, distances and traffic are affected.
Petrol or diesel	–	power to weight ratio, annual mileage, torque, fuel consumption, type of engine, performance requirement, gradability, standardisation.
Transmission	–	gear ratios, 2-speed axles, automatic and semi-automatic gearboxes.
Wheelbases	–	load suitability, body dimensions, axle spacing.

Brakes, suspension, cooling, security, air conditioning, regulations, etc., must be considered.

Having specified the essential mechanical features, draw up a similar specification for the body work. This will obviously vary through the wide range of possible work, i.e. bulk liquids, bulk powders, tippers, platforms, box vans, etc.

Figures 19:1 and 19:2 detail questions relating to the proposed operating requirements of the vehicles, with a draft specification sheet, which would be completed, once all the relevant facts were known.

New Vehicle(s)

Information required to prepare a vehicle specification

    (a) *Load information*
         1 Product to be carried.
         2 Average gross weight of load.
         3 What will loads be packed on or in?
         4 What will unit weight of average load item be?
         5 How will loading/unloading be done?
         6 Shape of load.

    (b) *Journey information*
         1 Average miles per year.
         2 Average miles per week.
         3 Estimated miles per day.
         4 Days vehicles used per week.
         5 Are vehicles to be used on 24-hour operation?
         6 Stops per day.
         7 How many operating bases will vehicles work from?
         8 Will all vehicles operate in similar conditions?

    (c) *Operating conditions*
         1 City
         2 Rural
         3 Inter-City
         4 Hilly
         5 Flat
         6 Mixed areas
         7 Motorways
         8 Unmade roads
         9 Desert

    (d) *Security*
         1 Will overnight storage be covered/uncovered?
         2 Are security guards used?
         3 Will access be adequate at base and depots?
         4 Are high value loads involved?

Figure 19:1   Operating requirements list

Maintenance requirements

The whole system of operators' licensing is based on safety, and this necessitates:

(a)   regular and effective maintenance, coupled with
(b)   systematic and thorough inspection of vehicles.

The Department of Transport has issued guidelines covering maintenance, and these are detailed in Figure 19:3.

    The most important aspect of ensuring that vehicles are in a roadworthy condition is a good system of inspection. This can be classed in three main categories.

CHASSIS

Chassis Make		Transmission	
Model		Clutch	
Engine		Rear Axle	
Fuel Used			
Wheelbase		Fuel Tanks	
G.V.W.		Automatic Chassis Lub.	
Payload		Anti-Theft Lock	
Cab Type		Air Cleaner	
Passenger Seat		Grille Guard	
Heater		5th Wheel ☐ Fixed ☐ Sliding	
Seat Belts			
Mirrors		Rear Bumper Stop	
BULKHEAD	☐ Full Height ☐ Half Height ☐ Full Width ☐ Half Width		
Power Steering		Other Equipment	
Brake System			
Tyre Size & Ply			
Spare Wheel			
Aux. Suspension			
Front Suspension			
Rear Suspension			

BODY

Body Type			Constructed of	
Body Size: L	Interior	Exterior	Floor:	☐ Soft Timber ☐ Single
W				☐ Hard Timber
H				☐ Alloy ☐ Double
Rear Doors			Side Doors	
Tail Lift: Size Type & Capacity			Shelving	
Rear Step (vans)			Rails	
Dropsides			Other Equipment	
(Lutons) Dropwell Tailboard and Bodyskirt				

PAINT

Chassis, Cab Colour		Artwork	
Body Colour		Notes (attach sample of sign)	
Signwriting			

ESTIMATED LIFE IN YEARS

CHASSIS		BODY		SPECIAL EQUIPMENT		PAINT	

Figure 19:2   New vehicle specification sheet

1 *Pre-delivery inspection.*   Very necessary before any new vehicle is put into service as unfortunately there is much to be desired in the quality control of many manufacturers.

2 *Roadworthiness inspection.*   This is a non-technical inspection and includes such items as:

(a) Condition and inflation of tyres.

(b) Effectiveness of lights, wipers, mirrors.

(a)   Maintenance arrangements should be such that a positive check is made at predetermined intervals of time or mileage on items which affect the vehicle's safety.

(b)   The main items which affect a vehicle's safety are those listed in the 'Goods Vehicle Tester's Manual', obtainable from HMSO.

(c)   Staff carrying out preventative maintenance must be aware of the significance of defects.

(d)   Inspecting staff should have the necessary authority to have defects rectified and keep potentially unsafe vehicles off the road.

(e)   Written records must be kept showing (i) when and by whom inspections are carried out, (ii) the results of the inspections, and (iii) when and by whom any remedial work is done, and details of such work. They may be kept in any form which allows the inspection history of each vehicle to be followed.

(f)   Experience with the type of vehicle operated and the work done will determine what is an adequate frequency for maintenance inspection.

(g)   Operators who contract out their maintenance arrangements will still be held responsible by the licensing authority for the condition of their vehicles.

(h)   Under-vehicle inspection facilities should be such that the inspector has sufficient light to see individual components, is able to examine them at close range and can, if necessary, handle them.

(i)   Pits, hoists and ramps are not always essential to meet the criteria given in (h). The essential requirement is that under-vehicle inspections can be carried out efficiently at appropriate intervals.

(j)   Means for measuring brake efficiency and setting headlamp aim are not essential, although it is obviously an advantage to have access to such aids.

(k)   Means must be provided for drivers to report defects on vehicles to the person responsible for their maintenance.

(l)   The mechanical condition of hired vehicles and trailers is the direct responsibility of the user.

Figure 19:3   Adequate maintenance – Department of Transport guidelines

(c) Operation of steering, brakes and other controls.

(d) Engine performance and smoke emission.

3   *Regular maintenance inspections.*   Frequency of these inspections, carried out by a skilled vehicle inspector, depends on the type of conditions under which a vehicle operates, but is usually in the region of four weekly (or 2,000 miles) intervals for vehicles which operate on good roads. For those vehicles engaged in off-the-road conditions, or other arduous work, the period can be considerably reduced. Figure 19:4 illustrates a typical layout of a vehicle inspection report.

Company		Fleet number		Date of inspection	
Depot		Make		Mileage reading at inspection	
		Body		Inspected by	

A	If satisfactory	B	Repairs required X	C	
1	Position of legal plate	26	Speedometer	51	Shock absorbers
2	Details of legal plate	27	Audible warning	52	
3		28	Driving controls	53	Stub axles/wheel bearing
4		29		54	Steering linkage
5	Emission of smoke	30	Play at steering	55	Steering box
6	Road wheel and hubs	31	Steering wheel	56	Power steering
7	Size of tyres	32	Steering column	57	Transmission
8	Condition of tyres	33		58	
9	Bumper bar	34	Air/vacuum warning	59	Mech brake connect
10	Spare wheel carrier	35	Build up of pressure/vacuum	60	Air/vacuum/brake wheel units
11	Trailer coupling/drawbar	36	Hand levers—Mechanical braking systems	61	Brake pipes/reservoir connections
12	Coupling on trailer	37	Service brake pedal	62	
13		38	Service brake operation	63	Obligatory front lamps
14	Condition of wings	39	Hand operated air/vacuum control valves	64	Obligatory rear lamps
15	Cab mounting	40		65	Reflectors
16	Cab doors	41	Condition of chassis	66	Functioning of direction indicators
17	Cab floor and steps	42	Electrical wiring	67	Vertical aim of headlamp
18	Driving seat	43	Engine mountings	68	Position of headlamps
19	Security of body	44	Oil leaks	69	
20	Condition of body	45	Fuel tanks and pipes	70	Trailer parking brake
21		46	Exhaust and silencer	71	Maintenance of service brake
22	Mirrors	47		72	Maintenance of secondary brake
23	View to front	48	Condition of spring pins and bushes	73	Maintenance of parking brake
24	Condition of glass	49	Condition of suspension units	74	
25	Windscreen wiper	50	Attachment of suspension units	75	

Tyre condition

Mark with X where replacement(s) required

Figure 19:4 Vehicle inspection report form
The second side carries space to record repairs required and completed

Specialized equipment		Enter details of work required	Work completed
Engine			
Hydraulics			
Frame			
Drum or tank			
Blower			
Mechanical transmission			
Controls			Signed
Miscellaneous			
Work required *A*			Signed
Work required *B*			Signed
Work required *C*			Signed
Remarks			

Passed for service _____ (Date)   Passed by_____

Figure 19:4   continued

Maintenance system

This must include:

(a) Planning and control.
(b) Maintenance work arrangements.
(c) Records.

Scheduled maintenance should allow for lubrication services, oil changes, and special attention and adjustments to components at agreed intervals. The frequency of the work must be related to the type of operations on which the vehicle is engaged. The main criterion is that the vehicle must be in a 'safe and roadworthy condition at all times'.

Major repairs

With a good system of inspection and maintenance, unscheduled major breakdowns and repairs can be kept to a minimum. By careful monitoring of components the critical mileage factors of most units can be established and a unit overhaul/replacement plan programmed to fit in with operating needs. A typical example, and which illustrates this policy, is shown in Figure 19:5.

Component	Stop/start city hauls (miles)	Long-distance hauls (miles)	Off road operation (miles)
Replace engine	200,000	250,000	150,000
Injector pump	100,000	100,000	60,000
Water pump	80,000	100,000	80,000
Starter	70,000	100,000	40,000
Alternator	40,000	40,000	40,000
Radiator	100,000	100,000	50,000
Lift pump	80,000	125,000	75,000
Clutch assembly	50,000	75,000	40,000
Gearbox	100,000	125,000	80,000
Universal joint	100,000	150,000	75,000
Differential assembly	300,000	450,000	200,000
Rear hubs	500,000	600,000	400,000
Rear brake shoes	60,000	75,000	50,000
Rear brake drums	120,000	150,000	100,000
Front brake shoes	60,000	75,000	50,000
Stub axle assembly	500,000	500,000	350,000
Track rod end	75,000	100,000	50,000
Steering box	250,000	300,000	200,000
Front road spring	300,000	400,000	100,000
Rear road spring	300,000	400,000	100,000

Figure 19:5   Component life mileages (estimated) (twin axle type vehicle)

Documentation and records

The efficient operation and administration of a transport department is dependent upon many factors, all of which are moulded together effectively by management with the aid of logical, but simple documentation and records. Some company systems are very simple and effective, other companies have highly sophisticated systems.

To keep control of all situations there must be paperwork and simple aids to assist in such matters as planned maintenance, workshop loading, stock control, vehicle records and legal requirements. The following list covers the more essential requirements:

1 Defect report   – Used solely by the drivers for reporting defects on their vehicles.

2 Maintenance schedule   – Details the work to be carried out on the vehicle at regular intervals (recorded in miles or weeks).

3 Planning board   – Enables the planned maintenance programme to be forecast well in advance.

4 Weekly maintenance
   call-in sheet   – Information derived from the planning board and passed to the operations department to plan for the withdrawal of vehicles for maintenance.

5 Job card. Should detail   – (a) Vehicle number.
                                 (b) Date.
                                 (c) Milometer reading.
                                 (d) Details of work carried out.
                                 (e) Labour and material cost.

6 Stores documentation   – Requisitions, parts location index, stock control, invoices, warranty claims, fuel and oil records.

7 Labour summary   – A summary showing the productivity and efficiency of personnel.

8 Progress board   – To check the progress of each job through the respective stages of repair and rectification and also to ascertain the loading of the workshop at any one time.

9 Inspection report   – Details the vehicle inspector's findings and work requirements.

10 Vehicle record card   – Details of the date and milometer reading of all services.

Legal requirements make it compulsory for vehicle maintenance records to be retained and available for official inspection by the DOE for 15 months.

Computer records

A computer is capable of sorting and analysing repetitive information at a very fast rate, and in consequence can be suitable for vehicle costs and other details. Although it is difficult to measure the cost benefits achieved by management information, there are several factors that indicate a simple computer programme can be the most effective means of providing information.

The basic headings are reasonably similar, no matter what the use of the vehicle. These are usually running costs, fuel, lubricants, maintenance, tyres, standing costs, depreciation, insurance, licensing and overheads. The maintenance heading can be broken down into further divisions such as engine, transmission, steering, brakes, electrical, body, etc., with further divisions if required.

To have effective management it is essential to have objective information, and intelligent use of the computer provides a good method of achieving this.

Workshop design

Depending on the scale of operation, workshops can vary in size from a two-bay operation category for up to ten vehicles to a major assembly and overhaul central workshop catering for all classes of maintenance, repair, body-building, painting and chassis frame alignment. In choosing a workshop, an operator must give very careful thought not only to the capital costs, but also the annual operating costs of the new facilities.

Another very important aspect to consider in workshop design is economy of space. This is an essential aspect of good planning as space is costly to heat, light, clean and repair, and has to be allowed for personnel walking to their jobs, stores and other critical areas.

Whatever system of repair is employed, be it unit replacement or otherwise, there has to be some means of lifting heavy units. For example, when removing an engine, allowance should be made in the building design to allow for a travelling gantry to be accommodated in the apex of the roof.

The relative merits of hoists and pits are difficult to assess without referring to particular conditions existing in any organisation. Simple types of pit are usually cheaper than hoists, but if underground installations of a comprehensive nature are contemplated, the pits may be quite as expensive as hoists. Hoists are better for some operations, such as servicing, inspection, and work whereby the mechanic can position the vehicle to a comfortable work position.

An adequate workshop facility is the barometer of a successful fleet operation. However, coupled with the need for this are certain other pre-requisites:

(a)   Management must furnish proper tools, facilities and working conditions.
(b)   Mechanics must make proper use of the facilities provided, with emphasis on alert, conscientious inspections.
(c)   Drivers must avoid abuse of the vehicle, and make prompt, accurate reports on malfunction.

(d)   Equipment makers must furnish durable, reliable products capable of being
       properly maintained. Petroleum suppliers must produce and recommend
       proper fuels and lubricants to meet all operating conditions.

Workshop equipment requirements

Adequate workshop equipment is a decisive factor in prompt fault diagnosis, rapid
servicing and repair times, and final adjustments.

It is impossible to specify minimum equipment requirements, as workshops
differ in size, layout, and the number of mechanics employed. What will be needed
will depend on its general operation but for guidance the list shown in Figure 19:6
includes major equipment subdivided into five sections: maintenance safety services,
performance services, general workshop and accident damage. Specialist tools
necessary for the particular makes of vehicles operated are essential, and the
manufacturers supplying them should be known.

Workshop staff

The ratio of skilled staff to vehicle numbers depends on many important factors, e.g.
age and mileage of vehicles, size and type, and arduous nature of the operation;
whether it is a first line workshop, or major repair centre; and extent of service
exchange to vehicle overhaul work carried out. Modern labour-saving workshop
equipment can greatly assist workshop personnel in carrying out the repairs and
replacements associated with a transport fleet. Not only does good equipment ease
the task of the mechanics, but does in fact enable the workshop manager to economise
on his manpower.

In recent years many organisations have introduced more sophisticated
diagnostic servicing techniques. This, coupled with staff trained to diagnose
mechanical (or electrical) faults, and to pin-point the basic cause – be it poor design,
inadequate quality control, driver abuse, or skimped maintenance – are all aimed at
reducing costs and at the same time improving the engineering of fleet servicing.

Figure 19:7 gives a suggested staff establishment for various sizes of fleet
(heavy transport). Figure 19:8 shows a draft organisation chart for, say, a 100-
vehicle fleet operating both a day and night shift.

Training

The quality of management, supervisors, foreman, mechanics and other skilled
personnel is of the greatest importance. This can best be achieved by continual
planned training, education, and development to ensure that staff are as flexible and
effective as possible in their jobs.

It must be emphasised, however, that the basis of training for appointments in
road transport engineering is by an apprenticeship in automobile engineering in the
vehicle field. This should include technical engineering and education in management
subjects.

Operation	Equipment	

Lubrication	Air compressors
	Lifts (electric and
	  hydraulic)
	Lift jacks
	Lift lighting
	Chassis lubrication
	Engine oil dispensing
	Gear and transmission
	  oil dispensing
		Oil meters
		Penetrating oil sprayers
		Waste oil disposal
		Specialised lubricant
		  power guns
		Radiator filler (hose reel)
		Tyre inflator
		Hose reel systems

Washing and ancillary equipment	Conveyor systems Pressure washers Arch washers	Self-service, coin-operated Portable suction cleaners Brake system service

Safety services

Brakes	Brake tester
	Portable decelerometer
	Brake pedal depressor
	  (with or without meter)
		Brake system service
		  (hydraulic and vacuum)
		Impact tool (wrench)
		Lifts/jacks

Headlight testing	Headlight tester	Headlight tester (sealed beam)

Steering and
wheel alignment
	Steering and wheel
	  alignment – complete set
	Turning radius gauges
	Wheel alignment gauge
		Camber, caster and king
		  pin inclination gauge
		Impact tools (wrench)
		Lifts/jacks

Tyre service	Wheel balancers Tyre bead breaker Tyre changers Tyre spreaders Impact tool (wrench)	Tubeless tyre test tank Vulcanisers Tyre inflation Air compressor Lifts/jacks

Performance services

Diagnosis and
tune-up
	Dynamometer
	Diagnosis test set
	Instrument type; or
	Diagnosis equipment with
	  an ignition oscilloscope
	  and meters
		Distributor tester
		Coil-condenser tester
		Exhaust gas analyser
		Plug service equipment
		Ignition timing instrument
		Compresssion tester

Electrical	Test bench Pole screw-driver	Volt-amps test set Ohm-meter Electric tachometer
Battery	Condition testers Fast charger/tester Chargers – fast	Chargers – slow Cadmium voltmeter

Figure 19:6   Maintenance services

Operation	Performance services *(continued)*	
Diesel	Fuel pump testers (bench or in situ) Fuel pump calibrator Fuel pump service vice Fuel pump element comparator Governor tester Injector tester (hand operated or motorised all types)	Injector dismantling jig Injector cleaning kit Injector reconditioning machine Injector microscope Needle adjusting jig Compression tester Smoke meter
General workshop equipment		
General repair	Air compressors Lifts (electric and hydraulic) Lift jacks Jacks – trolley Jacks – transmission Axle stands Hoisting equipment Creepers – floor Hose and cable reels Breakdown recovery equipment De-greasing tank Drills – electric and pneumatic	Grinders – electric and pneumatic Impact tools – electric and pneumatic Presses Steam cleaners Underbody sealing equipment Valve refacers Valve reseaters Work benches Pullers and extractors Lathes Cranes
Engine reconditioning	Air compressors Bench grinders Cleansing tanks Cranes Crankshaft grinder Engine stand	Presses Steam cleaners Valve refacers Vale reseaters Valve seat cutting and insert tool
Accident damage repair		
General	Air compressors Lifts (electric and hydraulic)	Jacks – trolley Axle stands
Chassis and body repairs	Body and frame straighteners Panel beating tools	Welders – arc, spot and oxy-acetylene Impact cutters Body checking jigs
Refinishing	Spray booths Fume extractors (exhaust fans) Low bake oven Suction cleaners Sanders – electric and pneumatic	Paint sprayers Air regulators/moisture separators Paint drivers – infra red Polishers – electric and pneumatic

Figure 19:6   continued

Number of vehicles in fleet	100+		75 to 100		50 to 75		25 to 50		10 to 25		1 to 10	
Workshop coverage	12 hour	24 hour	12 hour	24 hour	12 hour	24 hour	12 hour	24 hour	12 hour	24 hour	12 hour	24 hour
Spare vehicle capacity	10+	7+	7 to 10	5 to 7	5 to 7	3 to 5	2 to 5	1 to 3	1 to 2	1	1	–
Skilled mechanics **	10+	12+	7	9	5	7	2 to 5	3 to 7	1 to 2	2 to 3	1	–
Auto-electricians	1+	2+	1	2	1	2	1	1 to 2	–	–	–	–
Semiskilled mechanics ***	2	2	1	2	1	2	1	2	–	–	–	–
Vehicle inspectors	1+	2	1	1	1	–	1	–	–	–	–	–
Greaser/trainee	1+	2+	1	2	1	2	1	2	1	2	1	–
Apprentices	2+	2+	2	2	1	1	1	1	1	–	–	–
Coachpainters	2+	2+	2	2	1	1	–	–	1	1	–	–
Labourers	1	2	1	2	1	1	1	1	1	1	–	–
Storemen	2+	3+	2	2	1	2	1	–	–	–	–	–
Vehicle cleaners	1	2	1	2	1	–	1	2	–	–	–	–
Total labour force	23	31	19	26	14	18	8 to 11	12 to 17	4 to 5	5 to 6	2	–

** Includes chargehands and testers

*** Includes tyre fitter

Figure 19:7   Workshop staff establishment

357

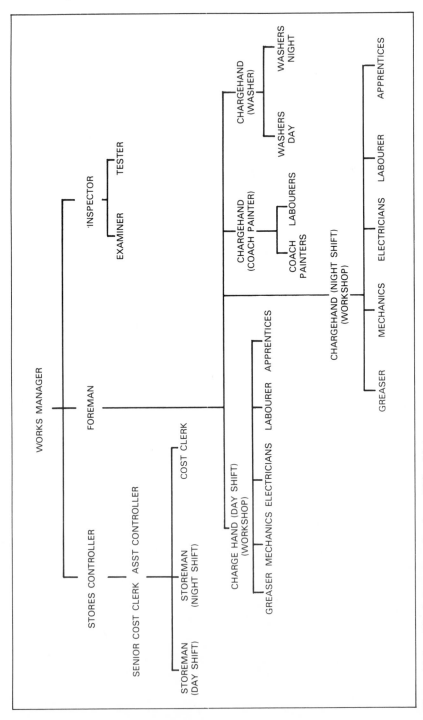

Figure 19:8 Workshop organisation – 100 vehicles

At the lower end of the scale, much of the routine work of transport maintenance is carried out by semi-skilled personnel, and a continuous training programme in the pattern of company maintenance and repair standards is necessary. It is hardly necessary to stress the wastage of materials and time that can occur through an indifferent approach to the job not by way of disinterest but lack of 'know-how'.

Most vehicle and component makers offer specialised training for operators' workshop staff. The bigger manufacturers generally have well equipped schools in which theoretical and practical tuition is given by professional instructors according to the best syllabus.

Spare parts

A very important aspect in connection with the maintenance of a fleet of vehicles is to ensure adequate facilities for the provision of spare parts, accessories, lubricants, fuel and such other items as are necessary for the repair and running of the fleet. Without careful planning, if the size of the transport operation increases, such growth can lead to a chaotic or unduly cumbersome parts department and its attendant administration section.

The size and layout of a spare-parts store will vary considerably with different fleets, and will be related to the extent of repairs undertaken and to the availability of parts from manufacturers' local agents. Body building, re-builds and painting, engine reconditioning and similar major operation in the workshops will greatly increase the range of spares necessary to be held in stock and the area of store required. A reasonable allowance would appear to be 6 sq. ft of floor space per vehicle maintained. An essential aspect of the parts operation is a good system of stock control to check maximum and minimum stock levels, turnover of stock, supplies, etc., and a parts location index to register parts held in the parts department and bin location.

A well functioning parts department must be able to handle a multiplicity of problems, and achieve:

(a) Sufficient supply capacity.
(b) Well balanced stock.
(c) Simple and reliable routines.
(d) Well dimensioned order quantities.
(e) Good control and steering aids.

Taken separately and together these factors will increase efficiency in and goodwill for the spare-parts department, as well as the operation in general.

In the very large parts departments the increasing number and variety of factors that are difficult to meter and survey have paved the way for computerised systems to perform comprehensive and complicated computations rapidly. Such a computer system should be built into the total spare-parts system, in partially manual, partially computer routines, and should be module built in order to conform to the individual demands that various users may put forward. A 'system of computer services' is illustrated in Figure 19:9.

Salvage recovery

All transport operators are aware of the increasing capital cost of each new vehicle they purchase and the vital necessity for ensuring that, when an accident does occur, whoever recovers that vehicle, recovers it without further damage. Also the size of the loads being carried today, and frequently their hazardous contents, has brought about the need for the most sophisticated approach to what used to be a simple winch job. Certainly the design of recovery vehicles has undergone a complete transformation in recent years, so that now they are fast and well equipped with twin-boom lifting gear,

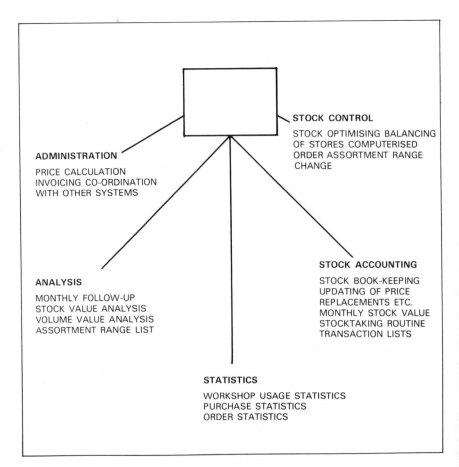

Figure 19:9   Computer services

nylon strops, air cushions, winch and all the other necessary tackle to clear the road without further damaging the casualty or spilling its contents.

Future trends in recovery vehicle design could soon follow continental and US designs, whereby hydraulic controls replace the coventional mechanical equipment. The advantages are that hydraulic controls are invariably finger light positive and have the ability to 'inch' by light application of the lever – something never possible with a mechanical recovery unit. An even greater advantage is the ability to inbuild safety cut-out valves to prevent overloading.

Air cushions, inflated from a portable compressor, are becoming standard equipment on recovery vehicles for the righting of overturned vehicles. Other essential equipment should include cutting tools, snatch blocks, spades, shovels, pick-axe, screw jacks, saws, chains, skid pans and wood blocks. It is also essential to include fluorescent jackets and crash helmets for crew safety.

There is now national coverage by several recovery organisations, which ensures prompt attention by rescue facilities to members' vehicles on a 24-hour basis. Some fleet users operate their own recovery vehicles for local incidents, and use a national organisation for the more distant jobs.

Vehicle cleanliness

Regular and thorough cleaning of vehicles is necessary to enhance the company image to the general public, and also to ensure that the underside of the vehicle can be seen without difficulty by the MOT inspectors and company maintenance personnel, and any wear or damage easily seen and acted upon.

Pressure on operating costs, the need for drivers to spend as much time as possible in actual driving, and the need for frequent cleaning, particularly in the food and allied industries, have made automatic washing machines economic for more and more operators. In addition, the rapid growth in demountable body and articulated fleets means that the number of bodies to be washed daily is no longer determined solely by the number of motive units.

The layout of a vehicle wash area has a most important bearing on the installed cost of any washing machine. If the area already has proper drainage facilities, the total washing equipment installation cost is significantly reduced.

Outside maintenance facilities

There are many occasions where it becomes an economic proposition to contract repair and servicing work out to the garage industry. The size and location of a fleet usually determines policy in this respect, and it remains very much a matter for the fleet user to assess his own needs, assess the costs of the alternatives, and then plan ahead accordingly.

For those operators who use a repair garage it is preferable to use a main distributor or agent for the make of vehicle operated, as the staff will be highly skilled on the particular manufacturer's products, considerable spare parts will be held, and warranty matters more easily progressed. Repair and maintenance arrangements should be agreed in writing with the repairer, and the garage should supply the operator with adequate records of all inspection, service and repair work carried out.

The effective working of a maintenance contract requires the fullest co-operation of both the repairer and fleet user in so far as the vehicle must be, within reason, made available to the garage when required at the specific servicing interval and time allowed to complete the job satisfactorily. By good planning and co-operation the risk of a vehicle being kept off the road unnecessarily is considerably reduced.

Continental operations

Europe, the Middle East and Asia are destinations now covered regularly by many British hauliers and own-account operators. This means exceptionally high mileages, rough terrain, extremes of temperature and vehicles being away from normal maintenance facilities for lengthy periods.

In recent years reputable service stations controlled by the major heavy vehicle manufacturers have been set up throughout Europe and to a lesser degree in the Middle East and Asia. These are well equipped to provide operators on international runs with any help they may need to deal with trouble as it arises. However, it is advisable to obtain an estimate of costs before any repairs are put in hand abroad, and the scope of the job made quite clear. Unless special arrangements have been made through the home distributor regarding payment, it is almost certain that the service station will require full cash settlement for the cost of the repair before releasing the vehicle. Special product training should be given to drivers engaged on overseas transport to enable them to diagnose faults, and carry out limited emergency repairs en route.

The following list of equipment and spare parts has been found adequate to cover most mechanical and weather problems likely to be encountered on long overseas hauls.

1   Tools:
     One jack and handle
     One wheel spanner and bar
     One vehicle tool kit
2   Lights:
     One torch
     One wonder lamp operated from vehicle battery
3   Warning signs:
     One red triangle
     One flashing warning lamp

4 Winter:
   One set of snow chains
   One shovel
   One pint methylated spirits (for the braking system)
5 Fire-extinguisher
6 First-aid kit
7 Driver's handbook
8 Spare parts:
   Spare wheels complete – tractor and trailer
   Complete set bulbs – tractor and trailer
   Fan belt
   Complete set water hoses
   15 ft airline hose with connections
   Set of fuel injection pipes
   Two screen-wiper blades
   One rear view mirror glass
   One flasher unit
   Box containing assortment of bolts, nuts, washers, split pins, jubilee clips, electric cable, fuses
   2 gallons of engine oil
   2 pound tin of heavy grease

From a security and safety aspect it is essential that all such equipment and tools are kept in a strong lockable compartment on the vehicle.

In addition to the equipment carried on the vehicle, detailed instructions should be carried advising the driver on the action to be taken in the event of a breakdown or accident. A driver should be told to telephone/telex the following information:

1 Telephone number and address where he can be contacted.
2 Location of vehicle.
3 Load destination (if contacting his own base).
4 Nature of breakdown/incident.
5 Vehicle or trailer make.
6 Registration number.
7 Chassis number.
8 Engine number (if there is engine trouble).

In the event of replacement tyres being required, the size and all other markings of defective tyres (except maker's number), and whether radial or cross ply, should be given. It is also advisable to include the telephone or telex numbers of the vehicle's parent base, and have telephone numbers of the senior engineering staff, so that contact can be made for assistance at all times.

In all cases of exceptional delay, due to breakdown or accident, the driver must ensure that his permit and 'T' document are formally endorsed on the reverse side by the nearest customs office or police.

Tachographs

The use of tachographs on a compulsory basis applied to drivers of all relevant vehicles from 1 January 1982.

The EEC law relating to tachographs is embodied in the following regulations:

(a)   543/69 dated 25 March 1969 as amended by 514/1972, 515/1972 and 2499/1977 on the Harmonisation of Certain Social Legislation Relating to Road Transport.

(b)   1463/70 dated 20 July 1970 as amended by 1783/1973 and 2499/1977, concerning the Installation of Recording Equipment in the Field of Road Transport.

The timetable for the compulsory fitting of tachographs in vehicles engaged on national transport operations was between 1 April 1980 and 31 December 1981. There is no requirement for the fitting of tachographs in the following cases:

(a)   Drivers of vehicles of less than 3.5 tonnes gross weight.

(b)   Drivers of vehicles exempt from 'O' licensing (except drivers of Crown vehicles).

There are three makes of tachograph available in Britain and the manufacturers are as follows:

Lucas Kienzle Instruments Ltd.,
36 Gravelly Industrial Park,
Birmingham B24 8TA.

Smiths Industries Ltd.,
50 Oxgate Lane,
Cricklewood,
London NW2 7JB.

Veeder-Roat Ltd.,
Kilspindie Road,
Dundee DD2 3QJ.

The cost of the instrument varies between £120 and £150, depending on manufacturer. They are usually subject to quantity discounts. Fitting charges can add between £90 and £120 depending on the type of vehicle. The time for fitting, again depending on the vehicle type, will be between 4 and 8 hours. Calibration and checking add a fixed fee (a standard amount set by the Department of Transport) to the job.

20

Security in distribution

John Wilson

.

There are no accurate figures available to show the total extent of thefts during distribution; the police hear only of those immediately noticed, or sufficiently sizeable to require reporting irrespective of time lag. Some show themselves as unaccountable deficiencies during warehouse stock checks, others in customer complaints of shortages, or simply as unexplained disappearances, generally put down to misdirection or faulty packing.

This is an international, not a domestic problem; in the USA, for example, the annual value of cargo stolen in transit was estimated in 1979 as being in excess of 2½ billion dollars (2 billion in 1972); in the UK the estimate was over £100,000,000. In each country the losses were mainly attributed to the criminal activity of employees; media prominence may be given to hijackings and the like but the major drain lies in the persistent pilferage which has made the phrase 'fallen off the back of a lorry' a joking reference to anything sold or offered low price.

Such figures as may be quoted are purely 'guess-timates'; there are too many obscuring factors for any accuracy. On the basis of reports to the Metropolitan Vehicle Observer Corps during 1978, which relate only to loaded vehicles and substantial losses, 159 were stolen with goods worth £1,590,000 in London itself. These could only be a fraction of the true cost to distribution as a whole in that area as they take no account of employee theft nor the innumerable occasions of petty stealing from vehicles during deliveries – to say nothing of the infinite variety of frauds that may be encountered. Although the emphasis in this chapter is on commercial vehicles, cars used by sales representatives are frequently selected for attack and in some instances the value carried in them is out of all proportion to the size of the vehicle.

Insurance cover

Too often insurance is the only precaution taken whereas it should only be one step taken to manage the operator's risk. A hardening of insurers' attitudes towards negligence, or failure by their clients to comply with conditions, is in the opinion of many long overdue. In some cases conditions have, at least on paper, become more rigorous as in one case by the inclusion of:

1   For overnight stops, vehicles were parked in a guarded car park, immobilised and alarmed, adequately sheeted or locked as applicable; or
2   If this could not be done, they should be left in recognised well-lit parking spaces, preferably compounds, and their presence made known to the local police – who would hardly appreciate this condition being widely applied!

It would be wrong to anticipate leniency towards claims will continue, even when transport insurance is only a small part of a much larger folio held with the client. No transport manager in his right mind should permit or condone laxity in procedure, documentation, supervision, etc., on the principle that 'the insurer will pay'. It is obvious that if an insurance company does decide to contest a claim, and reasonable precautions have not been taken, their refusal will be upheld. This follows from the case of Ingleton of Ilford *v* General Accident Fire and Life Assurance Corporation, [1967] 2 Lloyd's Report 179, where the policy excluded loss or damage by theft if the van was left unattended in a public place unless it was securely locked. The van and contents were stolen while the driver was in a shop making delivery of goods, the van was unlocked and the ignition key was left in. The insurance company was held not to be liable under the policy.

What a thief looks for

Since it is the prospective thief who starts the whole sequence, it is worthwhile trying to put oneself in his position, and thinking about what he will be taking into consideration when deciding to attack a particular vehicle.

In general, thieves dislike physical exertion; they want a quick, quiet, and if possible non-violent theft; they want to get rid of an identifiable vehicle as soon as they can; they would like to delay knowledge of the theft being circulated; they do not want to be caught with the stolen goods in their possession – in short, they want the odds well and truly on their side. A form of checklist of requirements for a prospective thief, intending to steal a loaded vehicle, would be:

1   Knowledge of the whereabouts of an attractive value load.
2   The ability to remove the vehicle and/or its load.
3   The opportunity to do so.
4   Sufficient time to carry out the theft without interference or attracting attention.
5   Adequate time to ensure being a safe distance from the scene before the theft comes to light.

6   An early market for the goods with reasonable reward.

7   Negligible risk of detection.

Major thefts are almost invariably the work of organised gangs who will have arranged the presence of nearby trans-shipment or storage facilities and probably a market for the goods before the theft has even been seriously considered.

A case in point – a loaded trailer was split from its tractor in accordance with insurer's conditions and left over the weekend in a poorly fenced and badly lit yard. The tractor was unlocked with the keys on the driver's seat (the insurers paid despite this!). Last known to be there late on a Sunday afternoon, at the time the theft was being reported to the police the following morning the trailer was being unloaded some 180 miles away into a container destined overseas.

Methods of stealing

A prospective thief has choice of target, time, place and method; the first three are peculiar to each incident, but there are certain basic methods which are regularly practised:

1   In the absence of the driver, stealing the vehicle complete or stealing from its load, while it is parked either temporarily or overnight.

2   Persuading the driver to stop by a subterfuge and then taking possession of the vehicle by threat of violence, or direct force.

3   By bribing, or threatening, causing a driver to co-operate with them in simulating the theft of his vehicle and telling a false story to the police (in the opinion of many this is the most prevalent method used).

4   Purporting to be bona fide carriers, persuading a firm to use them for carriage of a load.

5   Impersonating a driver to obtain possession of his loaded vehicle – infrequent, but effective.

It will be noted that the driver is the target of three of the five alternatives – which makes his reliability and trustworthiness all the more important. There are many variations on the main themes, and no doubt others will occur to thieves with fertile minds, but the more of these lines of attack and necessary accompanying requirements that can be negatived, the less likely that a particular load will be attacked.

Driver's role in security

Amongst all the employees in a distributive organisation, drivers have the greatest opportunities for dishonesty, either by themselves or in conjunction with loaders, checkers or office staff and, of course, there is the ever-present possibility of conspiracy with outsiders. If an operator uses a driver who cannot be trusted, then the most expensive devices and intricate procedures do no more than complicate his method of stealing or the manner of concealing his co-operation with outsiders. Where high-risk goods are concerned, a driver's integrity is essential, and a transport manager who engages a doubtful applicant must accept a good proportion of the subsequent blame.

Nevertheless, in most firms the recruitment of drivers remains on the same level as that of other staff. To a transport manager, a new driver is 'always wanted yesterday', the principle of expediency tends to be given priority, and the checking of references is too often regarded as an irksome last-minute necessity. In the carrying of high-value loads, this attitude invites trouble and the care taken should be commensurate with the risk to the operator. If such precautions result in the occasional loss of a driver who takes employment elsewhere, that is the price one has to pay for peace of mind. From the insurance angle, failure to take reasonable precautions in selecting drivers has been given as a good reason for nonpayment of claims. In this context 'reasonable precautions' has been interpreted as including whatever enquiries about the applicant are appropriate in relation to the standard of integrity that the post demands.

The great majority of drivers employed by firms of standing develop a degree of loyalty which precludes them from conniving in thefts from their employers. Even so, although approaches at motorway and roadside cafes are not infrequent, few are ever notified to the police.

It is a matter of statistics that most major losses are suffered when hired transport is used, where it is not possible for a firm to apply its own standards of driver selection. In using outside transport, therefore, it is all the more important to ensure adequate insurance cover, to agree conditions of liability, and to give specific instructions with regard to overnight parking and load security.

The degree to which, and the spheres within which, 'hired' labour is to be used should be carefully considered. Several organisations maintain pools from which their customers can draw temporary staff to substitute for permanent employees who are sick or on holiday, or to cater for a seasonal trade increase. The standards set by a company for its own drivers, and the checks it makes upon them, may not be met by these 'temporaries'. Fidelity bonds held by such organisations may not be considered by one's own insurers to be acceptable or an adequate basis for recovery in case of loss. If high-value loads are to be carried by such drivers, the insurers should be apprised and their prior approval obtained. They may well ask that a positive and satisfactory loss liability should be defined.

Where a firm's own drivers are concerned, careful selection should be supplemented by subsequent indoctrination and coupled with documentary and other procedures to minimise temptation.

Transport managers should realise that they may be biased at an interview in respect of an applicant who appears to have the best technical qualifications; security and interviewing are not disciplines in which a transport manager is likely to have had experience and, though he may regard it as a reflection upon his own competence and authority, it may be advisable for him to have someone present at interviews with experience in these areas.

Driver selection

The principle to be applied is 'horses for courses' – a driver who would be a major risk with a cargo of wines and spirits or tobacco could be efficient, and even trustworthy, putting concrete on motorways or driving farm tractors. Where there is doubt about the calibre of an applicant, it is doing him no favour to place him in a position of great temptation.

In these days of difficulty in dismissing unsatisfactory employees, even when they have misrepresented their previous record or their abilities, it is advisable to have an application form which leaves the applicant in no doubt about the necessity for accuracy in his answers. A sample of such an application form is shown in Figure 20:1.

Given fulfilment of the normal requirements of age, physique, experience and capability, the previous employment record gives an indication of the stability of the individual. Honesty apart, rapid changes of employment are consistent with a dissatisfied, disagreeable, or incompetent operative and also makes it unlikely that references will be of any real value. Long sustained periods with the same firm coupled with good reasons for each change of employment which can be validated are consistent with integrity.

Insurance companies are now suggesting that two references should be taken *before* a driver's employment is actually commenced, i.e. before he takes a load out on the road.

References should always be taken from former employers, not nominees of the applicants (in one case a father-in-law, uncle and cousin, all with convictions, gave impeccable references to an applicant newly out of a long prison sentence). Enquiries should not be addressed to an individual at a firm by his name – it is a bad practice of interviewers for convenience asking the applicant from whom at the previous employers the reference should be requested; this can lead to biased information being received. Similarly, telephone calls should not be made to a person and number given by the applicant. A BBC TV presentation showed how easily it could be arranged for an accomplice to be waiting at the other end of the telephone indeed, there have been incidents obviously based on this since the film was shown.

If, because of recruiting difficulties, it is necessary to engage a driver immediately to prevent him pursuing other applications, he should be used on internal work until the necessary verifications are obtained. More attention than usual should be paid to gaps in employment and explanations of these should be obtained at the interview. Reluctance to explain, apparent bad memory and evasion should be judged accordingly. The interviewer should bear in mind that the firm's long-term interests are paramount, and take the line 'when in doubt don't'.

It will be noted that the application form in Figure 20:1 contains the necessity

---

Driver application form – Confidential

Complete in ink; block capitals please
Applicant must produce current driving licence at interview
No approach will be made to present employer without applicant's prior consent

1   Full name _____   Date of birth _____
                                        Nationality _____
                                        Married/single _____
                                        Number of children _____

2   Permanent address _____

3   Next of kin   Name _____ Relationship _____

                    Address _____

4   Health; give details of

(a)   Any illness causing absence from work in last 5 years

(b)   Any serious illness, injury or operation prior to last 5 years

(c)   Any impairment of hearing/vision

(d)   Any physical disability

5   Prior employment: Give details of present and previous employments, most recent first, include military service

Name and address of employer	Job	From–to	Reason for leaving

Figure 20:1   Driver application form

6   Driving ability and record

    Note: disclosure of a conviction does not
          mean you will automatically be barred
          from employment; failure to disclose
          would, however, mean subsequent dismissal

(a) Have you experience of customer delivery? _____

(b) Are you experienced in the keeping of drivers' records? _____

(c) List types of commercial vehicles driven _____
    _____

(d) Have you driving experience with articulated vehicles? _____
    _____

(e) Give details of driving convictions if any _____
    _____

(f) * Have you been convicted of any offence involving dishonesty? If so,
      give offence, date and penalty _____
      _____
      _____

(g) Has any load, part load or vehicle in your charge ever been stolen? If so,
    give details _____

7   Hobbies _____

8   Any other matters _____
    _____

    I apply for employment as a driver and vouch that the preceding
    details are correct

    I understand that a misleading statement or unsatisfactory reference
    could lead to my subsequent dismissal

    I accept that my employment may involve overnight stay away
    from my base

    Date _____   Signed _____

*   Under the Rehabilitation of Offenders Act 1974, after a specified period of
    years a conviction is regarded as 'spent' or void and therefore need not be
    declared on an application form.

Figure 20:1   continued

to declare any criminal convictions; the object is not that these should necessarily be a bar to employment, but to allow the interviewer to use his discretion in full knowledge of the circumstances; some criminal convictions are so trivial, or so long ago, they can be virtually disregarded.

The validity of dismissal in respect of concealment of criminal convictions has been upheld by Industrial Tribunals, the definitive case being Torr *v* British Railways Board (1977) IRLR 184 (IRLR – Industrial Relations Law Reports) in which it was decided 'an employer is justified in dismissing an employee on discovering that a previous criminal conviction has been concealed and that false statements concealing such facts have been made on the application form'. It should be noted, however, that the Rehabilitation of Offenders Act, 1974, 'voids' convictions after a period of years, dependent on the duration of the sentence imposed (2½ years imprisonment or more is never 'written off'). This Act does not apply to some occupations of which, unfortunately, transport driving is not one. The principal effect is that an applicant need not disclose such a 'voided' conviction in writing, or at an interview, and no action could be taken on this omission, or lie, later. Equally of course, there is no obligation upon the prospective employer to bring the Act to the applicant's notice!

Any interviewer, no matter how experienced, can at times be misled by a convincing liar, so no new driver should be sent out with a load before his references have been verified and his driving licence, form P45 and National Insurance card inspected. The time expended on these precautions will not be wasted – if nothing else it will impress upon the driver that security is a basic consideration of his post. A degree of casual supervision should be continued after a man's employment has begun. It must be stressed, however, that the percentage of experienced lorry drivers, especially those in long-distance haulage, who are not entirely trustworthy, is remarkably small.

It is obvious that there should be a uniformity of performance on given runs, so if a new driver displays abnormalities in the time taken and the distances covered then note should be taken and a special watch kept upon him. Even so, variations in mileage and times at stopping places are more usually for personal reasons rather than more doubtful motives. Breaches of discipline militate against a firm's interest and it may be just as necessary to dispense with the driver's services on these grounds as on those of dishonesty.

Driver identification cards

Some years ago, incidents occurred in the London area where loaded vehicles were taken from guarded car parks by thieves posing as the legitimate drivers: obviously a considerable amount of planning must go into an operation of this kind, or else there is collusion with the driver to obtain suitable keys and information. As a result of this, National Car Parks Ltd circulated a request that firms using their facilities should give their drivers some form of identification. This did not achieve the measure of success that it deserved and the practice is far from universal though it is difficult to see what are the valid objections.

Spasmodic outbreaks of terrorist activity in this country have caused several organisations which feel themselves particularly vulnerable to insist on incoming drivers providing proof of identification, and this requirement may well spread. A number of firms supply equipment to produce cards with details and holders' photographs in sealed plastic cases, or will provide the service themselves. An example is shown in Figure 20:2. Such a card should carry a full or three-quarter face photograph of the driver, his full name and address and that of the employer, date of birth, height, weight and hair colour. His signature, together with that of a person of authority in the firm, should be appended and the card stamped with the firm's official stamp. This can be issued in a plastic holder to enable the driver to carry his personal documents with him.

Figure 20:2   Driver identification card produced by the instant Polaroid 103 Land system
The card is automatically sealed within a clear plastic laminate and is secure against tampering

Driver collusion

No one knows how many hijackings are faked, but they are far in excess of the genuine – these are estimates from persons in the transport industry, not those of sceptical police officers – and this is a major threat. It is a matter for conjecture how many casual approaches are made before a driver is found who is prepared to co-operate – at a price. Drivers hesitate to report these overtures; this is a pity, for they could be stamped out by police utilising the common-law offence of incitement to commit a crime.

It is immaterial that the solicitation or incitement of the driver has no effect upon him – if he is asked to help in stealing his load an offence is committed even though he refuses point blank. Proceedings would not normally be begun by the police unless there was a sequence of at least two such acts which could be substantiated to form corroboration.

A dishonest driver, by the way, incurs infinitely more risk than the thieves; it is unlikely that they will let him know their true identity or even see him after the incident if they can avoid it. Such payment as he receives will be trivial in comparison with what he loses by way of trust, and possibly liberty. Having achieved their objectives, it is more than likely that the thieves will simply ignore him, as his usefulness is finished. He dare not talk and he has no redress of any kind. And, if they are caught they will have little hesitation in putting him forward as the instigator.

If the risk justifies the extra cost, having two men on the vehicle more than doubles the protection against collusion. Careful selection is the major countermeasure, though it should be borne in mind that a driver who is contemplating participation in such a theft is apt to be transparently uneasy and worried before it takes place.

Observations on drivers

With experienced drivers this is a most difficult thing to do. No driver of any calibre at all will fail to spot a following vehicle within a matter of miles and, if there is no justification for the suspicion, the practice will cause strained relations with the transport fleet drivers. If it is considered essential to 'tail', several cars of differing types should be used so that there is no continuity in the following vehicle. Police co-operation should always be sought in these cases. They have intercommunication facilities between vehicles which enable observers to remain at a distance both from front and rear. Electronic devices of the radar type have been tried with some success, but this is a matter for the police.

Petty frauds by drivers

It is somewhat surprising that a proportion of drivers who would not dream of stealing from their loads sometimes indulge in practices to obtain what they regard as 'perks' which would, however, be regarded with equal severity by a court of law. The overnight allowance is a prime example and the consequential loss arising from the steps taken to obtain this far outweigh the financial gain. A driver who could reach his home base within his permitted hours deliberately does not do so, but parks up near his home where he spends the night, then runs in early the next morning purporting to have stopped some distance away.

The driver gains his overnight allowance but the employer loses time for unloading and reloading. An additional security hazard is that the lorry is probably parked in a street at risk. Whether or not a criminal offence in dishonestly attempting to obtain the overnight allowance by deception is proveable, the driver will certainly have falsified his records and can be dealt with accordingly.

False claims for parking expenses are a somewhat minor irritant but contain a more serious implication in that the vehicle is likely to have been left overnight at risk. A clear indication when these frauds are taking place is found by studying the chits submitted for expenses over, say, a monthly period – consecutively numbered receipts will be used when entirely different areas of the country are being visited and there may be ample evidence that the drivers have a communal book of receipts for making up their claims.

The same frauds appear in the more serious matter of fuel receipts, where those given by a garage may record exaggerated quantities supplied (the price difference split between driver and pump attendant), possibly in the form of blanks given to the driver for him to compile; or genuine receipts fraudulently altered by the driver – a 1 easily becomes a 4, a 7 a 9 and a 3 an 8. Surprisingly and fortunately, often a different shade of biro/ink is used. It is not unknown for a complete book of receipts to be sold by an attendant to a driver, particularly where they are from one of a chain of garages using its Head Office address only on the forms. This led in one instance to consecutive receipts being tendered in identical handwriting but different signatures for filling up at the furthest points of trips to Devon and Fife in Scotland!

These ploys will not be evident to someone who is authorising a single expense form for the driver – unless he retains a mental query when the next one is submitted and investigates. However, on the checking of a series, the frauds really stand out.

Precautions against hijacking

Hijackings of lorries receive considerable publicity which conceals the fact that they are relatively infrequent. A graph of the incidence of hijacking would be unpredictable with noticeable peaks when particular gangs were especially effective and sudden drops indicating a series of arrests. Indeed in the USA according to the US Freight Company, hijacking accounts for only about 5 per cent of their total transport losses. In the UK, the concentration still lies in the major centres of population, notably London, but the country areas are now by no means immune.

It is noticeable that drivers do appreciate their attention being drawn to incidents which they could visualise themselves being involved in, but a driver's prime responsibility is purely and simply that of driving and it would be both unfair and unwise to tender advice which he might follow to his detriment. In any case, drivers' reactions to unexpected incidents would be as varied as their physique and temperament. One thing they should not do: no one should argue with a firearm.

Examples of using direct force – by ramming, threatened ramming or obstruction by means of a barricade – are practically non-existent. They could involve a badly dented or immobilised vehicle and injury to the assailants – which are the last things that they would want. These are rare incidents and it is much more likely that attempts will be made to suborn the driver or stop the vehicle by a trick.

Stopping by trick

A driver cannot live in expectation of an impending attack at every routine happening. Nevertheless, there are several stereotyped approaches, of which impersonating policemen is the favourite, particularly in the Metropolitan Police area; here lies the advantage of internal bolts. A driver cannot with impunity disregard signals from a person in police uniform unless the circumstances make it obvious that no reasonable person would have complied. The police do accept that a commercial vehicle driver can insist on staying in his cab and driving to the nearest police station for examination of his documents. Common sense and discretion are the guiding factors on the driver's actions. Police uniforms are easily obtainable and there is a wide variety in the types of car in use; black is no longer the predominant car colour and the presence of a 'police' sign can be meaningless. However, police vehicles can be expected to be reasonably clean with absence of damage and rust, fully roadworthy; they carry intercommunicating radio, and few forces operate cars anything above the medium price range. As for the officers themselves: black shoes are always worn, with plain white or blue shirts and black ties; untidy appearance and very long hair are rare. In case of doubt the driver should speak through the cab windows with the door kept locked.

Fake accidents are difficult to cater for – especially where they purport to involve the carrying vehicle. The locality and circumstances could decide a driver whether he has or has not been in an accident or whether a trivial accident has been deliberately contrived. A collision with a car containing several men in a quiet area is very different to a bump in a traffic stream with a family car. In any case of doubt the driver should consider all possibilities before he leaves the safety of his cab. Where other vehicles are concerned in obviously genuine accidents, at the risk of seeming callous, a driver should again weigh the circumstances carefully before he obeys his natural instincts to stop and help; under no circumstances should he stop out of sheer curiosity.

The ingenuity of prospective thieves is shown by a series of incidents in the London area in which the stratagem has been to remove a vehicle's rear number plate while it is stationary, and later to drive alongside it in a quiet area and wave the number plate to the driver. He, thinking that it has fallen off and that he is being done a good turn, stops, gets out without setting alarms or immobilisers and is promptly at the mercy of the hijackers.

Hitch-hikers

There is a simple remedy for the dangers that can arise from hitch-hikers: do not carry them. This should be made a specific instruction from the firm and should be the subject of severe disciplinary measures if it is not obeyed. The danger is not always to the load. To a petty thief, the contents of a driver's pockets are also a target. Indeed, it is a matter for speculation how often drivers have been threatened, blackmailed, or cajoled into parting with money and have never reported the matter for fear of ridicule. Female passengers are the greatest danger of all: the girl-tramp frequenters of transport cafes can find it easy to persuade a weak driver to pull off into a layby where their accomplices are lying in wait. Their mode of life can also present a danger to health. Few respectable girls 'hitch' singly and the female in distress is the most hackneyed way of getting a driver to stop.

Other methods of hijacking

There is obviously a considerable and continuously changing variety of means that can be employed. Waving and flashing lights to indicate faults with the vehicle itself are common. Messages have been left at cafes which are known to be visited regularly by particular drivers, instructing them to divert to new premises. The latter should be queried if there is any doubt at all.

Selection of secure routes and schedules

There is a limited amount that can be done in this respect. If long-distance trunking vehicles are to operate economically and to a schedule suited to the customers' needs they are virtually confined to the main route between producer and customer. Regular variations are ideal in theory only, and no route which involves passing through quiet country lanes, as opposed to main roads, should be acceptable at all. Using a trunk road with other drivers on it denies opportunity to the thief to carry out his theft in peace and quiet.

So far as variations in time are concerned, commercial considerations will be paramount and, in any case, except in the transport of wages, there is little likelihood that a regular time schedule will be adhered to.

Radio linkage

A commercial security firm, Securicor, offers a system of radio contact with vehicles through the medium of their own chain of radio stations. A radio transmitter/receiver (transceiver) is installed on loan in each vehicle operating on wavelengths allocated to Securicor throughout the country. This enables a driver who is being attacked, or who has reason to fear that he may be attacked, to call the local control who will in turn notify the police. Other amenities that are offered by this service are those of passing messages, giving weather reports, and other information on such things as road diversions.

Overnight parking

This presents arguably the main danger. There are two difficulties in guarding against it: the lack of adequate supervised parking facilities throughout the country, and the difficulty in obtaining the co-operation of drivers. The government, through its Home Office Standing Committee on Crime Prevention, is fully aware of the problem, but regrettably, despite many official promises to the contrary, very little progress has been made in the provision of guarded lorry parks in strategic areas or cities, and there is no indication of any improvement in the immediate future.

At the moment supervised parks are limited in number outside London – the local police or road haulage associations will be pleased to advise on their location. Well-lit parks are a second best but, where very valuable loads are concerned, it may be worthwhile to consider coming to an agreement with a local firm or garage which can provide enclosed accommodation. Every large group of firms should insist that vehicles belonging to any member of the group should be accepted overnight into any of their factories which is convenient; there is surprising parochialism to overcome in attitudes on this point. Where vehicles are to be left at a depot or warehouse with alarm facilities, it is possible to arrange external points where the vehicle can be joined to the circuitry so that any movement of it will trigger off the alarm.

Using supervised parks usually requires payment by the driver for which he will reclaim. As mentioned elsewhere there is a temptation for him to park in the open and claim the allowances. This should be clearly laid down as a disciplinary matter which will be regarded seriously. In no circumstances should lorries be left in back streets near lodgings for the personal convenience of drivers. The regular presence of their vehicles there will eventually attract the attention of interested thieves in the area who can then pick their opportunity at convenience.

Police manpower resources are not, and never will be, entirely adequate for all calls, but if they are notified of the presence of a high-value load parked in a particular area they will try to visit it periodically and at least, if they see any interference taking place, they will know that action is required – even to checking the bona fides of the actual driver.

Anti-hijack instructions to drivers with valuable loads

1   Do not park in quiet country laybys unless the presence of other similar vehicles gives a measure of protection by sheer weight of numbers.
2   Do not visit transport cafes where there are recurrent incidents or thefts – let your colleagues know if you know of such places.
3   When having meals in a cafe, set immobilisers and/or alarms; leave the vehicle where you can see it or at least put it in an open, prominent position.
4   Use guarded car parks, or well-lit ones when the former are not available. Under no circumstances leave vehicles in back streets near to lodgings for personal convenience.
5   Notify the police of the presence of your load if you are in doubt about the safety of where you park.
6   Before leaving the vehicle for the night, check immobilisers, alarms, all doors, and locks. Sheet down loads tightly to conceal the contents and hinder removal; arrange the knotting so as to ensure that if there is interference it will be detected. Inspect your vehicle before leaving in the morning.

7   If in doubt and obliged to stop at an accident, or by signals from police officers, stay in the cab with the door bolted, offer to drive to the nearest police station in such circumstances if the 'policemen' insist you get out.

8   If your vehicle is involved in an accident, use your discretion as to whether it is deliberate or an accidental occurrence when you can safely get out of your vehicle; err on the side of caution.

9   Casual passengers and hitch-hikers must not be carried.

10   Waving and flashing lights to indicate faults, or any other actions to induce you to stop, should be viewed as suspect and even diversionary messages left at cafes should be so regarded.

11   Any approaches from strangers suggesting collaboration in stealing the load should be reported to your employers or the police immediately.

12   Do not gossip in cafes about your load and its value, your schedules and destination, or the protection fitted to your vehicle.

Vehicle observer corps

The menace of lorry thefts caused the Road Haulage Association to create this body in June 1962; it is now operating in several important centres in the country and is not restricted to members of the Association. Fundamentally, the scheme is one of immediate search on notification of the theft of a lorry and load. In each locality a permanent area control is established which furnishes member firms with details of the stolen vehicle as soon as they are known. These firms in turn supply cars and crews to patrol small predetermined areas of an extent that can be covered in a matter of ten minutes. After an initial check they report back to their own base and then make a fresh search. With the co-operation of a large number of firms all these areas, which make up an entire district, can be searched simultaneously. No action is expected from the crew finding the vehicle other than to inform the police where it is and to follow it, if seen on the move. This is a form of self-help in the transport industry which has had success, particularly in London, where experiments have been made in the use of a helicopter for searching. The RHA at Roadway House, 22 Upper Woburn Place, London WC1 (01-387 9711) would no doubt be pleased to give additional information to interested parties.

Vehicle protection

Numerous firms produce immobilising and alarm devices for cars and lorries ranging from the ultra-sophisticated down to relatively simple locks on steering columns which are now standard equipment supplied on new vehicles by most manufacturers. The fact still remains that the deciding factor is the integrity of the driver, no matter what facilities are placed at his disposal – but anything fitted by the employer for personal protection and for that of the vehicle and load is generally very welcome.

The following is only a synopsis of what can be done and it may be expected that transit insurers will wish to be consulted when the load is of excessive value.

Internal bolts

Circumstances could arise where a driver might be attacked in his cab. This would be difficult in the first place, since he may be 2 m (6 feet) or more from the ground. If the vehicle is required intact, breaking windows to get at him is out of the question.

The thief has to get into the cab. A very simple precaution is the provision of 75 mm (3 inch) tower bolts inside each door, to be shot home by the driver as and when he requires. They will solve that problem almost entirely. If, added to this, the driver is furnished with a push-button in the cab to activate the alarm system and his own means of possible counter-attack – for example, a fire extinguisher to aim through the window at his attackers – an attempt to get at him will probably soon be abandoned.

Again, it must be emphasised, no driver should resist when threatened with a firearm.

Vehicle alarms and immobilisers

An increasing number of commercial companies produce a variety of alarms and immobilisers. The electric circuitry of alarms, in particular, is not complex and firms can even construct their own variations which may be just as effective as the commercially made ones and have the advantage of being unconventional. It is possible to incorporate both alarm and immobiliser in one unit, but the disadvantages of this offset the advantages – if a means is found of bypassing the whole unit, both forms of protection will be eliminated together. Both devices are really delaying ones and any skilled and determined criminal with ample time at his disposal could eventually overcome them. The presence of an immobiliser represents a challenge and an inconvenience, rarely a complete barrier. The alarm is a temporary embarrassment. It is no use at all fitting an alarm siren on a vehicle which is then left in a position where no one can possibly hear it; even if it is heard there is no guarantee that anyone will take a great deal of notice of it. The lack of attention paid to alarm bells sounding at jewellers' shops near opening times is proof of public indifference to such noises. Above all, no system is better than the operator. An unco-operative driver can nullify the effects of the best devices; an uninstructed or incompetent one can prevent them from ever beginning to fulfil their function.

Types of alarm system

Modern alarms are almost invariably electrical and either use the existing horn of the vehicle or are specially fitted with a siren of a distinctive note. There are a variety of means of activation, the most common being that of the key-switch turned after closing the doors and windows and with a circuit separate from the electrical equipment of the car. Contacts on doors, windows, boot and bonnet may be included as desired. Occasionally the alarm is wired into the ignition system or connected to the mechanism to operate when an attempt is made to start the engine. Other types of activation, dependent upon the actual movement of the vehicles, are the pendulum type of contact, mercury switches, and vibrator contacts. These may have an additional value in being usable for protecting the load itself if they are sufficiently sensitive to react to movement on the vehicle or interference with either doors or sheeting. With this type of contact it must be borne in mind that the natural phenomena of wind or rain may occasionally be sufficient to cause false alarms. Few of the ways of totally protecting a load itself against interference have been entirely successful and a firm with a load of a consistent nature and shape might be able to develop its own alarm device connected to the locks, ties or sheeting.

Under present-day traffic conditions it is absolutely essential that any alarm siren should be loud and distinctive, otherwise it will attract little or no attention. A high-pitched or a warbling type of sound which causes irritation to the listeners is probably the best, but whatever is fitted should be tested under the conditions in which it will be required to operate.

Types of immobiliser

There are two main varieties of immobiliser; mechanical and electrical. The consensus of opinion in the past has been that the mechanical types are more reliable and more resistant to interference.

Electrical immobilisers. These work on similar principles to the alarm systems, but cut off the ignition, starter motor, or the fuel supply. Those stopping the fuel supply are particularly suitable for diesel motors where they operate a plunger to lock the fuel injection system. Operation is similar to alarms in the form of a key or a combination lock mechanism, set after the driver has left the cab. Variations have been introduced, dependent upon movement in the cab or an attempt to start the engine.

Improvements may accrue from the development of silicon chip technology particularly on newer vehicles using electronic ignition. Already devices are being marketed for petrol driven vehicles in which the ignition switch is replaced by something resembling a pocket calculator for coded operation.

Mechanical immobilisers. The physical methods applied are, more often than not, in the form of locks upon the gearshift, brakes or parts of the engine and steering mechanism. More complex methods involve the transmission and the differential or the hydraulic braking system. There is ample scope for ingenuity in devising exclusive types – if these are of the lock and rod principle, they should be in a position where bolt cutters cannot be applied to them and also be in a position where they are not obvious so that the thief will have to spend valuable time locating them before determining how to counteract them. The unassisted driver quite often has simple and very effective means at his disposal – removal of rotors, leads, or parts of the mechanism.

Even slipping a piece of paper between the points and terminals can stop a thief as effectively as any expensive mechanism.

Cost of equipment can vary immensely – the more complex the more secure, but also the more difficult to service and reset if accidentally operated. Simplicity is a virtue for the driver – if he has to carry out a complicated procedure he will be tempted not to bother.

Trailer protection

During the winter months of 1973-4 there was a considerable increase in thefts where loaded trailers were the objective. These were concentrated in the London area and periodically since then the same procedure has been followed.

The main form taken was of stealing an articulated vehicle, promptly abandoning the tractor, replacing it by a waiting one which had probably been stolen and changing the rear number plates on the trailer accordingly – thus providing the thieves with a safer means of transport should the theft be quickly discovered. A second line of attack was on loaded trailers left overnight, either in transit by drivers who used the tractors presumably for their own purposes, or those loaded overnight for picking up early the next morning and left in an accessible place. In those circumstances, without precautions there is nothing to stop a tractor being backed onto the trailer and removing it forthwith.

Trailers represent a problem since the normal immobilising devices are not functional when they are separated from the tractors. Chains around the suspension and various brake-locking devices are apt to be more dangerous than effective. A pivoted steel clamp with a hacksaw-proof padlock on the trailer pin is probably the most effective device (see Figure 20:3). A firm can easily make these itself and it is essential to remember that the lock must be close-shackled and resistant to cutting. These will not offer perfect protection, but having to cut them off will be a deterrent – the position is an awkward one and the trailer pin may be damaged in the process. A number of commercial firms now market devices of this kind but the principle is the same in each case – protection of the trailer pin.

These trailer-pin clamps can form an additional line of defence for the tractor in the event of the immobiliser, etc., being defective. If a driver can drop his trailer so as to leave his tractor between it and a wall with no room for manoeuvring, there is nothing the thieves can do without forcing away the clamp.

Load security

Where large vans are concerned there is no difficulty at all in wiring up the rear doors to the alarm system of the vehicle. In any case, these rear doors should be fitted with a sizeable close-shackled padlock and bar to discourage an attempt in the first instance.

Figure 20:3   Clamp and padlock fitted on trailer pin when disconnected

Such a fitting must be substantial and not the flimsy hasp and cheap lock that is very frequently encountered. If the value of regular loads demands it there is no difficulty in protecting the walls of the vehicle as well with closed-circuit wiring of the type which is used in burglar alarms.

Open lorries carrying goods covered by sheeting represent a much more difficult problem. All loads should be sheeted down tightly to prevent casual petty theft during the course of deliveries, and also to conceal the nature of the load. It is common practice to steal from loads parked overnight at transport cafes by undoing the tie ropes on the sheeting, taking out property from the centre of the load and resheeting down, so that the theft is not discovered until the vehicle is several hundred miles away. More often than not this type of theft is the work of a dishonest lorry driver also parked at the same cafe. Each driver has his own means of sheeting down and if he uses knots of a particular type or sequence, or in some way ensures that interference will be detected by him when he inspects his load before leaving, the chances of the police detecting the theft are greatly increased.

With a little ingenuity alarms can be attached to sheeting, with switches functioning upon movement, of, or on, the vehicle. But the easiest and cheapest way to stop thefts from loads is to put the vehicle on a guarded or well-lit car park.

Where deliveries are made of comparatively small packages to a number of customers and the carrying vehicle has to be left in public streets, it is highly desirable for two men to be used so that the vehicle is not left unattended at any time. A limited number of firms have experimented with carrying Alsatian guard dogs in the back of their vehicles – this is effective but has caused complications in some instances with members of the public!

Tanker vehicles

These fall into a special category. The sheer bulk of their contents seems to militate against the vehicles being hijacked. The main source of temptation is the possibility of repeated pilferage, especially petrol, and wines and spirits. Preventive action is really required therefore primarily in respect of employees.

Where fuel is concerned, a driver's obvious ploy is to ensure that he has a quantity left after making all his authorised deliveries – stealing at any time before then has danger of detection for him in some form or another. To do this he has to ensure that he has the co-operation, either intentional or unintentional, of the person who is supervising or accepting delivery – sometimes this is unbelievably slackly carried out.

If the form of measure is to use a dipstick, this is frequently left to the driver. Despite the fact that he may have been visiting a particular site for years, an occasional check should be made to ensure that he is using it correctly and not just accept his reading. Drivers often have regular runs and it is easy to develop a sense of confidence and familiarity with them.

The fraud is possible by 'bouncing' the dipstick which causes a splash mark higher than should be shown, thereby indicating more fuel than actually is there.

Similarly, the driver may check tanks of different size with the same dipstick, or use a shortened dipstick with a flange which prevents it reaching the bottom thereby showing 'dry' (driver taps tank to simulate striking bottom). In addition, where there are meters on the vehicle, these may not have been reset to zero or readings noted before delivery, which would allow the driver to keep what was already recorded.

With the progressively increasing cost of fuel, more firms will no doubt be tempted to follow the practice, already existent in several with their own weighbridges, of asking that a tanker be weighed before and after discharging.

Where wine or spirit is concerned there are three main methods of stealing:

1   Short delivery (wine left in the tank).
2   Dipping through the top of the tank and transferring liquid to a container.
3   Removing Customs seals to attach specially adapted couplings and pipe to the outlet valve.

Added to these possibilities there is the risk of dilution being used to cover volume deficiencies caused by the theft. Frauds can of course also occur during loading and offloading and the temptation is perhaps greater with these goods than most.

The vehicles should be surveyed to ensure that every possible means whereby liquid can be abstracted is either protected by padlocks of quality or is fitted with seals sufficiently reliable to give an immediate indication of interference. In the past, Customs padlocks and seals have not always met these criteria.

Seals

Until recently, these did not provide additional security but were simply a means of indicating that interference with the locking arrangements had taken place. Newer forms have now been introduced which are dual-purpose using a steel cable with a numbered one-way-lock steel body, quite reasonably priced and needing bolt croppers or something similar to remove them (see Figure 20:4).

For many years the conventional form was a wire with a lead seal which was crimped hard onto it and may or may not have carried an identifying number. With time and care these could be opened and refitted so as to avoid detection, but many new and improved varieties have come onto the market. Those made of plastic seem to be advantageous both in price and performance; they have to be broken to be removed, and their nature makes it easy to carry a clear identifying number or marking so that they cannot be replaced by an identical seal. A system whereby the number of the seal is shown on a driver's consignment note to be checked at the delivery point before unloading takes place can easily be inaugurated with little additional clerical cost.

There are of course numerous other obvious applications – on cash bags, coin containers, and rope lashings on the motor vehicles. In any instance where it is necessary to recognise interference at a glance their use can be considered.

It has been suggested that plastic seals can be opened and re-fastened by judicious use of heat; this needs privacy, time and patience, and the author has not

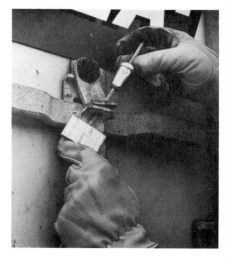

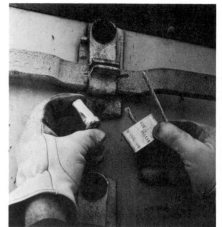

Figure 20:4   New type of theft-resistant seal

seen one which has not then shown clear signs of the interference. The real danger is simply that seals are cut and not examined – when the shortage comes to light, then they cannot be found!

It is imperative that drivers should be discouraged from breaking the seals themselves when making a delivery. This may be done thoughtlessly or to expedite offloading, but it thoroughly destroys the integrity of the seal and suspicion will fall on the driver should a shortage be revealed.

However good seals may be, they are a waste of time and money if the hasps or other fastenings to which they are attached are removable and replaceable without trace, or the doors/shutters can be taken off and put back without breaking the seals.

Procuring a load by fraud

This is rarely attempted on a large firm with well organised traffic arrangements and insistence on precise documentation. The procedure is that the prospective thief with a large lorry or articulated vehicle, either genuine or stolen for the purpose, and in any case carrying false number plates, calls at a firm on the pretext of seeking a return load for a journey, usually to London. The vehicle may have a fictitious owner's name, address, and telephone number painted on the cab, and the driver will be in possession of copy delivery notes and other 'proof' that his offer is genuine and honest.

The field of operation is usually that of provincial cities well away from London and the driver will have documents showing a London telephone number which can be contacted if the firm so desires. This number may be that of a telephone kiosk or some other place where an accomplice is waiting to answer. By the time a check on non-delivery has been made, the goods are beyond redemption and identification of the culprit is remote by both time and by distance. If the thief is purporting to be employed by a well-known haulier he may even take the risk of contacting a local transport clearing house to be sent where transport facilities are needed at short notice.

That any firm should fall for a fraud of this nature seems ludicrous; nevertheless it is a regular occurrence – perhaps the convenience of a prompt despatch at reduced rates is too tempting for the operator. The easy solution is not to use 'casuals' at all unless the carrier has been previously utilised. Even those sent from a clearing house should be suspect until the driver's licences and his vehicle have been thoroughly checked and examined to ensure they are in order. A further check that could be made is to establish the identity of the customer to whom he purports to have delivered in that area and check with that person whether what has been said is true.

If it is thought that this could not happen refer to the case of Garnham, Harris & Elton Limited *v* Alfred W. Ellis (Transport) Limited, [1967] 2 AER 940. This is a judgement given on the liability of a contractor who subcontracted the carriage of a valuable load of copper to what was subsequently found to be a non-existent firm. Damages were awarded against the contractor. Another large metals firm lost a complete load valued at tens of thousands of pounds in this way in July 1972.

A number of similar incidents have occurred since that time and few, if any, of the offenders have been traced. Some very prominent firms have suffered under circumstances which reflect little to the credit of their transport department; dockside imports have disappeared after allocation by shipping agents to a casual carrier whose bona fides were not checked.

An allied gimmick somewhat the reverse of that just mentioned is one in which the customer himself does not suffer. A fictitious firm with impressive name and letterheads, address, telephone numbers, etc., circulates large firms in a given area on the pretext of making regular deliveries there from industrial towns elsewhere and having difficulty in obtaining return loads; rates well below the normal are offered to any destination in or near any of the return routes. Subsequently, those obtained are subcontracted to local carriers; payment having been received from the customers, the spurious firm simply folds and disappears, leaving the subcontractors to whistle for their money.

Internal frauds involving transport

Once a vehicle has left a firm's premises carrying goods in excess of what should have been loaded, detection of the theft becomes difficult. On many occasions it will be impossible to determine whether stock deficiency is due to bad documentation or theft from inside the premises, either through intruders, or through progressive pilferage by dishonest employees. A driver and warehouseman acting in collusion represent a dangerous combination and could function for some time without detection. Any signs of undue affluence on the part of two friends in these categories should be viewed with suspicion.

There are only two physical ways of establishing whether a loaded vehicle carries what it should; by offloading and checking against the consignment notes or, where the load is composed of items of known weights, taring and grossing the vehicle over a weighbridge and comparing the net weight with the cumulative weight of the individual parts. The use of a weighbridge will have limited application with many products but where bulk metals or raw materials are concerned, it is always of value – if only because it will have a cautionary effect on those concerned.

Offloading is not popular with drivers and it could have repercussions in employee relations if nothing were found; it should only be done where there is virtual certainty of fraud or where it has been accepted that periodically such action will be taken. Spot checks can be made on odd items to establish that they are shown on the consignment note – in most cases, a driver will want to get rid of unauthorised material as soon as possible and his most likely sources of disposal will be local, so illicit items will be on or near the top of the load and readily accessible.

When a search reveals goods over and above what should be there, the criminal/disciplinary responsibility is by no means simple to prove; the driver claims that he was not responsible for loading and would have brought the undocumented items back – and will probably point out instances where he has done so previously (as a precaution!); the warehouseman may admit he has made an unintentional error and apologise – or blame someone else. Much will depend on where the excess is found – if in the driver's cab, a very good story will be needed; if part and parcel of the normal load, there is a limit to what can be done.

If suspicion is confirmed by positive stock shortages, serious consideration should be given to notifying the police, by appointment at a police station so that the thieves are not alerted and observations/enquiries have a chance to produce a result. At very least, police investigation usually results in a lull of thieving.

Role of documentation

Firms will have differing administrative requirements in this field, and no universal system can be recommended. Incidents have occurred, and no doubt will in the future, where goods in excess of an order have been deliberately labelled and consigned to a dishonest customer – this has even been known where no legitimate order of any kind has been in existence. Adequate documentation and good stock records which show up deficiencies immediately will effectively limit this type of fraud. Goods are inevitably lost in transit sooner or later, without indication of whether it is by theft, carelessness, or by misdirection; complete documentation will be necessary to support a claim on insurance and its absence may prejudice payment. Claims for reimbursement, particularly where outside carriers with trans-shipment points are used, may prove difficult to substantiate if the documentation has not been meticulous.

Each firm will have its own system of producing interlinked orders, job cards, advice notes, consignment notes and invoices in sequence. The opportunity of a fraud really arises at the consignment-note stage. If these can be created in a warehouse without the other documents coming into existence, it becomes possible to get goods out without detection. The automatic procedures which would normally follow from that department are never initiated. The existence of an interlinked system where warehouse staff can only despatch in accordance with notes sent to them will eliminate this possibility. Normal distribution of consignment notes is from a set of three – in different colours for ready identification. One note is to be signed by the driver and retained in the warehouse. The second is to be handed over with the goods to the consignee and the third is the driver's copy for signature by the consignee who accepts delivery.

In a fraudulent arrangement where the third goes back to the warehouse originator and the first is destroyed or concealed, the whole could disappear leaving no trace of what has happened.

The third copy of a set is most important in another respect. Claims of non-delivery of goods to a customer are commonplace and without this third copy, signed by the recipient, there is no basis on which to contest the claim. There may be no dishonesty on the part of the customer, whose records may be faulty, but he will be convinced that he is right in the absence of proof to the contrary. This third copy should therefore go back to someone other than the person responsible for making up the load and it should be filed and retained for a definite period, adequate to preclude possibilities of any claim being made. Six months is a reasonable time.

False signatures

These come to light when a customer refuses to accept an invoice for goods thought to have been supplied to him. When proof, in the form of a signed consignment note, is produced, for the first time it is found either that the signature is indecipherable and bears no resemblance to that of any of his employees or the name shown does not belong to any of them.

To complicate inquiries there will have been an inevitable delay between despatch and the realisation that something is wrong. Several alternatives exist: the driver may have forged a signature to cover his own theft or a genuine loss from his load – if he thought that might be held against him; a member of the customer's staff might be camouflaging a theft of goods inward; a total outsider may have posed as a customer's employee and deceived the driver; the goods may have been dropped with the wrong customer by genuine mistake and the latter has not brought the fact to notice.

There is a reluctance to accept that the loss is due to anything but mistake or bad records and the supplier, if the customer is a valued one, sooner or later has to come to the commercial decision and accept the loss despite annoyance and uncertainty. There will be little chance that his insurers will accept any liability in the circumstances.

If all firms would use an official receipt stamp as well as the initials or signature of the recipient, this increasingly frequent form of fraud would soon stop; unfortunately this is most unlikely and suppliers should take such precautions as they can.

The possibility of fraudulent acceptance should be among the matters impressed on drivers. A driver should be instructed to ask the name of the signer when he cannot read what has been written; he should then print the name alongside the scribble. In the event of any complaint of non-delivery, the first step should be to forward the signed note to the customer with a request for immediate comment if not in order – not to go through several stages of correspondence before this is done. Finally, the driver should be asked whether he can throw any light on the discrepancy at the earliest opportunity. A check should of course be made with other customers.

If no logical explanation, other than theft or fraud, can be established, the customer and supplier must decide whether to inform the police; in the case of substantial loss, insurers will not be sympathetic unless this is done. The best protection again lies in a commonsense, well-instructed and reliable driver, in this instance backed up by a laid-down and speedy system of dealing with alleged shortages in deliveries.

Checklist of advisable action in the event of delivery discrepancies

1   Driver must telephone, giving details and asking instructions, from customers' premises if shortage is noted during delivery.

2 If delivery is to your own premises, notify shortages or over-deliveries to suppliers promptly, and confirm the former in writing immediately.

3 Keep record of drivers and customers involved in reported short deliveries – pattern may emerge.

4 Driver must get legible signature on delivery notes – if not, should have instructions to ask name, and print it beside signature.

5 As soon as any shortage is notified by a customer:

    (a) question driver about it before time lapse dims his recollections of the journey; have in mind the possibility of unobserved theft from his vehicle during the journey;

    (b) examine consignment notes and driver's log sheets for possible mis-delivery and check with customers on run;

    (c) check your stocks to ensure no loading error has been made;

    (d) make sure your insurers are informed – do not of necessity wait until enquiries are complete if loss is substantial.

6 If loss is serious, visit customer, or cause him to be visited and discuss circumstances with him, suggesting possible stock check and examination of his 'goods inwards' and 'outwards' books, if he keeps them.

7 In contacts with customer, query any delay in reporting; have in mind possibility of theft during or after delivery, by his staff or outsiders – or the fact that his storeman might be rectifying a stock deficiency! Try to ascertain whether he is having any pilferage problems by his staff.

8 Ensure that the executive or manager, who will have to authorise 'crediting' the customer, writing-off the loss, etc., has sufficient information upon which to base his decision.

9 Do not treat delivery discrepancies as an unavoidable facet of distribution life. Look into them, even if no dishonesty is involved; the exercise will occasion more care in future and may throw up a better system.

Premises

The types of building used for distribution purposes are too diverse for other than generalised comment, but there are a number of things that can be done to reduce risk:

1 Limit number of access points to buildings.

2 Have each access point subject to scrutiny in some way – by receptionist, or in clear view of supervisor's office.

3 Loading/receival areas to be under clear, and obvious, view from a supervisor's office (or subject to CCTV).

4 Keep keyholding to an absolute minimum of reliable employees. Do not allow keys to be held purely for the convenience of the holder, or a driver to have them unless absolutely unavoidable.

5 Fit key-operated isolating switches to electrically operated roller shutter doors

and cranage. Secure hand-operated roller shutters by a good padlock on the chain. (Do not secure an electrically operated roller shutter by a central padlock and hasp to an inset ring in the floor – absence of mind might cause a 'U' shaped door or a burnt-out motor to result.)

6   Separately compound high risk items within the building – insurers will probably insist on this anyway. Obtain their advice on what should be done.

7   Consider:

   (a)   external floodlighting on solar switches,

   (b)   fitting an alarm system – local Police Crime Prevention Officer will advise,

   (c)   improving physical protection of premises against intruders.

8   If insured, check with insurers' surveyors that your measures are acceptable – in addition to the advice you may get from the police.

9   Lock off areas vacated during lunch and other breaks – especially during summer, when warehouse doors may be left open for ventilation in hot weather and remain open while all the staff are elsewhere at lunch.

10   If possible, make employees park their vehicles in full view of office windows; do not allow parking beside doors leading to storage areas.

The most important point of a security nature in connection with the construction of new premises is that the architect's attention should be drawn to the necessity of minimising risks. This so rarely receives attention that it is a major source of complaint by the staff of the Home Office Central Crime Prevention Centre. At no extra cost and no limitation on the efficient usage of the building, the job of a prospective thief can be made so much harder that he may be inclined to operate elsewhere.

Weighbridge frauds

The weighbridge, like any other mechanical device, is as good as its operator and no better. This is another post where honesty and reliability are of greater value than any other trait. If the operator is tempted to defraud his employers, he has ample opportunity to do so and the chance of early detection, if he is not too greedy, is small. However, modern improvements in weighbridge construction and recording have provided safeguards which make the deliberate misreading of weights almost impossible.

In addition to the new load-cell type of weighbridge with electronic print-out of tickets which are being progressively installed, there are many of the old 'dial recorders' and 'steelyards' which have been modified to automatic printing of tickets, plus a lot which still rely on visual reading and written slips. The dial recorder, by nature of its construction, can be fitted with a device for this purpose which is less subject to interference than a similar device on a steelyard. On the latter, the recording is complicated by the progressive movement of the blade, and it is possible for the weighman to stamp a card at a false reading. With the newest device associated with dial recorders, it is impossible to mark the card while there is any movement of the indicator or vibration upon the platform. In fact, a standstill period of 1½ seconds is required. The possibility of accidental or deliberate error is therefore eliminated.

It must be remembered that there are several ways in which a weighbridge can make a false recording without there being fraud. The worst offenders are weighbridges of inadequate length where double weighing has to take place. This is now technically illegal and errors of up to 200 kg (450 pounds) are common, even when both driver and weighman are expert in positioning the vehicle at the time of both taring (weighing the empty vehicle) and grossing (weighing the laden vehicle). The absence of flat approaches to either end of a weighing platform will further complicate matters. There is a legal requirement that these should be level, but this is rarely so with the older weighbridges, and this renders double weighing even more unreliable.

On an old weighbridge with the mechanism beginning to wear it is essential to ensure an even distribution of the weight – if there is excessive point loading at any part of the weighbridge this can lead to an over-deflection of the recording mechanism and a false reading. If water and dirt are allowed to accumulate on the weighbridge, or a sudden shower soaks it, an error of considerable magnitude can arise unless the operator adjusts his zero accordingly. The steelyard type is particularly prone to error if the operator lacks experience and expertise. Too quick a movement of the blade inevitably produces incorrect readings.

There is limited information on methods, if any, whereby false readings can be induced on the load-cell types. It has been suggested that this may be done by interference with the supply voltage – whether this is true or not, they certainly make fraud more difficult for the dishonest operator.

There are two main legal aids to security at weighbridges. First, the weighman, from his position by the dial or steelyard, must be able to see both ends of the weighbridge clearly. Second, the weighbridge office must be so constructed that the driver can see the readings being taken while his vehicle is being weighed, so that he can challenge them if he thinks fit. The virtue of these requirements lies in the facts that the weighman is able to see that the vehicle is correctly positioned which gives him the opportunity of questioning anything he thinks should not be on it, while the driver also has a potential check on the weight of his vehicle – although this is of less value for there is little chance that the weighman would be in collusion with anyone else except the driver.

Where large quantities of raw materials or scrap are being stockpiled or sold, a fraud in weighing a loaded vehicle can lead to a loss which is difficult to uncover or occasionally even to notice. This is a type of dishonesty which leads to overconfidence on the part of the perpetrators and will no doubt be practised regularly; the persistent drain should then eventually attract comment. One particular set of circumstances which is recurrent involves the purchase of scrap. Once the vehicle has been loaded at the seller's premises, the weight shown over a weighbridge will be that accepted for payment. If there is collusion between the buyers and the weighbridge operator it is easy for them to earn quick money by under-recording the gross weight. The prevalence of this type of offence is demonstrated by the number of occasions these facts have been repeated in court.

It is easy to establish that a load is underweight once suspicion has been aroused. Either the security staff or the police can stop a vehicle and send it back over the weighbridge or to another one. It is more difficult to prove that it is a deliberate act with fraudulent intent and not an accidental error that has taken place. If there are strong grounds for suspicion that this is happening, it is better to enlist the services of the police and try to ascertain where the driver is dropping the excess material that he is carrying. A defence of negligence and inefficiency is a difficult one to rebut unless there is positive proof of illegal disposal of materials. It may be possible to gain additional proof by the examination of documents over a period of time showing regular deficiencies in the amounts that should have been carried. Where a publicly owned, as opposed to a private, weighbridge is being used, an independent person from the firm should always accompany the vehicle to the weighbridge even if this causes inconvenience and loss of time.

The opportunity that a driver himself has of penetrating a fraud is mainly concerned with producing too high a reading for the tare (unladen) weight of this vehicle. He could, of course, remove materials from a load in transit and substitute disposable matter to be jettisoned after gross weighing but before offloading, but the procedure would be complicated, dangerous and unlikely to be carried out.

There are a number of ways in which a driver can falsify his weights, for example:

1   Fitting a large spare petrol tank which can be filled with water, to be emptied after tare weighing and before loading.
2   On lorries carrying sideboards and tailboards, having a 'bowed' tarpaulin over the empty lorry filled with water, to be tipped off before loading.
3   Carrying paving stones, old spare wheels, skids, old tarpaulins and so on, to be discarded prior to loading and reweighing.
4   Remaining in the cab during the tare weighing, or carrying dogs or family therein but all getting out after having loaded.
5   Where he has tared correctly and wishes to reduce his apparent gross weight, fractionally overlapping the weighbridge edge with a wheel. (The errors that this will show may be too sizeable to avoid notice.)
6   Where a driver is familiar with a short weighbridge, by carefully positioning his vehicle during double weighing, he may induce a false reading which is constantly to his advantage.
7   Where a driver has discharged his load and wishes then to inflate his tare weight he can do so by filling to capacity with fuel before reweighing.

When looking for places on a vehicle where objects can be stored to increase its apparent weight, favourite places are the same as those used for the concealment of stolen property. Figure 20:5 provides a quick guide to the most useful search points.

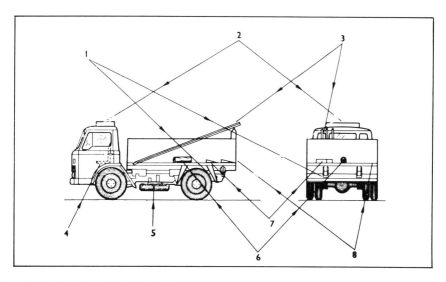

Figure 20:5   Search points in a commercial vehicle
1 Along chassis member under body
2 Under ropes in compartment on top of cab
3 Inside scaffolding poles
4 Under seat in cab
5 Inside spare wheel
6 In fold of tarpaulin
7 Under or inside skids
8 Tight against tailboard on loaded vehicle

It is as well for an independent person occasionally to cast an eye over what is happening at the weighbridge and ensure that the weighman is doing his job as he should (see Figure 20:6).

A precaution that an honest weighman can always take is that of calling out to the driver and asking him for the tare weight and comparing what he gives verbally with what is recorded upon the dial. A further check is that of noting and comparing the tare weight printed on the side of the vehicle – though this is often inaccurate. Where regular records of the same vehicle suddenly indicate a variation in weight, the reason for this should be challenged. In one regrettable instance this was noted after a lorry had called to collect scrap for the last time before being sold. It suddenly appeared to lose precisely 500 kg (10 cwt) after being constant for nearly two years. This happened when the police were making inquiries at the weighbridge at the time of taring and indicated that a profit of half a ton per trip had been enjoyed by the driver and his friend, the operator, throughout the two years.

It is a good idea to keep a record of complaints of deficiencies so that if the same driver's name appears at regular intervals a more intensive investigation can be

Figure 20:6   Weighbridge sited where it should be, immediately inside the gate

carried out. With a suspect driver the object should be to catch him rather than induce him to mend his ways temporarily, or he will remain a potential menace. If it is thought that he is carrying something to inflate the tare weight, observations should be kept upon him. If he is seen to throw material away before loading, he can be reweighed and then stopped, leaving him no defence to the charge of theft of goods equivalent to the weight he had thrown off. Be sure to let him reload or his offence cannot be more serious than attempting to steal.

A final word of advice

Do not accept losses without investigation. Even though this may not lead to a tangible conclusion, the fact that it is done may reveal system defects that can be remedied, it will cause those involved to reflect upon the possibility of personal error or carelessness, and it is likely to act as a deterrent to other intending thieves.

PART SIX

Distribution Operations

Overview

Great emphasis has been placed in the past on the physical aspects of the distribution activity, but ultimately nothing can work without the corresponding flow of information. Information is the amalgam which binds the whole distribution system together and allows it to function properly.

Skjøtt-Larsen takes this point up in Chapter 21 when he defines the various roles of a distribution information system, i.e. to trigger action, monitor and control, co-ordinate, and link systems together. In Chapter 22 Wilson discusses a major application area of a typical information system: the budgeting and control sub-systems. He regards the budget as the basis for management control and develops this particular view in some depth.

Gattorna then discusses the issue of a distribution performance audit in Chapter 23 beginning with the question: why audit anyway? He establishes the need for a structured, disciplined approach to reviewing a company's distribution performance and offers the audit as a satisfactory device. The emphasis throughout is on reviewing current system capability (in both cost and physical terms) and establishing whether or not the appropriate level of resources is available for the distribution task. He explains the audit methodology which has been developed through field experience, and concludes with the qualification that the audit does not of itself necessarily provide answers to all the problems identified in the investigation – but it does mark the beginning of the season for solutions and distribution planning process in general.

21

Distribution information systems

Tage Skjøtt-Larsen

The physical distribution system is oriented towards the market and has the responsibility for moving the items from the end of the production lines to the customers. The main functions embraced in the system are order acquisition, order processing, inventory control, warehousing and delivery. In some companies these activities are managed as almost separate sub-units; in other companies they are integrated into comprehensive computer systems with no barriers between each other.

Roles of the information system

An essential part of any physical distribution system is the information flow related to the operations. Without accurate and timely information the physical distribution system cannot respond efficiently and in a co-ordinated way.

The information system in distribution performs various specific roles:

1   It serves as a *triggering mechanism* by producing instructions and documents necessary to activate other components of the system. The order processing, for example, initiates a number of related activities, such as credit control, order assembly, updating of computer files, delivery operations, etc.
2   It *monitors* and *controls* the performance of the physical distribution system in order to ensure that previously established cost and customer service objectives are achieved. Information from the computer files of the operating units are summarised in various forms of management control information, e.g. periodic monitoring reports, requested reports, or special planning reports.
3   It *co-ordinates* functions both within the physical distribution system and

between this and other key decision areas in the company, e.g. sales, finance, production and purchasing.

4   It *links* the internal system to interrelated external systems, e.g. suppliers, customers and outside carriers.

The concept of the information system is not necessarily tied to the computer. The generation of documents and instructions and the updating of records may also be performed mechanically or manually. However, in larger companies, where the distribution operations often require huge volumes of data to be processed rapidly, there is great potential for using computer-based systems. This potential has been increased as a result of developments in micro-technology, making electronic data processing and transmission relatively cheaper.

The order processing system

Order processing is the core activity of the physical distribution information system. The inputs of the order processing system are customer orders, and the outputs are a range of documents and instructions, which trigger the warehousing and delivery operations necessary to fulfil the orders and ensure that the computer files are updated.

To illustrate the order processing system, a typical example, taken from a company producing consumer goods, is shown in Figure 21:1. Very briefly the sequence in the order processing system is as follows:

1   The customer orders are recorded on pre-printed order forms by sales representatives and mailed to the sales department.

2   The incoming orders are edited to ensure that the order data are in a computer-enterable form, and the order data are checked for accuracy.

3   The order data are entered into the computer system through visual display units and screened for credit limits.

4   The outstanding orders are compared with the inventory balance, and orders which cannot be fulfilled immediately are backlogged for later deliveries.

5   The computer files are updated and various documents are produced, e.g. delivery notes, order picking instructions, invoices, and monitoring and control reports.

6   The picking instructions are sent to the warehouse, where the orders are assembled.

7   The delivery notes are sent to the transport department, where load planning and delivery routes are prepared.

8   The orders are delivered to the customers, together with a copy of the advice note. Another copy is signed by the customer and returned as an acknowledgement of the receipt of the order.

All these steps will be found in most computerised order processing systems, but there may well be substantial differences in the way the sequence is arranged and the types of equipment used for entering and processing the orders.

One option is that the customer calls a data terminal operator by telephone. The operator enters the order directly into the computer via the terminal without any paper transcription. The customer or the representative may also record the orders on sense-marked order forms, which can be read by the computer without a preceding transformation process. A third option, which has recently been adopted by many retail chains, makes use of portable data terminals, where the clerks key in the order data on a tape during the working day. During the evening the orders are transmitted via telephone lines to a central warehouse, where the orders are processed. The goods can then be delivered to the stores the next morning.

The order transmittal can be further automated. Some of the major supermarket chains in the USA and Western Europe have installed POS (point-of-sale) terminals that encode the unit data the moment the customer checks out. When the stock level of a specific item has reached the re-order point, a replenishment order is automatically transmitted to the central computer where the order is processed.

Order cycle time

The total order cycle can be defined as the time that elapses between the moment the customer places an order and the moment the goods are physically delivered to the customer. Two dimensions of the order cycle concept are particularly important in the relationship between the company and its customers – the average length and consistency of the order cycle time.

An increase in the *speed* of the order cycle time, e.g. by installing a computerised order processing system, affects the costs in at least two ways. In the first place a shorter order cycle time reduces the necessary inventory levels held throughout the distribution channel and thus releases capital tied up in inventories. Secondly, a faster order cycle shortens the time required for the adaptation to changing levels of demand and thus reduces the negative consequences of stock-outs. A further advantage derives from a faster cash flow.

Closely related to the speed of the order cycle time is the *reliability* of the process. The reliability refers to the variations between the promised and the actual time taken for the orders to be processed. The reliability affects the necessary levels of safety stocks through the system.

In some companies there is a potential trade-off between a high-speed computerised order-processing system and a relatively slower transportation system, where the costs associated with the computer system may be more than offset by savings realised in the transportation system.

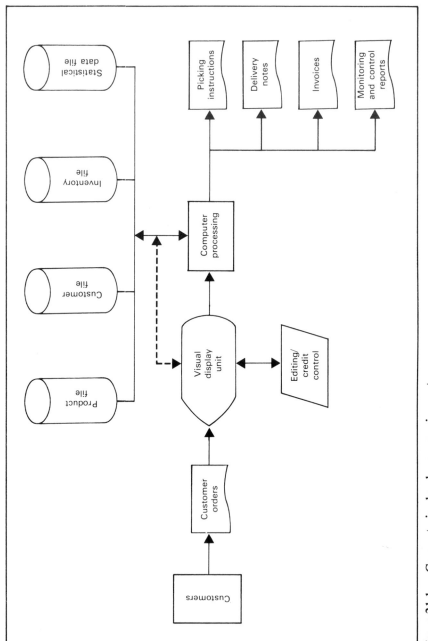

Figure 21:1   Computerised order processing system

Management planning and control

Information systems normally serve several objectives in the organisation. One important objective is to support the managers in planning and control of the physical distribution operations.

The information requirements for planning and control purposes differ from level to level of management. This implies that the information system must be designed to fit the information needs of managers at the various levels. Three broad categories of management levels can be identified:

1 Strategic planning.
2 Management control.
3 Operational control.

Strategic planning

In brief, *strategic planning* addresses long-range problems which are unstructured, non-repetitive and often demand changes in company objectives or major policy revisions. Examples of strategic planning decisions within the physical distribution area are choice of distribution channels, formulation of customer service objectives, choice between centralised or decentralised warehousing systems, etc.

The nature of the information needed at the strategic level is often company-wide in scope and tailor made for a specific purpose or problem. Often the sources of information are external to the company, e.g. indicators of fluctuations of the market, reports on the competitive situation, technological trends, etc. It follows from these characteristics of the information requirements at the strategic level that the types of reports must be customised to the individual company, its organisation and its managers.

Management control

Management control addresses problems of resource allocation which are more recurrent and structured. Examples of management control decisions are specifications of customer service programmes, choice of transport mode, formulation of inventory control procedures, etc.

Management control is concerned with the efficiency and effectiveness of the established plans, programmes and procedures. The information requirements are therefore concentrated on activities that are not going according to the plans. The focus is on exceptional reports which signal to the management that either *corrective* instructions have to be issued to ensure that the desired levels of performance are fulfilled, or *modifications* of the plans are needed.

Operational control

Operational control is concerned with repetitive, routine activities which are well structured and defined. Examples of operational control activities in physical distribution management are load planning, vehicle routing, fleet maintenance, and inventory control.

The data collected at the operational control level serve two major objectives. First, the control is concerned with execution of predetermined plans and decision rules. Therefore, the information has to be very detailed, accurate and up to date. Secondly, the information flow forms the data base for higher levels of planning and control. Therefore, the information needs to be specified and stored in a form that facilitates processing of summary reports and special reports for other purposes.

The three levels of planning and control are closely interrelated and so are the supporting information flows. In Figure 21:2 the relationships between management levels and the types of information are outlined. In general, the higher the management level is, the more selective the summarised information. Similarly, the lower the management level, the more accurate, detailed and up to date is the information required.

Design strategies

Various strategies can be employed in designing information systems for physical distribution management. Two major categories can be identified: the *bottom-up* approach and the *top-down* approach.

The bottom-up or evolutionary approach is an approach one often encounters in well established companies. The developing of the information system starts with building up separate subsystems for the various activities, e.g. order processing, inventory control, load planning, etc. Each subsystem operates its own data file for transaction processing, updating and reporting.

As the information requirements develop, the separate files are integrated into databases, and modules for planning and control decisions are added. At a later stage strategic planning models are added to the system.

The advantage of this approach is that the information is developed step by step in accordance with the information needs of the company and the capability of managers of using the information as a decision tool. The risk of designing a large-scale information system which is not accepted and used by the managers is thereby minimised. The disadvantages are the high costs of redesigning the subsystems every time a new feature is added to the existing system, and the risk of overlapping or unco-ordinated subsystems.

The *top-down* approach starts with specifying the objectives, the constraints and the environment of the organisation. The next step is to identify and define relevant decision areas and activities. Then models of the various systems are developed and the information requirements necessary to support the models specified. The final steps are to define modules required to manage data and assign priorities to the modules.

The advantage of the top-down approach is that it creates a consistent and coordinated information system. The disadvantage is that it is difficult to foresee the future information requirements of a dynamic organisation. Besides, the objectives of a company are often diffuse and contradictory and, therefore, not very operational as a basis for deriving information needs.

Integration versus independence

The balance between independence and integration is a fundamental characteristic of an information system.

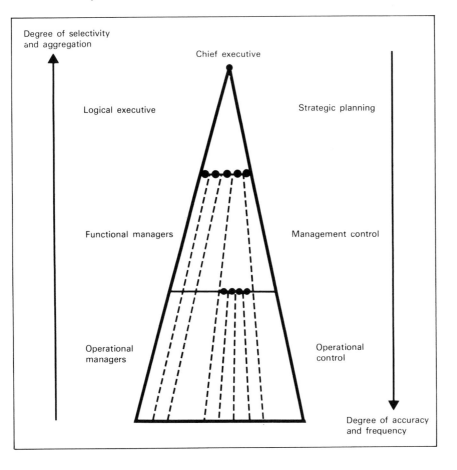

Figure 21:2   Information types and management levels

An integrated information system can be defined as a system in which there is a relatively high degree of co-ordination and resource sharing between the interacting subsystems. The general characteristics of an integrated information system are:

1   The output of one subsystem serves as the input to other subsystems. For example, customer orders entering the order-processing system are transformed into computer-readable form and made available for inventory control, production scheduling, sales forecasting, etc.

2   Data are consolidated in a common data base to which all interrelated subsystems have access. For instance, in a distribution network with several depots the inventory balance is held on a central inventory file instead of separate records being kept for each depot.

3   Closely connected activities are consolidated in the same procedure rather than split into separate procedures. For instance, order processing, credit checking and stock allocation are normally performed within the same program in a computer-based order-processing system, whereas in a manual system they are often separated between different departments, e.g. the sales office, the accounting department and the warehouse.

4   A high degree of resource sharing will often take place. For example, the central computer, the data base, the communications network, and the application packages are often shared among all the various subsystems.

The extent to which a logistics system should be integrated is an important management decision. A higher degree of integration often implies a closer co-ordination between interacting activities, a higher consistency of performance and greater efficiency. On the other hand, a higher degree of integration also imposes certain penalties, e.g. higher information costs, added complexity and less flexibility. The management choice is not one of absolute selection of either independence or integration, but a degree of balance which must be uniquely determined for each organisation.

The creation of slack variables is a common way of reducing the co-ordination needs between interacting activities in a logistics system. Slack variables allow the output of the supplying subsystem to differ from the input of the receiving subsystem, at least in the short run. Examples of slack variables are often found in such areas as inventories, warehouse space, size of vehicle fleet, delays in order-processing time. The creation of slack reduces the degree of interaction of coupled subsystems, but at the same time decreases the cost-effectiveness of the system.

One purpose of implementing an integrated information system is to eliminate or reduce the slack in the process capacity of the system and thereby improve both cost and performance levels. A computer-based order-processing system, for instance, is assumed to reduce the time delays in the total order cycle time and thereby to increase both the customer service level and the internal efficiencies. Similarly, the implementation of an on-line inventory control system is normally justified by savings in inventory costs and improvements in customer service.

Centralised versus decentralised systems

The development of integrated information systems initially tended to a centralisation of the computing power and the management planning and control systems. The advantages of centralisation derive from the economies of scale of large computers and the higher degree of resource sharing. However, a high degree of centralisation tends to reduce the flexibility of the organisation and imposes undesirable rigidities because of the necessity of standardising procedures and communications channels and centralising the management authority structure as well.

Recent developments in the field of mini-computers have, however, furthered hybrid systems that contain elements of both centralisation and decentralisation. The current trend in distributed processing systems has returned some of the computing power to actual users of the services. For instance, mini-computers can be placed at depots or central warehouses to serve local computing needs, such as preparation of picking documentation, updating of depots stocks, delivery routing, customer servicing, etc.

A distributed system offers the advantages of both centralisation and decentralisation. The more urgent local processing needs can be handled by mini-computers, while activities that interact relatively strongly with activities at other locations can be handled by a large-scale computer. The mini-computers in a distributed network will often have an on-line connection to the central computer and the central files, but in many cases the information requirements are satisfied by batch-processing.

Another effect of an increasing use of mini-computers is that the subsystems in the organisation will tend to be more decoupled. This will probably also affect the planning process, so that global optimisation models will be replaced by more decentralised model building.

22

Distribution budgeting and control systems

F. W. Wilson

It is now a generally accepted practice for the control system of a business to be based upon an annual operating plan or estimate. Before planning can commence, assumptions must be established on which the plan will be based. The assumptions will be derived from a detailed appreciation of the operations for the period under review and of the effects on the budget of policies laid down by the board. The assumptions should include a detailed review of the market and the categories of goods to be carried, the economic situation including competitors' prices, alternative systems, the availability of new traffics, seasonal fluctuations, the size of deliveries, the types of outlet to which delivery will be made, nominated schedules, the frequency of distribution, the availability of hired services, etc., all of which must be quantified for incorporation into the financial plan.

Whether the distribution service is an integral part of the marketing company or operating as a separate organisation, a free exchange of information is essential between the marketing and distribution organisations if complete compatibility between them is to be achieved and if an operation is to be developed that gives service of the required quality economically. Appropriate tolerances must be allowed for fluctuations in the volume of throughput because, however sophisticated the forecasting and marketing techniques may be, there is nearly always a certain degree of peaking and troughing in the distribution activity.

Establishing an operating plan for a distribution system

An annual operating plan consists of a series of separate but interlocking plans, which will generally comprise the following (in one form or another): operating budget, capital budget, financial budget, personnel budget.

It is usual to commence the plan with a review of the past year, and of the economic and other assumptions adopted, so that the ensuing figures can be seen in their proper perspective. In support of the annual operating plan, details of actual performances achieved over, say, the previous three years can be useful, so that changes can be shown as trends. In a progressive organisation forecasts for the years beyond that being reviewed for the annual operating plan would be made to demonstrate that the plan has been developed within the framework of the longer-term strategic aims. Capital expenditure is then seen in the perspective of the future operations of the organisation.

The annual operating plan is usually prepared some months before the commencement of the year which is being planned. An estimate should therefore be prepared of the results to the end of the current year's operation, for comparison with the budget as drafted for the current period. This kind of detail will enable the board members reviewing the plan to satisfy themselves that the plan is both sound and comprehensive. Care in the layout and presentation of the plan is also well worth while for the impression it conveys of sound preparation.

Operating budget

This usually has several parts but in principle it should include details of costs by functional activities including storage, handling, trunking operations, delivery, workshops, and administration. Against the totals of these costs should be presented the recovery which it is expected will be achieved, either in the form of revenue, in which case a profit by activity will be established, or, if costs only are to be recovered, the calculated value of interest on the capital employed in the various activities should be aggregated with the costs to arrive at a notional revenue. This latter point, whilst being one of finesse, enables the cost of the distribution service to be made more comparable with rates charged outside the organisation and establishes the economies of the system.

In an operating budget for a distribution organisation, handling a diversity of products, one would expect to find details of the revenue which is expected to accrue from each grouping of products, or customers, for comparison with the estimate of the costs of the operations. The basic operating budget will therefore consist of two main analyses of the results of the activity, one by functions and the other by customer or product, each of which complements the other in total terms. To facilitate the interpretation of the operating budget by the review team, it is also desirable to provide detailed information regarding utilisation factors of warehouses and fleet vehicles, trends of efficiencies by function, unit costs of distribution and ratios such as return on capital, revenue to capital, and profit or interest on capital to revenue.

Capital budget

This should be based upon the review of physical resources which will be required during the year of the operating plan and in future periods. The budget should show separately the expenditure which is required for expansion and that for replacement programmes. It may also be convenient to combine the repairs budget with the capital expenditure presentation, so that the relationship between repair costs and capital expenditure can be seen. No hard and fast rules can be laid down for the preparation of the capital expenditure budget, as the detail must conform to, and be compatible with, the expenditure control system of the organisation, which in turn is dependent upon the extent to which authority is delegated.

A review of the progress of capital expenditure authorised for previous periods should be presented, for although the approval of a capital budget may be a licence to incur expenditure, an organisation is usually only capable of making expenditure at a given and controllable rate. The budget should, therefore, include figures of any capital expenditure which is outstanding, so as to highlight any delays in the programme which may be occurring, indicating the extent of previous over/under-ambitious planning, or changes in the size of the team required to control the expenditure. Major projects which are proposed should be cross-referenced to an explanation for each project in the assumptions statement, so that the proposals can be related to the forces which are generating the need for the expansion of capacity.

Flexibility should be built into the capital budget to enable the purchases of equipment to be phased in as and when it is required. The delivery period of much equipment is of such length that it may be necessary to place orders well in advance and sometimes to make payments on account well before the period in which the equipment is required. Provision should therefore be made in the budget for the level of work-in-progress which is required for equipment such as vehicles. Re-equipment of the fleet is normally phased so as to match the size of fleet, at least to some extent, with seasonal fluctuations in activity. The whole question of vehicle replacement must, however, be treated as part of a long-term policy geared to producing the minimum annualised cost of capital outlay and of maintenance combined, using discounted-cash-flow techniques. Similarly, several years' forward planning may be required if the method of distribution or handling is to be altered to meet changing conditions. It may be necessary to start the replacement of part of the equipment in advance of the main implementation phase, so as to spread the total cost of the change and ensure compatibility of the various equipments without large costs for obsolescence.

All these considerations must nevertheless be subordinated to the overall constraints of the corporate plan for capital expenditure, which ultimately determines the strategic course of the business.

Financial budget

The financial budget links the operating and capital expenditure budgets, so as to determine the cash flow of the organisation and incorporate financial transactions, such as depreciation, taxation, capital allowances, investment grants, industrial training levies and refunds, and changes in levels of current assets and liabilities. The cash flow of the organisation, when established, enables its capital needs to be assessed and decisions to be made regarding the raising of new funds, or the use of surpluses.

Personnel budget

Without personnel the organisation will die, so that it is essential to have firm plans laid for future personnel requirements. As the organisation becomes more sophisticated and greater precision is required, the provision of personnel of the required training, experience and calibre becomes of paramount importance. The best-laid plans in terms of resources and money must be correlated with the provision of personnel. The budget should, therefore, incorporate a statement in terms of both numbers and cost of the various grades of personnel which are required, together with an estimate of the training, recruitment and removal costs which are required to maintain the provision of this essential resource.

As the organisation develops, it will attract a variety of specialists into its headquarters. The cost of the central overhead, mainly personnel costs, requires special attention and should be analysed departmentally, so that the trend of growth of the various headquarters activities can be discerned by the reviewing board, to ensure that growth of the organisation is accompanied by economy of scale of the headquarters operation.

Preparation of the budget

Preparation of the budget involves management at all levels in those organisations where delegation of responsibility is practised, since each manager must be accountable for the activity under his control. In a large organisation, therefore, the budget programme can develop into a complicated operation. Information must be delivered to the central budget controller in a disciplined manner, on time, if he is to meet the required timetable. Critical path analysis techniques may be useful in helping to maintain the timetable. The preparation of the budget schedules traditionally remains with the accounts department in the organisation, as the final budget summaries reflect the estimates of future costs and revenue.

The costs are derived from use of resources. The resources required for the distribution activity will have been ascertained as a result of an analysis of the sales budgets of the marketing departments (or companies). These represent the starting point of the whole budgetary process. The greater proportion of the budget preparation effort which ensues is based upon the use of known standard criteria developed from previous practice for which judgements are not required. The standards themselves must first be reviewed to ascertain that the efficiency levels on which they are based are still acceptable and compatible with the objectives of the organisation. The standards and basic data can then be distributed to all management concerned with planning the provision of resources, so that requirements for each location and cost centre can be calculated and agreed with each manager.

Parallel activity will be taking place to determine changes in cost level which are likely to happen as a result of external or internal factors, particularly in these times of inflation, so that standard costs can be brought up to date and applied subsequently to the resource levels which will be returned. At the same time replacement programmes will have been drawn up in terms of agreed policy. Agreement on the budgeted level of resources by regional and departmental management is essential if they are to take responsibility for their operations. It is at this stage that objectives for each manager can be assessed by his immediate superior and agreed in terms of efficiencies and utilisations, in advance of the costing operation which will be applied later.

Once levels of resources for the future operations have been determined, the preparation and finalisation of the budget becomes a comparatively simple arithmetical operation, since the elements of foresight and judgement which enter into any budget have been dealt with. Much of the time and preparation required in the production of budgets consists of the chore of the clerical work involved, so the sooner a budget can be agreed in resource terms the less likely it is that amendments will have to be made and the cheaper the budget preparation cost. A suitable computer model should be considered as the means to produce the budget as changes in any parameter can then be quickly incorporated.

The budget, when completed, will provide information for the ensuing year's plan both to higher management for their review of the total plan, and in detail by cost centres to each departmental and regional manager for the cost of the activities under his control during the ensuing year. It follows that the budget has become the focal point by which control can be maintained through a comparison of actual results with those that have been forecast. The budget has also become the means by which authority can be allocated and delegated.

The budget as a basis for management control

The preparation of comprehensive budgets has been shown to be a lengthy and, therefore, costly operation, requiring careful and sound preparation. All this work will have been wasted unless it becomes the basis for monitoring the actual results of the operations. The budget should become the focal point of control and be the basis on which the concept of management by exception can be introduced. The involvement of all managers in the preparation of the budgets and their agreement on the level of resources and costs required for the activities under their control means that responsibility can be delegated to them. Control must at the same time be maintained, and yet if it has to be maintained in detail, it has not been properly delegated. The solution is control by exception.

As long as actual results are close to the forecast figures, all is well. As soon as they differ by an appreciable margin, however, management should require to know the reasons for the variance. If it is adverse, prompt remedial action will be called for to rectify the position. If it is favourable, then the underlying reason must be identified so that, if appropriate, future plans can incorporate the tendency.

The original concepts of budgetary control were developed during periods when monetary values were for long periods relatively static. Thus the interpretation of variances between budgeted and actual results was relatively easy. In recent times, high levels of inflation produce continual increases in prices and result in much of the information contained in the budgets becoming obsolete before they are published. Flexibility must, therefore, be a feature of the budgets if they are to remain meaningful, and a basis for control. They should be capable of being revised to reflect change. Annual revision is too long a period in periods of high inflation. Quarterly reviews are now common practice. Any standards which are used in the preparation of the flexible budgets should also be capable of revision.

Variations in the level of activity will result in higher or lower costs. It is therefore of vital importance that costs which vary in accordance with activity levels should be segregated from those that remain static or fixed. In distribution much of the expenditure is fixed and the efficient utilisation of assets and resources is of paramount importance.

Information supplied to each manager should, whenever possible, highlight those expenses which are controllable by him against the budgeted levels of expense which were authorised for his area of control. Where a manager is responsible for a complete operation, such as a depot, a warehouse or a fleet of vehicles, it is important that he can be made aware of his total costs. If possible, the revenue earned by his operations should be set off against the expenditure, so that the profit and return on capital earned by his departmental activity can be monitored and related to his management operations. This has the double purpose of maintaining control of his total operation and of giving him the means of measuring his own performance. Computerised variance statements now allow a very high level of detailed information to be passed quickly and economically.

The largest expense incurred by industry is often the cost of labour. The managers immediately in charge of the labour force therefore need reports at very frequent intervals, probably daily and at least weekly, detailing the efficiency of the labour employed in the various cost centres, the utilisation of labour, in terms of the return for paid time, details of absence, sickness, holidays and idle time. If standard times are available for each operation, then it becomes feasible to pre-plan the work of the labour force so that the best use of its potential is achieved and loss of productivity through inadequate planning avoided. Management involvement in the immediate planning is essential if high productivity is to be obtained. As the industry at present is still largely labour-intensive, it follows that if proper control of the labour force is achieved, viability of the whole distribution operation will be assured.

Key ratios

Management needs information on the trends of key ratios to indicate changes in the

levels of activity, utilisation, costs of the operation and the revenue earned. These
ratios can consist of a selection of simple control figures such as the following:

Storage

Occupied/revenue (revenue per unit)
Occupied/cost (unit cost)
Occupied/space available (utilisation)

Handling

Activity level/wages cost (wages cost per unit)
Activity level/total cost (unit cost)
Activity level/revenue (revenue per unit)
Potential provided/activity level obtained (utilisation)
Standard hours worked/actual hours paid (efficiency)

Trunking

Activity level/total cost (unit cost)
Activity level/revenue (revenue per unit)
Standard hours achieved/potential time available (utilisation)
Standard hours worked/actual hours paid (efficiency)
Lost time/total time (lost-time ratio)
Miles/total cost (cost per mile)
Wages/miles (wages cost per mile)
Miles/fuel and oil (fuel cost per mile)
Miles/repairs (repairs cost per mile)
Miles/tyres (tyres cost per mile)

The lost-time ratio may be further subdivided so as to show the proportion of lost time
incurred through repairs, accidents, lack of driver, terminal times, etc.

Delivery

Similar ratios to those for the trunking fleet can be maintained. In addition, it is
important that the ratio of actual delivery time to running time is monitored, on the
premise that running time is an overhead to be kept to a minimum. This can very
easily be done using standard times.

Administration

Activity level/total cost
Activity level/salaries cost

Number of deliveries made/salaries cost
Number of lines delivered/salaries cost

Wherever practical, the costs of the administrative overhead should be analysed, so as to determine the costs of the various clerical activities, such as load summarising and stock control, and enable these to be monitored and controlled too.

Standard costs

Standards, used as reliable measures to give yardsticks against which actual results can be compared, can consist of time for an operation, usage of materials, the labour required and the costs of the various processes. If control is maintained only on the basis of past performances and the general trend, it is possible for one uneconomic level to be compared with another. Standards should be based upon performances which are at high levels of efficiency and are attainable. Standard costing is based upon the principle that actual expense can be compared with the cost based upon the previously calculated standards.

The standards are calculated at a budgeted level of activity, so that if the actual level is higher a fall in the unit cost of activity should result, and conversely a lower level will produce a rise in unit cost. In fact, only the unit cost of the *fixed* expenses will change, as those that vary exactly in accordance with the level of activity will remain in accord. In flexible budgeting, account is taken of the changed level of activity, or volume, and its effect is separate from other variances.

In a comprehensive system of standard costing, a complete analysis of the reasons for differences between actual cost and the standard costs is made. Some of the usual variances and the basis on which they are calculated are as follows:

Volume variance measures the amount by which under- or over-recovery of fixed expenses occurs because of changes in the level of activity from that which was budgeted.

Calendar variances are a subdivision of the volume variance arising from under-working because of holidays, etc.

Expenditure variances adjust increases or decreases in the cost of fixed expenses to the levels fixed in the budget.

Price variances adjust the actual cost of variable expenses to the price level envisaged in the budget.

Efficiency variances detail the under- or over-recovery costs which arises from differences in the rate at which work is performed compared with the standard rate.

Labour cost variances detail the difference in price of labour compared with that included in the standard, and also increases or decreases in wages earned as a result of the rate of working being more or less than the standard rate.

In a full standard costing system the profit and loss account would be drawn up as a statement showing the profit attained and the profit which would have been obtained if it had been earned at the standard rate. The two figures would be reconciled by giving details of the variances which make up the difference between them.

Although this system is economic to administer in times of steady prices, rapidly changing prices can result in such large and diverse variances that the maintenance of the system may become expensive.

It is characteristic of modern distribution that in the very short term the proportion of fixed costs is high because of the tendency to reduce the incidence of overtime by paying wages which incorporate overtime elements. This spreads the workload evenly over the working day to avoid queues of work. It may therefore be more economic in administration not to employ a full standard costing system but to restrict the use of standards for control purposes to those items of expense which vary in direct linear relationships to the level of activity, or to maintain the standards in a different medium such as time. Such a system would rely upon a strict budgetary control of the level of fixed resources while using standard costs as the control for variable expenses, and maintaining stringent controls over the efficiencies and utilisation of both personnel and equipment.

Control of specific activities

The efficiency of personnel in the warehouse, in the fleet and in the office must be carefully controlled. Because workloads fluctuate, control must take place upon a daily basis if it is to be effective. The workload for each operative, or group of operatives if jobs cannot be segregated, should be calculated in advance and a check made of the actual results when the job has been completed. The use of work-study standards provides a convenient measure upon which this form of control is based, and is particularly useful for the control of drivers (whose work cannot be directly supervised). Clerical work measures enable the performance of clerks to be monitored.

Control of vehicle utilisation

Full records of the use of vehicles must be maintained so that lost operating time can be identified. An analysis of the reasons for lost time will help management to take steps to minimise it. Lost time can arise from such causes as absence of the operative (sickness, strikes, holidays), and in the case of vehicles, excessive terminal time, repairs, accidents, or lack of work. If the cost performance is poor because of low utilisation, and lack of work is the cause, other than in the short term, then equipment should be removed following a specific investigation that this is the correct economic answer to the problem. The cause of low utilisation in the fleet vehicles may, however, lie in the province of the marketing organisation. Perhaps utilisation is high on certain days and low on others because of customers' refusal to take deliveries on those days. If the sales management cannot do anything to remedy the situation, the effect of unavoidable loss of utilisation may be reduced by arranging for vehicles to be serviced and repaired on slack days, and for the drivers to undertake clerical or other tasks in the warehouse.

Control of repairs

Information is required on the incidence of repairs for vehicles and warehouse equipment in terms of costs and the type of repair, mileage, year purchased, etc. The information is required so that if repairs or replacement of parts are required within the guarantee period granted by manufacturers then the manufacturer can be charged. Control is required in terms of individual vehicles or equipments so that decisions can be taken to replace rogues or to adjust the planned life of these mechanical assets. Information in summarised form is required at regular intervals so as to determine the incidence of repairs by various types of equipments.

Personnel control

In addition to the employee records which will be maintained probably in a central office, management will require information which will enable them to maintain control over personnel generally. Of particular interest will be details of numbers and grades of employees compared with establishments, hours of work, efficiency of working and the productivity attained, incidence of lost time or overtime suitably analysed to provide reasons for causes, and turnover of staff, giving details of reasons for staff leaving employment.

Revenue or product group control

The mix of goods which is distributed will undoubtedly be different from that which was originally planned in the budget. Monitoring of such changes will be required and whenever possible the assistance of the marketing organisation should be enlisted so as to avoid duplication and reduce administrative cost. In a sophisticated system, the work-study department will be capable of monitoring the effects of changes in effort as they occur. The changes reflected by their studies should be incorporated into the control system as soon as practicable. The work standards should, as published, separate the fixed and variable time elements contained in the standards so that the flexibility which this provides can be used for control purposes.

Information will be required regarding intake into the warehouse so that the effort can be planned in co-operation with the manufacturer, the spread of deliveries by location and by time, the number of deliveries and the size of the drops, the changes in the number of packs and pack sizes, and the incidence of losses and damage to various products, to isolate those that are inherently accident- or loss-prone. In distribution organisations which are operated as separate companies, management information will be required to relate the revenue earned to the costs expended so as to ensure that profits are achieved in accordance with an agreed plan. If possible, revenue should be allocated to each cost centre with a view to determining that each is operating as a viable entity.

Management must be regularly informed of the effects of changes in the level of distribution activity upon the viability of the organisation, so that action can be taken to remedy any adverse situations. Management must also be made continuously aware of the effects of peaking and troughing of traffics upon the viability of the distribution system. If necessary, support pricing policies must be negotiated to avoid losses through under-utilisation of resources during the trough periods and increased expenditure during peaks to meet demands which cannot be satisfied by the available resources.

Cash control

Cash control is generally confined to the central headquarters of the distribution organisation. Most businesses use a fairly simple pattern which permits the main elements of the cash flow to be quickly determined without further analysis. Strict control is required over the operations of the credit control function of the organisation to ensure that funds are not uneconomically tied up. In a separate distribution organisation, senior management needs to be apprised of the cash flow at regular intervals, probably monthly but at least quarterly. Statements which are prepared should accord with those prepared in the original budget or plan, to enable progress to be monitored so that funds are available when required.

23

Auditing distribution performance

John Gattorna

Introduction

The distribution activity is now generally acknowledged as a key contributor to the company's marketing performance and hence to its corporate performance. For this reason alone, and in view of the difficult economic times currently being experienced, more company managements are giving increasing attention to their distribution function. In many cases this new-found interest is unprecedented, the distribution system having grown like Topsy during the heady years of corresponding sales growth.

Under what specific circumstances, therefore, would an evaluation of the company's distribution system be appropriate, if not necessary? A short, though non-exhaustive, list of situations is given below:

1   When the company makes a significant change in its marketing strategy, e.g. with the decision to move a major part of the business over to wholesalers from a previous situation where customers were serviced directly (the opposite could also apply).
2   When the size of the company changes significantly, e.g. when new businesses (acquisitions) or products are added to the distribution system's task.
3   When the company's geographic mix of shipments changes appreciably.
4   Or, at worst, when five to ten years have passed since the last evaluation.
5   Finally, when any of the four major signs of mal-distribution are in evidence. These signs are:
    – slow turning inventories,
    – poor customer service as evidenced by the level of customer complaints,

– a higher than usual level of inter-warehouse transshipments,
– a higher than usual level of premium freight charges.

Of course what one has to be aware of is that these signs, although indicative of problems in the distribution system, may in effect be the manifestation of a cause or causes elsewhere in the company. For example, the customer complaints may in fact be due to poor definition of customer service objectives and strategies by the marketing executive, which leaves the distribution operations management to decide the best approach, without the benefit of all the necessary facts. The author has observed several distribution systems which in purely operational terms have been excellent, but have nonetheless come under criticism from other parts of the company for apparent shortcomings.

To review a company's distribution performance we need a structured and disciplined approach; for this reason, a device known as the distribution audit has been developed by a number of distribution thinkers, including the author. In essence, the distribution audit is a device for reviewing the environment in which the company is currently operating; it has both external and internal dimensions, both of which will be developed in this chapter. The audit attempts to find answers to two vital questions as follows:

1 Where are we in terms of resources, expertise, performance, etc., at this point in time?
2 How cost-effective is our current distribution system?

The audit is not radically new in any way – it simply brings a discipline, a logic, to bear on an old problem. Simply described, the fundamental reason for an audit of this type is to check whether or not the resources and capabilities of the corporate distribution function are compatible with the demands being made on it, or likely to be made on it, by the company's marketing executive. How many times can we recall a marketing effort, such as a special promotion, failing because the distribution function was unable to meet the physical task required? Often, in looking for reasons why this should have occurred, we find a lack of communication between the marketing and distribution executives.

So the distribution audit is the first stage in the distribution planning and control cycle as depicted in Figure 23:1. The distribution planning activity expressed in the context of the wider marketing planning activity is depicted in Figure 23:2.

Distribution audit environments

It is difficult to separate the external and internal operating environments of a company. However, in this treatment we shall cover both dimensions, although the main emphasis in the latter part of this chapter will be upon the internal environment, because it is here that progress must and can be made towards more meaningful managerial decisions in the distribution area. An examination of the internal

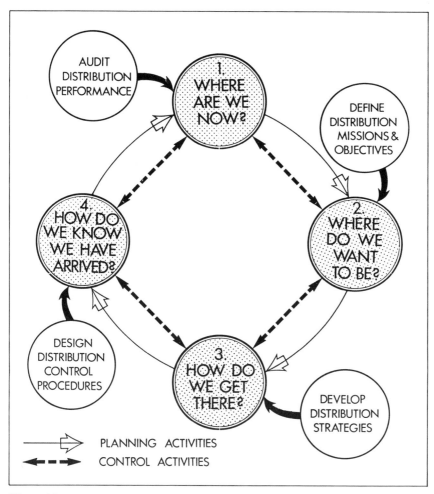

Figure 23:1   Distribution planning and control cycle

operations will also provide some useful pointers to the effective organisation structures which could be adopted in the future.

The key elements in an appraisal of the external environment are depicted in Figure 23:3 under the main headings of market profile, competitive profile, channel profile and government regulation. This wide-ranging set of headings is not meant to suggest anything other than the fact that the distribution executive in a company should be aware of developments and trends in those areas which are not necessarily his direct responsibility. There is no suggestion, for example, that the distribution manager should be an expert in marketing and market conditions. On the other hand, he will be a better distribution manager if he seeks to be informed in such matters as

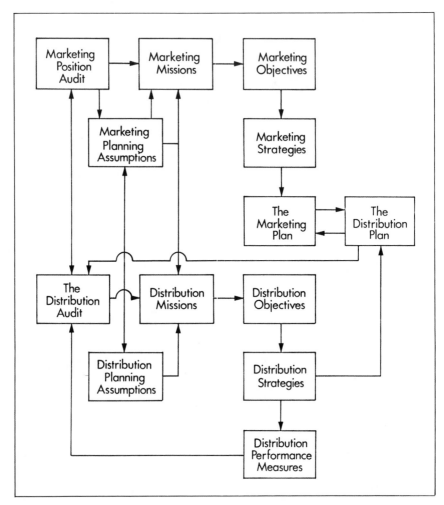

Figure 23:2   The distribution planning activity

emerging new markets, structural changes taking place in the markets he serves, etc., because these are the very factors which impinge upon his job.

The internal change appraisal, as depicted in Figure 23:4, is closer to home for the distribution manager, although here again he does not necessarily have to be an expert in the company's projects. But since product knowledge is so vital to the efficient completion of his job, the distribution manager is well advised to learn as much as he can about their particular properties and peculiar requirements. In the first instance, however, the real focus of the audit should be upon reviewing the *existing system capability*, for it is here that the distribution manager has the potential to make cost-effective improvements.

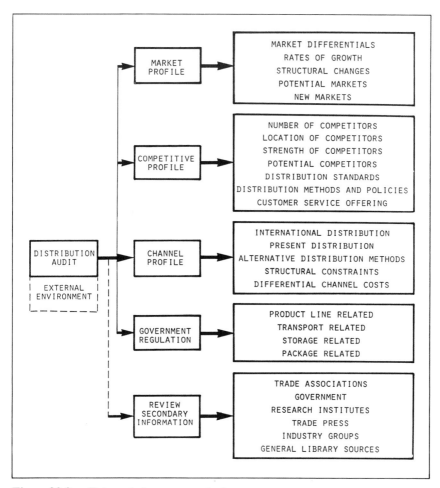

Figure 23:3   External change appraisal

Once an audit of this type is undertaken, for the first time it will be possible to discern the key operating variables in the particular distributing system under review and to set up a selective information system for the purpose of monitoring these variables at regular intervals (say quarterly) in the future.

Of course, one of the biggest obstacles to using the audit regularly is the difficulty of obtaining the necessary information with which to analyse and compare performance from period to period. In any event, the information system need not be over-sophisticated; above all, the cost of setting it up should not outweigh the potential savings. Some companies have found it useful to link the information collection responsibility to personnel at different operating levels in the organisation.

Finally, there is the question of performance standards. Without doubt the task

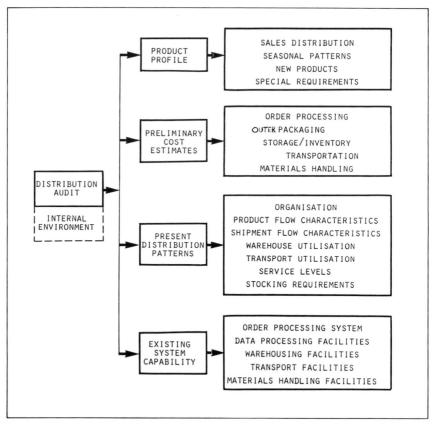

Figure 23:4   Internal change appraisal

of deriving sensible standards to operate by is very difficult, particularly where none previously existed. Three options are available:

1   Set standards on the basis of historical performance – this has inherent dangers.
2   Attempt to obtain some idea of competitors' standards – often to our surprise we will find that our competitors have thought less about this issue than we have.
3   Finally, we can opt to set some arbitrary standards and be prepared to alter these if they prove too high or too low in the light of experience. In particular, it will be possible to compare one location against another in the network, and be prepared to find explanations for the differences which will surely arise. The differences between locations are acceptable only as long as we are able to produce logical explanations for them, which in some cases may lead to corrective actions. This is the audit mechanism working at its best – not solving problems but highlighting potential problem areas which then gain the desired management attention.

Internal audit content and methodology

The control information which is available to distribution managers these days generally comes in financial terms, extracted from the company's set of operating accounts. Because of the particular dissection of such financial accounts and more latterly the ravages of inflation, the numbers which appear in the various reports are of little or no use in managing the distribution function on a day-to-day or even longer time period basis.

For this reason the data collected in the audit comprises both financial and physical quantities, the ultimate aim being to relate these two streams to each other. So two lines of investigation are pursued – one which endeavours to build up a true picture of the total distribution cost and the other which attempts to develop an understanding of what physical performances (in whatever units are relevant to the business, e.g. tonnes, pallets, cases, cubic metres, hectolitres, etc.) are actually being achieved for the monies being invested in the distribution activity. In schematic terms, Figure 23:5 tells the story very adequately.

The key ratio for which the distribution manager is responsible is the cost of distribution as a percentage of net sales. Some organisations use distribution cost as a

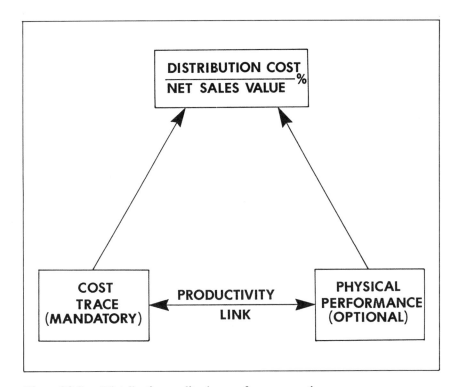

Figure 23:5   Distribution audit – key performance ratio

percentage of gross margin; others use distribution cost as a percentage of production cost; yet others use a combination of these. It really does not matter which key ratio is selected, as long as it is consistent if developed and is not subject to distortion.

As indicated earlier, it is useful to think in terms of managing the hierarchy of control ratios we are attempting to monitor by linking them to specific personnel or positions within the distribution organisation. The suggested hierarchy of control ratios is specified in general terms in Figure 23:6 and detailed specifically in Figure 23:7.

Of course the list in Figure 23:7 is fairly general and may not contain some of the ratios which the reader finds necessary to monitor in his business. Essentially, the process is one of building up information modules from the basic operating level of the company's distribution function, and ultimately selecting a relatively few key operational parameters to monitor in detail from period to period. These parameters will be different from industry to industry, company to company.

The *methodology* for carrying out the audit for the first time is important. In this regard the author has found the following seven-step procedure to be successful in use:

1   Flowchart all *trigger* communications from receipt of customers' orders.
2   Flowchart the corresponding materials flows.
3   Flowchart the subsequent reporting information flows (or feedback).
4   Review all the above flows for *gaps, redundancies* and *discrepancies.*
5   Select several performance parameters (or ratios) which appear to be crucial to

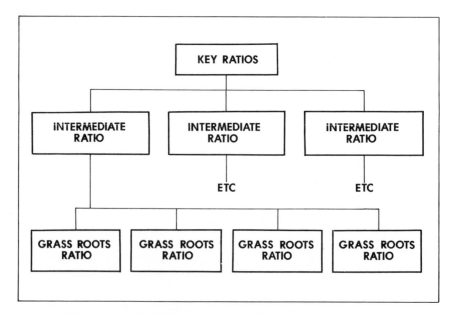

Figure 23:6   Distribution audit – hierarchy of control ratios

1. Facilities Utilisation
1·1   WAREHOUSE ACTIVITY FACTORS

1·2   OPERATING COSTS

1·3   CUBE UTILISATION

2. Inventory Management
2·1   INVENTORY CARRYING COSTS

2·2   STOCK TURN VELOCITY

2·3   STOCK SHRINKAGE

2·4   INTRA-COMPANY TRANSFERS

2·5   SERVICE LEVEL(S)

2·6   STOCK ROTATION

2·7   STOCK OUT PERFORMANCE

3. Transportation
3·1   OPERATING COSTS

3·2   TRANSPORT TASK PERFORMANCE

3·3   VEHICLE UTILISATION

4. Communications Systems
4·1   OPERATING COSTS

4·2   DOCUMENTATION ACTIVITY

4·3   CUSTOMER CONTACT

4·4   PERFORMANCE MEASURES

5. Unitisation Degree
5·1   COST BENEFITS

5·2   UNIT MODULES

5·3   PRODUCTIVITY MEASURES

6. Customer Service
6·1   ORDER/DELIVERY RESPONSIVENESS

6·2   DELIVERY CONSISTENCY

Figure 23:7   Summary of intermediate ratio groups

the company's business and begin to monitor these against previously derived standards.

6   In particular, look for any important inter-dependencies which exist between distribution and other functional areas of the business.

7   The end result of such a review can take various forms, e.g. reorganisation of systems and personnel; relocation of distribution centres; reassessment and redevelopment of the resources available to distribution, etc.

Perhaps the most difficult and certainly the most detailed task in undertaking an initial audit is developing the composite flowchart from steps 1 to 3 above. But it can be done and in itself is a very valuable undertaking. Figure 23:8 is an example of one such flowchart.

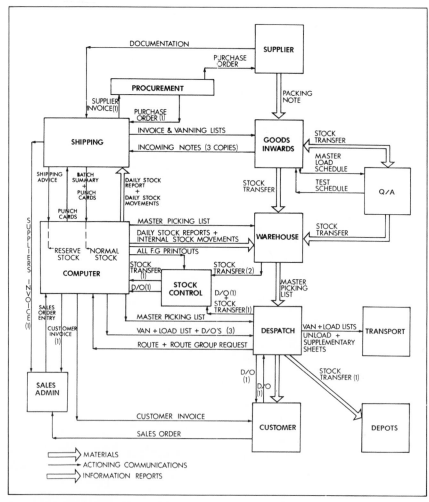

Figure 23:8   Distribution audit – materials and communications flows

Distribution audit output

It is necessary to approach any audit of distribution performance with an entirely open mind, because many unexpected findings do result, often in areas of the business outside distribution – in particular, marketing and production. The list below will provide an indication of what the audit is capable of finding – remember, the solutions to the problems exposed still have to be developed.

1   The varying cost of servicing accounts of roughly the same annual sales value is almost always overlooked.

2   Customer service vis-a-vis industry expectations and competitors' achievements is often unduly high and therefore wasteful.

3   Few companies appear to have developed minimum order and corresponding drop size (in value terms) policies.

4   Often the spares and repairs part of the business is using the same distribution network configuration as the company's finished goods products, and this is not responsive enough for customer needs.

These are just examples – there are many more. Generally, however, the audit findings highlight inefficient use of the facilities being applied in distribution, expressed in terms of under-utilisation, i.e. a percentage utilisation less than a desired level. Such under-utilisation is costly, although this is not always obvious, owing to the way the accounts hide such practices.

People, resources and implementation

The people resources required to undertake an audit of distribution performance for the first time are considerable, particularly if the existing state of the company's information system is such that the majority of the information required for analysis can only be extracted manually. In such a situation it is likely that the audit will take up to three months to complete, based on information collected over the previous year (in monthly periods if possible).

The skills needed by the audit team are as follows: cost accounting, systems analysis, marketing, and distribution knowledge sufficient to integrate the whole audit into an efficient package. To achieve the abovementioned skills may require up to four individual people on the audit team, and help from numerous other company personnel on an ad hoc basis.

The implementation of changes in organisation and procedures which are likely to follow on as a consequence of the audit also has to be carefully planned. In most cases a phased implementation is preferable to the rather more traumatic 'all out' approach.

Concluding comment

The audit is a device which to date has been seldom applied in a distribution context. However, we are going to see this situation change markedly in the next few years as companies struggle to find other avenues for cost reduction and more efficient use of operating expenses and resources at their disposal. The audit is the starting point from which system improvements can be developed in order to reach pre-determined marketing and distribution objectives. It provides a much needed life-raft without which we would continue to flounder around in the corporate swim, supported by poor (if any) information.

PART SEVEN

Distribution Issues

Overview

This section is designed to include coverage of those issues which do not fall under one of the previous section headings but are, nevertheless, significant enough to deserve special mention.

Bristow in Chapter 24 discusses that part of the distribution chain inside the UK which leads immediately to export. In particular he examines the various types of delivery point which are currently in use.

In Chapter 25 Pettit undertakes a wide ranging review of likely future trends in distribution/delivery operations. This comprehensive coverage takes in social, economic, legislative, and environmental issues, as well as changing distribution channels and the distribution services industry.

Lancioni examines the likely impact of future energy considerations in Chapter 26. In distribution-related terms he foresees reduced customer service offerings, larger order sizes, more economical scheduling and consolidation delivery of vehicles, adjustments in inventories to compensate for the lower service levels, and the development of more efficient recycling procedures for returned merchandise.

Apart from reviewing the current state-of-the-art in distribution cost analysis in Chapter 27, Ray's major thrust is towards the development of a method for determining customer account profitability which if achieved will become a powerful management tool in the relationship between a supplier and his customers.

Finally, Farmer takes a backward look in Chapter 28 to examine what happens at the input end to the logistics system, here defined as the summation of the materials management and distribution subsystems. He quite rightly implies that both these subsystems have to be co-ordinated and in phase if the company as a whole is to function properly. Hence having primarily concentrated for the foregoing twenty-seven chapters on the finished goods distribution subsystem (output) it is timely to end the text with a gentle reminder of the equal importance of the incoming materials subsystem (input).

24

Delivering goods for export

George Bristow

This chapter examines the portion of the distribution chain inside the UK which leads up to exportation by a route which, it is assumed, has already been chosen.

The existence of agencies and hauliers specialising in distribution for export shows that this is an important and distinct type of distribution. In spite of this, some firms treat export shipping as a function of the transport department, which is primarily engaged in home deliveries, as if it were a simple variation of the domestic delivery. Such is not the case. If the export side of its business matters to a company, it needs to study carefully the problems arising from exports which are not met with during domestic operations.

Type of delivery point

The very different conditions to be met at each type of terminal in export distribution require separate consideration. The major types of terminal involved are: specialised container depot, dock delivery, airport delivery, international railfreight or lorry terminal.

Specialised containerbase or depot

The containerbase, loading depot or its equivalent are modern additions to the range of possible international delivery points. A 'containerbase', or 'container depot', is a place where cargo is received and containers are loaded for international transport (see Figure 24:1). Increasingly, however, the same terminals are also loading road vehicles for Europe, and they now have their own delivery-vehicle queues and booking systems as they take over the export handling of a considerable amount of cargo. The door-to-door container from factory to factory offers both security and damage-free shipment. The container, or other type of unit-load equipment such as a TIR vehicle, loaded with other 'Grouped' cargo at an efficient, specialised terminal, provides a good second alternative for those shippers who have quantities 'less than container-load' (LCL); and also for those who have potentially 'full container-loads' (FCL) though inadequate loading facilities on site, but find that the international road vehicle can offer them the best terms for their export deliveries.

There is a primary network of container bases operated by consortia, major transport interests or wholly or in part by public authorities, supplemented by private terminals used and operated by road hauliers, freight forwarders, warehouse companies or small groups of these interests. The larger terminals are attended by Customs officers, so that they can be used for import clearance as well as speeding export cargo through ports without further check. The facilities in the UK are, however, far more sparse than throughout the Continent, where most major towns have Customs-attended terminals, and the larger the town the greater number of terminals both private and public.

If advance booking is required the proper conditions of delivery should be observed by the shipper who can no longer hope to find the congestion-free terminals which were supposed to arrive with the container age.

Figure 24:1   Packing for export: a container crane loading at ground level in a private container depot

Some containerised cargo is accepted only on an advance-booking system like the docks scheme described later. It is, of course, good to have a reliable turnround time despite the problems associated with making deliveries according to a timetable. With an 'open terminal' there is always the hope of being unloaded in a reasonable time without advance booking so that the call at the terminal can easily be part of a 'milk-run' delivery schedule. However, there is some risk of delay. In general, the freight forwarder and international haulier tend towards the open terminal method: the clientele is limited and it is possible, with experience, to assess the demand within reasonable bounds. As a selling point, too, open reception is desirable. Even so, large loads need advance notice to avoid unnecessary trouble. Very large terminals such as those operated by the Containerbase Federation must have advance booking if they are not to run the risk of recreating the old dock conditions (although more suitable surroundings must obviously make this less likely).

For the present, a shipper only needs to know which of the two basic methods is employed. If advance booking is the rule then he should book in advance and conform to the allocated timing.

Dock delivery (export by cargo vessel)

Widespread publicity is given to delays at major ports in the United Kingdom and remedies seem hard to supply. The shipping industry has long been aware of the problem and several solutions are offered. Unitisation at first promised to alleviate dock congestion, and has indeed been partially successful. But inevitably situations have arisen where the available container tonnage has not been able to meet the demand, with considerable delays as a result; also the container terminals developed for the new trade are all apparently working nearly to capacity. For the foreseeable future, however, the traditional type of receiving berth will survive with its peculiarities. An export delivery to a cargo berth of this type is normally (with the exception of bulk cargo meriting charter vessels) to a 'liner service'. The term 'liner' is not a description of the vessel but simply implies a regular service, usually from a regular berth or dock. Unfortunately, although the shipping lines attempt to adhere to the published schedules, bad weather and other adverse factors are apt to produce some variation. It is therefore usual to advertise 'receiving dates' which indicate the period during which cargo will be accepted and temporarily stored for shipment.

Shippers habitually opt for the last few days of the receiving period. Delivering as late as possible seems to secure the shortest overall transit time and to provide those extra days for the production department. It is also unfortunately true that, during periods of bad congestion, cargo received first is stowed in the shed and may be covered up by later cargo which is then shipped first on an over-committed vessel. On the other hand if too many vehicles arrive at the last moment for the available labour and equipment to cope with they will be turned away without redress for the additional expense.

Shipowners are well aware of the problem, but in a competitive business it is hard for them to adopt the tough measures required. A number of major ports have introduced a system of advance booking for deliveries. The dock authority accepts a telephone or telex advice of intended deliveries, and allocates a time-slot during which there is a very considerable chance that booked vehicles will be unloaded. This may mean waiting for a morning or an afternoon in the delivery rank but operators see that as a great improvement over three, four or even more days of waiting in endless ranks. Ship operators who are now largely containerised have also tended to offer reception of loose cargo at terminals away from the docks where the goods are containerised and transported in container to the vessel-loading berth.

If the export shipping department had an accurate knowledge of the true cost due to delays at each receiving point, it might well stop using the services of indifferent terminals and insist upon a change in consignees' routing instructions. Such detailed costing is, however, difficult; doubly so as the conditions at any berth will vary from day to day according to the amount of cargo tendered, weather conditions and the timing in the receiving period. Delays are reflected both in the rates and waiting charges of hauliers providing dock deliveries and in the actual withdrawal of companies from providing this type of service.

Airport delivery

Air freight strongly influences its associated transport pattern, particularly in that it demands speed of delivery, documents with goods, correct marking and control, and delivery times aligned to the service with considerable precision (see Figure 24:2).

The shipper of the goods will be working to one of three basic patterns, namely, airline processing of cargo, agent processing, or shipper processing. Of the three, the last is the least common and suitable only for a considerable volume justifying the employment of specialists by the shipper.

Cargo agents are said to handle in excess of 80 per cent of cargo from the UK, with this proportion steadily growing. Airlines also provide collection and processing facilities but would obviously be unable to cope with the present quantity of cargo without help, and some recognition of this is accorded in that IATA (International Air Transport Association) appointed agents receive a freight commission from airlines. The objective is to ensure that as much cargo as possible is presented as 'processed freight', by which is meant that the cargo is documented for international carriage (air waybill completed), weighed and measured accurately and labelled accordingly, marked with the unique air waybill number, and presented with all supporting documents so that it may be allocated immediately to the booked or next available flight.

Unprocessed freight involves the airline in the problems of inventory control during the preparation of documents, of transit storage, of picking and handling once a load for the aircraft has been established. Likewise, non-unitised or non-consolidated cargo entails drawing the cargo from the storage area and production of the final aircraft manifest. This is the reason for the 'cutoff' period, which is the minimum time that cargo must be in airline hands (shorter for processed than unprocessed freight) before departure of the flight.

Inventory control and associated operations, with the majority of consignments not exceeding 30 kg, help to explain the delay to be expected in turnround of the delivery vehicle, particularly at peak periods. Four- and six-hour delays mean lost vehicle and driver time, the possibility that the flight is missed, or that the driver's legal hours are exceeded, necessitating his return to base on the second day. These are all arguments in favour of employing specialist carriers or agents for air cargo.

If cargo is delivered for agent or airline processing, invoices go either in advance or with the goods. Instructions and documents should not have to be matched with goods at some later stage. It is advisable to have envelopes addressed to each processing airline, and stapled to the separate load sheets for each delivery. The processing agent will need similar treatment or provision for information to be made available via telephone or telex in advance, if maximum speed of transit is to be achieved. An express or emergency delivery to an airport will be useless if documentation has not been aligned to the operation and a booking secured. For the majority of the popular European destinations it is quite normal for too much cargo to be offered for the limited choice of services. British Airways European Division are the principal cargo operators with services to all parts of the world and a considerable daily throughput of cargo. This means that they are extraordinarily busy, and inevitably when problems arise there is a tendency to blame them.

In fact the lengthy waiting times often encountered at the cargo reception spring from causes not to be ascribed to the airline alone and by no means easy to remedy. Long-haul air-freight services periodically suffer from similar problems through

Figure 24:2   An igloo container for air freight being transferred to an aircraft from the forwarder's roller-bed box vehicle

conditions deteriorating at overseas destination airports. Our national airline is in the forefront of advanced cargo control systems, but air freighting is growing at a formidable rate annually and the problems of growth rub off onto the pre-air-freighting delivery stage.

International rail freight or lorry terminal

British Rail, in addition to their new liner train services, have developed terminals of which LIFT (London International Freight Terminal) at Stratford in East London and GIFT at Glasgow (Figure 24:3) are examples. At Stratford, located near a liner-train terminal, are a range of facilities largely rented to private operators, capable of loading cargo on either container or rail ferry wagons routed via the train ferries from Harwich to Zeebrugge or Dover to Dunkerque. The facilities are mostly leased to freight forwarders specialising in the 'groupage' of small consignments for European destinations. Delivery to the depots presents no great problem since the handling of small consignments is their planned function. Other smaller terminals operated on a similar basis and including Customs attendance, are being developed at strategic points around the country. British Rail sees an obvious interrelationship between its inland Freightliner facilities and international container movement. It originally expressed faith in the switch of European freight to containers and away from the more expensive train-ferry operation.

Figure 24:3   Interior of Glasgow International Freight Terminal (GIFT)
A consignment of whisky being loaded on to ferry wagons for transport to the Continent

Road hauliers or freight forwarders may also offer international services by road vehicle and roll-on/roll-off ferry to Europe. The delivery point may be a containerbase or a private terminal. Exporters are prone to ask why it is that road services are not more widely available. For the small but urgent consignment 'surely someone must have a lorry going to Stuttgart'. 'Someone' very probably does, but with a planned load and scheduled crossing booked because it is essentially an expensive operation. International road transport was at first more expensive than similar capacity by container or rail and therefore more suitable for the full load or large part-load. This is no longer true, certainly not in terms of cost efficiency.

In the 1970s the trend has been increasingly away from train ferry and rail-borne containers towards the use of roll-on/roll-off trailers (Figure 24:4) and now increasingly accompanied over the whole journey by the same tractor unit and driver ('self-drive'). The swift transit times that were originally envisaged for containers have in practice been extended by transfer delays and shortages on the ferry vessels, whereas a driver-accompanied vehicle has one man at least who is determined to make the round trip in the minimum time.

Figure 24:4   A typical TIR 12 m trailer going on board a ferry
Note the protected sealing point at rear centre of the cover

Collection services

The following paragraphs describe the principal methods of collecting export consignments from shippers' premises.

Express airfreight collection by an airfreight forwarder or specialist collection service.   Airlines are tending to opt out of this area of operations. Collection is usually by radio-controlled vehicles, so that cargo can be flown within a day of the collection request being received.

The fee is usually charged per kilogramme. This is expensive but, depending on the size of package, can be a sensible proposition.

Dock delivery service by road.   The haulier will give a rate and take the risk of unloading delays. (Check this condition first!) This method can offer a guaranteed cost in an uncertain situation and, according to the efficiency and the reputation of the firm, a reliable means of 'catching the vessel'. Rates are usually quoted per tonne (1,000 kg) with a volume equivalent of 80 cubic fet (2.27 m^3). It is not advisable to rely upon the carrier's insurance policy – f.o.b. insurance is not expensive and is a sound precaution. Hauliers' liability will not normally exceed £800 a ton pro rata except by special arrangement.

Rail pickup service.   This is usually not the quickest service, but properly used where rail can give good delivery, it can be excellent. The C & D rate for exports may include the dock charges and, for heavy goods, the rates will be competitive. This method should not be used for delivery at the last possible moment, especially with comparatively small consignments which do not give the railway a chance – the road haulier can usually work to tighter time limits. The main problem for railway operation is handling and sorting through many depots.

The modern accent on liner-train operation indicates a realisation of where rail has its strength – in long-distance quantity trunk movements. Some areas of the country are better served by rail for dock delivery, sometimes via a Freightliner container dedicated to, for example, 'Next South African sailing from Southampton'. Briefly, it is unwise to neglect what could be a good routing, but discrimination and consultation with the BR commercial and advisory services are to be recommended.

Road pickup by TIR (roll-on/roll-off) vehicle.   Full-load or major part-load traffic is the best suited for this service. *Transports Internationaux Routiers* is an international convention and agreement on the specification for a vehicle acceptable to pass across Customs barriers in a presealed and secure condition. The vehicle will in most cases be a 'tilt' – that is, with tarpaulin top, sides and ends, removable for loading or craning in (see Figure 24:5).

Originally a carnet/TIR was a guarantee document in the form of a book with tear-out certificates for each Customs control and with a blanket guarantee from a national authority that any duties liable or forfeited will be paid. With the accession of the United Kingdom to the EEC and the full introduction of the 'Community transit system' a 'movement certificate' with a covering transit guarantee takes the place of the carnet and is cheaper for the operator.

Loading direct to international rail ferry wagon. Ferry wagons may be loaded at private sidings by exporters fortunate enough to have a rail connection or a BR-operated siding. BR will offer very competitive prices for collection from a factory and loading at their own siding and will co-operate where shippers desire to supervise loading of what then becomes a complete ferry-wagon movement.

Loading direct to container. Container operators or steamship companies will usually offer very competitive rates for placing a container at a factory for loading, since their business is to get container cargo. Shippers should, however, bear in mind the problems of loading an articulated unit with a 20 x 8 x 8 foot container, probably with end doors. Loading by fork truck at trailer height is no easy matter for loading gangs unused to the operation. Containers can be obtained with shelving and other special fittings, including insulated and refrigerated units.

Figure 24:5   A tilt trailer in course of loading
The photograph shows how the cover, drop sides and side bars can be removed for loading

Choosing between own transport and outside contracted transport for delivery of exports to docks

Whether a manufacturer should use his own vehicles or contracted outside transport to effect dock delivery will depend on a comparison of their relative cost, effectiveness, speed, and utilisation of his own fleet of vehicles. The order of importance may vary from firm to firm.

Cost should be related to the service required. It is obviously a good idea to utilise unused vehicles normally engaged in domestic distribution. However, as has already been mentioned, there is a good case for using a contractor with known costs rather than incur unknown overheads.

Handling of delicate goods may be a major consideration. The service offered by an outside haulier needs to be evaluated against the alternatives. Does the quantity involved at the time merit the use of a complete vehicle or can the shipment be integrated with other deliveries without critical loss of time?

Speed is the twin to effectiveness. Air freight demands the utmost speed. Export by sea demands speed related to the time available before the closing date, bearing in mind what has been said about late deliveries.

One must ask is export delivery a major part of the total and worth taking into the main scheme, or is it a comparatively minor portion and is the fleet already well employed? If any part of the delivery work is to be contracted out, should it not perhaps be the export work? Dock delivery may mean a long-distance run combined with an uncertain waiting time or the problem of booking. Regulations about drivers' hours may mean an overnight stop and loss of the scheduled work for the following day.

Influence of contract of sale

The costs and conditions of delivering goods f.o.b. (free on board ship) vary from port to port, but sometimes a generalised 'f.o.b. UK Port' delivery clause may lead the export sales department to treat the costs entailed to any port or terminal as a matter of indifference. In practice an overseas buyer's specified routing may entail additional cost. A simple example might be a contract with the USSR – terms of sale f.o.b. UK port. The Russians, wishing to transport in their own flag vessel, may put a vessel into Hull or Aberdeen and the price would then have to include placing f.o.b. irrespective of location. In addition, the port may require stevedoring (loading of the goods into the hold) to be borne by the shipper or even the goods to be tendered at an anchorage in lighter. All this serves to emphasise the need for consultation between the transport section or shipping department and the part of the organisation which prices and sells overseas orders.

There is a further complication: the custom is growing of treating f.o.b. responsibility as ended when goods have been loaded on board a container or an international vehicle at a groupage loading terminal in an interior town, which may be very close to the factory but comparatively distant from the ferry port.

Insurance against loss or damage

Export distribution involves areas of risk not always found in the domestic market, and adequate insurance is one of the first essentials. The extent of the carrier's liability needs to be understood both in terms of its upper contractual limit and its scope. Within the limitations of this chapter the best advice which can be offered is to consult an insurance broker experienced in transport or marine insurance. On f.o.b., f.a.s. (free alongside ship) or even ex-works contracts it is not advisable to rely upon the consignee's order stating 'I will insure'. He may well do so but only for his own insurable interest, which will not commence until the defined point of delivery, and then only if goods are taken up. Contingent cover offers a complete protection.

A suitable f.o.b. insurance cover to complement the general 'goods in transit' cover is the most secure method of protection and it is not difficult to obtain reasonable rates for a general (described as 'open') cover upon which declarations can be made at a convenient time and all goods will be 'held covered' by the underwriter or insurance company concerned. Delivery by exporters' own transport should be evidenced by a suitable receipt, on file in the transport department. There should be a regular procedure to ensure that damaged or incomplete receipts are reported and investigated. This action is doubly important if the delivery terminal is not a client's warehouse but a dock, airport or freight depot where delivery of five instead of ten packages may not be noticed and where shipment of a part order may be the result, with serious consequences if the terms of a letter of credit are breached.

Documentation, packing and marking

Goods pass successively through the hand of hauliers, dock operators and steamship companies. However efficient their operation, a careless act or an oversight by an employee can lead to loss. Although physical security is only partly in the hands of the owner of the goods, there are certain precautions which he can and should take in order to reduce the likelihood of loss. Secure packaging, clear and appropriate package markings, accurate and complete documentation, and clear instructions for disposal of the goods are all critical factors.

The export shipment which becomes separates from its documentation is like the goat who ate his label and of whom the porter remarked: 'He doesn't know where he's going and neither do I!'

Loss, even for only a limited period, is serious in view of the need to satisfy the overseas client's delivery date. Goods may be safely in a warehouse at the dockside, but 'lost' if their identity has been mistaken or overlooked. On receipt of goods at the shipping point, the packages are accepted and usually placed into temporary store awaiting shipment or despatch.

The identity of the goods is established by the documentation handed over with them and the subsequent tallies of which they form part. The new National Standard Shipping Note (see Figure 24:6) has been widely adopted by port authorities throughout the United Kingdom following the initial experience with the PLA (Port of London Authority) shipping note on similar lines. This form, obtainable through Chambers of Commerce and approved printers, is mandatory in many ports, incurring penalties for non-use. The CAN (Customs Assigned Number) system requires the CAN number to be clearly shown on the Shipping Note if goods are not pre-entered.

In October 1981 H.M. Government conformed to EEC requirements in revising our export procedures. The EEC requires goods to be pre-entered with customs before shipment and in the initial outline proposals for UK shipment will be allowed against the production of a 'skeleton' document, which might for example be a copy of the Standard Shipping Note in the case of conventional shipments, bearing the essential consignment data and also a unique reference number. The reference number known as the ECI (Export Consignment Identifier) will consist of two parts, one of which indicates who is responsible for presenting a finalising entry. Thus exporters completing entries or their forwarding agents will each have a *Customs Registered Number* (CRN) and a unique consignment number chosen by the exporter or his agent. Shipment will be allowed against this document, giving the essential details, and the finalising customs entry must bear the full ECI for cross matching inside the British customs computer system.

The first need, then, is for a clear delivery note which indicates marks, contents and weight. The second need is for the next link in the chain of despatch also to be indicated and warned. For example, cases may be delivered to a steamer berth for West Africa, but to the order of 'Crown Agents', who will take out the bill of lading. If the name of 'Crown Agents' is not on the shipping note, as the delivery note is called in this context, the ship's return will be misleading. This situation can then only be rectified by the shipper inquiring for the goods and identifying them by their marks.

If cases are marked with multiple order numbers, or a complicated mark rather than with one which is reasonably short and clear, the dock return may be either inaccurate or abbreviated to the point of confusion. The following type of mark is recommended, simple, bold and black:

> AB Co
> JOHANNESBURG
> VIA DURBAN
> 1/5

(The 1/5 indicates that the case is number one of five – the others will be numbers 2/5, 3/5, 4/5 and 5/5.)

That marking is not without complications may be clear from an illustration based on the example. Direct through containerisation services are available to Johannesburg and also to Durban. If, therefore, the goods are being delivered for containerisation to Johannesburg, the port of entry should not be mentioned or the goods may be stowed in a Durban container, with the unnecessary additional on carriage costs arising. Loose cargo for Johannesburg via the Port of Durban should be marked as in the example.

Shipside tallying is no longer common and with a great deal of cargo unitised it is of great importance that the shipping note or delivery note clearly identifies the goods and copies the correct marks and numbers. More usually the receiving foreman makes a check of the packages for which he is signing and allocates a unique 'rotation' number which is fixed to both packages and shipping note. Thereafter the loading and control of the cargo tend to be from the rotation number rather than careful checking of the actual packages against the marks and numbers on covering documents.

SITPRO 1974

STANDARD SHIPPING NOTE

Exporter/Shipper (Name and Address)

| 1 CAN/Pre-Entry No./Other Customs Ref. | 2 S.S.Co Booking No. 3 |

Exporter's Ref.

F Agent's Ref.

4 For use of Receiving Authority only

Account No.   Receiving Date(s)   5

F.O.B Charges to be paid by (Name and Address)

Forwarding Agent/Merchant (Name and Address)

6 This six part set is printed on Baron self-copy paper and is suitable for use with reprographic equipment. The sixth sheet is the shippers file copy. The fifth sheet is to be returned to the haulier by the Receiving Authority

7 TO THE*

8

*Enter name of Receiving Authority   9

Berth and Dock

Ship

Port of Loading

Port of Discharge

10 Please receive for shipment the goods described below subject to your published Regulations and Conditions (including those as to liability)

11 Marks and Numbers	Number and kind of Packages; Description of Goods	12	Dimensions of Packages in Metres (m)	13 Gross Weight (kg)	14 Cube (m³)

Enter scale (if required)

This Note must be lodged WITH the vehicle at the receiving point OR at the Receiving Authority's designated office BEFORE arrival of the goods, according to local port practice. Only goods for shipment to one port of discharge on one sailing may be grouped on one Shipping Note. For multi-vehicle deliveries or any further information contact the Receiving Authority

450

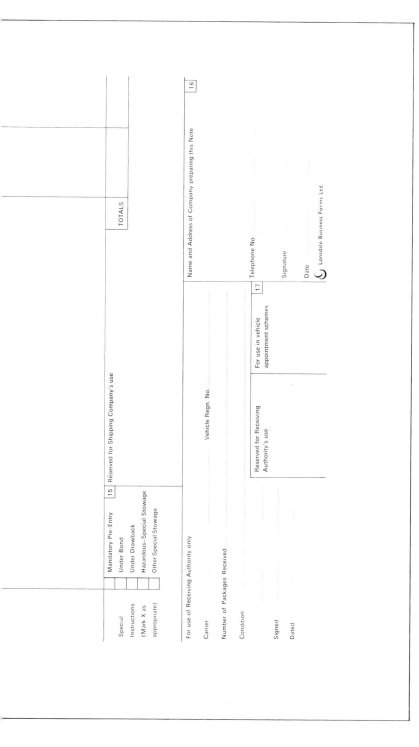

Figure 24:6   New National Standard Shipping Note
(Reproduced by kind permission of SITPRO)

25

Trends in distribution/ delivery operations

Sir Daniel Pettit

Everywhere over the last two decades, not least in the UK, we have witnessed profound changes in the field of transport and distribution without any particularly individual or dramatic breakthrough, and without noise or fuss, but with the progressive weight of many influences at work on the balance of costs and efficiency. Road transport has increasingly dominated the scene. In support of the freight lorry, itself subject to continuous engineering refinements, new methods and patterns of service have been developed, deriving from advances in technology and in handling equipment; from the changing nature and quality of products; from the developing needs of users and the growing expectations of consumers; from strong and opposing political, environmental and social forces; forcing change but varying sharply in intensity and direction throughout the period.

Not for the first time, the transport industry has been compelled to react positively to a world in ferment. In the last 20 years or more, it has accepted a massive range of challenge, enabling it to improve personal mobility out of all recognition, to overcome barriers to the movement of a much wider range of goods and services, to provide more speedy and convenient access to sources of raw materials, and to extend the scope and penetration of markets for finished goods, more time and cost effectively than ever before. These changes have had a particular impact on the character of the transport activity nearest to the consumer, that of retail distribution and delivery.

'Physical distribution management', as the control and direction of this transport sector has come to be known, increasingly operates in an environment which has witnessed the progressive and persistent decline of the small trader over the period, the rapid growth of self-service shopping and of the supermarket, and the concentration of buying power and financial muscle in the hands of selected retailers and wholesalers. Discovering a new source of power in their control of outlets, and of offtake in the market place, retailers, in particular, have progressively extended their capacity to exercise pressure on manufacturers in such vital matters as brand, quality, price, quantity, merchandising, display and the level of service required for a product. The retailer's new-found ability to decide shelf space allocation and product location in the store, and the extent to which he decides to co-operate with 'in store' promotions and merchandising, mean he has a decisive influence on packaging, on levels of inventory and the speed, frequency, and reliability 'criteria' of replenishment, and even on the manufacturing programme itself. Paralleling this, the distribution activity has equally become part of the essential arena of manufacturing and of the manufacturer's marketing strategies. So, the Physical Distribution Manager, wherever located, is at the hinge of the interrelationship between supplier and retailer. His systems can condition the level of profitability and performance of both.

Structural changes in retailing are, however, only a part, however important, of the equation with which the Physical Distribution Manager is increasingly concerned. During these two decades, the tools of his trade and the techniques and technologies at his disposal have equally been subject to great alteration. Pressures to challenge, to experiment, to modify, to reject, to innovate have intensified not only from the pressing demands of retailers and the competitive requirements of the market place, but from the intransigent march of economic and technical influences within the transport field itself. He has had to face the increasing cost of labour, the tougher demands of the work force for convenience at work and in living, the pressure on financial margins and cash flow in a highly competitive industry. More recently, and especially relevant in the context of controlling the quality, cost, and effectiveness of the delivery operation required, has been the insidious consequences of a world in the grip of progressive inflation and economic recession, coupled with a universal fossil fuel crisis of no mean proportions which will not go away until we discover new applications in the source and use of power.

To the rising burden of issues to be resolved if our modern industrial society is to survive must be added escalating vehicle and equipment prices, massive fuel cost demands, inflationary wages increases beyond the containment of productivity improvements, road, office and warehousing constructional costs of vast proportions, interest rates at levels which menace elaborate distribution systems, and the growing complexity of inventory requirements, working capital needs and cash flow required for the development of new products and activities. Conditioning all these issues is an environment increasingly difficult through legislative and community restriction, traffic congestion and costly pressures on the infrastructure of roads and of land use.

It is perhaps natural that all these trends in terms of cost, efficiency and service, and the ever-increasing demands of the market place, should put a premium on the need for a new generation of physical distribution managers, trained and equipped in the skills of logistics, aware of the demanding relationship between cost and service and the interrelationship between the manufacturer and the retailer, capable of assessing the demands on a company's distribution services of marketing policies and the products to be promoted. Major technological changes during the period have, in their turn, conditioned the growth of new patterns of delivery, seeking to contain the demands of the market place and the cost and service needs at work. They include the development of air freighting, throughout movement based on containerisation, roll-on/roll-off ferry services, freightliner, cellular container ships, inland freight terminals and motorways. In the field of handling and reception, there have been significant advances in palletisation and unitisation, new forms of packaging (for example, vacuum packaging), and the application of electronics to automatic and mechanical warehousing and pallet silos, and of telecommunication systems to the whole area of advertising, communication, display and recording.

Of outstanding significance system-wise, and still in its early stages, is the application of computer and silicon-chip developments across the total range of transport and distribution, marketing, wholesaling and retailing. Twenty years ago, Professor La Londe declared:

> The development of physical distribution management during the period in which computers emerged from infancy provided the basis of a unique marriage. It offered the potential for placing high-speed digital computers to work in day-to-day operations. The computer became a device which allowed management to cope with millions of details in an orderly and systematic manner. . . . Future historians will regard the simultaneous development of integrated physical distribution, computers and high-speed data-transmission as a most serendipitous event.

How right he is proving to be! In our world, the computer begins to offer the retailer a unique opportunity to organise all aspects of retail activity through the medium of computerised stock control based on central purchasing, to monitor sales and profit mix, and to establish levels of accountability and responsibility in an orderly fashion. Utilising his computer, he can know as much, and more, about his business and the reaction of customers to products as his supplier. Equally, of course, the computer offers the Physical Distribution Manager, in his particular field, an equal range of services which, when deployed in co-operation with his physical transport assets, provide a powerful combination to grapple comprehensively with current requirements. The compulsory introduction in the tachograph at the end of 1981 has added to the range of technology supporting his efforts, and those of his driving staff.

Pressure of rising distribution costs

It will be readily seen that, despite the many savings and improvements in efficiency made during the period under consideration, any review of trends in delivery operations must start from the realisation that the most significant trend to recognise is that there is never any respite from the apparently remorseless increase in the costs of distribution facing management, whether incurred by manufacturer, distributor or retailer. So it is that we must still hold on to Peter Drucker's 1965 comment and react to its challenge, namely, that 'physical distribution is the one big area where one can still do something about costs – it is the last commercial area of cost reduction'.

Statistical support of his view is consistently available and has been throughout the last two decades. A typical breakdown of the costs of one distribution company in the UK would still show some 60 per cent as a direct labour (clerical and manual) cost. Distribution costs in the USA and UK have been shown by survey to be of the pattern shown in Figure 25:1. Although these were collected some years ago, the findings are still as valid and as representative today. Indeed, the large increases in fuel and vehicle costs of the last few years and the expense of a deteriorating environment have only compounded and aggravated the labour cost issue (see Figures 25:2, 25:3 and 25:4).

Within the detailed activities associated with delivery, these cost trends dominate. In the USA total expenditure on logistical activities range between 20 and 50 per cent of gross sales, while here in the UK percentages are similar, with the characteristics of the products in this environmentally congested island – kilometres covered per ton, weight per drop, shelf life, perishability, quality control required – producing sharp and significant variations.

Legislative, social and environmental pressures

In July 1980 new national road traffic forecasts were issued by the Department of Transport covering the period 1985–2010 (see Figures 25:5 and 25:6). They stress the severity of the challenges continually facing the delivery operation and underline the urgent need for strong and positive responses and for continuous experiment in techniques and patterns of distribution.

Figures 25:5 and 25:6 illustrate that, by the end of the century, there will be 24–28 million vehicles on the roads in the UK, compared with some 18 million at the end of 1979, a rise in traffic ranging from some 33 to 55 per cent. Although goods vehicles only account for 8 per cent of total traffic, and so far they have broadly offset rising costs by improved techniques, their operations will undoubtedly be severely restrained in the future, especially on routes in cities already subject to considerable congestion.

We can also anticipate continued Government intervention by legislation, for example, to raise safety standards and maintenance; to contain size, noise and pollution levels; to control and restrict drivers' hours; and to constrain delivery patterns by trying to hold railway freight systems. The effective exploitation of the goods vehicle, itself increasingly costly, is bound to continue under severe and hostile pressure. The problem is further complicated by the need to respond to the retailers' own work schedules and the traffic engineering requirements of local authorities in unloading restrictions, unilateral waiting, urban clearways, pedestrian precincts, one-way streets, bans on night unloading and the like. The only certainty is of more disciplines and constraints as congestion increases, and an inevitable pressure on

Physical distribution costs by functional activity – USA

Functional activity		Cost of activity as percentage of sales
Administration of distribution		2.4
Transportation:		
Inbound	2.1	
Outbound	4.3	6.4
Receiving and despatch		1.7
Packaging and protective packing		2.6
Warehousing:		
Factories	2.1	
Distribution depots	1.6	3.7
Stockholding:		
Interest on investment	2.2	
Taxes, insurance, losses, etc.	1.6	3.8
Order processing and related		1.2
Total physical distribution costs		21.8

Physical distribution costs by industry – USA

Industry	Costs as percentage of sales
Food and food products	29.6
Machinery	9.8
Chemicals, petroleum and rubber	23.1
Paper and allied products	16.7
Fabricated metals	26.5
Wood products	16.1
All-industry average (approximately)	21.0

Physical distribution costs by functional activity – UK

Functional activity		Cost of activity as percentage of sales
Administration of distribution		2.0
Transport:		
Inbound	1.5	
Outbound	4.0	5.5
Receiving and despatch		0.5
Packaging and protective packaging		2.0
Warehousing:		
Factories	1.0	
Distribution depots	1.5	2.5
Stockholding:		
Interest on investment	2.0	
Taxes, insurance, etc.	1.0	3.0
Order processing		0.5
Total physical distribution cost		16.0

Figure 25:1   Survey results showing physical distribution costs in the USA and UK by functional activity and (for USA only) by industry

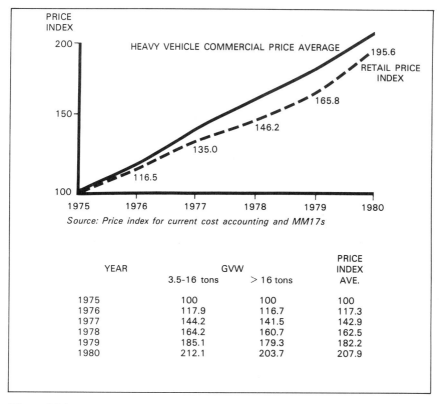

Figure 25:2   Heavy commercial vehicle price index (1975 = 100)

YEAR	GVW 3.5-16 tons	GVW > 16 tons	PRICE INDEX AVE.
1975	100	100	100
1976	117.9	116.7	117.3
1977	144.2	141.5	142.9
1978	164.2	160.7	162.5
1979	185.1	179.3	182.2
1980	212.1	203.7	207.9

delivery costs, which ultimately must reflect into the cost of the product, even allowing for the capacity of the industry to advance its efficiencies.

Consequences of environmental pressures

One of the most significant phenomena associated with the development of modern industrial society has been an increasing enthusiasm for constraints and techniques to improve the quality of life regardless of their impact on our capacity and ability to afford them. This interest has progressively impinged on the activities of the freight lorry, as it did earlier on the railway systems, the 'juggernauts' of the 19th century. It is a factor which must be recognised and reconciled, if not totally absorbed.

The 'Dykes' Act (Heavy Commercial Vehicles – Controls and Regulations Act 1973) is symptomatic. It is significant that while the 'juggernaut' controversy focuses on the very large type of vehicle – particularly TIR articulated units – the Dykes Act defines 'heavy' as 'more than 3 tons unladen weight', or over 70 per cent of the total

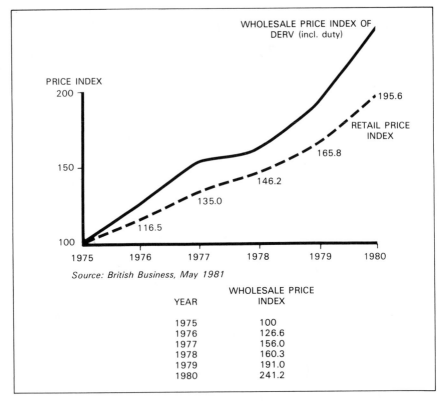

Figure 25:3   Wholesale price index of derv (including duty) (1975 = 100)

Year (April)	Earnings rate per hour (pence)	% Increase over previous year	Increase over 1973 (1973 = 100)
1973	73.5	–	100.0
1974	84.4	14.8	114.8
1975	113.0	33.9	153.7
1976	128.4	13.6	174.7
1977	137.5	7.1	187.1
1978	158.6	15.3	215.8
1979	194.5	22.7	264.4
1980	227.9	17.2	310.1

Source: 'New Earnings Survey', *Department of Employment Gazette*

Figure 25:4   Driver earnings in the road haulage industry

	Cars (millions)		Car traffic (index)	
	low	high	low	high
1978	14.1	14.1	1.00	1.00
1985	16.6	17.4	1.08	1.20
1990	18.3	19.8	1.16	1.37
1995	19.7	21.9	1.23	1.52
2000	20.9	23.7	1.28	1.66
2005	21.9	25.1	1.31	1.77
2010	22.7	26.4	1.32	1.87

Figure 25:5   Traffic projections – cars

	Light vans (under 30 cwt)				Other goods vehicles			
	Stock (thousands)		Traffic (index)		Stock (thousands)		Traffic (index)	
	low	high	low	high	low	high	low	high
1978	1,153	1,153	1.00	1.00	551	551	1.00	1.00
1985	1,340	1,369	1.10	1.15	552	587	0.98	1.04
1990	1,406	1,485	1.16	1.27	540	586	0.97	1.06
1995	1,467	1,613	1.22	1.39	534	594	0.96	1.07
2000	1,531	1,756	1.27	1.51	532	599	0.96	1.08
2005	1,598	1,912	1.32	1.64	530	603	0.96	1.09
2010	1,668	2,082	1.37	1.77	530	605	0.96	1.09

Figure 25:6   Traffic projections – goods vehicles

vehicle population, whose response to productivity improvement has been related to vehicle size. The Act gives authorities power to restrict vehicles to certain routes, to prohibit access to certain roads or areas, and to control parking. This has opened up the possibility of widespread regulation of freight movement by road. The Act is particularly relevant today (1980) as a consequence of what has become known as the 'Windsor cordon', under which the Berkshire County Council, in 1978, imposed severe restrictions on all lorries exceeding 5 tons unladen weight operating within the road system around Windsor. The appeal by the FTA, the NFU and the RHA against the ban was dismissed in the Court of Appeal. This judgement can have considerable significance in the battle to preserve environmental quality, regardless of the costs of providing goods and services to the population within the defined area. It is clear, if local authorities generally follow the Windsor precedent, that distribution problems will be exacerbated and indeed the cost of local delivery systems will be adversely and perhaps harshly affected. It is interesting to note that the trend of restriction could extend to rail freight equally, especially where dangerous goods, e.g. nuclear waste, is carried.

Clearly, decisions of this nature, if widely applied, carry great significance for trends in delivery operations. Anything which delays the process of delivery and adds substantially to cost must always come under close scrutiny. Reporting some 15 years ago, the National Board of Price and Incomes commented on the inadequacy of loading and unloading facilities at shops, warehouses and factories and declared 'This is a complex problem vitally affecting costs'. It referred to 'the serious problem caused by the wide discrepancy between hours per week the haulage industry is willing to work, and the number of hours the customer will make available'. It pointed to 'restrictions imposed by the 5-day week among customers, the awkwardness of midweek half day closing; the virtual impossibility of delivering later than mid afternoon on Fridays and the widespread disappearance of Saturday deliveries. . . . Limited delivery times unless carefully planned, create congestion and delay, affect the reliability of timetables and increase the cost of turnround.' The problem has persisted since then, although yielding substantially to tailormade delivery services linked to computer scheduling. Recent legal judgements could however cause a need to reconsider the whole basis of delivery scheduling, if the material needs of people in community are to be met without major cost increases for the goods and services required.

Consequences of the pressures at work

It is clear that the range of pressures on the retail delivery services which has applied over the last 15 years, and which is now complemented by a group of economic and environmental pressures with substantial commercial costs never previously envisaged, make it more and more imperative that there is the closest possible co-operation between retailer and manufacturer and between supplier and customer, and indeed between manufacturer, supplier, retailer and the ultimate consumer, who in the final resort has to pay the price for the goods and services required and the terms under which they are delivered.

Any pattern of distribution, any technique adopted, any technology promoted, must recognise the fact that the manufacturer, retailer and indeed consumer have to identify and accept a common aim to restrict and contain the costs, increasingly arising from areas outside their direct control, of delivering the goods which the market demands. We find ourselves therefore in a 'New World', a world which demands and indeed promises new relationships – of direct computer hook-ups between suppliers and retailers, and of close integration in forecasting, ordering, shipment, inventory and quality control, product development and innovation, packaging, launching, refurbishing and the like – in supply and demand. Under current cost, legislative and environmental pressures, and under the impact of a much wider market and manufacturing environment such as the EEC presents, the manufacturer and the retailer are, I believe, compelled to make common cause in many areas associated with physical distribution to their mutual benefit in commercial terms. Consider some of the current trends and the ways in which current pressures affect them.

Capital strength of retailing chains

It is true that with the economic concentration of the retail trade – which, continuing apace, forces the small trader to specialise in terms of service and convenience – we have reached a point where large-scale trading groups such as Sainsbury's, Marks and Spencer, Tesco, ASDA and the like, can generate professional skill and command capital resources equal to any that manufacturing industry has previously enjoyed. As we have already observed, against this background, the retailer is much more able to control his total environment, to exercise a firm and conscious choice of the source and pattern of supply, utilising statistical evidence provided by his own computer-based controls, to fix his own requirements in terms of price, quality, service and even product.

With a new range of initiatives thus available to the retailer, one of the first opportunities to emerge is the extent to which he controls, or indeed owns, his sources of supply and the pattern of distribution this poses for his retail chain. The crucial issue here could well be the extent to which the retailer is persuaded to invest precious capital in his own central warehouse, isolating the manufacturer away from branch delivery and restricting distribution through traditional wholesaling and other channels. Nothing illustrates so well the extent and depth of change in retail distribution and delivery patterns, and the pressures at work, as the growth of central warehousing and supply over the last decade, whether promoted by retailer or manufacturer.

Central warehousing by retail chains

As long ago as 1967, a survey commissioned by the Supermarket Association found that 60 per cent of all manufacturers' grocery deliveries were made to central warehouses and 40 per cent direct to branch. A further inquiry, also commissioned in 1967 by a leading manufacturer, to establish the requirements and preferences of multiple and co-operative retailers on the division of manufacturers' deliveries between central warehouses and retail branches, produced a number of interesting facts:

1   the drive to central warehouses was greatest in the co-operatives at that time;
2   a majority of multiple retailers favoured a high degree of central delivery, with a minimum of 30 per cent turnover handled this way and over 50 per cent being normal;
3   a majority used their own warehouses for auxiliary functions.

Opinion was sharply divided on future trends, with 57 per cent wanting more central deliveries and 40 per cent wanting more branch delivery.

It is significant that since that date there has been an even more powerful trend towards the so-called central or regional warehouse, the combination of cost, environmental and infrastructure pressures working strongly in its favour – especially since 1975 – coupled with the need for speed, reliability, quality control, and the containment of inventory cost in the channel of supply. The need for a closer and more direct relationship between the manufacturer (activated by his commitment to the development and marketing costs of new products) and the large retailer (committed to the need for substantial throughput on low margins) makes much of any intermediate delivery pattern irrelevant unless uniquely conditioned by the constraints of geography, by local circumstances, or by the nature of the product, all of which require separate costing and charging. That process has equally been stimulated by the perspectives of the computer, the range and scope of container operations, the horizons offered by the motorway and bypass infrastructure, and the ingenuity of technologies that break through old boundaries and frontiers.

Factors influencing decisions on central warehouses

It is true that the new factors influencing decisions in this area are most powerful, but the principle remains paramount that there is a scientific technique for decision-making in such a complex area. It demands the dispassionate examination of all current lines, commodities and product groups, and the separate determination of the delivery specifications for each. These specifications are determined by such considerations as branch storage facilities, quality control, perishability and shelf life. Within the grocery field, for instance, such delivery specification could take the following form:

> Salads, bread, fish – one daily delivery by 09.30.
> Frozen foods, poultry – two or three times a week.
> Zero cabinet stocks – two or three times a week.
> Prepacked meat – three times a week.
> Non-foods – weekly delivery.
> Grocery items – weekly delivery.
> Branch stores and consumable items – weekly or as convenient.

All these specifications reflect the item's keeping quality and the constraints of shelf life, and take into account any technical possibility of increasing this – for example, chilling – and whatever degree of presale preparation is necessary – such as washing, grading, price marking, pre-wrapping. At this stage, there are likely to be clear pressures in favour of direct branch delivery for certain items, but for perhaps 80 per cent of the average supermarket range the decision is very obvious – the goods can be assembled and co-ordinated at regional level.

It should be equally necessary to make a more detailed examination of the individual product group characteristics and determine how many brands and lines are to be handled, the variety of pack size, and the physical characteristics – that is, bulk to weight ratios and so on – within each group. This is likely to be determined from historical data, warehouse work study and so on, all allied to the buyer's assessment of the competitive characteristics of the product. One must establish the demand fluctuations at retail level, which may be imposed (seasonally, like turkeys), or induced by either the manufacturer (like detergents) or the retail distributor (say, cut-price cigarettes as loss leader). There must also be consideration of the effects of inherent taint and packaging and their effects on handling systems, which will influence decisions on segregated storage, clamp handling, palletisation and the like. From this sort of analysis, certain product groups stand out, subject to total cost considerations, as best delivered direct to branches – for example, cereals, tissues, detergents – though clearly their characteristics bear directly on cost and competitive factors.

There is a continuous proliferation of pack range today, which can be expected to continue in spite of pressures to rationalise inventory and save costs. This could probably bring the realisation that last year's decision for central delivery of canned goods or any other product might be better reversed this year to accommodate the central handling of hardware, shirts, or something else. In this sort of consideration it is vital to have an authoritative definition of the organisation's policy with regard to expansion and development in terms of size or geographical spread; obvious critical considerations are the type of merchandising, quality control, handling systems, etc., that the manufacturers are likely to offer now and in the future. The distribution manager must live from now on in a world of regular appraisal of everything he handles. There is no unique absolute answer.

The trend towards the concentration of buying power in the hands of multiples and supermarkets based on self-service is not inevitable, though current pressures encourage it. The manufacturer remains concerned to control his own costs of inventory, distribution and sales administration, and he still has his own objectives of market share and penetration to consider. He is under similar pressures to the retailer to establish a central warehouse policy of his own, to control his strategic promotional stocks centrally, and to use his local depot facilities for transit and delivery rather than for stockholding. In many areas of warehousing and distribution he has a new range of choice – modes, patterns, technologies – which have cost and price implications and which can be developed either in co-operation with retailers to their mutual advantage or, as alternatives, checks and counter-balances to limit or evade the new powers available to the retailer. Nevertheless, current trends suggest he has a progressive need to find a firm basis of accommodation with the retailer.

Wholesalers have been affected by the changes in distribution systems, by the steeply increasing cost of small-scale deliveries, and by the development of the voluntary wholesale groups. These factors have created a need for a new method of supplying small retailers at minimum cost. The principle of self-service has, therefore, been applied to the wholesale trade in the form of the 'cash-and-carry' wholesale warehouse from which small retailers, hoteliers, restaurant and cafe proprietors and the like can obtain supplies in relatively small quantities, using their own transport.

Manufacturers who have increasingly, as a result of rising costs, adopted policies of minimum drop sizes, now depend to a large extent on cash-and-carry warehouses to supply their goods to the small retailer. For example, in July 1974, Brooke Bond stopped direct deliveries of tea and coffee to 85,000 small grocers, and set a minimum drop figure at 25 packages. Since then, the process has intensified, with manufacturers progressively abandoning the small man to new suppliers such as cash-and-carry operators, who live in a resilient, flexible, independent world of their own.

Cash-and-carry warehouses

The first self-service warehouse in the UK was opened in Uxbridge in 1955. By 1966 there were 459 warehouses and by 1974 the number had risen to 600. But not only have they increased in numbers, the warehouses have also increased in size to an average of some 50,000 sq. ft or more as many older smaller warehouses have been replaced by much larger, often purpose-built buildings, and small cash-and-carry businesses have retired from the battle. In addition, while smaller and weaker brethren have fallen by the wayside, many cash-and-carry organisations have grown and diversified to positions of strength, or have come under the umbrella of larger groupings, some of international standing.

A better measure of growth than numbers is turnover: in 1969 turnover was estimated at £360 million, by 1974 it was estimated that it had increased to over £1,000 million, and since then business has increased each year by 15 to 20 per cent. This is a much higher rate of growth than that experienced by the grocery trade or food retailing as a whole. A major factor in this growth is that the range of goods stocked, based initially on groceries, has expanded into toiletries, confectionery, hardware, cigarettes, wines and spirits, textiles, domestic equipment, records and record players, furniture and especially toys and DIY.

This increase in the range of goods stocked has opened cash-and-carry trade to new custom from public houses, catering establishments, nursing homes, small hotels, industrial canteens, hairdressing salons, etc. Cash-and-carry wholesaling can be regarded as the response to the instinct of self-preservation by small businesses, in which the self-employed predominate, in the face of the pressures of large-scale activities by industrial and distributive trades. It is a splendid example of the vitality and readiness to change and adapt to the distribution sector; it has done much to prevent the long-forecast demise of the 'small' man business.

The essence of cash-and-carry is that it provides the small man, unwilling to join a voluntary group, with a wholesaling service at discounted prices, at a time when rising costs make it uneconomic for wholesalers or manufacturers to deliver the goods direct. In addition, many members of wholesale groups use cash-and-carry for particular items or to top up stocks. The key mode of distribution is the car or small van. The trader takes his van to the cash-and-carry when convenient, does his own picking and handling on self-serve lines and pays cash at the checkout. The cost reduction consequent on the cash transaction, and the savings in handling, breakup, assembly and delivery, mean that the cash-and-carry operator can offer favourable terms. He is also less vulnerable to trade union restriction than manufacturers, which clearly appeals to the small self-employed person.

The majority of warehouses operate on low stock levels (6 to 10 per cent) with rapid turnover and gross margins between 3 and 5 per cent. The main advantages to customers are the lower prices – the consequence, as has been indicated, of bulk purchase on favourable terms and, in most cases, of the minimisation of distribution, handling and warehousing costs. Cash-and-carry warehouses sustain a wide range of items, enabling a small trader to stock items not normally available through manufacturers' direct sales forces. Additionally, the small trader can hold his shop stocks at minimal level, and meet his own transport costs in a marginal way by his selection and collection at off-peak periods.

For the manufacturer there is an opportunity through cash-and-carry of reaching a wider section of the retail trade, and the facility to make more economic deliveries as compared with those to small retail shops. Since the average weight of delivery is increased substantially for the supplier, it is possible to reappraise the logistics of delivery (that is, direct ex-factory delivery as opposed to local depot stockholding), and to have a specialised sales/merchandising force concentrating on wholesalers' head offices and cash-and-carry outlets as an alternative to a retail representative/van sales force covering a wide geographical section of traders.

Other implications emerge. Because of the low margins on which the business operates, it is particularly sensitive to the costs of warehousing and handling. The warehouses, therefore, have to be based on high racking and palletisation. Custom-built cash-and-carry warehouses offer opportunities for palletisation, unitisation, and mechanical reception and handling not possible in old-fashioned wholesaling premises. Over 88 per cent allow manufacturers full access to merchandise on their premises, with 84 per cent permitting the erection of point-of-sale material. This, associated with the reduction in pack sizes to respond to the case-splitting requirements of small traders, has stimulated display packaging, and the adoption of shrink-wrapping units for cash-and-carry.

Finally, cash-and-carry has affected transport requirements in that it has led to the substitution of small-scale 'do-it-yourself' transport by traders for expensive, time-consuming distribution of small quantities of goods in much larger vehicles. It has to that extent altered the pattern of freight transport and thereby probably reduced congestion; it is in effect a 'break-bulk' depot of the type often advocated for urban areas.

Cash-and-carry, quite clearly, can be seen as one way of meeting the environmental issue of delivering to small premises in congested areas. The proprietor chooses his own moment to supply. Provided the cash-and-carry warehouse is appropriately sited, it has environmental advantages – if not always cost ones – locally.

Break-bulk distribution and other specialist services

While some manufacturers have turned to cash-and-carry warehouses as a means of distribution to small retailers, thereby reducing the costs of physical distribution, others (or indeed the same manufacturers in other areas) have adopted various types of break-bulk distribution. One method is to use a professional carrier for the whole operation or for the final stages of distribution – that is, the manufacturer or retailer may trunk bulk loads of their goods to a local depot from which a local carrier will distribute them in smaller loads, often along with other manufacturers' goods, to retailers in the area.

A long established example of this type of operation, and still practised, is that carried out by a number of hauliers for Boots the Chemists. In this, trunk loads are carried every night from Boots' central warehouses to regional distribution centres, where the loads are sorted to delivery vehicles for next-day delivery to the company's 1,500 shops throughout the country. The technique, considerably refined by the originators themselves, has been quite widely imitated in other fields in the last decade.

A wide range of services are available, including stockholding, inventory control and bonded stores to meet a manufacturer's or distributor's specific requirements. And, of course, such operations permit the use of maximum-capacity vehicles for the trunk run while avoiding their use in final delivery operations, often in congested areas. In recent years a number of specialist operators have grown up, such as SPD, Cory Distribution Services Ltd., the special sections of British Road Services and of National Carriers, to provide these services for particular areas of the market, such as soaps, foodstuffs, wines and spirits, and tobacco, and, more recently, through Carry Care and Chinaflow for the pottery industry and through Fashionflow and Tibbett & Britten for the garment trade. There are, in addition, the specialist security services such as Securicor for high-value products, and a variety of 'despatch' services for products such as computer tapes and newsprint, which have a very short life or require immediate use.

A variation on this theme is the 'distribution without warehouse' service by the British Road Services group, in which loads of goods are trunked overnight from a factory in medium-sized vehicles which are then used for daytime deliveries without any intermediate unloading or handling of the goods. An example of this is the distribution of fish from Grimsby. Each night, trunk vehicles leave Grimsby for all parts of the country. At transfer points during the journey, the fish is transferred direct to small vehicles for local delivery in the early hours of the morning. Many variations of this theme exist, using 'laybys' or local parking facilities, in so far as local regulations allow.

The distribution of foodstuffs is in the forefront in developing new methods and systems to meet the ever more exacting demands of the retailer. The need to overcome the problem of limited shelf life for many products, particularly in view of the trend towards a wider degree of date-stamping of products and the impact of quality control, linked with increasing consumption of frozen and temperature-controlled foods, has led to the development of temperature-regulated transport systems involving the provision of cold stores with a range of temperatures and conditions.

Not all distribution schemes entail 'break-bulk' in the strict sense; there are many variations and systems in use. For example, National Carriers operate a nationwide textile distribution scheme for Marks and Spencer which can be described not so much as break-bulk but bulk amalgamation and co-ordination of a wide range of goods, for delivery to the firm's shops to a tight time schedule and strict levels of service, geared to programmed and projected offtake.

The common theme in all these distribution schemes is increasing specialisation of the operations, of the equipment and not least of staff and management. The application of these specialist skills, after problems have been analysed and solutions carefully thought through, brings the benefits of both economical operation from a total distribution point of view, together with properly defined and sustainable levels of service. They are clearly attractive also as a means of concentrating and exploiting marketing plans and strategies.

A major component of the specialist's skill is the selection and use of the right type of equipment. Undoubtedly, one of the most exciting developments in recent years has been the emergence of the modern container and related systems. The developing constraints which economics, infrastructure and environment have more recently produced have encouraged the growth of such specialised delivery packages, and we can envisage many more developments from the basic container breakthrough.

Containerised delivery

In Chapter 15 the development and operation of the container as a distribution resource/technique is examined in detail. In the delivery field its value as a medium of distribution is clearly evident. The last 10 years have already seen a variety of exploitations. It has been noted that in the field of retail distribution the customer has become much more demanding in terms of supplier services. For the distributor this means that he must operate on shorter lead times with greater pack ranges and wide variations in offtake and promotional success. Throughout container movement from manufacturer to retailer certainly resolves some of these requirements, especially where inter-modal transfer is required.

The container commends itself in terms of security and control of damage; it enables one to operate with a shorter delivery cycle from more concentrated stock inventories, since it facilitates cheap, speedy and reliable bulk unit movement; it persuades operators out of multi-handling practices; and it reduces terminal time by providing for the co-ordinated availability during warehouse hours of a supply of containers for loading. In conjunction with the possibilities of computer scheduling, it has much to offer.

Problems remain, however, especially in the reconciliation of the container requirements for speedy long-distance movement with the more flexible requirements of local reception, supply and delivery. A major limitation to the wider use of the container for internal movements in the UK is the unfortunately inescapable fact that not only is this a small country, but with the exception of Scotland all its major producing and consuming areas are relatively close together. Eighty-five per cent of the population lives in only half of the area and is furthermore concentrated in the major conurbations.

However, the steeply rising cost of fuel may well favour an extension of container traffic, particularly as the use of containers goes far to obviate costly and time-consuming operations of transfer between road and rail. The speedy transfer of containers themselves still requires the provision of elaborate and expensive cranes at terminals, but much experimental work is being done to reduce the cost impact of such requirements.

The operational needs can be summarised in the terms of the specification laid down by one of the leading transport companies in the UK for its containerised delivery operations. Requirements are:

1   Speedy transfer of containers independent of fixed terminal points or facilities.
2   The minimum risk of mechanical failure, and preferably no loose equipment that can be detached, lost or mislaid from the container.
3   Single-man operation.
4   The facility to interchange between trunk and delivery vehicles and thus contend with a platform height variation of 760 mm (30 inches). This is essential, as factory-assembled container loads will normally be road-freighted down in pairs for subsequent local delivery.
5   The facility to use any non-specialised vehicle to preserve the ability to use 'spot hire' at minimum cost for traffic peaks.

Other problems arise in terms of payload, traffic planning, container utilisation and traffic imbalance. If a container is to be fully utilised in the interest of cheap long-distance traffic hauls, it needs to be well stowed – probably expensively by hand (though the longer the haul, as in America, the less significant, in the ratio to total cost, this becomes). If the container is to be transferred ultimately to a local delivery run of more than a few drops, problems of retrieval and identification of individual orders arise, and such problems militate against close stowing, since working space is needed. In addition, special features, designed to facilitate access to the load for local delivery, work against the standard container concept – side doors, roller shutters and so on.

A careful check of the work planned for local delivery is needed if the container is to be kept within regular close-working schedules, and this can lead to a classic dilemma. Should the container be effectively stowed with the benefits of the trunk haul economics in mind, or is the load to be tailored to what can be effectively delivered in a day at the delivery end, so as to enable the daily round trip to be completed with a minimum of container equipment? The problem of the return load and the imbalance of traffic on major routes can be equally crucial in the economic evaluation of container delivery services.

It must be stressed, therefore, that far from it being the basis of a comprehensive revolution, the container can in retail distribution matters have a limited attraction. One can easily fall victim to a 'simplicity syndrome', unless the delivery requirements are carefully specified and the container's contribution measured against them. The container is but one mode of transportation and distribution. It may well resolve many storage and distribution issues in cases where the long haul by sea and/or land is the preoccupation. Where the local delivery issue predominates, it can create as many snags as it resolves unless it is specially, almost exclusively, adapted to the need. Custom-built containers and combitainers operated out of central warehouses as a distribution facility for deliveries to shop premises to facilitate reception 'out of hours', or in locations suffering from traffic congestion, are examples of such use.

Even so, the container remains one of the most promising developments of the last two decades, and we have still a lot to learn about its potential. It has a major role to play in local distribution, as a lock-up store located in correlation to a regional or local warehouse and delivered as may be convenient to local environmental and commercial needs. It links with current developments associated with pallets or trays, which can be used as 'in store' display units on which pricing and merchandising have been pre-arranged, as we have mentioned earlier. As a technique which brings all modes of transport together – road, rail, sea and air – it clearly has much in its favour.

Automatic vending, food brokers

There are many other new developments facilitating the process of distribution and sales. Examples are the growth of automatic vending machines in institutions, garages, motorway cafés and places of all kinds where the public gather or live, as in high flats. After a very slow start in the UK, this development associated with the idea of convenience shopping and supply, especially in areas such as holiday resorts, leisure camps, railway stations, and motorway services stations, begins to command attention. In this connection it is interesting to observe the way in which the consumer – owing to the cost of supply – is being drawn nearer to the source of his needs, especially food requirements, as he finds himself commanding his own source of freight mobility in the motor car. He can now go himself to the source of supply, picking his own vegetables in a 'pick your own' environment, choosing meat in bulk for his own deep freeze, bypassing the distribution channel for many of the requirements of the home through a 'do it yourself' system.

National pallet pools

The possible further development of national pallet pools remains of interest. They already exist in a number of countries: a rental pool is operated in Australia and interlocking exchange pools are run by various European railways. In Great Britain there are some limited forms of pallet pools, privately organised. The prospect of further development in more national terms seems limited against a background of cost considerations. The use of pallets as a medium of materials handling and storage is, however, widespread, with consequent saving in time and labour by unitised handling in bulk. This development is, however, specialised and localised rather than national. It is doubtful if – at least until an effective computer control system emerges – a national pool of any consequence, however attractive in theory, is feasible in practice on any widespread scale.

Trend to telephone selling

In the last decade there has been a major development of the telephone as a marketing and sales medium. It carries substantial delivery implications. Today, a number of distribution systems depend to a large degree on telephone selling and pre-ordering. The UK pioneers were Birds Eye Foods, but today there is application in many industries, and at least one organisation offers a 'commando' telesales service, which can be utilised for specific projects or problems. The telephone is also the medium much in use for marketing appraisals and opinion research.

Telephone selling of products can be developed on a regular basis with integrated calling between representative and telephone clerk. It can be used for covering peak loading on a sales force during seasonal or promotional activities, and it can be an effective alternative to an auxiliary sales force for covering vacant territories, holiday and sickness relief, or even product launches through indirect accounts. Its main advantages derive from economy and flexibility. Speedy territorial coverage is possible, especially significant for a developing company or in territories where there is a wide geographical scatter. It is also of value in areas where traffic congestion and parking difficulties slow travel time for representatives. Since the telephone is an imperative instrument, it often commands attention more readily than a representative waiting in a crowded shop. But the law of diminishing returns applies, and as more companies adopt telephone selling, there is increasing evidence of irritation with telesales, unless inherent product characteristics, e.g. perishability, compel such an approach. Telephone selling is an effective method of ensuring full-range selling, unlike van sales. As it can be a supervised desk job, there is more of an analytical approach than for the representative in a face-to-face situation with his customer. Unlike the representative, it is not possible to see the actual stock situtaion or show the customer samples or promotional material – too frequently mailed promotional material is discarded before being digested – and without physical inspection the sales staff cannot make their estimation of actual needs and projected offtake.

Thus, although telesales allow greater contact frequency for the same cost and although it is possible to be extremely flexible in differentiating between categories and outlets within a geographical area, these advantages are offset to a degree by the complete inability to merchandise unless a separate and specific merchandising organisation is established. There are other disadvantages, such as the tendency to increased outstanding credits and bad debt levels without the facility of representative cash collection, and inevitably the competitive intelligence inherent in a representative sales force is not available to the teleselling organisation.

Nevertheless, in delivery terms against the background of pre-booked orders, there are opportunities for substantial benefits and economies in distribution arising from the full utilisation of van space, the planning of routes and schedules, and the co-ordination of deliveries. Sales and distribution administration is also simplified.

The current economic environment of wage and salary escalation, plus the stringencies of a fuel crisis and economic recession, may well encourage even more experimentation in telephone selling in the next decade, especially against the background of technological developments in computer and Post Office services such as Prestel, etc. It could well be (see later) that 'telephone ordering' becomes a technique associated with 'the home' as the work centre as well as the leisure centre of the future, as the 'local terminal/computer chip' technologies develop at the local level, and the practice of 'do it yourself/pick your own' comes to determine the lifestyles of the eighties and nineties.

Mobile shops

As national networks (road, rail, coastal shipping) come under the pressures of distribution costs in marginal areas, the mobile shop may continue to offer some potential for growth. With the increasing drift to the towns, shops can rarely be adequately sustained in rural areas any more than small units of any kind, whether they be public houses or farms. Even the village general store and the post office are coming under increasing pressure. As these trends emerge, problems of supply will encourage new forms of delivery and distribution. The mobility provided by the motor car will help, but as more people seek the quiet pleasures of the countryside for rest and relaxation, there emerges a real opportunity for the mobile shop to provide products and services (such as groceries, fresh fish, meat, hairdressing, book-borrowing facilities and even government services associated with the Post Office). Apart from rural areas and villages where shops are either closed or there are problems of reliability in supply, there are also opportunities for mobile shop activity in newly built areas (new towns and suburbs) where there are no supermarkets and stores. It is possible that the railway network could re-emerge as an infrastructure on which a new local delivery system might be organised, associated with a mobile shop system serviced from a local railway station. As a form of convenience shopping, attractive to the consumer, and as a delivery medium which carries low overheads and minimal stock and permits purposeful utilisation of facilities, the mobile shop has a part to play, especially in scattered rural areas.

Trend to mail-order business

Mail-order retailing marks the reaction of the consuming public to the limitations, inconvenience and constraints of High Street shopping, which have become even more distasteful as the cost of commuter services to the 'big city', whether by car, bus or train, escalate as energy costs increase. It offers a medium by which the purchaser can be introduced, on terms favourable to himself and on the basis of his own leisurely choice, to a range of products far beyond what can normally be carried in any supermarket chain. It is equivalent to a form of 'one-stop shopping' without the problem of carriage and collection, and the credit facilities provided broaden the opportunity of choice and 'minimise the cost of spending to the consumer'. From the operator's point of view there are the attractions of mass production and purchase, and while the planning and phasing of production/demand bring major problems of inventory control, which are only just beginning to yield to the computer, it is possible to share or offload many of the problems of distribution to manufacturers and to regard delivery as a purchased service from a wide range of distributors, including the Post Office and public carriers. There is no doubt, as visual display systems through the Post Office and television develop, this form of supply will grow significantly.

In the UK mail-order sales had grown from less than £50 million in 1950 to over £710 million in 1972, and they have more than doubled since then. The business tends to be seasonal, with a substantial upsurge in the last quarter of the year. General mail-order in the UK covers substantial turnover in clothing, footwear, furniture, household textiles, radio and electrical goods, leather and sports goods, with women's and infants' wear topping the list. It is estimated that over 40 per cent of all households in the UK buy through mail-order, with 50 per cent located in the North of England. Six mail-order houses account for about 85 per cent of the total business. But in recent years there has been a big growth in business by smaller, specialist mail-order houses, including the mail-order activities of big stores, and the development of mail-order services through the advertising media of weekend newspapers and magazines.

The channel of supply and distribution is manufacturer/wholesaler/mail-order warehouse and administration/agent/customer. Most mail-order houses have separately registered wholesalers to which, in some cases, are attached special PO despatch departments. Other parcels and small-freight carriers also make special arrangements for this traffic. Of recent years, the mail-order firms themselves have developed their own freight services. Goods are sold essentially through advertisement – television, radio, newspaper and periodical – and by widely distributed catalogues. The basis of large-scale mail-order business is the catalogue; those for the big mail-order houses contain 30,000 entries or more. The distribution of these catalogues to agents throughout the country is itself a major operation.

It should be observed that the order priorities when selling to wholesale and conventional retail outlets are different from those operating in mail-order. The wholesaler or conventional retailer rates his priorities in terms of price, then quality consistent with price, and finally a reasonably efficient service to customers. With mail-order the direct relationship of person-to-person sales is absent, and the operator cannot capitalise on the personal approach or point-of-sale appeal. To the mail-order operator the reliability of the service he offers, related to customer convenience, has most appeal. Quality is important in terms of consistency. The receipt of faulty or damaged merchandise creates a bad impression. The consumer has additionally to return the goods.

In this time-critical operation, therefore, the role to be played by the delivery service is a vital one, from whatever source it is derived. Cost can be significant, but the reliability and quality of the delivery service are most important. Timing must be right and criticisms based on damage or loss must be minimal.

There is no doubt that technological change could be on the side of the mail-order system of delivery. It links closely with the trends evident in computer technology, which could encourage the development of local terminal facilities in the home, which recognise the need to grapple with developing environmental restrictions, which compel a new look at 'consolidation' processes in regional depots and which, in any case, are in line with the drive to meet cost and technological pressures. Current pressures are also encouraging a fresh look at the process of 'trans-shipment and break-bulk' to local depots, a system which aims to contain environmental offence by large lorries by compelling local distribution in small vehicles. To date this system has rarely stood up to examination – as studies in 1978 by the Lorry and the Environment Committee have clearly demonstrated – and substantial cost improvements would be needed to validate it.

Development of new outlets and contacts with the consumer

As has been observed, the tightening control exercised by supermarket, multiple and operator over their suppliers on the one hand and their customers on the other, with the consequent constraints on the manufacturer in influencing the sale of his own branded products, have stimulated a dynamic search for new patterns of delivery, distribution and merchandising. This process has been further encouraged by the current crisis over fuel costs and the many areas of escalating distribution expense in an inflationary world suffering from economic recession. The search for containing and improving on delivery systems is being intensively pursued. It has been much encouraged by recent technological developments that reinforce the importance of the 'home' as the originator and satisfier of demand.

The fuel crisis is having a strong impact on the search for new or refined methods of propulsion and mobility. One of the most promising methods, which also carries positive environmental benefits, concerns the development of the electric truck in much more effective and sophisticated forms than the original 'milk float' design. Though the real breakthrough here remains dependent on the development of new type batteries, lighter in weight and capable of long-life energy storage, current progress has been promising enough in extending range and improving payload and performance, and in providing an infrastructure of service support to enable patterns of distribution based on electric propulsion to emerge. Chloride, Lucas, the Electricity Council and the National Freight Corporation (through its subsidiary National Carriers) have been prominent in these developments, especially concerned with local distribution in congested areas and conurbations.

Direct delivery to homes

There are already indications of the short-circuiting of the channels of sales and distribution, eliminating the need for the conventional stores as a medium of consumer supply. In cosmetics, glass and plastic ware, and frozen foods, manufacturers are establishing direct contact with homes, using a combination of telephone selling and personal contact through agents to achieve sales. Lead time, inventory and the total costs of distribution and administration can all be reduced by the elimination of the intermediary links between the manufacturer and the consumer.

The fact that distribution is effected in residential areas away from the major constraints of traffic engineering and traffic congestion, and that it can be smoothed by careful traffic planning and organised/synchronised telesales coverage to prevent peaking, also assists in controlling costs. Conversely, the technique necessitates detailed breakup and the minutiae of traffic control of large-scale fleets, since it lacks even the modicum of assistance in delivery that comes from the presentation of the customer at the shop and the selection and carrying of goods from there to the home.

A vision of armchair shopping of the future

Such activities can be said to grow naturally out of current trends but this development is consistent with the emergence of large-scale automated warehouses strategically sited within conurbations, and with the new technology of electronic telecommunications. A new level of sophistication could well emerge in the 1980s, altering conventional methods of merchandising. An article which appeared in *Harvard Business Review* as long ago as 1967 graphically outlined the main features of the change which could become commonplace in the eighties.

A substantial share of 'convenience' goods (frequently purchased items of standard quality and low unit price) will be sold through a relatively few central distribution facilities in each major area. Consumers will never visit these centres; instead retail transactions will be made by electronic telecommunications and push-button video devices installed in private homes and hooked on-line to data-processing networks.

Consumers will be able to sit at a colour television console in their own homes and order directly from the distribution centre. Regular orders will be pre-programmed and will be ordered by pressing a single key. Additional items to the regular order can be ordered by pressing keys in an agreed code listed in a catalogue supplied by the company operating the service. Consumers will not see the merchandise until it is delivered to their home.

To provide an efficient service, the central distribution unit will receive, interpret, process and deliver. The processing of the orders will necessitate the separating of the order into two parts: that which will be handled by the 'automatic' warehouse and that which will be handled by the conventional warehouse. Items standardised in shape and size will be handled by the former. When the supplies from both warehouses have been combined, and spot-checked for accuracy against the pre-printed invoice, the order will be sent to the packing room, where frozen foods and perishables will be packed separately from non-perishables before all the goods are packed into a single box ready for despatch to the consumer.

Computers will sort the order for delivery to the consumer as part of the service offered by the distribution company. The agreement with the consumer will also mean that the consumer's bank account will be programmed into the computer, allowing a system of 'telephone-cash' collection to be used thus eliminating the expense of collecting money and loss through bad debt. These savings will enable such distribution centres to maintain low prices.

The benefits of speed and ease of shopping, coupled with the fact that prices would remain competitive, will certainly be an attractive proposition to most consumers. Central distribution will offer a very strong challenge to conventional stores and will, in all probability, affect the established pattern of distribution by the 1980s.

The importance of the computer in the delivery field

Computers have been applied to the accounting, management information and some administration of transport and distribution companies for some time. Many companies now use computers for payroll, sales invoicing and analysis, purchase ledger, assets, inter-company charges and nominal ledger and trading. In addition, a number of companies use drive data with special systems to suit their particular needs. In the nationalised sector, for instance, British Road Services, National Carriers, Pickfords Heavy Haulage, Freight Computer Services and National Freight Corporation use the computer for financial modelling.

Examples are widespread. The national rescue freight vehicle service operated by British Road Services is based on a mini-computer and a disc file retrieval system. There are automated parcels sorting systems in which National Carriers, co-operating with Marks and Spencer, use computer technology to satisfy all Marks and Spencer's non-food delivery requirements. Many large firms are now experimenting with parcels sorting and product selection, leased on computerised programmes involving inventory control and route scheduling. Freightliner have now a well-proved container routeing and control system.

The main computer thrust of the eighties for distribution and delivery will be in the areas of operational control systems, in management information retrieval techniques, and for small companies in systems of a specialist nature. There is no doubt that all staff in all distribution activities will increasingly use computer keyboard operations as a way of life, especially as the new generation, brought up from schooldays to regard the silicon chip with the same familiarity as their fathers did the slide rule, will find no difficulty in applying the computer.

Once again we are finding that, in the world of delivery operations, the pressure of cost containment and gaining value for money is creating many new challenges and a host of new opportunities. To these, however, must be added the searching influences of many radical forces for change of unique intensity, stemming from inflation, worldwide recession, fuel shortages and the computer. We are poised for a great leap forward, a process in which the Physical Distribution Manager will pay no mean part in retail distribution applications.

26

Energy: its impact on distribution

Richard A. Lancioni

The current energy storage is a worldwide problem that will continue for many years to come, and business planners must accept that the era of stable and cheap energy has ended. For the distribution manager such a realisation is particularly hard to face, because the distribution function is responsible for providing the delivery service for customers. Rising energy costs have put the distribution manager and his logistics system in the forefront of the two-pronged battle to reduce energy consumption while at the same time seeking ways to maintain customer service levels.

Coping with the energy shortfall and with rising costs will continue to make the job of business managers and distribution executives a difficult one. Known reserves of energy are limited and no new large discoveries of petroleum are on the horizon. As shown in Figure 26:1, the amount of easily recoverable petroleum is limited. Oil can be extracted from coal and shale rock but the conversion methods are costly and not currently economic. Since the 1973 embargo the price of oil has risen dramatically around the world, with the price of a barrel of oil increasing by 3,000 per cent over the period. The astronomical rise has forced companies to alter their operations or face the alternative of going out of business.

Energy developments

New forms and methods of energy conversion are being developed each year. One of these is gasohol – a mixture of 90 per cent gasoline and 10 per cent ethanol. The idea was taken from a German process developed during the Second World War. Ethanol is blended with gasoline after refining. The mixture provides the motorist with the same or higher octane rating at approximately the same price as gasoline. Trucks and

Fuel	Known recoverable (quadrillion BTUs)	Total (quadrillion BTUs)
Coal	20–30	350
Petroleum	3.3–12.1	36
Natural gas	1.2	8–12
Natural gas liquids	–	1–2
Oil in bituminous rocks	–	–
Shale oil in shale rock	1.1	2,000

Includes all known, and allows for undiscovered, reserves

Figure 26:1   World fuel reserves

cars in Brazil run almost exclusively on the gasohol mixture. The advantage of using gasohol is that it is a renewable resource, since the alcohol portion is made from corn and other farm products.

Another potential energy saver is the development of synthetic fuels from coal and shale rock. As shown in Figure 26:1, the amount of recoverable hydrocarbons is quite extensive, but the feasibility, as mentioned earlier, and utilisation of these fuel derivatives are still in the developmental stage. Coal gasification, for example, has been around for many years and is currently being studied again as a source of fuel. In the process coal is pulverised into small granules, which are sprayed with a catalytic agent that speeds up reaction between the coal and the steam with which the coal is mixed. The vapour released from this process comes off in the form of natural gas, which is purified and then put directly into a pipeline system.

Shale rock also contains hydrocarbon deposits. The conversion process is similar to that of coal gasification in that the shale rock is heated to very high temperatures. The shale breaks down under the high temperatures, giving off a black, sticky crude oil. The waste products are removed and the crude oil is filtered out.

The need for conservation

Discovery of new energy sources and synthetic fuels is one way of increasing the energy supply, but opponents of this approach hold that conservation is a much more practical way of approaching the energy problem. They base their contention on the fact that it costs less to conserve than to produce from any new sources. Conservationists contend that conservation requires firms and individuals to abolish less energy efficient systems and substitute highly efficient ones. This practice, according to the conservationists, results in a change in individual and company behaviour regarding the use of energy in the long run. Manufacturing firms installing new equipment should not stress so much the cost of the equipment, but, rather, its energy efficiency aspects. The minimal cost alternative may not be the best, for the more energy efficient alternative may require higher short-run expenditures for long-run energy economies.

Country-to-country comparison of the usage of energy in manufacturing illustrates the significance of the conservationists' position. For example, steel production in Japan compared with the United States is much more energy efficient, while paper and cement production is much more energy efficient in Sweden and Germany than in the US and Japan. In an effort to catch up many US-based cement firms are installing new large dry kilns, which not only increase productivity, but reduce energy consumption by up to 50 per cent per ton.

Conservationists also point out that in the transport sector fuel savings can be realised by switching freight from fuel inefficient modes like truck and air to more efficient ones such as rail. In addition, consolidating loads before shipment can lower transport costs by reducing the number of trips, with consequent lower fuel consumption. Of course, the introduction of more fuel efficient cars has had and will continue to have significant impact on energy conservation. Conservationists look forward to a bright future if significant conservation steps are adopted. Figure 26:2 shows the energy intensities for the year 2010 as compared to 1975. The energy intensities reflect the potential level of energy usage in each consumptive category. The higher numbers recorded for 1975 compared to the levels forecast for 2010 demonstrate the expected reductions in energy consumption over the period.

Price as a regulator of consumption

The energy shortage has traditionally been blamed on price. The standard wisdom asserts that if the price of energy rises far enough, all energy sources, whether synthetic or easily recoverable fuels, will become more economically feasible and profitable to produce, thereby making more fuel available. But how far must prices rise? For the distribution manager, increasing prices force him to cut back on deliveries to customers. They also curtail inter-plant movements of material because of the increased cost of operating fork-lift equipment. Unless some reasonable price level is reached, constantly rising prices can only exacerbate the problems of the distribution manager. Price, therefore, is a legitimate vehicle for increasing supply, but careful administration, either by government or industry, is necessary to ensure that prices do not rise too rapidly.

Impact of energy shortage on distribution management

The energy crisis has had and will continue to have a damaging effect on physical distribution management. It is an area in a firm's operation that is highly energy intensive, for it handles materials movement, transportation, and warehousing, each of which consumes an enormous amount of energy. Specifically, the energy shortage

Use	1975	2010
Residential	0.84	0.63
Commercial	0.63	0.42
Government and education	0.42	0.35
Space conditioning	0.70	0.66
Air	0.53	0.52
Electric heat	0.71	0.66
Gas/oil heat	0.79	0.72
Refrigeration, freezing	0.62	0.58
Lighting	0.60	0.55
Agriculture	0.92	0.85
Aluminium	0.95	0.55
Cement	0.61	0.60
Chemicals	0.75	0.74
Construction	0.62	0.58
Food	0.66	0.66
Glass	0.75	0.69
Iron/steel	0.81	0.72
Paper	0.76	0.64
Auto	0.65	0.35
Freight truck	0.23	0.13
Air passenger	0.65	0.42

Figure 26:2   Energy intensity usage for 1975 compared to forecast for 2010

will affect distribution management in seven operational areas:

1   Customer service levels.
2   The size of orders.
3   Vehicle scheduling and transportation planning.
4   Adjustments in plant and field inventory stocks.
5   The need to establish consolidation programmes for transportation economies.
6   The development of more efficient recycling systems to handle returned merchandise.
7   Improved distribution planning.

Adjustment of consumer service levels

The shortage of energy has to some extent affected the customer service levels of nearly all companies. The reason for this is that firms do not always set realistic customer service levels, frequently providing more service than is necessary. When the energy shortage hit in 1973, all service policies were affected. The challenge facing the physical distribution then was to prevent service levels from deteriorating below an acceptable level. Currently, the distribution manager must align his service levels with what is demanded by customers and the energy supplies available.

In setting customer service levels, a company must first ascertain what its customer service requirements are. Assuming that he knows what his firm's customers want in terms of service level can lead a physical distribution manager to provide too much service. Determining what service level is needed by customers can be done by conducting what is called a *customer service audit*. The audit is a survey of a firm's customers which includes an inquiry into what their delivery requirements are, what inventory levels they need, what order cycle times are preferable to them, and what their tracing and informational needs are.

A customer service audit begins with a segmentation of the firm's customers into service categories, such as those requiring high degrees, moderate degrees and low degrees of service. After categorising customers, the physical distribution manager must then develop a questionnaire, which is distributed to the firm's customers. The customers are asked questions regarding their required delivery times, desired inventory levels, order processing and special handling and storage needs. After the questionnaires are completed, the distribution manager should tabulate the results and analyse them by customer classes. The survey findings will enable him to modify his current service levels and base them on the real requirements of his customers. In effect, the firm will be able to determine what it should be doing and not what it assumes it should be doing.

The firm may discover from the audit that its customers are asking for a higher level of service than the company can realistically cost justify and provide. At this point the physical distribution manager must negotiate with his customers, pointing out that the firm will not be able to meet the requested levels, owing to the cost limitations imposed by higher fuel charges. The firm's customers must be made to realise that the price of energy makes it economically undesirable to provide inordinately high service levels.

Once this negotiation is completed, the distribution manager can set customer service standards that both he and his customers agree upon. The standards will act as guides in managing the distribution operation. Before the standards are finally set, they should be tested for a period of time to evaluate their cost sensitivity. Once this testing period has ended, the physical distribution manager can then implement them.

It is imperative that once the standards are set the company should make every effort to achieve them. Customers, once given a delivery standard, depend on it. *Reliability* is the key element in a customer service programme. If a firm states a delivery time standard and does not meet it, the standard is meaningless.

Monitoring the customer service programme is also an important element, and the firm should establish a reporting system, with routine reports that are analysed by key personnel in the distribution group. If a deviation from standard arises, the firm should find out why, and correct it. Such a performance evaluation should be a continuous process.

The customer service standards established in an energy conservation programme should be fixed for long periods, and the distribution should see to it that they are updated and changed when necessary. As energy prices rise or energy supplies become short, or if the customer's service requirements change, so must the service standards. What is needed is a continuous feedback information system that will tell the distribution manager when changes are required. Figure 26:3 summarises the steps required in establishing an energy–customer service programme, beginning first with the audit and continuing with the feedback loop.

Order size

The size of the customer order may seem to have only a minimal effect on the energy conservation effort, but the larger the order size, the less frequent shipments have to be made to the customer and the less energy consumed. This may be a simplistic way of stating the relationship, but it can have a significant impact on energy conservation. A firm's customers generally do not want to order in large quantities, for it requires them to hold large inventories and do a lot of planning as to where the materials are to

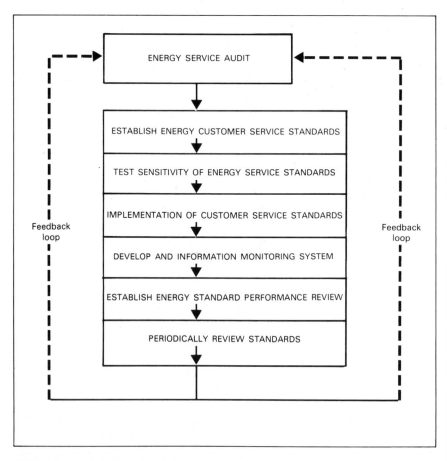

Figure 26:3   Customer service energy programme audit

be staged in advance of eventual usage. A customer may, for example, have to increase his storage capacity or invest more in materials handling equipment to accommodate the added inventory. Also, holding inventory is fraught with risks, including obsolescence, deterioration, investment, and opportunity cost risks. From the customer's point of view, there are a lot of negatives in increasing order size.

But for the supplier firm, the advantages are substantial in terms of reduced energy consumption and improved transit costs. Increasing order size can enable the distribution manager to get better transport service from a trucking company, the railway, or air cargo carrier, while at the same time realising lower freight costs. It therefore becomes necessary for the firm to work with its customers and develop programmes whereby large order sizes can be worked into the system. The transportation economies will be sizeable and the savings can be passed along to the customer.

Transportation usage and vehicle scheduling

The distribution manager can make substantial cuts in energy usage by analysing a firm's current vehicle scheduling programmes and the types of transportation modes it currently uses. The different modes of transport consume significantly different amounts of energy while hauling similar weights. Figure 26:4 shows that those modes currently in heavy use are not necessarily the most efficient. For example, moving freight by water is the most energy efficient form of transport, but its utilisation is very low. Likewise, railways, which rank second in terms of efficiency, are used to only a limited extent to haul freight when compared to truck. Air cargo, which is the most energy inefficient way to haul freight, is increasingly popular with distribution managers. The data reveal that, in general, shippers are not energy-conscious with regard to the type of transport they use to move goods to their customers. In the 1973–4 energy crisis shippers were forced because of shortages to switch to more efficient modes. In a study conducted during that period (Figure 26:5) it was found

Transportation mode	Efficiency rank	Energy usage (%)
Automobile	4	56
Aircraft	5	11
Intercity railroads	2	3.6
Waterways and pipelines	1	1.4
Local and intercity buses	3	.6
Intercity trucks	3	7.0
Local trucking	3	14.9
Other	3	3.8
The lower the efficiency ranking, the more efficient the mode		

Figure 26:4   Current transportation energy usage by mode

that 28 per cent of shippers switched from truck to rail and 16 per cent selected truck transportation over air transportation. The study revealed that, when forced, shippers can be more energy-efficient. But the switching to other modes was not without its problems. Figure 26:6 shows that those companies that switched from truck to rail experienced delays because of a shortage of rail cars to move their goods. Those who switched from air to truck found that their transit times increased and that their service levels declined. The shippers who switched to water found that it was slow and not adaptable to hauling other than bulk freight.

The energy shortage facing companies can be dramatically affected by improved vehicle scheduling. How frequently does a physical distribution manager schedule a shipment that is only half or partially loaded? How often does a vehicle make a pickup or a delivery over a route which is not well co-ordinated and planned? A vehicle uses the same BTU/ton mile whether it is fully loaded or partially loaded. Improving the routeing can reduce energy consumption by a significant amount. A large North American company with a private fleet comprising more than 700 trucks reduced energy consumption by 35 per cent through improved scheduling techniques. A large number of physical distribution managers have turned to computer models to assist them in vehicle scheduling. Many of these models are based on linear programming and can be developed internally by a firm's traffic department, or the

Mode	Shippers switching to the mode (%)
Rail	28.0
Common truck	24.0
Private truck	16.0
Water	12.0
Shipper associations	4.0

Figure 26:5   Change of transportation modes during energy crisis

Specific problems	% Encountering problems	
Extended transit times in using air	75.0	} 100%
Cannot accommodate backlogs when using air	25.0	
Increased load factor when using for hire trucking	64.0	} 100%
Increased transit times when using for hire trucking	36.0	
Shortage of railway cars when using rail	100.0	
Slow movement of freight when using water	100.0	

Figure 26:6   Problems in using alternative modes during crisis

software can be obtained from computer companies such as IBM.

Vehicle scheduling depends on four basic elements:

1   The number of vehicles needed to make the required deliveries.
2   Vehicle size.
3   The number of stop/pickup points on a given vehicle's route.
4   The sequence of stop-off and pickup points on routes.

The scheduling models have enabled firms to reduce the number of vehicles required in their fleets, reduce travel times and, most importantly, lower energy usage by reducing the number of miles travelled by each vehicle.

Adjustments of plant and field inventory

The level of inventory a firm carries and where it is located have an impact on energy usage. For example, staging inventory at a single location or at a limited number of locations may improve stock availability at those locations, but at the same order cycle times may increase. Alternatively, a distribution manager may ship orders direct to customers from a single location, in order to cut down on the local movement of orders from field stocking locations to customers, to save energy. Such a strategy may work, but it impairs a firm's ability to make inventory available over a wide market area.

What the distribution manager must do is to select an inventory strategy that will enable him to store the low turnover inventory material at centralised points and the high turnover items in field locations. This will reduce energy usage by reducing shipments out of the central location, which is generally a long way from markets, and increasing the number of short-distance moves from the field warehouses to the market demand areas.

Developing such a strategy may not be easy for the distribution manager. He needs, first, to develop an understanding of the different echelons within his distribution system of which there are three:

1   Level I, distribution – manufacturing plants to plant warehouses.
2   Level II, plant warehouse to field warehouses.
3   Level III, distribution from field warehouses to demand areas.

Each echelon is a link in the distribution flow and requires inventory staging and a centralised stocking point to service more than one level.

Another important element in developing an energy efficient inventory plan is the need to identify the high turnover and low turnover items in the company's distribution system. One of the most widely used methods for doing this is called ABC analysis. The technique is based on the 80/20 principle, whereby 20 per cent of the firm's inventory accounts for 80 per cent of its volume. The firm's product line can be segmented into A or high-volume items, AB or moderate-volume items, and ABC or low-volume items. The distribution manager would have to determine how far the inventory was to be classified. Based on the ABC approach, separate service or in-stock levels can be set for each classification: for example, 98 per cent for A items, 90 per cent for B items, and 75 per cent for C items. By relating inventory activity to market location, an inventory stocking plan can be developed.

The key ingredient is combining stock level and stock location into a co-ordinated plan. Along with inventory planning, the distribution manager needs to select an appropriate site for the storage of inventory. Selecting a location for a warehouse depends on a number of factors which include:

1   Land configuration.
2   Building costs.
3   Access to transportation services.
4   Market demand.
5   Expansion possibilities.
6   Taxes.
7   Access to market areas to be served.

Evaluating these factors over a number of different locations can be done most effectively through the use of computer models, which enable the distribution manager to select from a group of ideal locations. The models currently in use are of three types:

(i)   *Computer Simulation Location Model.*   This model type looks at the transportation costs, inventory levels, and order processing times over a number of different sites. The model then selects the locations for which these factors will be maximised.

(ii)   *Heuristic Method of Warehouse Location.*   This approach is a cost-saving approach to warehouse location analysis. It cuts down on computer time by limiting the factors to be considered. Inputs to the model include warehouse data, transportation distances, sales and demand data.

(iii)   *Algorithmic Model of Warehouse Location.*   This approach provides the distribution manager with an optimal location. The technique requires that the input data be precisely defined, and it takes a lot of computation and computer runs to derive the solution.

Developing an energy efficient inventory policy requires that the physical distribution manager totally evaluate the firm's distribution system. Setting stock levels at correct locations is an important factor if the company is to reduce its energy consumption.

Shipment consolidation

Shipment consolidation has often been viewed as a way of reducing transportation costs, but with the rising cost and shortage of fuel, companies have been realising energy savings through consolidation. Saving energy and reducing transportation costs through shipment consolidation requires that the distribution manager work with the firm's customers to adjust their service levels. Changing service levels is not an easy task to accomplish, but if the savings in cost and fuel can be demonstrated to customers, their willingness to co-operate will improve.

Establishing a shipment consolidation programme requires that the distribution manager do an audit of the distribution system to pinpoint areas where consolidation can exact some savings. The following is a list of steps necessary to determine the need for and to implement an energy-saving consolidation programme:

1   Conduct an audit of the distribution flows both in and out.
2   Evaluate the amount and type of freight moving from plant to warehouse.
3   Evaluate the type and amount of freight moving from field warehouses to customers.
4   Audit the breakbulk requirements at the different plant and field warehouses.
5   Discuss with the carriers the vehicle capacities available to haul consolidated loads between points in the distribution system.
6   Evaluate the transportation cost savings for consolidated loads between plant and field warehouses and field warehouses and customers.
7   Reschedule vehicle routeing (if the firm has a private fleet) to reduce total miles travelled.
8   Combine pickup and delivery wherever possible in the system.
9   Revise delivery times in conjunction with customer service levels.
10   Adjust order processing times to reflect the delays expected from the consolidation programme.
11   Develop an accounting system to determine cost saving and reduced fuel consumption.
12   Monitor the consolidation programme by establishing a set of time and delivery standards, with periodic feedback reports to the distribution manager.
13   Develop a procedure for minimising emergency order deliveries.

Shipment consolidation is the most immediate way a distribution manager can realise reductions in energy consumption. A large North American firm reduced its energy usage by 30 per cent over a 6-month period by extending order processing times by one day. It estimated that it could cut another 15 per cent from its fuel usage by increasing its delivery time by an additional day. In short, by going from a 6- to an 8-day order processing the firm could reduce its fuel consumption by as much as 50 per cent.

Recycling systems to handle returned merchandise

Handling a returned order is a costly process for a logistics manager. In general, a returned order can cost from two to four times as much to process as a regular order. The increase is due to the following factors:

1   Special handling of the item in the return channel.
2   Premium transportation costs brought about by less than truckload shipments.
3   Special warehouse handling and stacking.
4   Increased holding costs.
5   Special repackaging for the returned goods.

These elements not only increase the cost of returned merchandise, but they also increase energy consumption in the over-the-road transportation and warehouse handling of the item. What is needed is for the distribution manager to develop a standard recycling system for products that do not require handling in a special way. The distribution system should be modified to deal with returned merchandise when necessary in an economical and efficient manner. For example, in some return or recycle distribution systems, the product is returned all the way back to the original production point for reprocessing. Aluminium cans are recycled and remelted to make new cans. The return system begins with the establishment of a collection centre for the waste cans and their transfer back to strategic holding centres. The return transportation is generally by rail in fully loaded cars for maximum load advantage. Paper recycling is done in the same manner.

Recycling systems are of two types – the full recycle and the partial recycle system. These are shown in Figure 26:7.

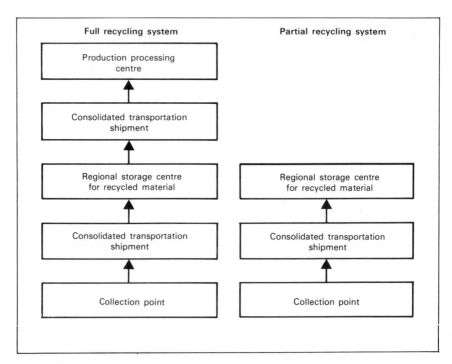

Figure 26:7   Product recycling systems

The full recycle system is normally used for products that can be profitably recycled, such as cans, paper, and steel. Recycled car bodies are an important source of scrap. The partial recycling system is utilised when it is too costly for the manufacturer to return the goods for reprocessing or for scrap. The item is moved to a regional holding centre and destroyed, or in some alternative form sold to company employees at reduced prices. In both systems it is essential that consolidated loads be employed to reduce transportation costs and energy consumption.

Improved distribution planning

Without a doubt the distribution manager who plans for shortages and develops plans to deal with them will be better off in the long run. The energy crisis will be with us for many years to come, and it has to be accepted as a variable that must be a part of the distribution plan of a company. Losing market share through reduced service brought about by poor planning cannot be tolerated in a competitive environment. The stakes are high and the distribution manager must control the situation. What is required is a comprehensive and systematic attempt to forecast customer demand and raw material availability, and integrate and co-ordinate the planning function into the production–marketing–distribution system.

Such an approach will enable the firm to control the raw material flow and adjust its production and distribution system to meet the variation. Allocation of fuel was imposed on firms by the government after the 1973–4 oil embargo. These levels cannot be exceeded in time of fuel shortage. Generating too much demand in the market place for a product and not being able to service the demand is a counter-productive strategy. Demand generation should be kept in line with the firm's distribution service capability. Fuel supplies will continue to limit a firm's distribution operation. Incorporating available energy supply levels into the distribution plan will enable a company to be realistic in determining what it can hope to accomplish in the market place.

Summary

The energy crisis will continue to have an impact on distribution systems. If the company is to compete and make a profit, it must adjust its marketing and distribution policies to the available energy to support them. Conservation is a necessity, but survival is imperative. Both must be achieved together.

Further reading

R. Ballou, *Basic Business Logistics,* Englewood Cliffs, N. J.: Prentice-Hall, 1978.
B. J. Lalonde, 'The Energy Gap and Distribution Strategy', Unpublished Paper, Ohio State University, 1974.

D. Lambert and J. Stock, 'The Corporate Energy Policy: A Management Planning Perspective', *Journal of Long Range Planning,* 1978

R. Lancioni, 'Carriers in A Crisis', *Handling and Shipping,* April 1976.

R. Lancioni, 'Facing the Energy Crisis', *Distribution Worldwide,* 1975, pp. 46–9.

R. Lancioni, 'Profile of a Crisis', *Distribution Worldwide,* 1974, p. 53.

R. Lancioni, 'The Transportation System and the Environment', *Journal of the Society of Logistics Engineers,* Spring, 1979.

William Lucado, 'The Energy Situation: Implications for Strategic Planning', *Business Horizons,* April 1975.

27

Profitable distribution cost analysis

David L. Ray

Distribution in the current economic climate

The recession that advanced upon the world economy in 1974 and has been in evidence ever since, except for short periods of respite, has changed the face of distribution and given it new prominence. As one of the earliest indicators of economic change, the distribution area was quick to suffer the impact of the recession. In the last quarter of 1975, for example, manufacturers' stocks showed the biggest quarterly fall on record. That stocks still remained around 6½ per cent higher than usual in relation to output, at this time, emphasised the effects of the downturn in activity.

In practical terms, it is not too hard to envisage the effects of recession on distribution costs, with under-utilised assets and the higher service level requirements of fulfilling more frequent but smaller order-quantity deliveries. Against this background, many companies with distribution resources are being forced to examine their distribution costing information systems as a prelude to decisions regarding the rationalisation of their operations. Others which have in the past devoted more attention to distribution, an area often consuming around a third or more of their company's resources, have been in a better position to control the new cost surge. A review of the more progressive thinking behind manufacturers' distribution costing procedures seems opportune. It is worth assessing the progress that has been made against the remaining shortcomings and potential still largely unfulfilled.

Distribution and financial accounting – counteracting some old criticisms

Most management account systems place great reliance on the financial accounting system as the major source of information. Ray[1] illustrates in diagrammatic form (Figure 27:1) the possible cost information flows.

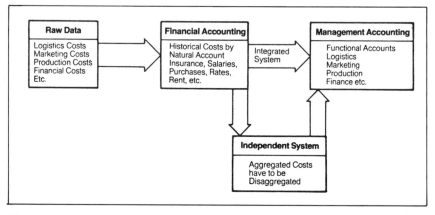

Figure 27:1   Cost information flow

No company of any repute should nowadays have to depend on sifting through financial accounting statements to collate a scattered collection of distribution costs. Gone, largely, are the days when aggregated natural account totals had to be broken down for functional classification. Integrated accounting systems are the order of the day, and distribution costs, appropriately coded, are pulled out in the requisite form by computer program.

So, three old dragons can be vanquished in respect of the progressive UK manufacturer's distribution costing: there has been a dispensation with financial statements, abandonment of natural account information and curtailment of manual disaggregation and functional reclassification tasks. Interdependent but more meaningful internal reports have taken their place. However, dispensing with financial statements is one thing; using financial accounting information is another. Having shaken off the shackles of manual system operation with speedy and more accurate computerisation, we find there are other basic problems to overcome. Some of these concern the inputs into the financial accounting model, which, geared to financial/taxation functions and external needs, provide an inadequate data base for distribution costing purposes. Problem areas include:

(a)   financial accounting procedures generally;
(b)   the matching concept;
(c)   use of historical costs.

Other difficulties exist, owing to the profoundly different roles of management and financial accounting. Although not caused by the use of the financial data by itself, these must be allowed for when monitoring and controlling costs, and for decision-making purposes.

Financial accounting procedures

The flow of information, as shown in Figure 27:1, leads to distortions in the costing system whenever there is any manipulation to the financial accounting. Gordon *et al.*[2] bring the phenomenon of the smoothing applications of judiciously selected accounting procedures to our attention, and both Schiff and Lewin[3] and Lewis[4] make similar observations.

In practice, the variability of yearly performance in profit terms is often smoothed out. In good times profits may be played down by, for example, increasing depreciation, valuing stock at top prices, or carrying over sales into less favourable periods. This attention to 'year-end' results is in direct contrast with the logistics operation, which is a continuing process. The lesson here is to be extra wary of cost information coinciding with year-end and interim financial results. Key figures such as sales and depreciation should be checked and if necessary adjusted or omitted. Distribution's own activity figures of throughput will be more useful in cost-efficiency exercises and replacement cost values more applicable for decision-making.

The matching concept

For profit-measurement the financial accountant uses the matching concept, whereby costs are related to revenue earned in the accounting period. In the shortest accounting period, normally 4 weeks or a calendar month, there is a strong temptation, particularly from those outside distribution, to measure distribution costs against monthly sales revenue. This should be resisted and the sales figure ignored, even in instances where goods coming directly off the production line are whisked away to the customers.

The sales revenue figure may contain advance payments (a buyer aiming to beat a price rise) or back payments which have been written off as bad debts. Even if adjustments have been made and the sales revenue figure is directly volume-related for the period, it may be no indication of distribution activity. Distribution costs precede sales and 'pipeline' costs include that of goods movement from plant to warehousing, plus packaging and storage expenditure. The answer is for distribution management to apply its own matching concepts, measuring warehouse and transportation activities against period costs, and ignoring financial sales figures.

Other problems arise with certain large distribution revenue expense items causing distortions in the period comparison: e.g. bulk purchases of fuel oil are sometimes written off in the month they are received, and large repair bills are seldom accrued. Monthly costs are distorted when the garage submits, eventually, a large backlog of repair charges, or the fuel-tanker arrives. Simple procedures are to accrue each period for outstanding repairs and to charge out from a fuel stock account for the period consumption.

Historical costs and comparing like with like

Historical costs can always be criticised on the grounds that they are only related to past events and may be a poor indicator of the future. Nevertheless, in many circumstances they can be the best guide to estimating ahead.

For revenue expenditure and current asset purchases, historical costs are usually perfectly adequate. With fixed assets, though, it is a different story. Comparisons are made, one depot with another, one vehicle fleet against another, hire charges against own account costs, contract hire versus direct purchasing, and so on. In each instance, some information will be needed from the distribution costing system. If the correct evaluations and decisions are to be made, like must be compared with like, or as near so as possible.

We have all heard of the company that regularly compares its own transportation costs with contract-hire quotations and always finds itself cheaper. A more amusing instance featured an inter-depot comparison, where a particularly desk-bound distribution executive noted that a specific depot regularly topped the performance list. Determined to tap the benefit of its superior operating methods for the good of the entire distribution operation, he visited it. He found archaic premises and an antiquated run-down fleet of vehicles. No rent was being charged for these company-owned premises and only a minimal depreciation for vehicles. In reality, owing to operating conditions, this field depot was the least efficient.

Solutions include charging notional current market rents where long-term low-cost leases or outright ownership exist, in order to represent realistic occupational costs. For vehicles, a current replacement cost allowance coupled with escalating maintenance charges as vehicles age tend to equate with any new alternative.

Financial accounting summary

Most of the major problems related to financial accounting inputs have been or are being overcome, but a further task is to educate outsiders not to scrutinise distribution costs solely on financial accounting data. But this is only one dimension. There is also the matter of ensuring that data other than the strictly financial (such as economic and other distribution cost related information) is included and collectively used properly and sensibly.

Distribution cost analysis in UK manufacturing

Companies use their distribution management accounting for all the generally accepted purposes. These embrace:

(a)   performance measurement and cost control;
(b)   cash flow analysis;
(c)   distribution audit;

(d)   channel selection;
(e)   capital investment and replacement decisions;
(f)   short- and long-term planning;
(g)   facilities location and system design.

The generally accepted procedure is to separate distribution costs on an activity basis into elemental subsidiary cost centres (as shown in Figure 27:2) except that (i) transportation costs usually distinguish between trunking (large direct deliveries and inter-depot movements) and the (smaller vehicle) local delivery work, and (ii) inventory costs rarely include the holding costs of finished stocks.

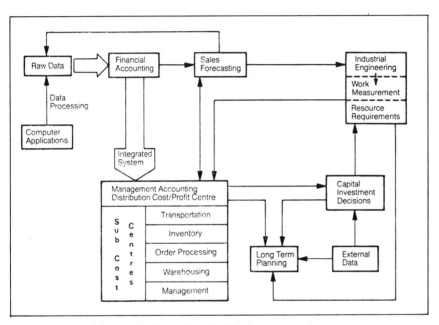

Figure 27:2   Information flows for distribution accounting

Companies rely extensively on sales forecasting to work out short-term resources, and most use industrial engineering measurements to formulate more exact establishment labour and vehicle needs. They are generally well versed in techniques for investment decision-making, usually following set procedures. Some firms have a much larger role for long-term planning than others. Most plan ahead for 4 to 5 years and forecast specific inflation rates for distribution. Others, with spare capacity or fixed location problems, tend to plan only in short steps.

However, the major part of the costing effort is devoted to short-term needs, notably monitoring costs and performance and attempting to control expenditure especially in relation to the peaks and troughs that affect a vast amount of industrial activity. These tasks are demonstrated in Figure 27:3.

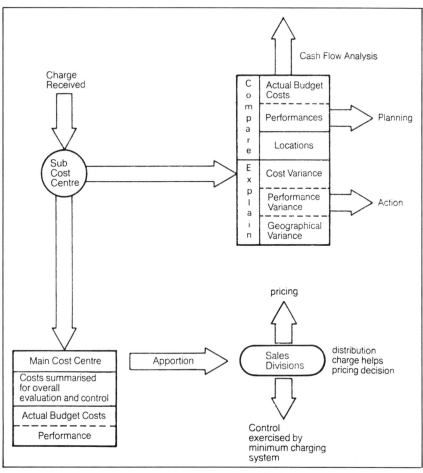

Figure 27:3   Monitoring costs and performance for planning and control

Subsidiary cost centres

Activities form the basis of these cost centres. Here, actual and budgeted costs are compared, along with outputs (work done), to provide a measure of performance and productivity. The cost information gives a period and year-to-date position and a basis for projecting future cash flows and planning costs. Where similar activities are duplicated from several locations, an additional dimension of geographical comparison is added (depot, warehouse, trunking, delivery activities).

Main cost centre

Costs regarded as 'distribution' are charged to the distribution cost centre, via the subsidiary cost centres as depicted, and are summarised for evaluation against physical outputs and planned performance (distribution budget). Usually in many large UK producers, there follows a large and time-consuming exercise. In the course of specialisation or diversification, organisations have been divisionalised. The task then remains, as illustrated in Figure 27:3, of apportioning distribution costs, between sales divisions on a usage basis, by the best means available.

Pricing system (charging out) features

Certain UK companies have shown much imagination in their charging out or apportioning of distribution costs to user divisions of their organisation. A common and significant feature is their aim purely to recover costs on a break-even basis, with no intention to use the distribution function as a profit centre by charging commercial rates.

Apportioning costs on an equitable basis requires more information than is provided in a summary, and this is obtained from the analysis of the subsidiary cost centres. In apportioning costs between divisions, methods vary from one company to another. The consensus is that total divisional throughput is only one of the important variables. Consideration is also given to average drop size of delivery, share of warehouse capacity coupled with stockturn (speed of turnover), and to the ease or difficulty of handling a division's products. Sometimes customer differences have to be discounted as well. If the pricing system is sophisticated enough, the user division which receives the charge will be able to relate costs to particular products (or types) and relevant customers, thus providing the necessary information for product and customer profitability analysis.

Minimum charging

A further feature is the use of a minimum charging system to exercise control of distribution resources. The distribution function is geared up (or pared down) to fulfil the needs of the annual plan, which itself is based on the sales projections of the selling divisions.

Over-optimistic forecasts will lead to the tying up of precious capital and the under-utilisation of distribution assets, the cost of which are highly fixed in the short-term. Levying a minimum charge of, say, 75 per cent of the original divisional distribution budget to cover the fixed cost element (generally around 70 to 80 per cent in UK own-account operations) of divisions failing to meet sales targets ensures that erring divisions are not penalising the more successful ones. Of course, these penalties can be relaxed to the extent that other divisions take up any slack.

Identifying deficiencies and refining the analysis

The picture so far presented seems one of both competence and adequacy, but a closer scrutiny reveals the more glaring weaknesses. Great progress has been made in the last decade after a period of much neglect, which caused Peter Drucker[5] to describe distribution as 'The Economy's Dark Continent' and D. D. Parker[6] to depict it as 'the last frontier for cost economics'. However, a large question mark hangs over both the ability of distribution heads to control distribution costs – because of inadequate recognition of distribution's all embracing role – and the power to improve company profitability, owing to unrefined distribution cost analysis.

Although many improvements have been made in the distribution area, much has been illusory. Costs have not necessarily been reduced, but may just have been moved sideways from one activity to another or from distribution to another area of the firm, or even to an outside institution. One way of reducing costs has always been to lower the level of service given. But what effect may this have on sales (through stockouts) and thus profitability? There have been few signs of any positive effort to relate distribution costs to some measure of achieved service. Work is going on in this area but it is difficult to get an all round agreement on what constitutes 'service level'.

We can identify three areas in particular where improvements and refinement would take us a long way towards improving the value of distribution cost analysis for the manufacturer. These are:

(a) the use of total distribution costing and trade-off analysis;
(b) DCA of product and customer profitability;
(c) service-level pricing.

Total distribution costing and trade-off analysis

The total distribution approach has been well documented[7] and widely discussed, but seldom has distribution been managed in that way. In fact, without a total costing system, attempts at optimising the distribution function are near to impossible.

Total costing recognises the interacting nature of distribution and that distribution activity costs should not be measured in complete isolation but as a total system. Without such, decisions will be made whereby the chosen distribution system will be no more than a set of optimal subsystems – something rather removed from an optimal solution.

There is also recognition that some companies may not identify certain costs as distribution because of their organisational structures, or perhaps certain activities fall in a 'no-man's land'. Additionally, there may be other cost areas of the firm clearly not a distribution responsibility but nevertheless affecting or affected by the distribution operation. All these distribution-related costs need including in any total analysis, regardless of formal responsibility or whose budget they may belong to. Typical of the distribution-related costs which are usually omitted are:

1 Financial – inventory holding costs of finished goods.
2 Production – materials inward deliveries
                  – production scheduling cost effects on ⟶ stockholding size, order
                     size delivered, order processing costs.

3   Marketing –   service level costs ⟶ frequency of delivery
⟶ size of delivery (minimum order size).
– product range proliferation ⟶ effect on stockholding and part/mixed pallet quantities.
4   Management services – electronic data processing and computer facilities.
5   Sales – order collection cycle ⟶ order processing costs
⟶ size of delivery

What is relevant from the above list will vary by industry. Arguably, not all these costs are completely related to distribution, e.g. some of the inventory carrying costs are not caused by distribution but by production. This, though, is not the point. Once goods come off the end of the production line, distribution activity begins. Holding costs need attaching to products for profitability measurement, and it can be done singularly in a distribution costing framework.

Inventory holding costs are, of course, opportunity costs of capital. Other opportunity costs above those already suggested for inclusion in any analysis (replacement costs, notional rents), should also be incorporated. These include cost of hiring distribution, using different channels, leasing vehicles and equipment, or whatever is appropriate for the company in question.

Trade-offs

Once all the relevant information is built into the system, cost relationships can be measured and trade-off analysis applied. 'Trade-off' is the popular word for an exchange of costs. Alterations in a company's systems are undertaken whereby cost increases in one activity are exchanged (traded) for larger cost reductions or revenue increases in another, producing a net gain. Sometimes changes concern outside institutions, and these might be induced to share any net gain for mutual benefit.

Advantage must be taken of the opportunity that an adequate system of distribution cost analysis presents to measure trade-off relationships, and discover improvements otherwise obscured under a conventional compartmentalised approach.

DCA of product, customer, and regional profitability

Ideally, the manufacturer would like to pinpoint the profitability of each product, customer, and zone, but most profitability or contribution analysis stops short of distribution. Under mass-production techniques, the cost of manufacturing one batch or run usually varies little, excepting breakdowns or overnight increases in input prices (labour and materials). But, product contribution calculated at this stage can be quite erroneous.

How much is made on a product (if anything) depends very much on the order size in question, the customer and his quantity discount, and the region being delivered to. Going a stage further and incorporating distribution costs for a net contribution can be equally misleading. What is required is a refined form of distribution cost analysis, as demonstrated in Figure 27:4.

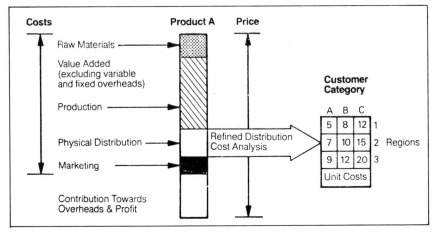

Figure 27:4   Marginal cost analysis – Product A

In practice, the whole exercise may become unmanageable unless some form of groupings (product and customer types) are made. Certain issues arise from an exercise of this nature:

1   Should distribution's role include aiding corporate profitability by presenting contribution analysis? As Figure 27:4 illustrates, production, distribution, and marketing cost analysis are all required. Who collates the information from the separate inter-company functions?

2   Further, what are the actual mechanics for working out unit cost figures as shown in the above box?

3   Should distribution differentials form the main basis for customer discounts and play a major role in product price differences?

Certainly, if distribution cost analysis is modified to produce more sensitive results, this superior information should be used by management to increase profitability. Refined knowledge will indicate unprofitable small accounts which might be better channelled through intermediaries or surcharged. Increased discounts may be possible at the other end of the scale to encourage larger orders, with further economies for distribution. In general terms, the emphasis can be on devoting additional time and attention nurturing those product groups and customers found to be more profitable.

Service level pricing

One of the problems of controlling distribution costs is that to some large degree the size of distribution expenditure depends on marketing decisions. Service levels are set particularly in terms of frequency of delivery, minimum order quantity and availability of stock. If service levels are increased irresponsibly or without knowledge of the likely effects, distribution costs can easily escalate.

Schiff's evidence[8] suggests the distribution information produced is not used properly, for marketing men have not been concerned with the effects their decisions have on distribution costs. Salesmen are usually rewarded through sales volume and not account profitability. Hence, a salesman can reward himself by picking up the 'rubbish' accounts which a more progressive outfit have chosen to ignore.

How can the distribution executive get the marketeers to show more astuteness? The answer lies in fixing a distribution charging system geared to the service level given. This is not easy, as it is practically impossible to encompass all service-level dimensions. However, the system can be built around the more important factors known to vary, with the assumption or past experience that others will hold steady. For example, given that accuracy in order taking and picking shows no great disparity and stock availability will be close on target, service level changes will relate to alterations in delivery frequency, changes or relaxation of minimum order quantities, and market demand fluctuations. If service level changes because of these factors, the effects will show through in terms of drop size (and order size).

Given acceptable cost apportionment methods (which allow for division differences), one can start the year with a total distribution budget and individual divisional distribution budgets, calculated on expected activity. Past events and future forecasts will suggest the number of drops likely to be made. Obtained from this is an average drop size and cost per drop, which form the central part of a drop-size pricing system. Divisions can then be charged on an actual (dynamic) basis for each delivery. The larger the order, the cheaper the unit cost of the delivery made, up to a point. The basis of the pricing system is a price curve derived simply from the inversely proportional relationship between number of calls required and average drop size in relation to the estimated sales volume.

To recover the budgeted cost for each sales division, the drop-size curve is used as a price-list curve. Budget costs and average estimated drop size provide the starting point on the price curve. Unit costs become cheaper as drop size increases and higher as drop size falls. Given a normal distribution of drop sizes (in statistical terms), budget costs would be recovered if all went to plan. (In practice, the drop-size curve would probably be skewed.) The drop-size pricing curve then needs modifying to allow for:

(a)   a minimum price below which the cost structure tends to be inflexible (for large drops);

(b)   a flattish part of the curve for the range around the budget drop size;

(c)   a rapidly rising curve to discourage very small drops occurring.

The three graphs can be illustrated as follows in Figures 27:5a, 5b and 5c.

The above pricing system is already successfully used in the UK by the Distribution Division of Berger Paints. Their philosophy is that they will provide whatever service level is required, but first the marketing department is told the likely cost.

'You pays your money and takes your choice'

For those distribution executives who do not recover distribution costs by charging them out, just one word of advice. Do! If the distribution costs remain on the distribution budget, who cares except you?

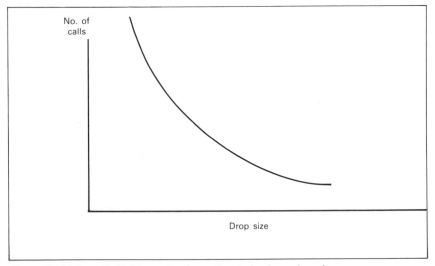

Figure 27:5(a)   Calls/drop size (re-estimated sales volume)

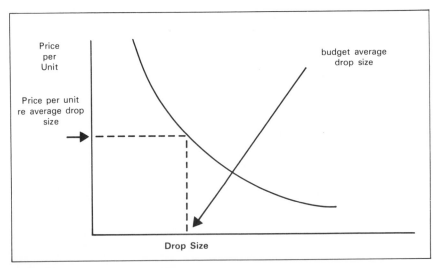

Figure 27:5(b)   Basic price list

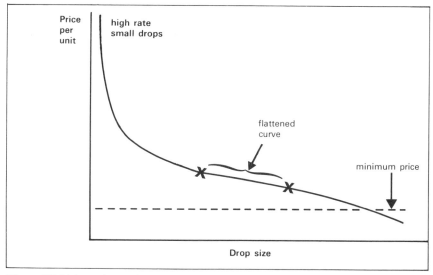

Figure 27:5(c)   Amended price list

Conclusions

Evidence of certain distribution costing systems by some of the more progressive distribution-minded UK manufacturers shows some considerable advancement from the general criticisms which have been laid at the door of distribution costing. There is a particular awareness of problems and selectivity in the use of financial accounting data, which has been used to advantage with improved decision-making. There is a greater appreciation of cost causation factors, and a more sophisticated approach to cost apportionment methods where inter-divisional activities occur, which can only lead to better pricing decisions.

However, in general, the march towards greater productivity and profitability through refined DCA is only approaching the halfway stage. Certain inhibitions still prevent the inclusion of important economic costs and more adventurous distribution costing. There is still too much of a compartmentalised approach and an unwillingness to seek and analyse existing cost relationships. One sees a reluctance to evaluate the return being earned on the organisation's distribution assets. Allowing for the risk factor (as compared to manufacturing and selling), is the return high enough, or are the company's earnings being diluted?

Some, surprisingly, fail to answer this basic question. Altogether though, much progress has been made in this difficult area, and more than has so far been given credit for.

References

1   D. Ray, 'Current Practice in Distribution Costing', *International Journal of Physical Distribution,* 1975, Vol. 6, No. 2.
2   M. J. Gordon, B. N. Horowitz and P. T. Meyer, 'Accounting Measurement and the Normal Growth of the Firm', *Research in Accounting Measurement* (American Accounting Association, 1966).
3   M. Schiff and A. Y. Lewin, 'Where Traditional Budgeting Fails', *Financial Executive,* May 1968.
4   R. J. Lewis, 'A Business Logistics Information and Accounting System for Marketing Analysis', *Marketing and Economic Development,* American Marketing Association, Sept. 1965.
5   P. Drucker, 'The Economy's Dark Continent', *Fortune,* April 1962.
6   D. D. Parker, 'Improving Efficiency and Reduced Cost in Marketing', *Journal of Marketing,* April 1962.
7   M. G. Christopher, *Total Distribution,* Gower, 1971.
8   M. Schiff, *Accounting and Control in Physical Distribution Management,* National Council of Physical Distribution Management, 1971.

28

In-coming materials management: a case of reverse distribution

David Farmer

Introduction

Any comprehensive view of a business system must include consideration of input as well as output. For example, in a manufacturing system there is a need for input of parts and materials to allow manufacture and subsequent distribution of those manufactures. Further, in any physical distribution system or logistics system, by definition, purchasers of the goods which are being distributed must exist. This chapter is concerned with the purchasing and materials management element of the system.

The approach taken should serve several purposes in respect of the readership of this text. It should help to apprise those concerned with physical distribution management (PDM) of the many implications of materials management which affect their own performance. It should help them to relate more effectively to the various aspects of the input systems of their own customers. It should provide those who are contemplating the development of a systems approach within their own organisation with an alternative starting point for the introduction of such a philosophy. Then it should provide the reader who is, as yet, uncommitted to the systems philosophy with a view of its potential in an alternative environment. Apart from anything else, it may also serve as a reminder of the importance of input management long and short term, in strategic as well as operational terms, to the efficiency and effectiveness of, for example, the majority of firms engaged in manufacturing.

Purchasing and materials management

Conceptually, the relationship between materials management and the remainder of the system may be illustrated as in Figure 28:1. The scope of materials management in this view can be seen to be the obverse of PDM. It embraces the management of the flow of materials from the supply market into the firm. It may be defined as:

> The concept concerned with the management of the flow of materials into an organisation to the point where those materials are converted into the firm's end product(s). Responsibilities include collaboration with designers on material component specifications, purchasing – which includes the search for, and location of, suitable economic sources of supply, incoming traffic, goods receiving and inspection, supplier quality control, inventory control (raw materials and components and, possibly, work-in-progress) and material control. In some cases internal materials handling would also be included.[1]

Clearly, if a systems approach has not been adopted, then the various functions which are embraced by the definition would generally be seen as separate departments, or as elements within more traditional departments, e.g. Production Control.

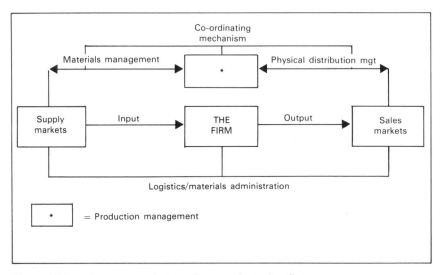

Figure 28:1   A conceptual view of a manufacturing firm

As with all systems approaches, the main thrust of the materials management concept is to avoid sub-optimisation; to look for systems efficiency and effectiveness; and to help ensure the achievement of common objectives rather than those that apply to elements within the system, which may be competing one with another. In addition, it should be concerned with 'supply marketing', which implies an orientation towards the environment within which the firm operates as a buyer.

This latter part of the task may be seen as the linking mechanism with the many

PD systems with which it is in contact. This is suggested by Figure 28:2, which illustrates the mutuality of these relationships as regards efficiency and effectiveness.

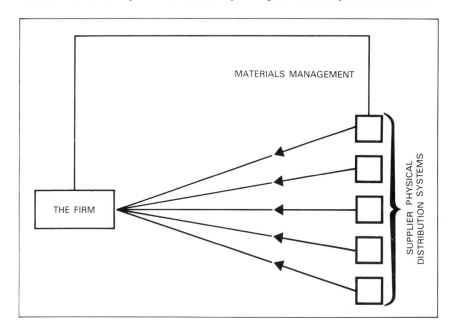

Figure 28:2   The link with supplier systems

The scope of activity is, thus, considerable, and, as has been argued elsewhere, it has important potential in terms of the efficiency and effectiveness of the total system. While many firms in the recent past tended to treat the supply segment of their business as mundane and strategically unimportant, things are changing fast. Firstly, the shortages and price escalation associated with 1973–4 alerted many more managements to the importance of their supply markets. The fall in the value of sterling and the resultant impact on the cost of imported materials and components emphasised that importance.[2] Then, the economic pressures in many markets, where the forecast upturn in trade did not take place, were such that they tended to focus management attention on major costs. Since purchase costs generally account for more than 50 per cent of the total income of the average manufacturing concern, this enhanced attention is hardly surprising.

The potential

Several studies have sought to explore the potential of the materials management approach. Zenz,[3] for example, from extensive research published in 1969, stated:

Materials Management provides concise delegation of responsibility and authority, eliminating the possibility that departments may have overlapping responsibilities. In so doing it recognises the importance of the manager principle of accountability by providing a materials management who is responsible for all aspects of materials decisions – a condition lacking in conventional organisation.

Ammer,[4] writing 10 years earlier, had listed the possible conflicts which exist between objectives relating to materials in a conventional departmental organisation (Figure 28:3). Ammer's thesis was that effective co-ordination through the adoption of the materials management approach would eliminate many of the problems associated with these conflicts. Since the conflicts are recognisable to all who work in the materials area, the promise is considerable.

	Primary objective	Interrelated objectives that are adversely affected
1	Minimum prices for materials	High inventory turnover, continuity of supply, consistency of quality, low payroll costs, favourable relations with supply sources.
2	High inventory turnover	Minimum prices, low cost of acquisition and possession, continuity of supply, low payroll costs.
3	Low cost of acquisition and possession	High inventory turnover (sometimes), good records, continuity of supply, consistency of quality.
4	Continuity of supply	Minimum prices for materials, high inventory turnover, favourable relations with suppliers, consistency of quality.
5	Consistency of quality	Minimum prices for materials, high inventory turnover, continuity of supply, favourable relations with suppliers, low payroll costs, low costs of acquisition and possession.
6	Low payroll costs	Maximum achievement of this objective is possible only by sacrificing all other objectives.
7	Good supplier relations	Low payroll costs, minimum prices, high inventory turnover
8	Development of personnel	Low payroll costs (other objectives might also be affected).
9	Good records	Low payroll costs (other objectives might also be affected).

Figure 28:3   Possible conflicts between departmental materials objectives

Fearon,[5] too, sees the potential of the concept. In reviewing the progress of materials management up to 1973, he argues that 'The Materials Manager, placed in a position to exercise direct control over all materials functions, can maintain the necessary overview and can assure that needed balance of functions is, in fact, achieved'. He goes on to argue that this balancing of functions results from two subsidiary objectives of materials management. The first of these is 'To co-ordinate the performance of the materials function into a total materials system, in which the whole is greater than the sum of the parts'. The second objective is then 'To provide a communications network among the several materials functions that provide a quick, accurate, and comprehensive transfer of data, regarding demands occurring anywhere along the system'.

Fearon's list of benefits which firms believed they had realised from adopting the materials management approach tends to confirm the view put forward by Ammer. He includes the following in this list: elimination of buck passing, better interdepartmental co-operation, lower prices for materials and equipment, faster inventory turnover, continuity of supply, reduced material lead times, reduced transportation costs, less duplication of effort, better morale, development of personnel, reduced materials obsolescence, improved supplier relationships, and better records and information. If Ammer's conclusions held considerable promise, then this list of Fearon's suggests an even greater potential. And since Fearon had the benefit of reviewing the literature on the subject up to 1973 (including Zenz's comprehensive study), that potential appears to be achievable under competent and committed management.

Since Fearon's article appeared, the pressures on material supply, including cost and availability, have grown probably at a faster rate than ever before. In the UK the 1973 oil crisis, with its aftermath of material shortages and frightening levels of inflation, forced managements to pay greater attention to supply factors. The area in many concerns which had been thought of in operational terms was now emphasised as of strategic concern. Inventory costs in the light of extremely expensive money became a focal point of activity in every organisation of any size. Purchase prices seemingly continued changing in an upward spiral as internal inflation was fuelled by the decline of the pound against other currencies. The importance of materials to the economy of manufacturing concerns was now not in question.

As the present author has shown,[6] most of this action, unfortunately, was reactive rather than proactive, so that the measures taken to alleviate the problems which occurred most significantly in 1973–4 were of a defensive nature. Since that time the downturn in world trade has eased the pressure on supply availability if not on the financial implications. Consequently, many organisations have had the opportunity to reorganise themselves to take advantage of the lessons learned from 1973. Whether UK firms have tended towards a materials management organisation in so doing remains to be seen.

What is not in doubt is that these pressures were significant in motivating changes in the market end of materials systems in manufacturing concerns. A study undertaken by Dr Keith MacMillan and the writer[7] showed that 'Raw Materials

Shortages' and 'The Oil Crisis' were the two most significant factors in causing buyers and sellers to work more closely together.[8]

The advantages of the improved liaison cited by respondents were, not surprisingly, closely related to those suggested by Fearon. They included 'better liaison Purchasing/Production', 'better utilisation of own production facilities', 'better utilisation of stores, warehouses, and stockyards' and 'better relationships with sources of supply'. It would appear that improved liaison between parties in the total system is crucial to such benefits. However, there is little doubt that the advantages will accrue most readily and most quickly where the internal organisation is in a position to control its activities as it mates with those of its suppliers. The materials management approach would appear to offer a sound base from which to relate to supplier organisations. However, as has been suggested, materials management requires the commitment of top management to the concept and professional, capable management of the area if the objectives discussed earlier are to be achieved. The materials manager should be of a calibre commensurate with the importance of the task he has to undertake. He should be able to relate to colleagues within his own organisation, and in those of suppliers, at the highest level. The objectives, goals and policies towards and within which he needs to work should be clearly defined. Like his marketing colleagues he needs to be consumer-oriented but with the added responsibility of extending that orientation into his supplier's systems.

Ericsson,[9] writing about materials administration, suggests that several other requirements need to be present in the company system if the approach is to be effective. He argues that management expertise should exist within the company to enable the approach to be adopted, and that management should have available to it the appropriate information-processing equipment and techniques. Further, costs – especially those connected with the materials system – should be capable of being analysed and accounted for with a reasonable degree of accuracy; and top management, as well as those concerned with the materials system, should be wedded to the concept.

These requirements for system effectiveness are just as applicable to either PDM or materials management; and while it is true that many current accounting arrangements, for example, are unsuitable for systems approaches there would appear to be a better chance for successful adaptation on a subsystem basis as a first step. It is probably true to say, however, that the relevant deficiencies at the input end of many company systems are greater than in the majority of others. Nonetheless, the potential rewards – once recognised – are so great that the motivation to implement the materials management approach should ensure that these deficiencies are made good relatively quickly.

The significance of materials

The UK Census of Production for 1974 showed that the purchases of all UK manufacturing industries amounted to a total of £49,000 million. Direct labour costs, on the other hand, totalled £10,500 million – a ratio of 4.7 to 1. The 'average' manufacturing company thus disposed of more than four times the amount it paid for its direct labour on purchasing materials, components and services.

Another relevant statistic relating to manufacturing costs is that the 'average' company disposed of some 56 per cent of its income in buying materials and components. The impact of this statistic may be seen from the following illustration:

> Company X has an annual turnover of £1 million, made a profit of 10 per cent on its operations last year and spends £500,000 per annum on materials and components. If company X, through more effective and efficient materials management, was able to make a saving of 5 per cent in its material costs, it would *earn* a further £25,000, making a major contribution to the company's profit. Thus:

Income	Profit		
£1 million	@ 10 per cent		£100,000
Purchases £500,000 – saving 5 per cent =			£25,000
		Total profit	£125,000

Assuming that at the same profit level the company wanted to make an equivalent profit without the contribution from the materials area, it would need to increase its turnover by 25 per cent. In the light of this simple illustration, a 5 per cent saving in material costs can equate in profit terms to a 25 per cent increase in turnover. The converse is also true.

It may be argued that this is an over-simplification of the situation. Such complications as utilisation of resources, additional marketing cost and possible effect of materials cost savings against larger volumes are ignored. Nonetheless, even when all are considered the basic fact remains that a £1 saved on materials costs is a £1 extra profit. A pound increase in turnover can only contribute a percentage of that sum to profit.

Some aspects of materials management

Many systems problems stem from product decisions. Indeed, virtually all the main business decisions in manufacturing organisations are influenced by the basic product question, What products should we have in our range? The complexity, quality level and number of products which result from such questions impinge upon procurement to a considerable degree; and it is extremely important that relevant attention is paid to this aspect of system management.

There is a positive procurement role in which the key objectives include working with other managers in the system to:

1   reduce the time taken to get the product into the rapid growth stage of the Product Life Cycle;

2   elongate this stage;

3   extend the profitable part of the maturity phase.

Too often, as in the following case history, procurement is reactive and, not infrequently, related to some kind of supply assurance crisis.

The case in question concerned a medium-sized manufacturing concern. Traditionally, the purchasing staff did not consider a new product in any depth until engineering had released the item for production. Over the years this proved to be prohibitive to the purchasing operation in terms of its power in the supply market and to production in meeting the right schedules laid down in respect of vehicle launches by the motor manufacturers. All in all, both purchasing, manufacturing and related functions sub-optimised in respect of costs in order to meet time schedules. As one senior executive put it: 'We survived as a result of buyers' miracles and they were extremely expensive'.

The point was that, while buyers may have been able to meet the necessary lead-time through emergency action, that action was detrimental to their negotiating position in respect of purchase costs. There were also other difficulties within the company system on new products as regards design and production engineering release dates. The serial progression through these functions included the possibility of resultant error, particularly as regards time, with production and purchasing departments having to take 'emergency action' on many occasions to attempt to solve the problems which emerged.

A new system which successfully obviated many of these problems was devised. Purchasing staff were represented in product development discussions, where they received 'advance authorisation', perhaps as long as three years before the product launch. At the relevant meeting the purchasing representative obtained pre-production dates and quantities and the first production lot date. From this data, the department then indicated in bar chart form their best estimated lead-times for tooling, samples, authorisation and pre-production releases. The chart was then built up with data provided by marketing, engineering and production staff, and the completed chart was sent to all relevant managers and was updated periodically. Among other things, purchasing staff indicated:

(i)   when they needed drawings for enquiry purposes to meet schedule;

(ii)   when they required requisitions at the various stages;

(iii) when they needed to place orders on the various suppliers.

It is claimed that the procedure resulted in much closer co-ordination within the company system and, in particular, with suppliers; further, that the 'team' aspect in the reduction of purchase prices and total material costs has been stressed by all parties. Since these cost improvements benefited individual product centres, this served to promote such collaboration.

The role of procurement in the organisation

No attempt will be made here to discuss the general aspects of organisation for procurement. This topic is well covered in the book listed under Further reading at the end of this chapter. Instead, discussion will be related to the total system and the function of procurement within it. The emphasis will be on the need to recognise the importance of liaison between functions in the system and of having the right people to perform those functions; for, whatever form of organisation is adopted, the quality and attitude of the people engaged in it is extremely important.

Procurement and the environment

It is important for the organisation to be aware of the potential impact of changes in its environments. The events of 1973, 1974 and 1979 have emphasised the impact of the supply market environment on the system as a whole, suggesting the importance of effective market study in the procurement area as much as in respect of sales. Such study should include a general scenario relating to the following aspects: mergers, key suppliers' activities and plans, alternative suppliers' activities and plans, other buyers' activities and plans, government legislation. It will be necessary to have (i) staff in the procurement area who have the necessary attributes to undertake this work, and (ii) a suitable mechanism to ensure that the resulting pertinent data is fed into the corporate decision-making and planning system, both long and short-term.

At the strategic level this might include consideration of such factors as the need to integrate vertically, or abandon certain products. In other cases it might call for participation in plant location, production methodology and make or buy decision-making. The essence of strategy is in the ability to concentrate strength against competitive weakness. The considerations listed above are among those which may have a considerable effect on the recognition as well as use of such strengths.

The case cited earlier on product development indicates the potential of procurement liaison in this area. The situation described before the new arrangement was adopted is also typical of the kind of difficulties caused by lack of effective liaison at the various stages of product development. It should be the task of procurement to keep product designers in touch with developments in the supply market. Not only should this include data on new materials, but also projected comparative economics of available alternatives. Among other things, consideration of potential changes in currency parities and transportation methods might be included. In the multi-national company environment it could also involve consideration of the availability of material at the various company manufacturing locations. Other factors might include an analysis of material/product availability with respect to potential demand, not only as regards the company itself, but also other users and potential users. Changes in the supply/demand balance can also have a considerable effect on production economics and on end-product selling prices. Given the proportion of material cost to total cost in many products, sound supply market information may be critical to the selection of the right formula for a new product.

The roles suggested by the foregoing discussion are not the kind which many people apply to procurement. However, in many cases, if the company system is to be effective, they need to be undertaken efficiently and effectively. Such roles necessitate staff who have a corporate perspective, who understand the objectives of the business as a whole, and are aware of how they might contribute to the achievement of those objectives. They need to monitor potential changes in their external environment and plan and act with a view to minimising the adverse effects of those changes while seizing every advantage.

Internal liaison and suppliers

The foregoing may be considered as examples of aspects of the strategic role of procurement. There are other important liaison roles in respect of what may be termed operational activity. A manufacturing organisation receives materials/ components which it converts into finished products. As has been suggested, one task of Procurement is to ensure that those materials and components are there when they are required at the most economic cost to the buying company. This means close liaison, e.g. with production, production control and cost analysis departments.

Production is perhaps the function with the most obvious liaison requirements. A failure in supply which results in idle men or machines is always expensive. Not only is there the direct cost of idle men and machines, but when equipment stops, overheads are not being recovered, and the finished product may be delivered late to the customer, with consequent damage to relationships. In addition, if goods are delivered late, payment will be made at a later date, which may in turn affect cash flow and, in extreme cases, solvency. These dangers are among those which result in many organisations attempting to ensure against supply failure through, for example, increasing inventory. However, there is often a tendency to over-compensate in this direction, which is extremely expensive in itself.

Clearly the level of inventory is an important factor in ensuring adequate in-flow, but it is only one means. Close liaison between production and procurement departments can often result in reasonable levels of inventory while providing the necessary level of service. Time is often extremely important in this connection. Production needs to give the procurement department sufficient notice of its needs to allow the latter to obtain the required materials when needed at the lowest cost. In turn procurement needs to keep the production department advised of changes in lead-time in order that material may be called-off sufficiently early to meet the new conditions. In addition, procurement needs to ensure that the goods are delivered in keeping with the requirements of production in respect of such aspects as handling methods.

Then the liaison between the two functions needs to be closely controlled in respect of changes in call-off. Last minute changes, continual urgent requests, and failure to advise users of supply delays, all go to destroy confidence within the communications system. Some last-minute requests are inevitable, but too many changes of this nature are a sign of inefficiency as well as an irritant in the system. And this applies not only inside the company but also with respect to the suppliers.

In the ideal world this aspect of procurement would simply mean calling forward 'sets' of components/materials from suppliers in accordance with the company's own production schedule. There is no doubt that much can be done in terms of making such call-off automatic. For example, period contracts may be placed with suppliers in which the estimated daily/weekly/monthly call-off is stated. The supplier then sets up to meet that demand but delivers against an 'actual' schedule provided, say, one week in advance. This approach works well where there are limited variations in supply and demand. It can also work well where there are changes, but communications within the production–procurement–suppliers system need to be effective. Such circumstances require fast response to changes, intelligent anticipation and prompt action. The growth in interest in the MRP concept reflects these ideas.

While liaison with the production department has been cited here, similar interrelationships might be described with respect to other functions. Other examples are the finance department in respect of budgets, cash flow, sanctions, capital expenditure, inventory levels, stock evaluation, invoice clearance and control and letters of credit; costing in respect of suppliers, price analysis, and own product cost calculations present and projected; and marketing as regards product formulation, packaging and, particularly in time of shortage, material availability.

These roles and many others require effective management and staff within a suitable organisation. It is hoped that this short discussion of the place of procurement and its role in the total system will be helpful in assessing the type of staff needed to carry out those tasks. Given the appropriate standard of attention and expertise, the benefits to the wider system should be clearly apparent.

Notes and references

1   Similar models have been suggested by, for example, Bernard Lalonde and Donald Bowersox.

2   This is true even of many companies which do not themselves import directly, in that, for example, their own purchases may be from organisations so affected.

3   Gary J. Zern, 'Materials Management: Threat to Purchasing', *Journal of Purchasing,* May 1969, Vol. 4.

4   Dean Ammer, 'There are no "Right" Answers to Materials Management' *Purchasing,* 16 February 1959, Vol. 46.

5   Harold E. Fearon, 'Materials Management, A Synthesis and Current Review', *Journal of Purchasing,* February 1973, Vol. 9, No. 1.

6   David H. Farmer, 'Corporate Planning and Procurement in Multinational Firms', *Journal of Purchasing and Materials Management,* May 1974, Vol. 10, No. 2.

7   David H. Farmer and K. MacMillan, 'Voluntary Collaboration v. "Disloyalty" ', *Journal of Purchasing and Materials Management,* Winter 1976, Vol. 12, No. 4.
8   The 'merging' of the supplier's PDM system and the buyer's materials management system in these cases was implicit if not explicit.
9   Dag Ericsson, 'Materials Administration', *The Scandinavian Journal of Materials Administration – Trial Issue,* November 1975.

Further reading

P. J. H. Baily and D. Farmer, *Purchasing Principles and Management,* 4th edition, London: Pitman, 1980.

Index